THE
ELMHIRSTS
OF
DARTINGTON

THE
ELMHIRSTS
OF
DARTINGTON

THE
CREATION OF AN UTOPIAN
COMMUNITY

MICHAEL YOUNG

ROUTLEDGE & KEGAN PAUL

LONDON, BOSTON, MELBOURNE AND HENLEY

First published in 1982
by Routledge & Kegan Paul Ltd
39 Store Street, London WC1E 7DD,
9 Park Street, Boston, Mass. 02108, USA,
296 Beaconsfield Parade, Middle Park,
Melbourne 3206, Australia and
Broadway House, Newtown Road, Henley-on-Thames, Oxon RG9 1EN
Set in 10 on 12pt Sabon by
Rowland Phototypesetting Ltd, Bury St Edmunds, Suffolk
and printed in Great Britain

Library of Congress Cataloging in Publication Data

Young, Michael Dunlop, 1915–
The Elmhirsts of Dartington.

Includes bibliographical references and index.
1. Dartington Hall (Totnes, Devon) – History
2. Collective settlements – England – Totnes (Devon) –
History.   3. Utopias.   I. Title
HX696.D37Y68   335'.9423'592   81-22639

ISBN 0-7100-9051-X   AACR2

with
ANTHEA WILLIAMS
and
ROBIN JOHNSON

CONTENTS

ILLUSTRATIONS

⸺◦❍◦⸺

ix

CHAPTER 1

INTRODUCTION

———⊃∘◉∘⊂———

People often ask – if a boarding school,
why an estate? If a well-run estate, why
a school? Or an arts department?
Faith and Works, 1937

Visitors coming for the first time can drive off the road from London at
Buckfastleigh and miss altogether the first indication that they have arrived
at Dartington. Only if they take their eyes off the car ahead will they notice
a grim stone church standing on its own, with hardly a house in sight, as if
some nineteenth-century ecclesiastical planner absent-mindedly stuck it
down on paper without venturing out of his deanery; and only if they slow
down sufficiently might they see, almost hidden by grasses, the small blue
signpost leaning drunkenly to one side:

DARTINGTON HALL TRUST

← COLLEGE OF ARTS
← SCHOOL

Parking in the church car park and continuing on foot they will see a
rounded hill topped by a collar of trees and then half a mile away over the
top of the bank a sawmill gantry and by its side a box-like building, surely
twentieth-century. White. In Devon old buildings are grey. On the left
there is an old one in the right colour, very strung out. In the car park for
that, labelled OLD POSTERN, are four orange kayaks and a boy pumping
up tyres.

Through the trees to the right of the road, on an escarpment, stands
another large building, looking from this distance like a very overgrown
house except that it has a square clock-tower with a clock that always says
twenty past ten. Not factory, nor office; it must be the school or the college.

Fields of rich green are broken by sharp lines of red earth where one of the fields has been ploughed, the only animals Friesian cows like cardboard cut-outs with all their heads held down to the same angle against the grass, all pointing in the same direction. Men in Mini Metros and women with round faces on puttering Hondas, as they get up speed for the hill, force the pedestrians into the hedge. A small girl walks cautiously holding her violin case on the hedge side, away from the traffic.

Another architectural puzzle lies on the right-hand side, a little like a ship set in concrete, white again, with long slit windows almost the whole length of a wall, not to look out of because they are too high for that, but to let light in. Its size suggests luxury; so does the ostentatious absence of anything that could be thought of as decoration. Again, not a Devon style. This is an idea dating from the era when houses were machines for living in. Such machines were never cheap.

From the top of the hill, looking back, a distant silhouette of Dartmoor. Ahead the road forks before descending. Going one way there is a gate. Whatever is hidden behind it can only be approached on foot around the side of a stone pillar past a notice which says 'Trail Users. These are the Hall and Gardens. To return to the Cider Press please retrace your route.' The garden, which is what it turns out to be, is an unusual one, in the shape of an immense irregular amphitheatre. Beyond the gate the ground falls away at first gently and then more precipitately, down a series of terraces like a stepped green waterfall. At the bottom is an expanse of lawn and, rising up again on the other side, more terraces leading to a line of soft grey buildings which are the focus from every point of view. With its high arched windows, this must be the Hall itself, flanked on the left by another church tower. The old drive is serpentine, following the contours, and so are the walks wherever they can escape from the pressure to straighten themselves to the command of the rectangular terraces and the buildings. William Kent, the landscape architect who made other gardens in other places, said that nature abhorred a straight line.[1]* This garden masks the hand of man. Come around any corner, sit on any of the many garden seats, and there again are the buildings seen through a lace-work of tree branches, over the tops of magnolias or around the sides of rho- dodendrons. On a fine day in summer the garden is peopled, by a man with a whirring motor mower, boys with bamboo rakes shaped like fans, other boys with yellow plastic tanks on their backs spraying ground elder with weed-killer, visitors moving slowly along the many paths, and what are presumably college students rehearsing plays or practising dances.

The verticals are the abundant trees. A garden of trees as much as of plants – on the top terrace gnarled Spanish chestnuts, their trunks

---

*This and all other numbers in the text refer to the sources and notes listed at the end of the book.

strengthened with pitch; four tall London planes stepping down the other terraces; a statuesque Monterey pine; an evergreen oak with skirts as enclosing as a hovercraft's. The dominant colour, green, is all the more pervasive because there are so many shades of it. Other colours are in clumps, cherries in the spring, then azaleas and magnolias, rhododendrons later, then roses and hydrangeas, always planted together. One colour alone is constant through the seasons, the bright red of the flag which flies above the Hall. The wire snapping against the flagpole in the wind sounds from all over the garden like a giant jackdaw.

It is hardly a surprise in such a place to find so much sculpture: a half-reclining woman looking out over the garden with Henry Moore's mark on her, a statue of Flora bearing a plaque 'For Leonard and Dorothy Elmhirst from the Community of Dartington on Foundation Day 1967', two granite swans and a bronze donkey, a small semi-circular temple rather like a mausoleum engraved with the names of all the Trustees at the time it was built.

Penetrate further, around the back of the Hall, and there is a large medieval courtyard, with buildings of the same grey stone surrounding a cobbled oval drive and lawns out of which grow more cherries, two Scots pines, a Florida cypress, and where there are dozens more students of all ages. Up the steps under the clock tower there is a wooden door.

Half expecting a room of ordinary size, the vastness of the Great Hall is an immediate surprise. How large is it? There is almost no way of telling because none of the ready reckoners of size – ordinary window or table, chair or bed – are there to give scale. It swims all the more because there is such a 'boundless wash of light',[2] on the one side from the three arched windows which can be seen from so many points in the garden and on the other from the four which let in light from the courtyard. The bare walls are whitewashed. They rise from wooden floors, and at one end from a dais in front of an ox-long fireplace, on and up to the oak timbers of the roof.

The eight richly-coloured heraldic shields on the carved angels under the hammer beams of the Hall bear the arms of the successive owners of Dartington Hall. There is a notice to say so. Before Richard II there are three shields, for the Saxon Lady Beorgwyn[3] who dates to the ninth century at a time when South Devon was liable to be raided by parties of the West Welsh from Cornwall; for Robert Martin and his heirs from the twelfth to the fourteenth centuries; and for Lord Audley in the fourteenth. Then come the Plantagenet shields of Richard II and of his half-brother, Sir John Holand, Earl of Huntingdon and Duke of Exeter. Richard's badge – a chained white hart on a red rose – decorates a central boss in the vaulting of the porch tower. After the royal pair others held the land for comparatively short times until the Champernowne family who owned it from 1560 to 1925. Finally, for modern times not one shield but two for the

3

joint founders of modern Dartington, Dorothy Payne Whitney and Leonard Knight Elmhirst. No space for any successor.

As well as the shields there are eight banners. They were woven from wool by Elizabeth Peacock to represent the main departments of the Dartington estate as they were in the 1930s at the time the banners were made. A pattern of white wings for poultry; great blocks of stone for building; tree trunks and green branches for woodlands; suggestions of spinning and weaving for textiles; rays of light falling through fruit trees for orchards; upspringing golden corn for farms, and for the central office a net holding many and various elements together. Against the back wall, presiding jointly over the whole, rise Education represented by a range of hills rising to a far horizon and the Arts by figures also mounting to some heavenly summit.

Our visitors might be able to piece together a little more by using their eyes alone. But to find out what is happening inside the buildings they would either have to enter them one by one and talk to people or consult the records. Then they would find that the Dartington Hall Trust, despite that notice by the church referring only to a college and a school, owns a textile mill, a glass factory (Dartington Glass, at Torrington in North Devon), a furniture and joinery works, a number of shops, a substantial share in a large building contractor, farms, woodlands, a horticultural department and of course the promised college and school. The Trust, directly or through its companies, employs about 850 people. There are in addition nearly 300 students and nearly 300 pupils. It owns 2,000 acres of farm and amenity land and 1,200 acres of woods. The annual turnover is about £14 million. Even though the elements are no longer the same as in the banners, it is still a strange mixture, like the architecture.

How did it all come about? This book tries to sketch an answer. It is a memoir of a kind, and inevitably a personal one since the Elmhirsts were part of my life from 1929 when I came to the school as a pupil until they died. I have been a Trustee, for many years with them, for many years without them, since 1942. Detachment is something I have no claim to. The book is a memoir of them and also of the institution which they made, or suffered to be made.

Dorothy recognised that personal and institutional were so much fused they could not be separated. She said:[4]

> The story of Dartington is no longer my personal story. It is the chronicle of a great common effort on the part of many others, fired by Leonard's imagination. At the start, it was an act of faith on our part to take over an old estate in a rural area, being at that time rapidly depopulated, and to believe that we could transform it into an active centre of life. And life with many facets. For we never intended to

make Dartington an economic experiment merely, concentrating mainly on farming and forestry and rural industry. From the beginning we envisaged something more – a place where education could be continuously carried on and where the arts could become an integral part of the life of the whole place. We believed that not only should we provide for the material wellbeing of our people here but for their cultural and social needs as well. And in our dream of the good life we counted on the human values of kindliness and friendship to bind the community together. We hoped that in this way a certain quality of life and human relationships would emerge, relatively free from fear and competition. If any of these aims have been realised it is largely through finding the right people to help us and entrusting them with responsibility. As the place has grown and developed over the years it is to these countless others that we offer our grateful thanks.

'Relatively free from fear and competition' – I would emphasise that.

In the course of writing I have had the sense that how much I can say depends on how much the Elmhirsts will allow me to say. I lost any assurance I had almost as soon as I embarked on the book. I realised then how little I knew of those whom I thought I knew so well. I did not know about their lives before they entered mine in 1929, except anecdotally, and I did not know very much after that either. The letters, the records, the impressions gathered from people who also knew them in different contexts and with different angles of vision from mine or who had some expert quality in one or other 'department' of their lives that was denied to me – all diminished my own claim to know them.

What then do I mean when I say that how much I can tell of them depends on them? They are not alive and so cannot obviously give me permission to say this or that, or refuse it, any more than I can go to Dorothy and say 'I am puzzled why as a child you lived with your Uncle'. But I am writing the book in their house, in the room below Leonard's study. The footsteps I sometimes hear above me could be theirs. They are not banished as inhabitants of the place just because they are dead.

What they allowed of themselves to be impressed on paper is what I have to go on. Leonard appears very tolerant. He left a lot of himself behind. Dorothy, born in Washington, the daughter of a man later expected to be the Democratic candidate for President, born, that is, to a kind of public life, on a public stage, was almost the opposite. She was secretive in life, and perhaps wanted to be in death. I wondered whether she was saying 'Don't write about me. I do not want it', and whether I should stop. But gradually snippets appeared like the notes written in the Bahamas about the tears she shed there when she remembered her mother dying. She has not completely hidden herself.

Another way of putting the question is to ask it in another way – how much will the part of them that is in me allow me to say? They *are* me, or a little part of me, and have therefore formed the attitude which, even if I cannot define it, will inevitably influence what I select about them as being in some way significant.

There is plenty to select from. People who live in large houses do not have to throw things away. They can hoard paper and objects which others of more modest means would discard. Leonard and Dorothy lived, when younger at least, in an age when letter-writing took up a part of almost every day. There was no telephone, and when it was introduced their first number, Totnes 8, was used far less than its modern counterpart is today. Leonard and Dorothy retained the habit of letter-writing until the end of their lives and filed the letters they received. Leonard's parents devotedly kept the letters he wrote to them, and these found their way to Dartington from the family home at Elmhirst, near Barnsley in Yorkshire. Dorothy's correspondence, notebooks and diaries for the period of her life up to 1925 are divided between Cornell University, where her first husband studied architecture, and Dartington.

After 1925 most of their letters, except to each other and to family and close friends, were no longer handwritten but typed by secretaries. Every morning Leonard would be in his study after breakfast promptly at 9 a.m. to read the incoming mail, with Dorothy next door in the Morning Room, which was her sitting-room. Like joint managing directors they kept the doors between the rooms open so they could think together, bringing each other the odd letter or having a little discussion about something which had just been thrown up by the morning mail. Leonard would shut his door only when he was about to start dictating. After that was over he, and Dorothy, could devote the rest of the day to other things, without having their time fragmented by the telephone. External communication was reserved for the beginning of the day.

The Records Room is in what used to be their private house, which has no front door, being all mixed up with administrative offices, as it was when they were alive. The Tudor beams are still in the low ceiling, although the house was extensively remodelled in the eighteenth century. The leaded casement windows look out over the garden which became such an absorbing interest for both of them. About 800 Records boxes are installed on shelves covering its walls. Leonard's boxes number about 500, containing over 100 million words by and about him; Dorothy's about 80 and Dartington departmental boxes about 220.

As well as letters Leonard wrote extended essays on several periods of his life before 1925, often drawing on the diaries he kept at the time. Some of these have found their way into print, as an introduction to *A Fresh-*

6

man's Diary,[5] his brother Willie's diary at Oxford in 1911–12; *The Straight and Its Origin*,[6] Leonard's account of his two years at Cornell University from 1919 to 1921; and *Poet and Plowman*,[7] about his work in India with Rabindranath Tagore in 1921 and 1922. The quotations I have put at the head of each chapter are taken from three Dartington publications – from the *Outline of an Educational Experiment* (1926), from the *Prospectus* (1926) or from *Faith and Works at Dartington* (1937). They were each written by, or in collaboration with, the Elmhirsts.

Many people have been extremely generous with their time and knowledge. Devoted work has been done by Anthea Williams as my assistant and by Robin Johnson, the Dartington archivist, who has made the Records Room bear fruit for me as for others. Without their skill and patient work I could not have managed at all. Marjorie Fogden shared an office with me throughout and was unfailingly helpful. The Dartington and Elmgrant Trusts gave support which enabled the work to be done, and individual Trustees – Maurice Ash, Ruth Ash, Sir Alec Clegg, Alfred (Pom) Elmhirst, John Lane, Peter Sutcliffe and Christopher Zealley – freely discussed my interpretations with me, without necessarily agreeing with them. Michael Straight gave me most valuable comments, as did Mary Bride Nicholson and John Wales. Victor Bonham-Carter has been an indispensable authority. I have drawn on the book, *Dartington Hall*, that he wrote with W. B. Curry;[8] and on the more detailed but unpublished *Report on Dartington Hall 1925–1965* that he also wrote. W. A. Swanberg, author of *Whitney Father, Whitney Heiress*,[9] which is about Dorothy's earlier life, made available a manuscript of his book before it was published. Karolyn Gould also did a great deal of research on Dorothy's life before she came to Dartington and gave me the benefit of it. Dr Gould Colman, archivist at Cornell University in New York State, guided me around the Straight and Elmhirst papers there. Jack and Ann Collingbourne gave me help on Leonard and Dorothy's involvement in the estate at Dartington, Peter Cox on the arts, Pom Elmhirst again and again on many points and especially on Leonard's family, Bob Hening on architecture, Imogen Holst on music, Margaret Isherwood on Dorothy's interest in religion, Paula Morel on many subjects, Edward Stettner on Herbert Croly, Anthony Stevens on the Withymead Clinic, and Frank Walters on Dartington's finances and other matters.

Valuable information and ideas were given to me by Miriam Adams, Ronald Anderson, Irene Rachel Barker, Jean Bolt, Roy Bolt, Stuart Bunce, Gladys Burr, Cecil Chapman, Clare Chapman, Lois Child, Ernest Clake, May Crook, Ena Curry, Roger Dixey, Gwen Elmhirst, Richard Elmhirst, Susanna Elmhirst, Marjorie Fogden, Hardy Gaussen, Helen Glatz, Susan Hammond, Tom Hancock, Michael Harley, Ronald Hawtin, Edgar

Hodge, George Honeywill, Kathleen Hull-Brown, Ken Hunt, Francis Huntington, Edith Jefferies, Krishna Kripalani, Kenneth Lindsay, J. J. MacGregor, Lady Ranu Mookerjee, Sybil Newman, Max Nicholson, T. S. H. Piper, Christine Raikes, Wyatt Rawson, Alison Robbins, Dick Rushton, Peter Snape, Willi Soukop, Beatrice Straight, Emily Thomas, Nancy Wilson Ross, Charles White, John Wightwick and Heather Williams. Leonard's sister, Mrs Barker, was sometimes called Irene, sometimes Rachel and sometimes Irene Rachel.

I had many useful comments on drafts of the book from Victor Bonham-Carter, Peter Cox, David Davies, Susanna Elmhirst, Imogen Holst, Sasha Moorsom, Milton Rose, Alan Sillitoe, Prudence Smith and John Taylor, as well as from individual Dartington Trustees.

Lois Child, Susan Hammond, Juliette Huxley, the Liddell Hart Archive at King's College, University of London, and Cecily Oppenheim made available letters that were not at Dartington. Sue Chisholm, Daphne Piccinelli and Dorothy Ward typed successive drafts with an efficiency and speed which put me to shame. Rosemary Burn and Elizabeth Grove of the Dartington College of Arts Resources Centre managed to conjure up books for me from all over the country. To all these people, and many more, my heartfelt thanks. Needless to say, none of them bears any responsibility for any mistakes or other faults in the book.

All the photographs reproduced in the book, except that of Willard Straight's drawing of Dorothy (which is at Cornell University), are from the Dartington Hall Records Office. Some acknowledgements are made in the illustrations list to individuals – Michael Dower, Susanna Elmhirst, Jill Franklin and Juliette Huxley – and to professional photographers – Brian Heseltine and A. F. Kersting.

CHAPTER 2

THE ENGLISHMAN

The object of our venture at Dartington
Hall is to provide a School for the
children of parents with moderate means,
where the spirit and intention of modern
educational methods may be combined with
what is best in the present English
School System.

Prospectus, 1926

At no time in his life could Leonard be mistaken for anything other than an Englishman and a gentleman, rooted in Yorkshire. When he had the chance to fulfil his dream he never had any doubt that his Utopia should be set in the English countryside.

Queen Victoria's Diamond Jubilee in 1897, celebrated as enthusiastically in the Yorkshire village of Laxton, where he was born, as anywhere else in the Empire, from England to Canada, from Australia to India, gave Leonard his first memory of a public event. He and his older brother, Willie, were put early to bed and then woken up after the grown-ups had eaten supper. They drove in the family dog-cart to a spectacle which united the nation in a different kind of communion from the one Leonard was by this time well accustomed to observing in church. The common factor was Colonel Saltmarshe who led the procession of torch-bearers to the beacon on the banks of the Humber. Saltmarshe Hall was set in country that had been literally that until Charles II invited the Dutchman, Vermuyden, to supervise its drainage. The geometry of his ditches still surrounds the house. On Sundays, Saltmarshe sat at the head of the congregation in the front pew. When he stood up to read the lesson it seemed to Leonard that he was addressing not the parish but his troops. Onward Saltmarshe soldiers, marching as to war.

Leonard was born in the Vicarage four years before, on 6 June 1893.[1] His father, William Heaton Elmhirst (Father William to distinguish him from Brother Willie), was the first-born in a family of six, who followed *his* father into the Church from Repton and Jesus College, Cambridge. His mother, Mary Knight Elmhirst, came from a parson's family with like fertility though not with like social standing. She was the more devout of the two. The eldest son bearing the traditional name for the eldest, Father William entered the Church without any anguish. The stipend from the curacy at Laxton, £120 a year, not princely, was enough to maintain a wife and settle her commandingly into her vocation of childbearing. The gap between Brother Willie and Leonard of 17 months was about average. By the time the family left Laxton in 1903 seven more children were born in the room where they were conceived. One, Tiny, died. A photograph of Mary in the early days of her marriage shows her small and pretty, an eager look in her eyes, a high forehead, no-nonsense hair brushed straight back. She is wearing a black dress buttoned up high enough to leave the shape of her neck to the imagination, only a touch of lace at her sleeves' end to suggest the arm beneath.

Her husband's relatives called her the 'hardy annual', although not so hardy that she could breastfeed any of her children. They were all raised on the bottle, which in the view of the youngest brother Alfred (known to all as Pom) made him and the other brothers except Leonard into heavy smokers. Her failing was in spite of being put on a bottle when pregnant. 'Dr Bottle', as the family doctor was called by the children because he nearly always left medicine behind him, prescribed Guinness for her; she must therefore have been drinking it regularly for a good part of twelve years. Leonard knew it was Guinness because his father taught him how to make a sort of paint by adding brown sugar to the dregs from the bottle. When daubed on trees, the Guinness attracted moths. Leonard would walk around the garden at night with a candle lantern, and, guided by the smell, pick them off their deathbeds for his collection.

For his first years he had to share Mary only with Brother Willie. 'After the little ones had been put to bed, and there seemed to be more and more little ones all the time, Willie and I would at last claim Mama for ourselves.' The nightly ritual was for her, Brother Willie and Leonard to sing hymns to her own accompaniment on the piano. She was a good singer. After the hymn came the story, often from the Old Testament. She preferred it to the New. David and Goliath was a particular favourite. The two boys could re-enact it easily in their day-time games because it was customary before harvest to erect a platform in the nearby field on which a boy would stand with a sling to frighten away the marauding birds. Leonard remembered Mary's embarrassment over the story of Joseph and Potiphar's wife, which in countless families all over Christendom has reinforced the sense of sin, secrecy and excitement about anything to do with sex. She could not bear to explain why Joseph was sent to prison, nor for that matter where baby rabbits came from nor why she was always 'ill' before another baby Elmhirst was due to arrive and Leonard and Brother Willie had to be sent away from home. If it was not the Bible it was the *Pilgrim's Progress*, until eventually the competition from the younger children became too intense and they had no private time with her at all.

These readings were moments of happiness, more so in retrospect than being invited into his parents' bed in the morning from the cots where he (and Brother Willie) slept in their bedroom. To an elderly man, writing an account of his childhood, more vivid than the good days was the despair he felt when he woke up in the night after he had wet his bed, and the disgrace when he had to refuse the invitation to hop in with his parents alongside his brother. His inadequacy was drummed home by his being diapered the next night and expelled to a cold mackintosh sheet in the governess's room. The only compensation was the following morning when the governess asked him to help her on with her stays. He remembered bracing his little body for the heave and then the click as the whalebone ends snapped into their sockets, and the big body became Miss Hall.

His mother was all duty. On his first Monday at prep school a letter arrived from her and on every Monday for decades thereafter. But her heaviest duty by far was to her husband. When he stood at the bottom of the stairs and shouted 'May' she came running from wherever she was, kitchen, scullery or bedroom. Leonard had two great anxieties, whether he might forfeit for a moment his mother's respect and affection; and whether the family would ever survive intact her being so teased by his father. Leonard called it 'unmerciful', a harsh word for a Christian household. His father related in her presence how he could not decide whom to propose to, Mary or Kate Dymond, how there was so much to say on both sides that he decided in the end to toss up, heads for Kate, tails for Mary. Since tails it was, there she was. Leonard wondered who was more hurt by this, he or his mother.

Father William was especially demanding at honey harvest. Honey was one of his special joys, stings and all. Mary was conscripted for days before, getting the knife sharpened for de-scaling the cells, scrubbing out the swinger, cleaning the honey jars, and putting the labels and screwcaps in order. As the harvest approached, her fright grew. She was allergic to bee-stings. But he would not let her off. She *had* to stay and help. 'Good for your rheumatism', he said every year. His bullying got worse as she grew older. Her hearing gradually gave way and her failure to follow the conversation irritated him so that he would keep shouting at her.[2]

Leonard's affection was edged with disappointment. Why could she not stand up better for herself? Why so meek? Daddy, or Papa as he called him later, commanded respect and terror, the ruler of the house, with licence to beat and hector. Leonard was not beaten himself except once by the wrong person, his mother. But he remembers his astonishment at seeing his august elder brother coming out of Daddy's study, weeping after a beating. It cannot have been much compensation for Brother Willie to have, as the oldest, the same right to beat his younger brothers that he had as a prefect to cane fags at school. He was also supposed to be present, and watch, when his father beat any of the younger brothers. When Pom saw him standing there while he was being beaten he said to himself, 'Willie, you are not on my side.' Pom also said that 'his responsibility was rammed into him as the heir by both parents and grandparents. He was not therefore so lovable. He tended to keep us young ones in order, whereas Leonard would play with us.'[3]

William, Leonard, Christie and Tommy were in one set; Vic, Richard, Pom and Irene Rachel in another, the boundary between them being the dead brother, Tiny. His death made twice the normal gap between Tommy and Vic. Leonard became the leader for the four youngest; he was ready at any time to play games with them. His return each term from prep school was a family event. He was always inventing games. One was called silent hide and seek. In the drawing-room after tea on winter evenings the children were restless and noisy; the father, trying to write letters, was also restless, because they were noisy. The game solved the problem, as politics does, by compromise. Leonard sat in a chair with his eyes shut. Everyone else had to go and hide somewhere in the room but noiselessly. Leonard, without moving, would guess where they were. He also acted as arbitrator, as when Pom broke Vic's bike and Leonard chaired a meeting of brothers to decide how to pay for a new frame. He bought unusual things like a Sparkbrook Sceptre, a marvellous green bicycle with two speeds such as nobody had ever seen before, and, later on, a strange double desk with a cabinet above it.[4]

Father William's harshness was softened by his desire to share his two great interests with his sons – sport and nature, with shooting decisively bridging the two. He was an athletic man with powers almost awesome to his children. He persuaded Mr Hatfield, the farmer next door, to let him make a cricket pitch out of one of his fields. There he coached the village boys on summer evenings and brought in Willie and Leonard to bat before they went off to bed. Their admiration for his physical prowess once got the better of their discretion. They were by the pond in the field. In the distance Father William was tending his Canterbury bells by the beehive. A question suddenly riveted them all. Would he or would he not be able to clear at one jump the wooden fence between the garden and field? One of them let out a great yell, as though drowning. 'Coming', shouted Papa.

'We stood with our eyes glued on the fence. To our delight he cleared it with some inches to spare, asked who had fallen in, was told we were only playing a game.' Miraculously, as Leonard thought, he did not punish them but went quietly back to his flowers. Perhaps he could see in their eyes the admiration mixed with the guilt.[5]

Papa was diligent as a parish visitor, surpassed only by the vicar himself, Mr Simpson, and his wife, who regularly cycled past the garden gate dangling from their handlebars small cans of soup for the poor. Leonard sometimes rode with his father on Neddie, the donkey. His father would point out whatever he noticed on the way, buds, trees, osiers, cottages, crops, and chat to anyone he passed, usually in a friendly way, but once when a small boy threw a stone at his horse he slashed the boy's bare legs with his horsewhip. The rides were the beginning of an apprenticeship to country life which was completed at prep school and later when the family moved in 1903 to Pindar Oaks, a rented house on the outskirts of Barnsley, within reach of the Elmhirst family estate. There, said Leonard, 'Every spout, every stove, every sink, every bit of plumbing, every drain, every fence, every wayleave on that little estate, some twelve farms and fifty cottages, are for me as real and significant today as they were in the days when I would spend hours standing by him while he negotiated with tenants or builders, or ditchers or hedgers, or did his own digging for rabbits or planting trees.'[6] This was the apprenticeship he liked to recall when he became master of his own estate in Devon.

Father William's obsession was shooting. He thought it a disgrace not to be able to pick the two old birds out of a rising covey of partridges for his first right and left. Pop, pop. Dead, dead. The Elmhirst family were like that. One of the ancestors, Robert Elmhirst (1794–1835), was another keen sportsman. His rigour against poachers has been fully documented. In 1833, a year after the Reform Act, he established his rights to the shooting on the Midhope Moors by hiring wardens and gamekeepers, a private police force twenty strong, and bundling every poacher off to the magistrates after inflicting his own punishments. The bilberry pickers from Sheffield were a particular nuisance:[7]

> On one famous occasion he ordered his keepers to grab the fattest picker, throw her to the ground and drag her by the legs across the bilberry bushes in an attempt to teach her who was who and what was what; contemporary lack of undergarments must have made the journey both painful and embarrassing.

Father William boasted he never spent anything on meat in the shooting season. Since at Laxton he was neither landlord nor tenant of anything except the garden he had to rely on the landlord's rabbits. One evening he took Leonard out stalking and from behind one of the oak trees daubed with the Guinness and brown sugar, taking aim with his .22 repeating rook rifle, he killed one of the squire's rabbits. Just then William saw someone coming along the road and pulled Leonard down into the ditch beside him. There they lay trying not to breathe until the man had passed. If he had been discovered and Father William brought before the magistrate the fat bilberry picker might have had her revenge.

On most occasions shooting was legitimate. Father William may have been only a curate but he was also, as everyone knew, the heir to an ancient if small estate. William took his family name from it. He had a Cambridge degree and College colours. He was known to be an excellent shot. So he was invited by Colonel Saltmarshe and other local squires to join their shoots. From the earliest age at which they could stand, first Brother Willie, then Leonard and, one by one, all the rest were trained as beaters like 'prize gundogs or spaniels',[8] enough of them eventually to make up, according to some observers, the most perfect team of beaters ever seen. Their father had only to raise his hand from a distance and they all wheeled, marched, and wheeled again. 'Keep a line', was a stern and frequent order, and with good reason. If you didn't you could be shot by a gun ignorantly or carelessly following a bird flying down or across a line of beaters. As trophies of the chase the house at Elmhirst was decorated with a stag's head, fox masks, a hare's head, a stuffed weasel, a stoat and case upon case upon case of stuffed birds.[9]

There were plenty of other family customs. Parents and children walked together around the garden before Sunday lunch and again before Sunday tea to observe the results of the last week's work. 'This walk must have been Sunday routine for the family from time immemorial, for Elmhirsts always had gardens. I remember no Sunday spent with any Elmhirst great-uncle, great-aunt or grandparent when these two routine visits on Sunday were not paid to all plants, trees, dogs, chickens, horses and ferrets.'[10] Leonard and the rest also visited their grandparents at Worsbrough in the house that had their own name. When there they went to the Worsbrough Parish Church and sat in the family box pew. Many of the Elmhirst ancestors were buried directly beneath it, the custom until 1853 when an Act of Parliament forbade any more burying inside churches. You could smell them. He did not mind. Others did. He remembered one Sunday in 1920 when Father William took a Cambridge friend to Worsbrough Church; half way through the service the friend whispered, 'Your ancestors are too strong for me' and went out for air. Leonard told me, in the 1950s, that he almost looked forward to the time when he would be buried in the churchyard, next to his father, mother and his grandparents.

English rural society was firm in its grading. At the top, perfectly secure, were Colonel Saltmarshe and his two fellow squires, one of whom at

Metham doubled as the Reverend Mr Simpson while the other at Yokefleet was Mr Empson. To them and their families an almost feudal deference was displayed. When a village boy met any of them he swept his hand from his forehead groundwards as if with a feathered seventeenth-century hat in hand. All the girls also curtsied low when any of the quality rode by. When Willie and Leonard followed suit and raised *their* little caps or tam o'shanters to everyone they passed including Mr Hatfield, the farmer with the cricket field, they were firmly corrected by their father: they were to *be* saluted, not to salute. The essence of hierarchy is that behaviour between classes should not be reciprocal. By the time Leonard revisited Laxton in 1919, although the salaams and curtsies had disappeared, the delineation of class was not in other ways much less marked.

The order of precedence between the stations of life was demonstrated to full effect in the church which everyone had to attend. The first to approach the communion rails for bread and wine were always the squires, their ladies and their children, followed by the curate's family, the land agents and the leading farmers, the keepers and craftsmen and then the smallholders. The labourers and servants waited to the last for their turn to partake of the body and blood of Christ.

Industry had no accepted place. The richest local family were the Andertons who owned lime kilns and a fertiliser factory near Howden. They were neither invited to the houses of the others, nor give any invitations. They were 'in trade'. The barrier was maintained as firmly from the one side as the other. When one of Mr Simpson's nephews came on a visit, he walked along the road with the daughter of Mr Watts without his Uncle's permission. Mr Watts trained hackneys for the top of the London market and so was also in trade. When he saw the two of them out walking he ordered his daughter indoors and horsewhipped the young man on the spot. Since the nephew's position was such that he could not marry Miss Watts any attention to her had to be publicly and humiliatingly deterred. William and Mary told the two boys the story with every sign of approval, as if (Leonard thought) warning them never to notice girls 'below' them.

The other important figures in their social universe were the governesses. There is some dispute about their number. Brother Richard told me there had been twenty-eight by the time he left home, the high turnover being due to the alacrity with which Mary sacked the young and pretty ones and Father William the middle-aged or frumpy ones. There is no denying who was first in the long line – Miss Clarkson, the one remembered for her dreaded drowning punishment. She would pick up Willie in her strong arms, turn him upside down and immerse him once, twice, thrice face down in a basin of cold water. Leonard thought it was only his slyness that saved him from a like fate. Miss Hall, of the whalebones, came next. She insisted that all her charges should eat every single morsel ever placed before them; if at lunch they would not it reappeared at tea. She also complained, Leonard thought unjustly, that he had lied about blowing out a candle, and that was the time he was smacked by his mother. He did not blame his mother. Another governess's standard threat was to invoke Napoleon: 'If you don't stop it, Boney will surely get you.'

And then, in 1900, came someone quite different. Miss Glendinning was in charge of Willie and Leonard for one and a half years, and of Leonard for two glorious terms after Willie went to school. Mimi (as Leonard called her) was young. She was enthusiastic. She made the schoolroom exciting. She had time, so that Willie, Leonard, Christie and later the younger ones could all talk to her about their fears and be encouraged in their dreams. Her greatest asset was that, unlike Mary, she was not in the least afraid of Papa and *could* stand up to him. She even became an adviser on his sermons without making Mary jealous or fearful of Hell-fire for a husband who appreciated other women. She was able to win concessions. She asked for play materials and told Papa she could get suitable ones from a shop in Hull. For the first and only time he was persuaded by her to let them catch the boat at Blacktoft on its way from Goole to Hull. One morning the three of them boarded the great steamer with its immense paddles – could ever any wheels have been so large? – churning up the bran soup of the river. Standing aft Leonard thought they were bursting out into the great world when the river, at the junction with the Trent, suddenly broadened into the wide expanse of the Humber estuary and swept down towards the sea.

When Leonard was sent to school, against her strong advice to keep him at home a bit longer, Mimi left. For a boy who was not allowed to raise his cap to Mr Hatfield the parents would not consider a day-school. Mimi could not bear the heartache of losing one after another of her 'children'. Leonard corresponded with her in New Zealand for the next sixty years and in her old age she remembered him as[11]

> One of the most observant persons she ever met. She recalled with pleasure an example of his precociousness when a child of only seven or so. Accompanied by his elder brother and younger members of the family they were being conducted on a nature exploration of the woodlands. Their study of plant and animal life was being so disturbed by frolics and fun that Leonard appealed to his governess to send 'the little ones home so that we can study the woods without interruption'.

His father's religion was certainly time-consuming, if not devout. Every weekday all the family trooped into morning prayers in the drawing-room. The domestics filled the back row of chairs. While the porridge kept warm on the range the Reverend William stood before his weekday flock to intone the daily prayers. After porridge came 'scripture' at the village school also taken by him; and last thing at night prayers at mother's knee.

The weekend routine was even more formidable. Saturday night was cleansing night. Every member of the family had to wash his body and his hair in a tin bath. On the following day family prayers were extra long, with a chapter from the Old Testament as well as extra prayers. After breakfast on Holy Communion Sundays Mama and Papa cut up the squares of bread together. Then came Sunday school, morning service in church, children's service at 3 p.m. After tea Papa would saddle up the horse himself for the ride to Yokefleet to take evensong; he did not believe any servant should have to work more than absolutely necessary on the Lord's day.

He had entered the Church because his father expected him to, and he needed the money, not because he had a calling. After his father died he decided to leave and become a full-time landowner instead, which he did in 1903. He was happier with gun than Prayer Book. His wife was the only sorrower. When it was decided that Brother Willie was to become a solicitor so he could be of use to the family in that capacity and Christie a land and mining surveyor for the same reason, it mattered all the more to her that the tradition of the two families should be preserved by at least one son, Leonard, following his two grandfathers.

It was a shock to be sent to boarding-school in the summer term of 1902. Leonard was eight. St Anselm's at Bakewell in Derbyshire was a conventional prep school of the kind which has often been described before. He suffered from the sadism, the brutality, the mindlessly imposed conventions of received educational practice as so many other sensitive boys suffered, pretending in his letters home – what else could he do when the Head read all of them? – that all was well. 'We have BEATEN Stancliffe at last, it was a nice match.'[12]

Only in later years did he reveal the truth. 'I crept up early to bed, said my little but immensely comforting prayers, the only comfort I had, and listened to that swirling group of swifts that nightly screamed their way around the silent dormitory as, so often, I cried myself to sleep.'[13] The Head, Mr Storrs Fox, reported to his father that when he first came he was 'very tears-near'.[14] He made sure the tears should not always remain near. On one occasion after the Head beat him with tremendous force on his hands Leonard could not use them for the rest of the day and had to find volunteers to undo his buttons when he went to the lavatory. One mark remained on his hand till his dying day. His form master made offending pupils stand on the top of their desks to be ridiculed. Leonard remembered small new boys standing there until the piss ran down their legs and formed pools around their shoes, which brought on more jibes from the master. The prep school I went to twenty years later, before I reached Dartington, was much the same.

Only in his third year did Leonard find any happiness. It was outside the classroom. He was with a group of boys out for a walk with the Head. Suddenly Mr Fox turned and said 'Elmhirst, tell me what that bird is singing up there'. Quick as a flash came the answer. 'Missel-thrush, Sir.'[15] The song saved him. Mr Fox was so pleased that there and then, as if knighting him on the field of battle, he appointed him one of the school's two 'mousers', with the immense privilege of cleaning out the droppings in the aviary that was Mr Fox's treasure. He also had to trap the birds' food supply. From the time Leonard was appointed he was paid a halfpenny for each mouse he caught, twopence for five sparrows, twopence for a rat, sixpence for a cat. 'Tails to be produced, except for the sparrows.'[16] The more mice were killed the more satisfied the Fox became. Leonard was allowed to roam around on his own to visit his traps. When the Head came down the stairs with 'a proper bate on',[17] which he often did, Leonard no longer needed to fear his hands would be mangled by the terrible cane. Some other poor boy would be the victim. Mr Fox needed Leonard's hands to mangle the mice.

For his last eighteen months his letters home were for once a true record:

> 13 May, 1906. Last Wednesday we went for a walk to Lathkill Dale, I think it was one of the best walks I've had: when we got into the dale I saw what I thought was a dabchick's nest so Mr Fox let me undress and go in after it, I walked on the weeds going to it but the mud was deep and I went into it getting back so I had a bathe in a weir made for fish, and I had a swim. Soon afterwards we found a water hen's nest with nine eggs in. . . . Stancliffe have got chicken pox but if they have only one case we shall be able to play cricket against them.

In the autumn of 1907, aged 14, he went on to Repton, his father's old school. It was housed in a grim red-brick building on the banks of the Trent. For most of the next five years he had the same miserable time as at St Anselm's, with no hope of being appointed mouser. His first diary there is labelled '1907 1st term MISERY, REPTON'. He hated the fagging, especially the beating that went with it. It was not often he could write: 'Went a walk by myself along the Trent, saw two herons.'

The habit of going for walks alone was enough in itself to make him an outcast. He must have written about it to Mr Fox and Mr Appleton, a junior master at St Anselm's. They both referred to this unfortunate practice in letters to him. 'I was rather sorry', said Mr Fox, 'to hear that you were going for lonely walks on Sunday.'[18] 'By the way,' wrote Mr Appleton, more forcefully, 'I wouldn't go for a walk by myself, if I were you. Go out with somebody else. People will think you are an odd sort of chap, if you make a practice of going out alone.'[19] England depended upon cultivating the fear of not being thought an odd sort of chap. One of Leonard's great grievances against Repton and St Anselm's, brought out again and again throughout his life, was that they did not, like Eton, give boys private bedrooms in which they could take refuge from each other. It determined him, when the time came, to make Dartington in that respect like Eton and unlike Repton.[20]

The classroom did not offer any escape, particularly for a boy who was not regarded as a high flier. Leonard was nearly always in the bottom half. His school report for the Lent term of 1911 is fairly typical:

> Distinctly slow and easily puzzled in Classical Subjects, but shows more interest and capacity in History and English, though in these too he is often confused.

Only in drawing ('Excellent – he has done some beautiful work from nature'), above all drawing birds, in carpentry and in singing did he perform relatively well.

Among the masters, until his final year, he had no particular friends, and of his housemaster, Mr Cattley (called the Cossack), he was almost as frightened as he had been of Mr Fox before the missel-thrush saved him:[21]

> I should like to visit Repton again, but I suppose it is so full of nightmare memories of the five most dismal years of my existence that I always hesitate even when in the neighbourhood. . . . When I am really worried and asleep, the form of the great Cossack still comes creeping up the stairs ready to hail one off to dire punishment of some kind or other.

As at St Anselm's the relief came at the end, with his move into the Sixth Form to study history, the subject he read at Cambridge. In charge was a newly arrived master, D. C. Somervell, well known much later for his abridgement of Arnold Toynbee and as a climber of Everest. He was 'a breath of fresh air in a very stuffy atmosphere'. He dared to question the prevailing religious conformity by proposing that people should not only read but live by the teaching of the Gospels.

A new headmaster also made an impression – William Temple. He afterwards became a controversial Archbishop of Canterbury. Most of the boys condemned him as a 'bloody socialist'. Leonard on the other hand regarded him in the same light as he did Somervell, or indeed anyone who stood for any change whatsoever in a system which had inflicted such pain upon him.

For Leonard, despite Somervell, Temple and the missel-thrush, ten years of boarding-school had been almost unrelieved misery. He was not tough enough to bear the cruelty without being inwardly, and sometimes outwardly, hurt. He was not clever enough at academic study to get any deep pleasure out of it. He was not talented enough at games to shine at them either. Only his love of birds and butterflies flying so free in the sky brought him solace. But he was never broken by the system of which he was the victim. He was a rebel in the making – and if against boarding-schools perhaps too against much else that lay behind them.

Leonard did not choose Cambridge in 1912, when he was 19. It was chosen for him, just like his two schools. For Father William the only question was which College. Father had been at Jesus and had found that, despite its unpromising name, the college housed many besotted sports-men who were, sadly, interested in far lowlier sports than shooting. In his last two years he decided to stay in lodgings so he could the more easily see his more agreeable friends in Trinity. He assumed Jesus was as Jesus had been forty years before; he was probably right. So Trinity it was, with its Wren Library, its Great Court and its Nevile's Court, all of which Leonard thought could not be matched by anything at Oxford.[22] He became a 'Trinity man' expected to assume a definite character, of seriousness, to distinguish him from King's men or Christ's men or John's men. In later life it was sometimes as though he had not been at Cambridge but at Trinity, the smaller and more select university within the larger. He once hurried me along King's Parade and Trinity Street as though there was nothing worth stopping for until, upon entering his own domain, he slowed down to a shuffle and beamed with appreciation.

But in his letters home he sometimes seemed a little weary, as if he had waited too long for revelation that did not come. The choir in King's College chapel sounded merely 'ripping'.[23] He might have been trans-ported by Cambridge if he had been 'clever', to use one of the favourite words at the university, then as now. He was not. He needed no great prowess to gain admission. The entrance exam was a formality. He plodded his way through the History Tripos, very methodically, to his expected destination of a third-class degree, and through most of the Divinity Testimonium which he needed to complete if he were to be ordained without going to a theological college. He was content enough with his application, to judge by a businesslike letter written in 1915:[24]

> A little arrangement and calculation and every thing falls into its
> proper place. By this I mean such things as timetables, putting down
> on paper the books of different kinds under their headings which have
> to be read, or which I want to read by a certain time. Thinking over
> before hand what is to be fitted in and where.

He was like many another young man destined for the Church. He could, after saying all those offices in and out of home, recite long passages from the Bible, especially from the favourite Old Testament, and engage in learned argument about the kinship networks of Shem or Japhet. He was his mother's son. She kept making it clear she pinned her hopes upon him. She meant him to be a priest, not a sporting parson like her husband but a proper God-fearing priest who would set a fine moral example to others in and out of her Church. She breathed into him some of her strong will which on this point was not overridden by her husband's dominion. She even persuaded Father William to side with her. Any doubts Leonard suppressed, or rather pushed aside for the sake of immediate good works and her good opinion.

William Temple was partially in league with his mother. Temple recommended the Student Christian Movement because, as Leonard later recalled, 'its inter-denominational approach encouraged contacts between all the non-conformist bodies, Baptists, Wesleyans, Quakers and Presbyterians, and that this would serve to give me a view beyond the rigid walls of the state-supported Anglican Church'.[25] Leonard became a more and more active member and proselytiser. He told his father at the beginning of his second year how pleased he was at the way things were going:[26]

> There's a great movement at present in this college to try and wake up people in a Christian direction.... The proposed activities are many. ... Circles are to be promoted everywhere.... Five or six people meet once a week, and discuss, generally with the help of a book, politics, missionary work, social problems or the Bible from the Christian standpoint.

He also worked hard in Trinity's mission in Camberwell, in South London, as well as in the YMCA in Cambridge and in a summer vacation in Eastbourne.

His Director of Studies, the Rev. F. A. Simpson, was a lovable man who liked giving his students port older than themselves. He was not exactly orthodox. 'How can one believe in the divinity of Our Lord', he would ask, 'when He was so unconscionably rude to His mother?'[27] Leonard visited 'Simbo' (as he was called) almost right up to their deaths in the 1970s. At the time the catalyst of doubt was not him but Goldsworthy Lowes Dickinson. Goldie, as he was known, had grown sceptical long before Leonard became a member not of his college – Goldie was at King's – but his university. He had also learnt what a profound shock it could be to young men who had it to lose their faith; he therefore refrained from anything that might bring on such a crisis. He would instead throw out a gentle question whose significance might or might not be recognised: the true believer would not recognise, the would-be sceptic might. As a moral philosopher Goldie had just as much respect for Socrates as for Jesus, and if he thought it would not perturb too much he was prepared to say so, or at any rate invite his students to consider whether they agreed. When the questions did stick in the minds of his listeners they did so all the more surely because he was such an affectionate, unselfish, intelligent, witty man. These qualities, according to E. M. Forster, 'were fused into such an unusual creature that no one whom one has met with in the flesh or in history the least resembles it, and no words exist in which to define it'.[28]

Leonard was never bashful. He already had the confidence to go straight up to people he thought interesting, like Goldie, and engage them in conversation. I remember him much later on the *Bremen*, queen of the Norddeutscher Lloyd's Atlantic fleet, tackling Henry Ford, the original one, with this same quiet confidence, on a subject he knew almost nothing about, the design of the internal combustion engine. Dorothy looked gracious and vague. She was not interested. Leonard was, by then, in almost everything. Henry responded by drawing a diagram of a poppet valve on the back of the menu and then of the stern of the *Bremen* which he was in an engineer's ecstasy about. In order to reduce the resistance of the ocean to its swift passage, it had the shape of a raindrop. Dorothy did take a little notice of that. Henry gave me the menu.

Goldie did not stop Leonard going on with the YMCA but now he was doing his duty with less assurance. He noticed with a kind of envy a few soldiers who had the courage to walk out of the YMCA hut in Eastbourne when he got up to 'take' Prayers during the summer of 1915. The brave ones 'were obviously men looked up to and admired by most of the rank and file. The very atmosphere of the hut would change when they entered.'[29] From that time on he was always asking himself whether people of faith were 'better' men than those without even if he usually went on to answer in the conventional way. Some years later, writing to Dorothy from another ship sailing towards the rickshaws waiting for him on the quayside at Hong Kong, he gave it as his opinion that people who believed in the existence of a Deity 'are not merely pleasanter companions than the faithless, but leave the world no worse and often better and happier than when they found it. I don't think this can be said of the sceptic, the atheist or the agnostic, for they are so uncomfortably negative.'[30] Doubt there might be, but still well mixed with Laxton.

One of the required books for Goldie's series of lectures on Political Science was the then very fashionable *The Great Society* by Graham Wallas,[31] a professor at the newly-founded London School of Economics and Political Science. It was an 'analysis of the general social organisation of a large modern state', and an application to society of the findings of psychology which Leonard knew little about then but took an ever-increasing interest in as he grew older. What startled Leonard most was

1 Willie on the ground and Leonard, aged 4, with their Elmhirst
grandparents, 1897

2 Granny Elmhirst with her grandchildren, 1906. Seated front, from
left to right: Vic, Leonard, aged 13, Richie, Granny Elmhirst with
Cecil, Jack (these two were the sons of Herbert Elmhirst, Leonard's
uncle), Christie. Rear, from left to right: Tommy, Irene, Pom,
Marjorie and Nan Mann (daughters of Mary Mann, Leonard's aunt),
Willie

3 Leonard with Flossie, undated

4 In descending order:
Willie, Leonard, aged 17,
Christie, Tommy, Vic, Richie,
Pom, Irene. 1910

5 Leonard (right) and Vic at
Cornell University, 1924, while
Vic was studying there

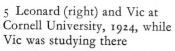

6 Leonard and Tagore, seated
centre. Santiniketan, 1924

that Wallas could proceed without mentioning the very matter which was causing so much disturbance in Leonard's mind. It was as though the great, even the good, society could exist without religion at all. In a note[32] written fifty years later Leonard said he asked Goldie what the difference was between Wallas's concept of a common humanity shared by all individuals and the general principles laid down in the Gospels for the Kingdom of God. Goldie suggested in reply 'that so much of the determined pursuit of rigid orthodoxies, still current at Cambridge, was out-of-date, and that a new and much more sensible form of rational and religious behaviour must be found for the whole of human society to live by if man was to survive'. Perhaps they also discussed Wallas's main conclusions. These became more and more the currency of liberal thought, and Leonard's, repeatedly rediscovered as the century has worn on:

People happiest in small social units.

Skills of social psychologist needed to help people understand how best to live together.

Lack of personal satisfaction for people working in industry, compared with craftsmen.

Wider educational opportunities needed for working classes.

Need to eradicate war from relations between states.

Leonard's concern was whether it was necessary to be a Christian in order to be a christian; whether the ritual and observance had to be; whether what mattered was the kind of life people led every day, not what they did just on Sundays. Awkward questions but not so much so at that point as to make him forego the career his mother had chosen for him.

Another question thrown up by the war was more teasing – how could one square the teachings of the Church with the identical blessings heaped by Christian bishops of every country upon their armed forces? Goldie for one became more and more outspoken:[33]

I can well believe that your work with the troops is uphill. You will find, perhaps have found, that the fact of being officially connected with any religious organisation cuts you off from all the decent English. They will not take their religion that way, and personally I think they are right. The Christian churches will not, I believe, ever recover any influence, nor do they deserve to. The greatest crisis in history has found them without counsel or feeling or guidance, merely re-echoing the passions of the worst crowd. Civilisation is perishing and they look on passive and helpless. Not from such comes the inspiration men are waiting for. If there is to be a religion in the future it will grow up outside the Churches and be persecuted by them – as indeed is now the case at home.

At almost the same time Goldie was writing to Leonard, Willie was killed in the battle of the Somme in 1916. Christie had gone before in the Dardanelles in 1915. This had a double effect. It made the catastrophe of war very personal and turned Leonard into the son and heir. The demography of the family had decreed he should take the cloth. Now, as the oldest, he was entitled to, or could even say he had a duty to, accept the inheritance and eventually to manage the family property at Elmhirst. According to his sister, Rachel, Brother William's death changed her father's (though not her mother's) view that Leonard ought to go into the Church and, in time, changed Leonard's as well.[34]

At least up to the time he left Cambridge in 1915 at the age of 22 Leonard seems to have been oddly undisturbed by the war. He had two reasons for not trooping with his fellow-undergraduates to their deaths in Flanders. He was labelled would-be priest, and his health was not all it should be. He was 'passed as unfit by the family doctor for military service in 1914'.[35]

When he graduated, however much he may have been a shrinking creature inside, however afraid he may have been of meeting other Cossacks, on the surface he was all the confident Englishman. His mediocre academic performance mattered hardly at all. He sprang from an ancient Yorkshire family which had owned land in the dale of Worsbrough since the first half of the fourteenth century. He was from a social class made up of interlocking personal networks that he knew his way around. He had been to a public school where he learnt the manners of that class. He had brothers and a sister who admired him exceedingly; he was already foremost in their affections before Brother Willie and Christopher were killed. Cambridge had not fitted him for anything in particular but had nevertheless left him with the belief that, as a BA Cantab., he had 'experienced the best education that the world can give'.[36] The world was not exactly at his feet. It was being torn apart. But he was, on the surface at any rate, a remarkably poised 22-year-old.

He had worked for the YMCA in Cambridge and it did not need a lot of introspection to decide that he should continue to do so, in a place rather less benign. Thinking of himself as a missionary in the making, he volunteered for India; and by October 1915 he was with the YMCA again, at Ahmadnagar in the Deccan. The ambivalence between the conformist and the non-conformist was with him all the time. He explained it later to his mother, in 1918:[37]

> I find there are two me's at present, A and B, we'll call them. A is keen to turn out as fit and trim as he can, to be first out for a commission and to justify his education. He's beginning to drop into his slot and to

appreciate the training, the drilling and the routine. B hates the whole thing, especially the bayoneting and bombing businesses. Luckily the B side hasn't much time to think or consider. Do you see? The boots are getting really quite comfortable.

In Ahmadnagar the A was sahib and the B anti-sahib.

The sahib lived like one, in a large house that had once been a General's, served by a *dhobi*, a washerman who washed all his clothes for two shillings a month by beating them on a rock; a *mahli* or gardener who also watered the tennis-court; a *chokra* or boy who ran errands; and then some servants called by their straightforward English names, a cook 'who has to be always kept up to the mark or I get the same two dishes for supper night after night' and a sweeper who 'bows very low whenever I come in sight, but never speaks unless spoken to'.[38]

> 6.30 woken by my servant bringing tea, toast and an orange. I climb out of my mosquito net, consume the aforesaid viands, take a bath and dress and 7.30, cycle out to the fort, 16th century affair to which all civilians would retire in case of mutiny. There I am taught how to handle the big guns in case of need, merely a policing precaution, voluntary, but it helps me to get to know other civilians.[39]

The anti-sahib was also peeping out. He was expected to bring the Tommies into contact with local Indians, which meant he had to find out something about them:[40]

> They sit in their workshops all day doing beautiful and highly skilled work, weaving, brass-beating, shoe-making, and then gather round their fires in the evening, sing their own songs, and make their poetry. . . . Everywhere there is need, appeals come from students, men and women in villages and towns. A little sympathy and effort to understand wins the Indian's heart straight away, but he hates being dictated to. . . . I long for the time if it ever comes when I can come out here and work wholly amongst and for Indians, for at present I can only study and get to know them in my spare time.

At such moments he was more fag than prefect. He criticised the colour prejudice in the minds and behaviour of other Englishmen, including some of the missionaries who so disappointed him in this as in other ways. Although he had never got nearer to *Das Kapital* than Wallas, without knowing it he joined with Marx in criticising the government for encouraging Manchester with its cheap manufactures to kill off India's craftsmen and craftswomen.

After only a few months in the General's house he was summoned, in February 1916, by E. C. Carter, the American Head of the YMCA in India,

and offered a real sahib's post, as his private secretary. BA Cantab. may
have been doing its work. Leonard accepted at once and went off in May
and June to learn shorthand and typing at a hill station at Kodaikanal in
South India, a holiday resort for missionaries and other civilians.

Unluckily for Leonard, his boss was promoted Head of the YMCA for
British and American troops in France. Without a job, he decided to move
to a much less cushy place than Calcutta, where he had been since July. In
November 1916 he arrived in Basrah in support of the 'Mesopotamia
Expeditionary Force' and after a stay there moved to another YMCA post
at Amara on the River Tigris. Britain (or England as it was still called) was
fighting Turkey for control of the Middle East. Leonard took a conventional view of that bit of the war. He contributed to a YMCA pamphlet on
The Land of the Two Rivers. He talked about 'the Turk' as he did about
'the Indian', and as he was later to talk about 'the American':

> The Turk has a genius for misgovernment, oppression and
> sticking-in-the-mud. Wherever he goes he makes a desert. It has,
> therefore, fallen to the lot of the British during the past century to
> undertake the greater part of the development of the region. British
> sea power, the diplomatic efforts of British residents, and British
> commerce have combined –
> (i)   To suppress the slave trade and piracy.
> (ii)   To preserve peace and develop trade in the Persian Gulf.
> (iii) To open up the Tigris and Euphrates to navigation.
> (iv)   To survey the coasts and rivers, and produce navigation charts
>   and the like.

Leonard was not out in the desert shooting at 'the Turk'; but he was
sharing with the troops the tribulations which gave 'Messpot' its own
unsavoury reputation in the British Army. It did not seem like the place
which had been the cradle of man. The day's temperature – 112 degrees in
the shade one day, 121 degrees another – was always recorded meticulously in his letters home.

Leonard's task was to keep the 'Tommies' as contented as he could.
He approached this job in a proper sahib spirit. 'The general atmosphere',
he wrote to brother Richard, 'is terrible. Not men like trees but like
animals walk the earth and care for nothing but the next meal, the next
prostitute or the next bottle of beer, small blame to them, but such is war.'[41]

He did not have much with which to counter women and alcohol,
demons worse even than the tormenting desert sandflies, but he did his
best:[42]

> Last night after dinner at 6.0 over at the YMCA Mess I climbed into a
> ballum and was poled down the creek and rowed across the river by

starlight. Such a wonderful sight. Lights from the ships' coloured reflections in the water and a silhouette made by the ballum shi. Then up the bank and along the road to the flying corps. It was a cold night and as I was thinking out what to say at my lecture with slides on Derbyshire, the sentry's challenge rang out – it always gives me rather a shock, and in fear of my life I yell out 'Friend'. I was met then by the Secretary and proceeded to deliver the lecture in the matting hut which serves as YMCA. If appreciation is measured by applause, well, I was satisfied.

The puzzle in that is why he had to think out what to say. In the following month, on 27 March,[43]

I take my slides out to another camp 2 miles away and deliver the lecture on Derbyshire. I do enjoy doing it, one lives all the old times over again, half term holiday to Dovedale, choir trip to Chatsworth, walks from Bakewell.

There were not many other enjoyments, apart from strange sights like mirages which covered the bottoms of telegraph poles and camels' legs in their shimmer, but reflected the top halves upside down. He was frequently ill and in hospital, each time more so than before. On doctor's orders he was eventually invalided out of Mesopotamia, back to India in August 1917.

During his period in the land of the Old Testament Leonard was even more tormented by religion than by the heat. Gradually, he moved away from his mother and nearer to the father who had never been much of a believer. In January 1917 he wrote to him:[44] 'In the last few months my whole outlook on life has changed . . . the effect of it is that for the time being I do not see the way open to taking orders, and I could not honestly put my name to most of the things the Church demands.' Even to his mother a little later he wrote[45]

the old creeds, formulas, hymns and doctrines no longer sum up my experience or satisfy my reason. They have not gone for good, and I think the fact of dissatisfaction is not necessarily bad. It only means that when one has to work out a whole new philosophy of life, one tends often to be destructive at first rather than constructive.

Writing to Harold Angus, a friend in India, he named his heroes (or counter-heroes) – Dickinson, Bernard Shaw, H. G. Wells and Michael Sadler, son of the family doctor at Barnsley and later Vice-Chancellor of Leeds University. These were all men who combined intellect with the simplicity and frailness of the child, each one a man who 'devotes both brain and heart to the enlightening of his fellow men and the building up of the greater kingdom'.[46]

By 1917, when he was 24, he had firmly committed himself against a career in the Church, the final split being precipitated by the differences he had with the YMCA. He had seldom been comfortable with Sunday prayers and services. He had been no more comfortable in the pulpit than his father, even though his was in a hut in the desert. But until Amara he had stuck to the regulations. Only there did he take the decisive step of substituting music for religion. For Sunday evenings he organised a concert and sing-song instead of the usual 'hymnal orgies'. It was a great deal more popular. It lightened by a little the lives of men who were fighting in the desert against the heathen. Leonard felt he was fully justified.

Not so the padres. They complained, strenuously. It was almost blasphemous to sing anything other than a hymn on the Sabbath. The YMCA authorities heard about it and descended. A certain Mr Dixon travelled up from Basrah as an inquisitor and put Leonard through a long examination, of which he kept a record.[47] 'You wish then to hold services which dispense with all hymns and prayers?' 'Why not hold your meeting on a week day?' Leonard stood his ground. He had finally made up his mind.

The long conflict resolved, on his return to India in August 1917 Leonard went to convalesce where he had stayed after an earlier illness in September 1916, with a distant cousin, Molly Richardson, and her husband, Ted. He was Deputy Head of the Indian Education Service in the United Provinces, and their home was at Naini Tal, in the hills near Allahabad. A fellow guest was Lionel Curtis, a Fellow of All Souls and editor of the quarterly magazine *Round Table*; he had been sent to India by Lloyd George, rather as Stafford Cripps was to be sent by Churchill in the next war, to work out a scheme for advancing India to self-government as a Dominion within the British Commonwealth. Curtis was already famous as a member of Milner's Kindergarten, one of the group of gifted young men from Oxford who helped to create the Union of South Africa as a Dominion after the Boer War.[48] Curtis was a determined and skilful negotiator. He was attacked from two sides, by the orthodox Indian Civil Servants for amateur meddling, and by Congress, who said he wanted to keep them in the British Empire when what they demanded was freedom. But he found a middle way. Leonard was employed as his temporary secretary, typing out draft after draft of a report which was in the end embodied in the Montagu-Chelmsford Act of 1919. It was the first time Leonard had been in the anteroom of history.

Curtis was a sahib, but not one open to the denunciation of Leonard Woolf who as a magistrate in Ceylon not long before attacked his fellow sahibs as a 'stupid degraded circle of degenerates and imbeciles'.[49] Perhaps because there was a bit of the anti in Curtis, and he saw the same in his new secretary, he introduced him to another man with an even more pronounced streak of it. Sam Higginbottom was to prove more crucial than Somervell or Goldie.

Sam was brought up in poverty in Manchester in the 1870s and 1880s. Like Leonard, he was propelled by his mother but in his case her influence stuck and he became a missionary. Lacking all education, he thought he would have a better chance of getting one in America, by working his way through school and college. After Princeton he was sent to the Allahabad Christian College to teach English and Economics; luckily he knew no economics so took his students out of the classroom and into the fields. He saw more than they. He saw the desperate poverty of the peasants. He saw how undernourished and therefore unenergetic they were. He worked out why their agriculture did not produce more. He had really found his vocation, and to pursue it returned in 1909 to the USA for still more education, leading to a degree in agriculture at Ohio State University. Back again at Allahabad he bought a tract of derelict land for his own agricultural institute. He experimented there with new methods, he taught students, he had a colony of 300 lepers doing gardening.

Leonard was delighted by him. Sam required him to act as his secretary, which he did for five months; he also encouraged him to work on the farm as he had done at Elmhirst. He wrote to his father:[50]

> You don't know how one misses the kind of useful manual labour that you taught us so well at home, out here. . . . Labour is so cheap that you have grown men to pick up and throw you tennis balls, in the hills four men to carry you, a body servant who puts your braces on, folds your clothes, will tie your laces and darn your socks. . . . It's not *done* to do manual labour, to carry your own bags, even a parcel, or to dig your own garden, and one's very apt to get swept along in the tide of 'good form'.

He was impressed by Sam's fierce attacks on both his fellow missionaries and government officials: they cared little or nothing about the land which shaped the life and death of hundreds of millions of ordinary Indians. Sam never concealed his feelings. He was forthright, impetuous and tactless, all qualities which Leonard could do with more of.

A man at last that Leonard could follow. He was doing obviously good work, showing peasants how to grow more food, and doing so undeterred by the indifference and hostility of nearly all British civilians. Sam saw the effect he was having and advised him to do as he had and go to the USA for a really practical education in agriculture:[51]

> Leonard, you should study agriculture but not in England. They'll turn you there either into a scientist or into a hobby-farmer who walks

round with a walking stick. You'll never know farming as a business. Oh, as an art and a science and a tradition, yes, but not as a business. For that you'll have to go to America. Go to a good state college of agriculture and learn the game.

To understand farming as a business you had to know something of agricultural economics. Sam together with his two American assistants all said Cornell was next best after the college they had each been to.

In March 1918 Leonard left for England. As soon as he boarded ship, losing no opportunity, he scanned the passenger list, marked down a member of the elite Indian Civil Service from Bombay (with the magic initials ICS after his name which were so well known they never needed to be spelled out, denoting as they did what was supposed to be far and away the best civil service in the world), and presented himself, his shorthand pad and his typewriter to the august man. He was hired, for the voyage. On arrival in England, where conscription had been introduced and health standards lowered, he enlisted right away and went from his recruit's training at Romford to Bushey and into the Officers' Cadet Battalion of the Coldstream Guards. During his initial private's training at Romford he wrote to his father:[52]

> I feel just as if I'd come to school again, only instead of the 'old man' Cossack is a certain Sgt Baker of the C. Guards, a regular terror calculated to put the wind up, create a vertical breeze in or raise panic with any bunch of raw recruits.

For the rest of his life one of his party tricks was to imitate Sgt Baker drilling his men, Leonard playing both parts, the NCO bawling his incomprehensible orders and the terrified knees-up recruit marching up and down the room, with stiff back and held-in chin. At the final shout he stamped to Atten-shun with enough of a thud to make the glasses shiver on the dining-table.

In January 1919 he was posted to Dublin in the army education service. Its head was Frank Salter from Magdalene College whom Leonard had known at Cambridge. Since there were no officer's posts he became a Sergeant and lectured on India and, I imagine, on the dales of Derbyshire.

He was demobilised that summer. He spent it with his family, learning to milk a cow, shooting rooks, building a rockery, tending cauliflowers and strawberries, mapping bird nests in the garden, manning a stall on food values at a local show and revisiting Laxton. He was offered a job by a Mr Bourne, father of a fellow-cadet at Bushey, and an owner of Bourne & Hollingsworth's department store in London, as their buying agent in China. He asked advice from two of his eminent acquaintances, Curtis and Michael Sadler; recognising the countryman in him they both said he should study agriculture in America.

He was still trying to make up his mind during a miners' strike. Barnsley was a coal town. He wrote in his diary:[53]

> The miners round here are still on strike, but hermit-like I am loath to go outside the gates. . . . 'It's not paint I want', said a miner tenant to Daddy, 'it's a loaf. I've five children and no earnings, and we're all starving.' So it is with many another. And we, we do not feel the pinch at all. One wonders that there is not far more violence. Troops have been drafted into Barnsley but they are kept very much in the background. A few houses have been raided and we have put extra locks on ours, but what must they think to see limousine cars travelling in and out of Round Green and young men full of idleness, apparently full also of unearned income. Within a few hundred yards of us the children have gone hungry to bed, yet we and most of our neighbours carry on as though nothing out of the way was happening.

He finally chose Cornell after considering Leeds, and Cambridge a second time. It would be constricting to stay with, or near, his parents. Taking a hand in running the family estate would have to be postponed. When he made a few tentative suggestions about management to his father the response was emphatic:[54]

> When I was your age (said my father) I decided to make a number of suggestions to my father not unlike the ones you are now making to me. Do you know what he said to me? 'Will, my boy, I'm not taking my trousers off until I go to bed.'

I have followed Leonard through his 26 years from Laxton to St Anselm's, from Repton to Cambridge, from Mesopotamia to India and back to Britain. It is a succession of narrow escapes from conformity. The convention he wrote about from Allahabad was a force which few Englishmen could resist. The country was ruled by a King not only of England but of the Dominions beyond the Sea, Emperor of India, Defender of the Faith. Even more than by him, it was ruled by good form attuned to the role of a small country which seemed the most powerful in the world. The dreadnoughts of the Royal Navy and the Guards, the cotton mills of Manchester and the money of the City, Oxford and Cambridge, cricket and missionaries, were compacted with the Anzacs, the Royal Canadian Mounted Police and the countless regiments of the Indian Army from the Rajputana Rifles to the Bengal Lancers.

Leonard, while he had absorbed an English tradition of public service, just escaped the full grip of it. His father was a parson who was not one, not quite, nor quite a 'landowner' either. If he was to model himself on his father, what was the model to be? He was also saved by his lack of talent. If he had excelled at classics or cricket he would not have been forced off into those dangerous walks on his own along the banks of the Trent. If he had won his way into intellectual university circles he could have been snared for life. If he had not been destined for the Church he probably would have squeezed into the Army and been killed like his brothers on the Western Front or the Dardanelles. If he had actually gone into the Church he would, as his mother hoped, have been more dedicated than his father. If he had fitted into English India he might have become a proper sahib. If he had been content with his first degree and not wanted to add something more practical he would not have gone to America. He was a gentleman but not a perfect one, a sahib impressed by influential men like Curtis and ready to manipulate his MA Cantab. and his connections with the powerful, and an anti-sahib in sympathy with Sam Higginbottom. Appearances were partially deceptive. The man who went off to Cornell looked the perfect gentleman, a confident member of one of the most confident social classes there has ever been – with his double-breasted blue suit for the formal occasion, with a white handkerchief puffed up from the breast pocket, his open smile and his bristly moustache which made him look like the Guards officer he was not.

CHAPTER 3

THE AMERICAN

Mrs Elmhirst is well known in the United
States for her support of the arts and as
chief proprietor of the *New Republic* and
Asia.

Faith and Works, 1937

At no time in her life could Dorothy be mistaken for anything other than an
American. She was born in Washington some six years before Leonard, on
23 January 1887 in a house on H Street, a short stroll from the White
House. Her father, another Father William, William Collins Whitney, was
a grandee at the time of her birth, Secretary of the Navy in the Cabinet of
President Grover Cleveland, the first Democratic President since the Civil
War. She was greeted as the Navy's, even as the Republic's, Baby, the only
one born to a Cabinet of middle-aged and old men. The President wrote to
William, 'Allow me to congratulate you and to say how glad I was to hear
this morning that our Cabinet "buds" had been increased by one.' William
was for a few days the most famous father, her mother at 42 the most
famous mother, she the most famous baby in America. Dorothy was the
right kind of symbol for a nation even then still feeling the shock of the
War; every second man in Washington had served in it.

For her parents she filled a gap left by the death three years before of
her sister Olive, named after her uncle Oliver. The government made her
all the more welcome because Whitney was such a prominent member of
it, a birth being almost as good for popularity as a wedding. Mr and Mrs
Cleveland chose her name, Dorothy, for its meaning, a 'Gift of God',
presumably to the Administration as well as to the family. Her photograph
was in every newspaper. The baptism in St John's Church was attended by
the Cabinet, the Supreme Court, the heads of the Army and Navy, General
Sheridan and her father in a double-breasted Prince Albert coat made by

his London tailor. Also there were her eldest brother, Harry Payne, then aged 15, her sister, Pauline Payne aged 13, and her other brother, William Payne, 11, known just as Payne. A 'verse' was produced for the occasion, no doubt composed by some Navy poet:[1]

> I'm proud of our Washington folks
> For manning the church that day
> To christen 'Our Navy Baby' Dot
> When the little craft got underway.

Her granddaughter, Dorothy, presided in 1976 over another occasion linked with the sea. It was to commemorate the opposite of a launching, the berthing on dry land of a long-lasting tugboat built in December 1890, when it was named *Dorothy* in her grandmother's honour while 'Our Navy Baby' was still remembered.

Grandmother Dorothy's family could hardly have been more brilliant. Her father was not only charming, good-looking and, above all, clever; he was successful at everything he did. After he became an attorney he went into New York politics as a popular anti-Tammany reformer, the enemy of Boss Tweed, and from there into national politics. Cleveland, also from New York State, was his choice as Democratic candidate for the Presidency; at the Convention in Chicago he helped to capture the nomination for him. 'He had moved quietly but effectively among the delegates, and already many Westerners were regarding him as a leader of the eastern Democrats, a man apparently without personal ambition and in politics for the love of it.'[2] A politician thought without ambition must always be at a singular advantage. His reward was the Cabinet post. In it he earned a reputation for innovation, as the maker of America's first modern Navy. After the President he was the most powerful member of the government, something like a mixture of Cordell Hull, Foster Dulles and Henry Kissinger in later administrations. After Cleveland's defeat he was talked of as a leading presidential candidate.

Instead he went back to business, to add more power and more money to the store he already had. He had started out with no money himself, as did Dorothy's two husbands when it became their turn to take the stage. Although he married into it, most handsomely, he did not want to be dependent just on his wife's fortune. Flora Payne was from a wealthy family in Cleveland. Her brother, Colonel Oliver Payne, who had been William's classmate at Yale and the man who introduced him to his sister, became the first Treasurer of Rockefeller's Standard Oil Company. The Payne family was rich even before that. With her money William could afford to buy a large house in Washington and equip it with a retinue of servants, a large garden for parties and a carriage to take him to the White House whenever he wished. Flora was *the* hostess of Washington, determined not to be like one of the Bostonians whose 'measured long pace and cold breath'[3] she detested. She is said to have entertained 60,000 guests during William's four years in office.

William became bored with parties but not with money-making. It was a period, before taxes had to be reckoned with, when a few 'persons of violent and undertaking natures, who, so they may have power and business, will take it at any cost'[4] amassed extraordinary fortunes from the industrialisation of America. Not of a violent although he was of an undertaking nature, William joined zestfully in the bitter struggles between the Vanderbilts' Grand Central and the Harrimans' Pennsylvania Railroad, between this oil company and that. As a speciality, he traded on his knowledge of Tammany politics and, with Thomas F. Ryan as a partner, bought franchises from the New York City Council to run streetcars and railways. Their Metropolitan Street Railway Company was before long in control of much of New York's public transport. He and Ryan did what all the other 'robber barons' did: after having acquired control of the company they watered the stock and sold it off to the public for many, many times what they had paid for it. He made more millions out of helping to put together the British American Tobacco Company, Consolidated Edison and the Guaranty Trust Company. Very rich though he became, he did not become as much so as the richest of all, the Astors, the Vanderbilts, the Harrimans or J. P. Morgan – John Pontifex as he was sometimes called. He did not climb right to the top of that pyramid perhaps because (unlike them) he devoted his energies to other purposes as well.

Sociability, for instance. Riches alone did not give entry to New York 'society'. To be acceptable, pedigree was needed as well. Neither William nor Flora could be faulted. They could trace ancestry (and were careful to do so) back to Whitney Castle on the Welsh Marches and to places in England inhabited by Paynes and Whitneys long before the *Mayflower*, and as well to passengers on the ship that, according to the myth of origin, bore the founders of America across the Atlantic. Dorothy had pride in her pedigree, as Leonard did. A copy at Dartington of one of her books on her family history, *The Paynes of Hamilton*,[5] is inscribed by herself as 'Dorothy Payne Whitney Straight, great-granddaughter of Elisha Payne'. The similar book for William was *The Descendants of John Whitney*.[6] On this score William and Flora, and hence their children, were welcome in any part of high society. Being rich as well they were not just welcome, they were very much sought after.

William spent a great deal of time on horses and horse sports, building himself at Old Westbury on Long Island a vast racing stable a sixth of a mile long with a private race track to go with it.[7] One of his famous horses was Volodyovski which won the English Derby in 1901 in the presence of one of his friends, Edward VII, whose mistress, Mrs Keppel, William entertained in New York and who introduced Dorothy to the King. The passion for horses also showed itself in the building of the racecourse at Belmont Park and his reorganisation of the one at Saratoga Springs.

He was as much at home in Paris as London, in Rome as Baden-Baden. Driving down to the pier near his New York home and boarding a transatlantic liner with a party of friends was a standard method of getting a rest, away from Wall Street and the dinners and the dances. When they reached Europe they travelled in style from one luxury hotel to another, from one friend's luxury house to another.

William also prided himself on being a connoisseur of the arts. Henry Adams, one of the great observers of his time, said that the lives of the very rich were 'no more worth living than those of their cooks'.[8] Unless the talk were of money some of them could only grunt monosyllables at their sumptuous dinner tables. For this they were criticised mercilessly by the old rich. The new rich reacted by purchasing culture, or its artifacts – the 'spoils' of civilisation as Henry James called them. Some of the houses they filled with treasures ransacked from Europe still exist, notably in Newport, Rhode Island. One of them, 'The Breakers', where Dorothy often used to visit her friend Gladys Vanderbilt, is on the outside a copy, not grotesque but dull, of a Renaissance palace. Shiploads of European workmen and European materials were sent to make it. Some rooms have mosaic ceilings made by Italian craftsmen; others are in the style of Louis XV or English 'baronial'; the whole is on the scale of a Pyramid. The bathrooms offered a choice of fresh or salt water and there was a bank of servant call-buttons above each bath.[9] The ballroom would look empty with fewer than 400 people in it, a bathroom with less than two. The 'Four Hundred', which included the Whitneys among the elite of American society, were the number supposed to be able to fit into another ballroom, Mrs Astor's.

Dorothy's memory of her father was rather of the art-lover than the lawyer, the politician or the company promoter:[10]

> He built a very beautiful house in New York – with tapestries – a kind of Renaissance palace, one great salon hung with old Venetian velvet, another with Cordova leather, still others with old Gobelin tapestries and all through the house were hung great pictures, Raphaels, Rubens, Van Dykes, early Florentine statues, carpets from Persia. He surrounded himself with these things because he loved them passionately. . . .
>
> My father's great recreation was music and every Sunday night throughout the winter he would invite a small group of appreciative friends to gather together for music. Joseph Hoffman and Fritz Kreisler used to play sometimes together, sometimes alternate

Sundays, and they would bring other musicians of their acquaintance to give an occasional concert. Though only 12 or 13 years of age myself I was sometimes allowed to come down on these occasions and I can well remember being curled up on a cushion in a far corner of our great music room and feeling that it was all a world of magic.

She was also proud of her father's creation of an 11,000-acre nature reserve at October Mountain in Massachusetts and his development of his 70,000-acre estate in the Adirondacks. He re-introduced beavers there in the 1890s.[11]

Being a man of so many parts William was widely envied. Henry Adams has testified to this in *The Education of Henry Adams*:[12]

Few Americans envied the very rich for anything the most of them got out of money. New York might occasionally fear them, but more often laughed or sneered at them, and never showed them respect. Scarcely one of the very rich men held any position in society by virtue of his wealth, or could have been elected to an office or even into a good club. . . . Whitney was not even one of the very rich; yet in his case the envy was palpable. There was reason for it. Already in 1893 Whitney finished with politics after having gratified every ambition, and swung the country almost at his will; he had thrown away the usual objects of political ambition like the ashes of smoked cigarettes; had turned to other amusements, satiated every taste, gorged every appetite, won every object that New York afforded, and, not yet satisfied, carried his field of activity abroad, until New York knew no longer what most to envy, his houses or his horses.

If William had been more single-minded Dorothy would certainly not have turned out the way she did. If he had been only politician she would not have become an heiress. If he had been only millionaire she would not have taken an interest in politics as well as the arts. If both her parents had not been blue-blooded she might not have had the confidence to become her own woman.

There is more background than foreground to her childhood. She did not record memories as Leonard did – indeed claimed not to have any, or hardly any. She had almost no recollection of her mother, which is perhaps also a sign of how much affected she was by her death. She wrote about it in 1959 when she was over 70, on holiday in the Bahamas:[13]

My early life seems deeply buried. My mother died when I was six. I can only recall two memories of her – one at Newport when she stood beside me at a window while we watched for the return of my nurse from church on a rainy Sunday afternoon, and the second, when I was

taken into her little sitting room – on the upper floor of our big New
York house – to say goodbye. She was lying on a couch – that is
about all I remember – but she must have been very ill – for it was the
last time I saw her. Then – perhaps soon after – time is
indistinct – Ma Bonne and I went to Lakewood and I remember,
while sitting on the floor, her telling me that my mother had died. The
emotion is buried – I can only remember the occasion and the words.
Strange – as I was writing these words tears flooded me – from some
deep part of myself – and I had to stop. Perhaps after all the emotion
is not so deeply buried. The years that followed are almost a complete
blank.

She learnt later that there had been strains in the marriage of her
parents. In one letter William wrote to Flora, after she complained about
his attentions to Mrs Randolph, whom he was later to marry, 'Well! We
have made quite a failure of it but for the sake of the children and society
we will say nothing.'[14]

Dorothy saw little of her parents before or after her mother's death. Her
brothers and sister being a good deal older, she cannot have seen much of
them either. The public life of her home was on a larger scale than what it
later became at Dartington. She was a small child in a large house. Space
over which they can exercise their dominion is one of the chief assets the
rich can buy, indoors and out. It is less of an asset for their children if suites
for each member of the family separate them from each other. She was
brought up like a Princess and, like other Princesses, remembered with
special affection the small places she could nestle into – the nursery on the
top floor of the palace in the centre of New York which was like the
nursery in which her youngest children, Bill and Ruth, had their own little
household on the top floor of the Hall in the centre of Dartington; or the
'children's cottage' (there was to be one at Dartington too) where she took
cover with Gladys Vanderbilt when she was staying with her at 'The
Breakers' and which had the merit of being no larger than an ordinary
family would need. She gave a homely touch to the 'Whitney Mansion', as
it was regularly called in the 'court pages' of the New York Times, by
stringing a piece of rope from her bedroom to the one next door where
Gladys lived in a French château. They could signal by pulling on the rope.
A private telephone.

In her nursery the earliest treasured figure, her Mimi, was not her
mother but Ma Bonne, as Dorothy always called her, an elderly and devout
French maid who was with her for many years. She used to take Dorothy
regularly to St Patrick's Roman Catholic Cathedral in the heart of New
York, only a few minutes from her home. She remembers[15]

when Ma Bonne disappeared for a while into that fearsome brown box – and Ash Wednesday when Ma Bonne led me up towards the altar and my forehead was smeared with ashes. I remember a kind of game I played when I would pretend to be praying on my knees beside my bed and she would come in as if surprised. We would laugh together.

As it fell to Ma Bonne to tell her about her mother's death so it was she more than anyone who prevented her from feeling too much the orphan, completely deserted by her mother and half deserted by her father. It may also have been her devotion in the incense-filled cathedral which first awakened Dorothy's interest in religion. She certainly gave Dorothy an authentic French accent.

Whether saved by Ma Bonne or not, she seems to have been a happy child. One of her earliest memories, going back to before her mother's death, was of her brother Payne:[16]

My brother Payne chased me up the stairs, saying that bears were after me – and I remember the exquisite excitement of feeling both safe in somebody's arms and at the same time exposed to such a dramatic danger.

Susan Sedgwick (Mrs Paul Hammond), a lifelong friend, was in 'Mr Roser's School' which was in feudal style set up right inside the Whitney mansion. She remembers Dorothy being quite as gay as any of the other children. The mansion 'was exciting because it had elevators in it, which were quite new then. Dorothy and I and the others used to run about and play with the elevators. She was frivolous like the rest of us; the reserve came later.'[17]

Nearly four years after her mother's death, in 1896, her father married again. His bride was the same Mrs Edith Randolph, widow of Arthur Randolph, an Englishman and a Captain in the Queen's Own Hussars, whose home was in Somerset. William was 55 and Edith in her thirties, an American noted for her beauty, 'a brilliant brunette with clear skin',[18] as her second husband described her. It caused a family rift. Harry wrote, 'Of course your marriage was a great surprise, and when it was all done it seemed harder to get along with even than in the thought of it last winter.'[19] Flora's brother, Oliver, was profoundly shocked by what his old friend had done. He regarded it as a betrayal of his sister's memory and did his best to wean his nephews and nieces away. He did not succeed with Harry, despite Harry's difficulty in accepting the marriage. He did with Pauline and Payne. If they would come over to him he promised, as he was a bachelor, that he would leave them his whole fortune, which was much larger than William's. He also threatened to disinherit any children who refused his offer.

Dorothy remembered well the occasion when she had to make her choice. She was 10 at the time, and was called by her father into his long downstairs drawing-room. He said that Uncle regarded his remarriage as treachery to her mother and that Pauline and Payne also could not forgive him. Harry was unwilling to break with him. 'What did I choose to do? . . . But I said – I think quite unequivocally – that I wanted to stay with him – And from this time on, the family was broken in half.'[20] She never mentioned Colonel Oliver in anything she wrote after that.

Dorothy liked her stepmother before the marriage and afterwards 'loved her dearly – She was the first person I can remember who kissed me good night'.[21] Her two children, Bertie and Adelaide, of about Dorothy's age, were companions for her in the house.

This happiness was not to last long. One day just over a year later at Aiken in South Carolina, where her father had one of his houses, Dorothy was riding immediately behind her stepmother as they passed under a low bridge with a construction underneath it. 'She must have failed to see it for suddenly I realised she had been struck by it and fallen off her horse. She was unconscious and obviously fatally injured.'[22] She lay paralysed and semi-conscious for two months.[23]

> I remember passing the open door of Papa's room every evening and seeing him beside his desk reading all the medical books he could lay hands on. He hoped always to find some answer to the cruel and implacable fate that was in store for her but the injury to her back proved beyond the possibility of repair.

She was moved to Westbury and died there in 1899. Shortly before her death she told Dorothy about menstruation in the hope that it would not be too much of a shock for her when it came. 'My poor father! – He loved her so much – and she had brought the gaiety of life to him and to me and I see her always now with light around her.'[24]

Dorothy, now with no mother *or* stepmother, almost immediately had a substitute for both in 24-year-old Beatrice Bend who was appointed her 'companion' and governess. She was 12 by then, and Miss Bend immediately took her away from Mr Roser's School where she had started and sent her to Miss Spence's instead. Miss Spence, also English, was called 'A Famous Educator and Remarkable Christian Character'.[25] One lifelong interest started there; Dorothy had to learn reams of Shakespeare by heart. It did not turn her against him – quite the opposite.

Miss Bend remained her companion until Dorothy's marriage. They went everywhere together. According to Mrs Hammond she belied her name: an intelligent woman with a very strong character, both worldly and selfish. Dorothy always spoke more kindly than that about her, saying for instance that it was Beatrice who taught her the delights of books and ideas. She named her first daughter after her as she named her second after another close friend, Ruth Morgan.

After her father died in 1904 the 17-year-old Dorothy, with Beatrice, went to live with her brother Harry and his wife Gertrude (older sister of her friend, Gladys Vanderbilt) at the same house on 57th Street where she had lived before. They were her guardians, as determined as Beatrice to find her the right partner and to freeze out the wrong ones. There was plenty of competition. She was attractive enough, with sparkling light blue eyes in an oval face, wavy brown hair piled high on her head, and her soft voice and her manner, to have drawn men to her even if she had not been an heiress. But she was. Her father had given her three-tenths of his estate;[26] her share was worth not far short of $6 million in 1904 and some $8 million four years later by the time she was 21. The money made it difficult for her to choose for fear that men were choosing it, not her. At the same time other men more worthy kept away for fear of being thought the fortune-hunters they were not. The portrait of her as a young woman still hanging in the Hall at Dartington shows that she must have been formidable to men as well as attractive. She is dressed for the painter in the elaborate costume of her *Mayflower* ancestors; smiling she is, but also very solemn, a woman with a weight of responsibility and tradition.

At this stage of her life it was no disadvantage to be an orphan. She had no parents to push her into what they thought a good match. Instead of parents, she had Harry and Gertrude and, though they supervised her entrance to the marriage market, their example was more of a put-off than a come-on. In love when they married in 1896, it had not lasted. Gertrude took up sculpture, an interest which led her much later to create the Whitney Museum of American Art in New York City. In 1907 she discovered Harry had been having a serious affair with another woman for five years, and that he intended to continue with it.[27] Watching them, Dorothy sensed the friction and she knew from others about the unhappiness between her own parents. It made her cautious.

Also, with that fortune, she had no need to marry. Before she was 20 she had her own house at Westbury on Long Island and another in New York City, with their own staffs loyal only to her or to Miss Bend. But she was happy to join in the same round as the other girls she knew. The play started in earnest when she was 18. Before that the only boy she saw a lot of was Howland Auchincloss, father of Louis Auchincloss, the novelist and lawyer. Her official debut was in January 1906, in Harry's enormous ballroom. All the many branches of the Whitney and Vanderbilt families came, along with Alice Roosevelt (daughter of the recently elected President) and most of New York's high society. After hearing Caruso sing Faust at the opera they arrived in a house filled to bursting with American Beauty roses. The men were given American Indian head-dresses and fur hats to wear, the women tomahawks and Red Riding Hood hats and capes as well as the more usual favours of silver picture frames, matchboxes, face-powder cases, brocaded bags for opera glasses and *boutonnières*. Dorothy, younger and shorter but as elegant, stood next to her sister-in-law to receive the guests, and led the cotillion when the dance started after midnight. The newspapers pronounced it a great and original success.[28]

From that time on Dorothy was prepared to give a chance (or the appearance of a chance) to a good many young men, while she was waiting for the right one. In the following year, when she was 20, after a trip to Scandinavia, Russia and the Tatra Mountains in what was then Austria, she wrote down her specifications on a sheet of notepaper from the Grand Hotel at Venice. They go much beyond the meagre accounts she gave of herself in her diary:

> When the right person comes along, I wonder if one has doubts, even then! Many of us are immediately carried off our feet and swept away into an irresistible current of love – while to the rest of us love comes walking slowly, and yet with sure steps he overtakes us and folds his arms about our shrinking forms. How little can we know ourselves, and yet I feel that love would come very slowly and gradually into my heart – and not with a sudden inrush of emotion. Of course the man one marries cannot be all one dreams of having him – and I am fully expectant of disappointments. I can't help longing for certain things – he must be strong and he must be tender – he must be honest and generous, and also kind and thoughtful – and oh – if he only will love me tenderly, take care of me, put his arms about me.. . . .
>
> Married life is full of rifts and troubles, of course, and I have seen too much of life to imagine that it is all a rosy dream. But if two people understand each other and each has patience and confidence – the troubles will be cleared away and will not become black and mysterious shadows. Perfect faith in each other – that, above all things, is the truest, surest foundation and I can't imagine anything more wonderful than this sort of an understanding between two people. Nothing then could really go wrong.
>
> I don't think I could fall in love with a man who had no ambition or no aim in life – because I feel a great longing to become a part of his life and help him when possible to do his work – and then besides if he lacked all ambition I couldn't admire him and admiration for my husband would be – [word left out]. I wonder if a woman really can be a help to a man she marries. I have always thought so until a few weeks ago, when all sort of horrid feelings came to me at Tatra, and I imagined that I was not apt to be happy. If I demand so much in a man in the way of mental capacity and desire for work and

accomplishment of what is worth while – doubtless that man will be
far beyond me in every way, and after a few years I may drop out of his
life having ceased to be of any help, and then each of us will go our
own way. Perhaps the chances of happiness would be greater were I
to marry a man with no career who would need me more in his daily
life – while on the other hand, a man with a good mind and the feeling
of living and being 'up and doing' would stride ahead of me and never
need the hand which I would long to give. If those two were weighed
in the balance, of course I should choose happiness with the man of no
career – for surely happiness is the aim of life.

I have only seen one man that comes near to what I long
for – only one man that I would really like to marry – at least I think I
would! Sometimes I feel 'oh, no' – not even you – but altogether he
fills up most of the holes and niches and I know he is much too good
for me.

Karolyn Gould concluded that the Venetian man was Grosvenor
Atterbury, an architect who designed model tenements for the poor, and a
poet as well.[29] In 1907 he was reported as sketching in the garden while
Dorothy read aloud to him. Beatrice for once was out of the way, in bed
with measles. More to the point, he was on the S.S. *Adriatic* in June 1907
when she started the European tour which led through Tatra to Venice. He
also heads the league of Dorothy's admirers which Karolyn Gould compiled for 1907. She gave scores to forty-three men according to the number
of times Dorothy saw them. Atterbury was ahead of his nearest competitors of that year, Lloyd Warren, another architect, and Delancey Jay, who
had been at Eton and Harvard and was also in the US Foreign Service.
Atterbury saw her 42 times, as against 25 for Jay and 20 for Warren. Even
so, he was after Tatra turned down; for all his virtues he was a lot older and
a bit shorter than Dorothy. Another, later failure was Piatt Andrew. Piatt
was second-in-command at the US Treasury and so was able to use the
Treasury yacht, *Apache*, for his courting. He invited Dorothy for a
three-day cruise on the Potomac and James rivers. He did not invite
Beatrice Bend; she came all the same. On the third day he finally proposed
and was gracefully rejected. Dorothy knew it was coming and enjoyed her
talks with the intelligent Piatt all the more because she knew. She played
the game of Jamesian heroine till the end and the disappointed suitor
remained a bachelor for life.[30] 'Who so list to hunt, I know where is an
hind.'[31]

Her photograph album[32] shows her perched on sleighs or lined up with
the young men in fur coats and fur hats at some skiing resort, standing on
the spacious steps of spacious houses in South Carolina, reclining on the
decks of yachts in Long Island Sound, sitting at polo grounds or race-

tracks like her father's at Belmont Park. The men are always smartly dressed, the women even more so, with their enormous hats swathed in drapery and flowers. There is also picture after picture of wedding scenes. The bride is always supported by at least six and often nine bridesmaids, all in the same embroidered, beribboned dresses frothy with lace and burdened with enormous bouquets which they have often deposited on the floor for the photograph. The people are usually laughing or smiling, not embarrassed before the camera or anywhere else, one would imagine, and Dorothy is smiling as flirtatiously as the rest of her friends, with none of the camera shyness which afflicted her later at Dartington.

She was always on the move. She would be off with a family party to Aiken on 'Wanderer', the private railroad car which Harry had inherited from their father. There friends would materialise from Fifth and Park Avenues. Or it would be the Adirondacks, or Newport, or Long Island and, again and again, Europe, meeting there the same circle in gondolas on the Grand Canal or climbing the lower slopes of the Matterhorn, riding in Hyde Park, in a pleasure-boat steaming around the Ile de la Cîté or in yet another five-star hotel in Vienna, Rome, Florence, Athens or St Petersburg. It became the custom for Dorothy to make one grand tour after another, all carefully planned by her serious-minded companion and prepared for by much reading, not only of Henry James. She was away in Europe six months of the year in 1906, in 1907 and in 1908 and then in 1909 went on the fateful trip which kept her out of America for fifteen months. Between 10 August 1904 and 31 December 1909 Dorothy spent 965 days in the USA and 1,005 days out of it. Shortly before the long trip in 1906, she had met her future husband. Even by then her 'seriousness' was recognised in her circle. She enjoyed cotillions but also classes and serious discussions on serious subjects with serious people. She could respect the demand of the Edwardian age for high ritual and shape in personal life, she could benefit from the generous sense of time and the reticence and irony that went together so well. She shared a common sense of *noblesse oblige*. But she was also uncommonly serious, for a girl so pretty and so rich.

At 18 she was a founder member of a Book Class to which many of her serious women friends also belonged. They read a book a month and met for a long session to discuss it at one or other of their grand houses. In 1906 the books included works by Henry James, George Eliot, Balzac, Tolstoy, Meredith, Hardy, the Brontës, and three Shakespeare plays. The Book Class continued to meet for the next sixty years. Dorothy attended when she was in New York, which was not all that less frequently in the 1930s, when Dartington had begun, than it had been in the 1900s.

She was also a regular attender at Grace Church when she was in New York even though she thought some of the sermons ridiculous. Of one she said, 'It was about the angels and I had to giggle internally all the time.'[33] She became steadily more critical of standard religious observance. She quoted with approval in her diary, but I do not know from where, the statement that

> There is only one true religion – the ministry of the head to the
> devotion of the heart. You need no priesthood here but the priesthood
> of conscience; you need no costly erection of churches, but the open
> world of God's house of worship.

She went to classes in philosophy, economics, Greek literature, lace-making and basket-weaving. She was fond of lectures on heavy subjects like the Causes of Human Hatreds, Tolstoy, the Hague Peace Conference, the Relationship between Chemistry and Biology, Subliminal Drama, the Standard of Living and Labor.

She also gave much of her time, when she was in the USA, to good works. The Junior League was one of her organisations. It was for fashionable young women from New York Society. She became its Treasurer in April 1906 and its President a year after. Dorothy later had the idea, around 1916, of forming the Association of Junior Leagues of America. She was the first President in 1921–2. From the beginning she introduced to its meetings the same sort of serious lectures she enjoyed hearing elsewhere and, with fellow-members Ruth Morgan and Daisy Harriman, pushed it into making investigations of the industrial and living conditions of the poor, and into doing something about them, for instance building tenements and supporting settlement houses. Dorothy's diary for a fairly usual day, 15 February 1909, says 'Beatrice and I visited a lithographers factory and then went to the opening of the new Municipal lodging house'. Without at all giving up the round of weekend parties and dances Dorothy also became active in organisations of an increasingly radical nature, like the suffragettes and the Women's Trade Union League.

American emulation of Europe (and especially of England) was at its height and it accounted for more than the suffragettes. The symphony orchestras, opera companies and repertory theatres of New York were sometimes better than the originals in Europe. A new ruling class was quite deliberately attempting to establish and secure its position on the European model. Resorts such as Newport, palaces like 'The Breakers', balls for the Four Hundred, all had their functions to perform. The men looked on marriage in the European manner, as a means of consolidating their wealth; their wives were more concerned with social distinctions. Titles mattered more to them than wealth – hence all the daughters who were married off to bankrupt English or Hungarian noblemen in need of American money to maintain their estates. Dorothy saw all this going on, Consuelo Vanderbilt being forced to marry the Duke of Marlborough and her close friend Gladys Vanderbilt becoming Countess Szechenyi. Her eldest sister, Pauline, also married into the English aristocracy and Pauline's daughter as Lady Baillie made a gift of Leeds Castle in Kent to the British nation. Most of Dorothy's contemporaries, the mischievous, fun-loving girls who grin at the cameras from all those sleighs and polo-grounds, ended up as wives of stockbrokers if not of Lords and Counts. Why not Dorothy? Serious-minded, and a radical. How could it be? There are perhaps four main strands of influence.

First, she believed quite solemnly, in a country whose people have in this century been much more solemn on this subject than in Britain, in her duty to society. She did not question (any more than most people questioned) her right to inherit wealth; but she did think that right carried a duty. This same belief on the part of very many other wealthy Americans has found expression in thousands of Foundations, Galleries, Museums, Hospitals.

Second, she had a father who had been a notable reformer in his younger days. An effective opponent of crooked machine politics, he had helped to destroy Boss Tweed of Tammany. He was also remembered as a reformer of the Navy. But the ways he used to make money were much criticised. He was not more unscrupulous than many others: he used the methods common in his time:[34]

> Thus in setting up the American Tobacco Company the artful allies, Whitney and Ryan, had begun by issuing to the public an initial capital of ten million dollars, which was increased in 1890 to 70 million dollars; then finally when they changed the Company into a New Jersey Corporation in 1904 they celebrated with a revised recapitalisation of 180 million dollars. According to one of the fantastic legends of Wall Street, Whitney and Ryan together had used little more than 50,000 dollars in promoting the Tobacco Trust and capturing the stock.

He also used his inside knowledge of Tammany and New York politics to squeeze concessions for his streetcar empire.

Whether or not Dorothy knew anything of this while her father was alive is doubtful. She was probably too young. But she cannot have avoided knowing when a public scandal about his business deals broke in 1908. His Metropolitan Street Railway Company went into liquidation. Many people who had bought the watered stock lost their money. It was on the front pages of all the New York papers. Many critics, his biographer says, would have forgiven Whitney 'if it were not for what they termed his unscrupulous methods in acquiring his fortune'.[35] Hirsch says Dorothy told him her father wanted to make it up to the two children who stood by him.[36] She was in a roundabout way taking over the guilt from him. It was for her he did it. She may have felt she needed to do all she could to redeem his name.

Third, she was an orphan and so had no parents to veto her eccentricity. Neither Flora nor William would have allowed her to support the Women's Trade Union League.

Fourth, she came to maturity in a period of reform in America. Theodore Roosevelt was elected President in 1904. He was the first great trust-buster, just as Grover Cleveland had along with her father been a reformer some twenty years before. Roosevelt enjoyed all the more general support because he was a Republican. Dorothy came from a Democratic family, but she must have been influenced by the mood of the times, as also, perhaps, by the election of the Liberal reform government in England in 1906. England helped to prompt some of the causes like the Workers' Education Association she helped to start. Dorothy was drawn into campaigns to end corruption in city government, to aid immigrants, to ease poverty. Roosevelt himself became a personal friend.

Dorothy met her future husband for the first time just after her coming-out dance in January 1906 at a dinner given by E. H. Harriman (the railway tycoon and the 'little giant of Wall Street')[37] at his home on East 66th Street. Mary, Harriman's daughter and sister to Averell, was one of her closest friends, also a member of the Junior League and another of the rare rich girls who wanted the League to do something for the people who worked in the sweatshops or in the railway yards from which her father extracted his money. Dorothy had probably heard that a Mr Straight was to be at the dinner and that he was courting Mary, two years older than Dorothy.

Willard Dickerman Straight was a man of no fortune at all. His father, Henry Straight, taught natural sciences at a training college in Oswego, New York, and was an upholder of progressive educational ideas. He died in 1885, when Willard was five. Emma, his mother, was a spirited woman who supported her children by taking a job in Tokyo as a teacher of literature and drawing. The Superintendent of Schools in Tokyo had been one of the students at Oswego. 'Those two years in Japan exerted a profound impression upon a susceptible boy with a taste for adventure, an almost tempestuous disposition to have his own way and an avid interest in picturesque and startling surroundings.'[38] Emma died of tuberculosis in 1890. Willard was adopted by a lady doctor and eventually entered Cornell University to study architecture. He was, like Dorothy's father, a man of diverse gifts, highly talented as draughtsman and painter, singer and guitarist. A drawing he did of Dorothy is reproduced as Plate 12. His professor, Morse Stephens, recommended him upon his graduation for a job, which he got, in the Imperial Maritime Customs Service in Peking which was headed by an Englishman, Sir Robert Hart. After that he became a Reuter's and Associated Press correspondent during the Russo–Japanese war and later US Consul General in Mukden. There he was also unofficial representative of the same Mr Harriman who invited him to dinner and who was anxious to promote and finance railway development in China.

Dorothy could not have known all that. But she cannot have failed to notice his charm, or his extreme good looks (including the reddish hair which his daughter Beatrice inherited). According to Susan Hammond, women were drawn to him. 'He was the sort of person you would like to have notice you.'[39] Perhaps because she had heard of the relationship with Mary, and there were other young men there whom she knew, Dorothy did no more than write in her diary that a 'Mr Straight' was one of those at dinner.

The next encounter was not until some three years later, in 1909, in Washington. Much had happened to both of them in the meantime. Willard, now 29, had moved up in the diplomatic service and was Acting Head of the Far Eastern Bureau of the State Department. In Washington Dorothy sat next to Willard at one dinner and then at another. After the second the whole party went off to a dance at the White House. There were two more encounters on Long Island before Willard left again for the Far East. Having resigned from the diplomatic service, he was to be the official instead of the unofficial representative of the J. P. Morgan and E. H. Harriman interests in Peking, pressing the Chinese government to accept a loan. Dorothy was the more interested in him because, having travelled so extensively in Europe, she was now planning a visit to China. This did not interrupt her social round. In 50 days after 6 January 1909, Dorothy attended 40 dinner parties, lunched out 44 times, received 50 different gentleman callers to tea, went to 7 suffrage meetings and heard Florence Kelly speak at the annual meeting of the Consumers' League.[40]

On 13 July that year Dorothy departed from New York, again aboard 'Wanderer', having spent some time between all the engagements, in her customary spirit of self-improvement, preparing for the journey. On her private car and then on the S.S. *Korea*, when it sailed from San Francisco for its long voyage across the Pacific, she took with her her faithful maid, Louisa Weinstein, also Beatrice and her mother, Mrs Bend, and a small library of books about the Far East.

In Peking Willard vacated his large house for the visiting party. They could not have had better quarters. There was a gathering momentum from the arrival on 1 November until 7 November which Willard and Dorothy celebrated for many years as an important anniversary. A Sunday. The air bright. The women, accompanied by Willard and Mr Prather Fletcher (who later married Beatrice), drove to the Summer Palace and then to the Imperial Jade Spring where they had a picnic lunch between purple hills on one side and golden Peking on the other. What the two of them most remembered was their long talk by lantern light when they returned to the city.

By 15 November, their time up, Willard was calling her Princess in his diary and almost right away, in a letter, more romantically, *Princesse*. Dorothy was taken by everything about him including the loneliness he often felt as one who had been an orphan too. She wrote to him from Hankow:[41]

> Oh Wise Man of the East: You have made us very lonely and very homesick for the purple hills and for your own companionship. I don't think I realized what a sad break our departure was going to be until I stood on the wall with you yesterday and said goodbye to the great city and the distant hills — and hardest of all, to you. And then when we stood on the station platform and the whistle suddenly blew and we all said goodbye, I had a lump in my throat that was very hard to smile away, for the veil was being drawn there over two of the happiest weeks I have ever known. . . . I can only thank you for being the sort of man you are, and I think that after yesterday morning when we burned incense for the last time together before your Buddha and we solemnly promised to have faith always that there can never be in the future such a thing as lack of understanding between us.

Dorothy had not written anyone a letter like that before in her 22 years. He replied:[42]

> I cannot write the things I feel — but you understand — I think we both did that morning as we looked out over the mist shrouded city — then back to the Golden Roofs — as we walked down from the wall — and through the busy gate — to the station gate — and then for the last time — turned from the bridge and the broad street — to the distant hills of 'Borderland'.

Borderland was a place he had invented for a song he had sung her, a paradise somewhat like the purple hills of Peking. Willard had to stay at his post trying to negotiate the loan which the Americans, the British, the French and the Germans wanted to make to China. He could not leave until the end of April 1910. He travelled to London to report. At the Morgan Grenfell office in Old Broad Street he was told he could have three days off. By 6 the next morning he was knocking at her door in her Milan hotel:[43]

> There were no pretences then. After one brief word of greeting he told me why he had come. Standing against the door of our little sitting

room with his hat still in his hand he poured out the yearning of his heart. . . . I, who had been living for six months in anticipation of this day, suddenly found myself weak and uncertain. Confronted with the reality I drew back in hesitation and doubt.

Later in the morning, in the cathedral, she said that while she had great affection for him she was not sure.

He dashed back to London for another crucial round of talks in the loan negotiations, and then had a day off to meet Dorothy at Aix. She would not give him any firmer answer but he won a further advantage. Since he had now to return to New York she agreed to use his private code in their telegrams to each other. BORDERLAND already meant love. The other words were[44]

AIKEN	–	I miss you frightfully
ANTUNG	–	Are you well?
BOY	–	Willard
HOOROO	–	Everything fine
GRAZIA	–	Thanks for your telegram
LIEBESTRAUM	–	God guard you always
SHEMMO	–	How are things going?
TAOHSIEH	–	Thanks for your letter
RAINBOW	–	Success

She sent him a cable to New York saying LIEBESTRAUM BOY BORDERLAND.[45] Hundred upon hundred of such cables rest in the library archive at Cornell.

But she was still not sure. Harry and Pauline were against it, thinking Willard an adventurer. She made her final decision conditional upon his success in China when he got back there. One criticism of him was that he was impatient, would not stick at anything any more than he had persisted in his relationships. Therefore, he had not yet achieved anything major, on his own. It was a test for him:[46]

I know how dreadfully hard and lonely it must be for you . . . and the negotiations with the Chinese must be such discouraging work. . . .
But I have great faith that you will put the loan through . . . and then – oh Willard – won't that be wonderful! . . . Wouldn't it be the greatest triumph ever, if you won!

He replied, 'If ever anything comes of this it will be because you said "Steady" and because for your sake I want to win.'[47] Whether for this reason or not, he did. The loan agreement for $300 millions at 5 per cent over a period of forty-five years was signed in Peking on 15 April 1911 by the Ministers of France, Germany, England and the United States. Willard sent her a cable containing the one word RAINBOW. She replied[48]

GRAZIA HAPPY SHOUTING FOR JOY GOOD FOR US AIKEN LIEBESTRAUM BORDERLAND

Willard was also given much of the credit in the newspapers of New York, London and Paris. This improved Harry's opinion of him.

When she at last accepted the *New York Times* played up the story of the boy 'Who Became a Figure in Finance, Politics and International Affairs, and Who Won the Love of Two Heiresses'.[49] To get away from more of that they chose to have the wedding not in America but in Geneva on 7 September 1911, if not the same month at least the same day of the month as their talk by the Peking lantern light. He was 31, she 24.

Dorothy continued to doubt up to the last minute. She admitted in her diary to terrible headaches. She did not set down what she much later in 1927 wrote to Irene, Leonard's sister, about the hold of Beatrice upon her:[50]

> It was only when I began to love Willard that the test of her influence came – and it was much more controlling and powerful than I ever dreamed it to be. I suddenly found myself closing up again with Willard, dreading the sight of him and finally almost refusing to see him. He came back to me only two days before we were married and even then I was as hard and cold as a stone.... I never realized what was the matter with me until long afterwards. I only knew I didn't want to leave Beatrice and that the prospect of breaking from her was somehow tearing me to pieces. But I never fully realized the terrific psychological effect that the conflict was having on my relation to Willard. It only became clear to me, some time afterwards, what indirect and hidden results issued from the struggle.

It was as if in leaving the tutelage of Beatrice she was suffering again the anguish caused by the loss of a mother and a stepmother. Up to the last minute it must have been touch and go whether she would call it all off.

But she stayed firm. They were married. From Geneva they went to Venice and then on the Trans-Siberian, headed once more for Peking. Willard had more work to do on the loan. They filled a large scrapbook with drawings and verses from Willard, exclamation marks from Dorothy and wedding photos and telegrams. They were very comfortable in the large compartments on the train's two-week journey. They alighted at every station to buy goods from peasants and take fast walks into the town. At one Siberian station Louisa, the maid, 'gaily took a walk and . . . the train pulled off without her. When we discovered what happened, Willard telegraphed her to take the next train and he sent back her bags, some money and some books to read – so that she came along two days behind us quite comfortably.'[51] Dorothy had three electric lights in her compartment. Willard read Carlyle's *French Revolution* to her while she pasted things into her scrapbook or wrote up her daily diary for Beatrice, who was not physically with her for almost the first time in twelve years.

The day they arrived in Peking saw the last rising against the Manchu Dynasty. There were provincial revolutions in Hankow, Hanyang, Wuchang and Canton. Would the revolution reach Peking, and in what form? Officials of the legations buzzed around each other sucking up the latest rumour; Dr Morrison, correspondent of the London *Times*, rode up and down Legation Street telling everyone the end of the Manchus was at hand. The newly married couple managed to make the best of it, in Borderland for them if China in revolution for others:[52]

> Willard and I rode together this afternoon from 3 o'clock to 6.30 . . .
> it was too heavenly to be on a horse again and we had a perfectly
> glorious ride over the plains, strewn with the ruins of tombs and
> temples. It did us both no end of good. During dinner – which we
> were having by the fire in my sitting room – a soldier arrived from the
> Legation . . . with two large army revolvers – deadly looking
> weapons. We are really commencing to feel rather business like – for
> Willard is going to sleep with a loaded revolver by his bed – and I have
> another – unloaded by me. It would be rather exciting to be attacked
> by a wild mob in the night.

There was as it turned out no fighting in the streets. On 30 October the Emperor capitulated to the threat of an attack upon the city by 27,000 rebel troops. On that same evening, instead of the soldiers, two visitors came to dinner at the Straight's:[53]

> We had a dinner party for the Sidney Webbs who have just arrived in
> Peking for a week's visit – bringing among other letters of
> introduction one for Willard! . . . He is only about five feet
> high – with a shaggy beard, little eyes and a huge Jew nose . . . I'm
> afraid that I am the only one who found any charm in Mrs Webb. . . .
> She has rather a sweet face and to me she was very attractive – but not
> one of the men could stand her. She talked in an absolutely positive
> way about things – which put a damper on the conversation as no one
> wanted to argue with her. Their attitude was one of great intellectual
> superiority – and they seemed to take no interest in any remarks but
> their own. They got on Dr Morrison's nerves to such an extent that he
> left right after dinner to send off a telegram and never came back.

Dorothy on the other hand liked the couple so much she gave three more dinner parties for them.

The new government of Yüan Shih-kai was shaky but it was not until the following March that the Straights were forced to leave their beautiful house. A local mutiny filled the streets with looting soldiers. Willard and Dorothy, Louisa and Dr Morrison made off to the legation. They got trapped in a cul-de-sac and could do nothing but watch helplessly as the soldiers ran by with their loot, smashed shops or set fire to bazaars and a theatre. They were eventually rescued by a party of twenty American marines. There was a lot of publicity about them in New York and Harry Davison, Willard's boss at J. P. Morgan, thought that the murder of such a well-known couple would do no good to the reputation of his bank. The future of the loan was also uncertain. He recalled them.

This did not upset them. Dorothy was expecting her first baby. Any fears she may have had that when Willard had her money his love would wane were being rapidly dispelled. He became more fond rather than less.

Her first baby was born at Westbury on 6 November 1912, the day after President Wilson's victory at the polls. The baby was named Whitney but at first called Bill. Just before the birth Dorothy had an interview with one of her father's lawyers, William H. Page, to review her will and make sure her first child would be fully protected if she herself did not survive. Her second child, Beatrice, was born in 1914 and her third, Michael, in 1916.

Willard went to work at 23 Wall Street, the Morgan head office. He had returned with quite an achievement to his credit for someone so young and he was given his little triumph, a trip on J.P.'s great yacht, *The Corsair*, whose name J.P. liked partly because it gave him the chance to joke about being descended from Captain Morgan, another famous pirate. His annual salary was doubled to $20,000, which would have been all they had to live on if it had not been for Dorothy. It was her money that made it possible to commission the same architect, William Adams Delano, whom her father had employed, to design and build a large new town house for them, on Fifth Avenue, at No. 1130.[54] It was known for long after as the Willard Straight house.

Harry Davison, Willard's immediate boss in the bank, regarded him as promising and showed as much, although there were still unanswered questions in his mind. Had he done so well in China only because he understood Chinese, Chinese politics and Chinese intrigue so intimately and because of his dazzling skill at making people like and trust him? Had he also the making of a banker? Would he get down to the humdrum? Until the answers came Willard would have no chance of the Morgan partnership he coveted. Willard became more and more restless as time passed without his getting it. In 1915 he resigned.

Dorothy was all the more needed when his life did not go smoothly. He needed her maternal sympathy and support, remaining prone to fits of anxiety when he was separated from her even for a day or two. She used her power to ward off his depression and also to try to stop his falling victim to his other chief weakness: to give things up, or want to, if he did not rapidly succeed. The battle she had helped him win in Peking was constantly renewed.

If he leaned on her for emotional support he began increasingly to do so in other ways as well. His biographer, Herbert Croly, speaks of her influence:[55]

> His mind had never fully faced the existence of social problems, such as the problems of poverty, labor and education, with which the state might not be entirely competent to deal. It was these problems in which his wife was most keenly interested and which his companionship with her and his life in an industrialised society imposed upon his mind. His increasing interest in them rendered him less interested than he had been in what he could accomplish by a business career, and less satisfied than he had been with public administrative work as an alternative to private business.

They were both greatly impressed by Croly's book, *The Promise of American Life*, an American counterpart of Wallas's *The Great Society*. He had published it in 1909 with the object of giving a political philosophy to the Progressive Movement which flourished in the first years of the century. It was still being much read when they returned from China. The politician they both admired most at that time, Theodore Roosevelt, was also much influenced by it, as indeed the book was by him. It put into more intellectual form his attack upon the 'malefactors of great wealth'. They had added political to economic power to such an extent as to make a mockery of democracy. 'The great American industrial leaders have accumulated fortunes for which there is also no precedent on the part of men who exercise no official political power.'[56] Dorothy did not take any exception to the implied criticism of her father, nor Willard to that of J. P. Morgan. Nor did they mind being themselves labelled as belonging to the 'class of economic parasites' who inherit money without earning it. 'The creator of a large fortune may well be its master; but its inheritor will, except in the case of exceptionally able individuals, become its victim, and most assuredly the evil social effects are as bad as the evil individual effects.'[57]

They invited Croly to come down from his home at Cornish in New Hampshire, where he had been editing the *Architectural Record*. He said he would like nothing better than to edit a political journal which would espouse the radical ideas he had put forward in his book. They could hardly hear what he said – he was extraordinarily shy – but they nevertheless took to him and he to them.[58] All was decided at a conference at

7 Dorothy in 1895, aged 8

8 Dorothy (left), and two friends,
probably at Saratoga, New York
State, 1906–9

9 Dorothy, probably in Burma, 1910

10 Dorothy in Japan, 1909

11 Willard and Dorothy, probably 1911

Westbury of the Crolys, Judge Learned Hand and his wife, Felix Frankfurter and Phil Littell. Before long the weekly, *The New Republic*, was on the newsstands. Walter Lippmann, Walter Weyl and others were soon on the staff and joining in the weekly editorial conferences with the Straights. Within a few years *The New Republic*'s circulation had risen well above the 20,000 mark. It has survived until today as a foremost radical journal. Four years later Straight added another to the magazines supported by his wife when he converted the little journal of the American Asiatic Association into the fully fledged periodical, *Asia*, a good deal later joined in the group by *Antiques*.

When America came into the war he pulled every string he could to get himself into the State Department or onto the General Staff, and failed, just as he was to fail in 1918 to get himself front-line duty in command of a battalion or on the staff of a division. The post in France when it came was not all that brilliant – in charge of the War Risk Insurance Bureau for the US Army. But while he was with the Bureau arranging for American servicemen to insure their lives – running the European end of probably the biggest insurance company in the world, with a staff of thirty-four officers and sixty-five enlisted men – he was still reasonably content.

Dorothy was busier than he was, on the Mayor's Committee on National Defense, with the Red Cross, working for a time in a YMCA canteen, still a suffragist along with colleagues like Mrs Belmont who said, 'Just pray to God. She will help you.'[59] She also helped to start, and was one of the main financial supporters and a director of, the New School for Social Research. It still flourishes.

While Willard was in Paris Dorothy made the first of many gestures, as though she wanted to gather unto herself other lost children, even if at the expense of her own. Willard's sister Hazel was now Mrs James Sanborn, and pregnant. Her son, Bobbie, needed attention. Dorothy adopted him into her home, not to any warm welcome from Whitney.

Willard's contentment at the Bureau did not last long. When the work was finished he floated from one short-term job to another as a staff officer when what he really wanted was combat duty. He was 'badly down on his springs', his health as poor as his spirits, when, while he was waiting for a better job to turn up, he wrote to 'Miss chairman of all things':[60]

> And that brings me to my first great principle – which you must impress upon Whitney and Michael. In fact if I had the chance only to give two pieces of advice to a youngster – I would – assuming of course he was gently bred – tell him – *always to get his foundations solid – before he started to climb* – and to by constant practice and the most consistent effort – *train himself to have his bowels move each morning as soon as he was dressed*. You've no idea what these

things mean. . . . From the latter I am suffering constantly – and it's only a question of training. As to the former – that has been my great handicap in life. I've always been finding myself in places more important than I was really competent to hold. I've never had the foundation for the jobs I've had – except perhaps the political foundation for the Chinese loan business – and for my job in the State Department.

Dorothy, however much she agreed with him, protested in her reply that he was appealing for the specialisation which is what mastery of fundamentals always brings. People who could specialise happily were seldom creative, as Willard had been when he could overcome his main weakness, his lack of 'stick-at-it-iveness'. 'As to the second precept – it is such a fixed habit already that it is almost funny to see the [boys] rush upstairs every morning after breakfast as if they were bent on a mission! Poor Willo – I know your troubles, and I shall certainly try to avoid them for the children.'[61]

He never achieved his ambition of active service. But when the war was won things improved for him. He no longer felt allegiance to Roosevelt; he was wholly behind Wilson now in his commitment to a League of Nations of which his own country would be a member. Willard had known Colonel House, the President's chief assistant at the Peace Conference, and had repeatedly asked him for jobs. At last came the offer he wanted, a post on the Colonel's staff. The Colonel also wanted Dorothy to come to Paris to take a house where delegates could meet outside the conference chamber. She agreed. One of Willard's first assignments was to visit M. Clemenceau, the Premier of France, to tell him when President Wilson would be leaving New York.

He was making the final arrangements for the conference when he fell victim to the world-wide influenza epidemic. He was looked after by two friends of Dorothy who were in Paris with the Red Cross, Daisy Harriman, cousin of the little giant of Wall Street, and Ruth Morgan. The flu became pneumonia. On 1 December he died. He was only 38; Dorothy became a widow at 31.

Dorothy cabled Daisy:[62]

PLEASE THANK PERSONALLY FOR ME NURSES, DOCTORS AND ALL WILLARD'S FRIENDS WHO HAVE DONE SO MUCH. I AM VERY GRATEFUL FOR THE CARE AND LOVE HE HAD. NO WORDS CAN EXPRESS MY GRATITUDE TO YOU. I SHOULD LIKE TO HAVE WILLARD BURIED IN FRANCE SOMEWHERE WITH AMERICAN SOLDIERS HE LOVED AND ADMIRED SO MUCH. WILL THIS BE POSSIBLE.

PLEASE DO NOT WORRY ABOUT ME. I KNOW THAT HE IS
SAFE AND THAT IS ALL THAT MATTERS.

Dorothy had planned to take passage on the S.S. *George Washington*
two days later, with the President.

She did go not long after, with Flora Whitney, Harry's daughter, whose
fiancé, Quentin Roosevelt, had been killed in the last days of the war, to
stand by Willard's grave in the war cemetery at Suresnes. She went to
Langres Cathedral where Willard had had a moment of telepathic communication with her while he was at the Staff College. After the organ
stopped, when the service he attended at Easter, 1918, was over, he said, 'I
stood there with you.'[63] She felt the same towards him a little later that
year. On an always remembered occasion (as much so as the first ride into
Borderland) when she had been at Southampton on Long Island she had
one day looked out across the sea in yearning and had been so conscious of
Willard that she could almost see him.[64]

It was not so easy to feel the same sense of spiritual union after the
death of his body. She longed to regain it, and tried every means she could
to re-establish the communication she had at Southampton. She had been,
like her sister, Pauline, and many others, interested in Christian Science
and hoped to find some solace in that. Later on, for the same purpose, she
tried séances. She went to Towson in Maryland for them and sometimes
the medium, Mary K., came to her house in New York. However much
scepticism she may have felt, she kept a detailed record of the questions
and answers in her notebook.[65] Willard, through the medium and the
control, told her he had been 'there' with her on several occasions. She
often asked him how she should bring up their children, and particularly
what Willard wanted her to do about their education. He told her not to
worry:

Do you think our children are developing in the right way?	Yes, splendidly. You need not worry over them, they are doing just as I would have them.
What kind of life will Whitney have?	He will have a life of great worldly interest. He will mix in the world – stand out but more as a good businessman and good fellow – a companion – he will be restless and fond of pleasure as well as work.

What about Michael?	He will be more literary and I want to see him develop in that way. He will have a very deep mind, and problems of all kinds he will have to be taught to meet.
What sort of training will he have?	Social, literary, economic and so forth.
What about Beatrice?	She is quite different – and will be harder to bring up, she will like to be frivolous first, so give her happiness. Later when she is older she will develop, I think, more like you. It is harder for me to judge . . . she is so young.
Has Beatrice any artistic talent?	Yes – I think she will have.
What should I try to get Whitney deeply interested in?	He will not be a literary type – he will be more of a sports and businessman, so fit him for that.

The notebook for 1919 in which all this is written opens with an inscription in Dorothy's hand. 'By this shall all men know that Ye are my Disciples – if Ye have love one to another.'

By 1919, when Leonard was installed at Cornell, Dorothy's personality was fully shaped in the way that Leonard's was not. The loss of two mothers had not dulled so much as sharpened her sensitivity to the feelings of others. From her father to whom she had been loyal, she learned loyalty. Her money, and so her power in a worldly sense, came from him. She did not regard it as something either to be squandered or hoarded. Her wealth was responsibility as well as prop to the state of life she had been brought up to.

Plenty of rich people have the same sense about their wealth. Not so many sympathise with radicals who attack all privilege. In this Dorothy was not so much in accord with as reacting against her father. She was more like him when he was the young anti-Tammany reformer than when he became part of the Tammany machine and used it with little scruple on behalf of himself and her. She was happier in opposition to the Boss Tweeds than in alliance with the Thomas Ryans.

If she had no mother she did, after Ma Bonne and along with Louisa, have a Beatrice Bend. Her high-mindedness was in tune with Dorothy's. Beatrice saw to it that she was educated not just in the cotillion but in literature and, through travel, in the history and culture of several continents. It must have been partly from Beatrice, although of course by no means wholly, that she gained confidence in her own judgment. She would listen to other people, endlessly – some people thought her chief talent was as listener. She could be swayed. But on any aesthetic or moral issue she was by 1920 already fully capable of making up her own mind. Once it was made up, it was not easy to shift.

Willard was many things she liked and needed – he was gay, brilliant and, above all, in love with her. But, at least in the world of ideas, the influence was mostly one way, her upon him. She persuaded him to take an interest in radical causes and start *The New Republic*, not he her. He remained something of the new arrival. He had to try to make himself accepted by the Eastern aristocracy, for instance by buying a string of polo ponies and posing in the saddle of his favourite one with a mallet resting on his shoulder, as though he was to the game born just like Dorothy's brothers.[66] They knew, as she knew, that he was not. In wartime he was the conventional husband, insisting that everything must be subordinated to winning, and deeply critical of the one-time pacifists on his own magazine with their harping on war aims. She was the unconventional wife, looking towards the peace settlement and sharing the liberal hopes of *The New Republic* staff. He was the representative American; she was not.

Without these differences they might have been less devoted to each other. The letter he wrote to 'My Dear Bill', as the eldest son, on the eve of his departure for France, was as much to her as to him. It was only to be opened if he died. Even allowing for the special nature of the occasion, there is no reason to doubt he meant what he said:[67]

> I trust for your sake, and the sake of all three of you, your mother will be there to guide you. All the best in you comes from her, all the finest in you will be brought out by her. You are blessed as no other children have been blessed in your mother. May your worship for her – for it will be with you as it is with me, reverence and real worship – guide you and lead you to treat all women with chivalry. Save yourself and tell Michael to save himself, that you may go clean and unashamed to her who will be your wife and the mother some day of your children.

Dorothy acknowledged this letter in a note printed in his biography:[68]

> He opened the real treasure house of life for me. The love that he gave was, indeed, a sort of veneration, a veneration which at times, quite contrary to his intention, completely humbled me before him. It was so utterly generous, so big, so inclusive that I could only marvel before it and question my own power of receiving. But just because he taught

me to see life with new eyes, just because he liberated my spirit and brought me life and the abundance of it, now that he has gone I cannot feel that the joy and meaning of existence have gone too.

If there were to be another man in her life, to confirm the meaning of existence for her, he would have to be an unusual one. He would have to be able to cope with the melancholy which she was now prey to, which had been well hidden in the bright-eyed girl who went sleigh-riding or played tennis or danced till dawn. He would have to be a man not overawed by the maturity of a mother with three children who had already been through one life, nor dazzled by her wealth. While needing to be very different from Willard because otherwise she would be too prone to sadness, he would have to be someone who could, in his own way, compare with him.

CHAPTER 4

TOGETHER

To release the imagination, to give it
wings, to open wide the doors of the mind,
this is perhaps the most vital service
that one being can render another.

Outline, 1926

Friday arrived, and sharp at 11, there was Mrs Straight, tall and slim,
all in black except for a little sable fur around her neck and a very
fetching hat, which almost covered her face. . . . Mrs Straight was
then in her early thirties. She was not only charming to look at, but
there was a graciousness and style about her bearing, and, withal, a
very bright gleam in her eye. When I mentioned the business
shortcomings of professors, her face lit up and the laugh she gave will
not easily be forgotten.[1]

Leonard drew on his old diaries to describe this first meeting on a Friday in
September 1920, at the Colony Club which Gertrude and Helen Whitney
had helped to found in 1900. It was *the* women's club of New York. Men
were not admitted at all by the front door. Leonard was directed to the
small one around the corner. He had been through it twice before,
fruitlessly, on Wednesday and Thursday, to keep appointments made for
him with this seemingly inaccessible woman, and on each day waited an
hour for her to appear. Twice he had left the men's waiting-room to
telephone his go-between, Oswald Garrison Villard, the editor of *The
Nation*, which vied with *The New Republic* as the country's leading radical
journal. Each day he told Leonard not to worry and to be ready to return
the next day instead. If the first trial for Prince Charming, it was not the
last. He had to propose marriage three times as well, at long intervals.
When they first met he was 27 and she was 33.

His purpose was the same as the other hundreds who flocked to Mrs

Straight. He wanted money, though not for himself but for the Cosmopolitan Club. Foreign students at Cornell could live there. Leonard had been elected its President in his second semester as a student, much to his surprise: he was often called 'that bloody Britisher', or 'limey', or 'Lloyd George' and attacked by people from all around the world who thought British Imperialism to be the Devil's work. Villard had been a visitor to the Club a few months earlier to talk on an always fresh topic, 'The world situation', and Leonard, dropping into American in his diary, said that afterwards he 'walked him' down the hill to the train. Villard told Leonard that, given all the rampant prejudice at that time in the country, he did not know of any other campus in America where there could have been such a free expression of opinion. Leonard jumped in right away:[2]

> I'm so glad you feel that way, Mr Villard, but the sad thing is that the Club is likely to be sold up altogether in the near future and to be closed down. The debt amounts to around $80,000. Would you be knowing, Mr Villard, of anyone in the country today who might be interested in the saving of the Club?

Villard said Dorothy.[3] Leonard took the name to New York along with the list of Cornell alumni he had been told to approach for funds. None of them offered any. By the end of a week's canvassing Dorothy was his last hope.

In preparation, enquiring about her, he discovered the very welcome fact that her late husband had left funds in his will for making Cornell University 'a more human place'. Many Cornellians had resented the implication that it needed to be. Not Leonard. He reminded her (almost as if he were one of those messengers she tried to conjure from the deeps in the years after his death) of what Willard had said, and then, without pressing further, asked her merely to visit Cornell for herself, to form her own views. He believed if only he could get her to Willard's old university that would be persuasion enough. He left the Colony Club, still by the side entrance, but this time well satisfied with himself. 'I think and trust', he wrote to his mother just afterwards 'that I've landed the lady who will see us out of our mess to the tune of some thousands of dollars.'[4] In his letters home from that time on for years to come he called her 'The Fairy Godmother'.

Dorothy made up for her failure to keep the first two appointments in New York by following up with a quick visit to Ithaca. On 12 October Leonard met the overnight train on the Lackawanna Rail Road from Hoboken. After breakfast at the Club he did the same as with Villard and 'walked her by a little goat path, and under a fence, to the left, just as you cross the gorge from Cascadilla, and so to the Telluride. There was no Law School in the way in those days. I had to comment upon the unsuitability of her Fifth Avenue shoes for negotiating the sides of steep gorges.'[5] The day passed in talks with professors for Dorothy and classes for Leonard, and ended with him putting her in her Pullman car for the return journey. Wisely, Leonard again did not press: he did not ask for a decision on the grant. Money was at the top of his mind, not on the tip of his tongue. But after the bells of the train had faded into the distance he hurried back to find out from one of the professors if the Sibyl from New York had spoken. Yes, she had. She had more or less decided to build a Union Building as a memorial to Major Straight. 'Was nothing said about the Club at all?' asked Leonard anxiously. Yes, it had been. She had said she would make the Club 'her own affair'.[6] Leonard, though delighted, had to make sure what she meant with a further flurry of letters. Her reply did not come till 26 October:

> I hardly know how to thank you for the very wonderful day that you and Professor Burr gave me there. I have lived it over many times in my imagination and I have been unceasingly grateful to you both for all the effort and trouble that you expended on my behalf. . . . I am always a little amused and intrigued by the picture of you milking cows and picking apples – when your abilities seem so obviously directed towards other achievements. . . . And now about the Club; *of course*, I'm going to help.

It was not easy for the young Englishman to interpret the letter. Was this how she wrote to everyone?

He heard nothing further until the following April. By then he had already met, in Rabindranath Tagore, another person who was to have an influence upon his life second only to that of Dorothy, as well as to become another link with her. Leonard knew a lot about him already. He had once been carried away by Tagore's book, *Gitanjali*, when he read it in the garden of a Farnham pub in 1915. He had heard much about him when he was in India in the war.

He could hardly fail to, for Tagore was already world-famous and born into a family[7] which had been that for three generations:

> I was born in what was then the metropolis of British India. My ancestors came floating to Calcutta upon the earliest tide of the fluctuating fortune of the East India Company. The conventional code of life for our family thereupon became a confluence of three cultures: the Hindu, the Mahomedan and the British.[8]

His grandfather, Dwarkanath Tagore, born in 1794, became one of the merchant princes of Calcutta which, under British rule, became the commercial centre of India; he was popularly known as Prince. Also the

Rockefeller of India, he financed in 1816 the first centre of modern education in India, the Hindu College, which became the Presidency College of Calcutta, and was the first Indian member of the Asiatic Society of Bengal founded by Sir William Jones 'for enquiring into the History, civil and natural, the Antiquities, Arts, Sciences and Literatures of Asia'.[9] The Prince's son was acclaimed Maharshi, a combination of saint and sage.

Rabindranath, son of a Maharshi, grandson of a Prince, was born in 1861, the fourteenth child, five years after Leonard's father. Rabi, as he was called, was brought up in the family's huge mansion at Jorasanko in Calcutta. He suffered from a variety of schools. One of the worst was Normal School. It was in the same British tradition as Repton; hardly better was his next school, the Bengal Academy. His revered father did not have much time to spare for him, except that he once took him on a journey to the Himalayas, where he went frequently for meditation. They stopped for a few days on one of the family estates at Santiniketan (as it later became known) near Bolpur in West Bengal. To most visitors its flat open fields seemed like a wasteland. To Rabi, released from the confined life of Calcutta and in the presence of his father, the place was like paradise. He described it as 'the darling of our hearts' in the song he wrote about it for which, as usual, he composed music as well as words. Not long afterwards he began to write poetry regularly. His first long poem, over 1,600 lines, was published when he was 14. After that poems and dramas poured forth almost without stop.

What eventually won him special acclaim in England as well as India were his *Gitanjali* songs. Published in London in 1912 with the aid of Sir William Rothenstein they led directly to his award of the Nobel Prize for Literature in 1913. The formal proposal on his behalf was put to Sweden by another Englishman, Sturge Moore. Tagore was the first non-European to be so honoured. A large deputation of 500 distinguished citizens of Calcutta came by a special train to Santiniketan to offer him congratulations, and were promptly snubbed for their pains by the new prize-winner.[10] All this Leonard must have known when he met him in New York.

The meeting between them was arranged by Mrs William Moody, a member of the Cornell Board of Trustees, in a dingy apartment in Waverly Place, off Washington Square, in March 1921. Tagore came there after breakfast. Leonard observed him as carefully as he had done Dorothy:[11]

> The colour of his skin and its texture were both notable. Pale burnt almond was the nearest I could get to a description of the colour. The eyes perpetually lit up with gleams of humour, almost of mischief, as he talked to his old friend. This was no mystic sage. This was no

64

gatherer of disciples, but a very human, human being. His hair was worn long, down to the shoulders. Like the beard it was naturally wavy and 'silvered o'er'. His outer gown of a deep reddish brown hung just like that of a university professor's, nearly to the ground. Under it was a second of the same material and colour, but which buttoned across, after the manner of the Buddhist sages and of contemporary Tibetans.

Mrs Moody introduced Leonard. Tagore said there was no need, without saying why. Leonard found out later. Sam Higginbottom was on leave from India that summer. When his Mission turned down his suggestion that Leonard should be given a job at his agricultural institute at Allahabad – Leonard was not a firm enough Christian – Sam then proposed Leonard to Tagore. Just the man he needed. Tagore trusted Sam and American colleges of agriculture. He had sent his son, Rathindranath, to the College of Agriculture at Illinois University, Urbana, in 1906. So, without any preliminaries, he began to speak of his plans for revival of the villages, Hindu, Muslim and Santali, around the school he had started at Santiniketan. The base for the experiment was to be a farm he owned nearby, outside the village of Surul:[12]

> Twenty years ago on the edge of one of them, and about a mile and a half from my school, I bought a farm. I have for some years been looking for someone who would be willing to go and live on the farm and who would begin to diagnose their village troubles, and perhaps give them the tools, and perhaps the ideas, whereby they could re-establish their economy, their social balance and their creative arts. Would you be interested? Yes? Then would you come back to India with me tomorrow?

Tagore was far more impetuous than Leonard. 'It is a wonderful offer', Leonard said, but not 'tomorrow': he needed time to complete his course at Cornell. Once he left the presence, he realised that neither he nor Tagore had spoken about money, for Leonard or the project. All the more reason to talk about it to Dorothy.

Soon after, in April 1921, when Leonard was walking the streets of New York with a Mr Chen, a Chinese scholar whom he had known at Cornell, he decided to risk calling on Mrs Straight without an appointment. It might be less risky than having one:[13]

> At her lovely house on Fifth Avenue, there were large glass doors. I rang the bell. A most august figure appeared at the top of the steps and beckoned us in. Her butler was certainly impressive, but not over welcoming. After some delay he allowed us inside the palace, which it

certainly appeared to be, and put us into the lift, saying that 'The Mistress was ready to receive us'.

Leonard told her about the invitation from Tagore and Dorothy said she had seen Tagore too 'and I'm interested'. So perhaps there would be money for that as well. Leonard pressed her to come to Cornell again. She promised she would.

In June she invited him to Old Westbury, and although he would only have $1 left in the world after paying the fare, he accepted. It was yet another millionaire's palace. He partnered Dorothy at tennis and won. Most of the time he spent telling Harry Lee, her head gardener, that he should ventilate his poultry house properly, wire his laying nests, plough up the hen run and cull his flock.

Things went better still on a second weekend a fortnight later, except that he was just as short of money. Also, the decent clothes he had come to America with were by now very worn. He darned a pair of socks, washed a few detachable soft collars, ironed them with the sort of electric iron they did not yet have in Yorkshire, and rubbed clean his own, frayed evening collar with an India rubber. The bow was missing from one of his evening shoes and the toe almost split off. When he departed for New York and had again paid his return fare he had this time $14 left over for his food for the whole summer and nothing with which to pay his tuition for Summer School.

An economist, a trade union leader and an editor of *The New Republic* were staying at Westbury as well. Leonard was pulled away from them by Whitney, for an apple fight and then for a bird's nesting expedition on which Leonard could display some of his old mouser's skill. The following day when he taught Whitney too about poultry Dorothy thanked him for spending so much time playing with her children. On his last night Dorothy and he, by a sort of mutual invitation, went off 'to the woods' on her estate[14] – Leonard would always say, 'to the woods', as though their attraction was magnetic. They sat on a rug together and talked of the Cornell Union building, of India, and of her. Leonard wrote afterwards in YMCA vein, 'The trouble now is that she has been deluded into imagining that she can put a degree of faith in me far beyond anything I can really merit or live up. This was the greatest spiritual experience of my life so far.'[15]

He had started off to hunt her money; he was now falling in love, helped by the affection which surrounded her:[16]

I had never had experience of how, without any sense of unnecessary waste, or of splash for its own sake, everyone on the staff seemed to be inspired with one idea, to liberate their mistress, as best each could, to engage in the multiple of interests which she was determined to comprehend and to promote. A ducal, or even a royal palace, could not have been operated on better oiled wheels. From the august butler, of whom I had been so scared as he beckoned me within the portals of 1130 Fifth Avenue in New York, to the least of the serving staff, gardeners, grooms, and chauffeurs, I could sense no trace of servility or of friction, but only a devoted loyalty, and of respect and affection.

This second weekend marked the start of a closer relationship. They wrote to each other frequently until Leonard left for England. As early as October 1920, just after Dorothy's first visit to Cornell, Leonard had written:[17]

> I found it extraordinarily hard after I saw you in New York to sit down to another term of hustle and scrape, but now I'm in it, and now that I know that there is at least one person who understands, I really feel encouraged to go through and to try to win out.

Dorothy on 11 July 1921:

> It *is* such a satisfaction to talk to you! You have done so much for me, Leonard, so much more than I could possibly ever do for you. I needed your companionship terribly: in fact, I was really starved for it. Since Willard died there has been no one to whom I really wanted to talk, until I found you. And now I know that you understand and care enough to need my friendship too, and it makes me very happy.

Leonard on 19 July:

> I seem to have adopted you as mother and sister and everything else. . . . Except for a few bright spots life has seemed rather a grim affair till of late. My little store of faith is none too great and somehow you have acted as a stimulant for it.

But in response Dorothy pulled back. Leonard's 'everything else' was perhaps too much. 23 July:

> I like to think that the help we have given each other is an immeasurable, imponderable thing; that it will crop out in unexpected ways and places all through our lives. I know it will be that way with me. It's very sweet of you to want to help me and I'm surprised to find how much I need it. . . . Love and understanding are the great gifts we humans can bring to each other and we all need them so dreadfully, in spite of our fine self-sufficiencies. For some reason or other the harmony of spirit between man and woman seems greater than any other and so I am going to count on you always, and be grateful to you always for all that you have added to my life.

She paid her second visit to Cornell, a couple of weeks later, on the same train. After a morning of conferences about the Willard Straight Hall to be they were alone:[18]

> We had decided to take a picnic supper up into Enfield Glen, and having gathered a basket of food prepared by Alice Blinn, we were dropped around 3 at the foot of the Glen. Then it started to rain, and poured until the evening, when we were picked up again. It was from my angle a perfect picnic. With the help of my old Army blanket I rigged up a tent that kept the rain off my guest, though a good stream ran down my own back. The matches of course got wet, so we had to do without the corn, the steak, and the coffee. We still had plenty to eat and we were still reasonably dry when the car arrived to pick us up. She made the best comrade I have ever had and seemed to enjoy every minute of the adventure until, at 11 o'clock, I put her on her train. I still know her less than ever, but much better than ever before.

Dorothy sent her thanks almost immediately:[19]

> It's hard to tell you what a good day you gave me. It was wonderful, all of it, from beginning to end. You were an angel to have planned all those nice interviews, and breakfast and lunch parties, and the hot water, and everything else, but the nicest part of it all was the picnic. Even the rain added to the fun of it and made a distinctive occasion in my life. Having seen your ingenuity in building that tent, I have no further doubts remaining as to what you can accomplish in India.

Leonard hardly had time to get this letter before he was off again, to spend five days with her and her children at Woods Hole on Cape Cod. They became closer still.

It was almost a tearful goodbye. Dorothy drove him to Boston station on his way to Montreal for the boat home. Leonard wrote to her immediately afterwards, 'I just wanted to hug you tight at the end, but I'm a cold-blooded Englishman and I was scared lest I should make the parting more harrowing than it was.'[20] Dorothy replied, 'You must know how grateful I was to you for being a "cold-blooded Englishman", as you describe yourself, for I couldn't have allowed you to be anything else.'[21] Dorothy in the same letter said that Leonard should marry, have children and not sacrifice himself to her. A month later, on 27 September, she explained she could not link her life with his because he had his work to do in India, because her three children would be an imposition on him and because she still remembered the past too much. She also felt very committed to her work in the USA and had a strong sense of duty. Leonard was apparently accepting Dorothy's own definition of their relationship when he wrote:[22]

I used to think that the great friendships between man and man were of a higher nature than those between man and woman because certain animal passions were absent, but higher still and more worthwhile is the friendship of man and woman where the passion, even as an additional link, is left far behind and the one helps the other, suffers and rejoices and laughs with the other because of a common ideal.

These lofty sentiments did not last.

Leonard had turned up at Cornell in October 1919 without being sure he would be admitted and with only £50 to his name, money borrowed not from his father but from a friend in England. He was three weeks late for the start of the semester after being held up in London by a shipping strike. On the day of arrival he registered for the degree course in agriculture, saw his supervisor to arrange his programme of studies, applied for a tuition scholarship and found a room to live in. Outside was a beautiful campus, fashioned by some convulsion of the earth's surface into sharp hills ranged on each side of a gorge. Such strange geography has not even now been overlaid by man. Cars cannot go up and down those steeper slopes though they can slide down the hill to Ithaca and thence to the airport. It is relatively unspoilt now; how much more so in 1919.

One of the things that impressed Leonard about his course was the businesslike approach of the professors; Sam Higginbottom had been right. Leonard had his first taste of what he called 'down-to-earth teaching' in his first lecture from the Professor of Poultry. He remembered him as saying:[23]

> When you set out to go and look at which poultry farm to buy, one rule I lay down absolutely, don't take your wife with you. . . . She'll see her favourite bush on the lawn in front of the house, and you're stuck with that farm for good. . . . Or there was a tree that took her eye. Or there was a view from the parlour. . . . Don't let her in until you've really found the soil and site and that it's suitable to poultry.

Dorothy did not come to Dartington until after Leonard had done his prospecting.

In his first year Leonard spent one afternoon a week on a farm to learn about ploughing, milking, liming, drainage and harness mending. In June 1920 he worked for two weeks on another farm belonging to one of his professors doing a wide range of routine jobs: milking, mixing cow feeds, cleaning out the cow barn, putting fertiliser into sacks and mending drainage pipes. The hard work led to stiffness and blistered hands and Leonard used to retire exhausted up the ladder that led from the garage to the loft where he slept. To find space to put a bed in, on his first night he had to clear up 'tin chimneys, old stoves, bee appliances of every kind, mouldy sacks, broken jam jars, bee's wax, nails, shavings, old clothes, rats' nests and filth of every kind'.[24]

During his first summer vacation, in August and September 1920, he was employed as a hand on the Meridale Butter Farms in the Catskill Mountains, again on the recommendation of Sam Higginbottom. He lived in the farm workers' lodging-house with some twenty others of mixed nationality, being given charge of one cow to milk, and of nineteen young heifers and a few bull calves. He had to clean out stalls, replace bedding, feed, groom, clean out feeding mangers and drinking buckets and halter his charges one by one, before taking them out for exercise in a field. He also helped to prepare sixty-seven cows for an approaching auction sale under the direction of a fitter engaged for three weeks especially to give the cows the finest cosmetic treatment.[25]

The rest of his studies were hard for someone who had not done any science for ten years. In his first year he studied botany, bacteriology, chemistry, dairy science, veterinary physiology, animal husbandry, farm mechanics, animal breeding and poultry. In his second year poultry, dairy, apple growing, poultry management, farm management, veterinary bacteriology and the scientific handling of milk for market purposes. After his final examination he took a course in rural education.

His letters home and his diary no longer worry about the purpose of life or his own religious belief or disbelief:[26]

Somehow I never felt so free of care before: on the road of life with the goal before me; the old religious enthusiasms, austerities, burnings and strivings gone; the intellectual doubtings and strugglings of India and the war put on one side. I am on the top of life now. New pages of human existence, volumes of human experience lie on the shelf beside me to be had for the reaching down.

During his first term, in the autumn of 1919 and the early part of 1920, he was paying his way with three different jobs. Living in a room in the Cosmopolitan Club of which he was soon to be elected President, he acted as kitchen boy in return for free meals. For two hours in the evening, six days a week, he looked after the office at a hall of residence. He had the use of a typewriter there and so he put an advertisement in the local paper for typing work, which he did between answering the telephone and booking rooms for meetings. The kitchen was the most strenuous: six hours a day, up very early to get the coal out of the cellar and light the fires, producing coffee and pancakes for everyone at breakfast. Leonard had suggested he should do this to save the cook having to leave his farm too early on freezing mornings. In return, the cook made a pumpkin pie especially for him every week. The next cook told him that no kitchen boy had ever provided her with such a clean sink.[27] During his second and third terms, in 1920, he found less tiring and better paid work as a part-time instructor of Freshmen in English. He gave up his English classes in December 1920 so that he could concentrate on preparation for the exam. When he passed it his grades were

Animal Husbandry	C
Botany	B
Dairy	C
Poultry	A
Rural Engineering	D
Farm Management	C
Rural Education	A
Pomology	B

Not very good: a 'gentleman's grades', I was told when I visited the university.

After these two years Leonard had a bit of American in him; from then on he was always more a Cornell than a Cambridge man. He was more proud of his agricultural degree, grades and all. Adding Cornell to Barnsley, he now knew enough about farming to escape for ever from being a complete amateur at everything. Cornell's mark on him was shown in the dairy farm he later started at Dartington as well as in its poultry department, its orchards and its science laboratory; and even more in the work of the International Conference of Agricultural Economists which had its beginning at Dartington. The mark showed too in the impression made on him by the university's extension service which linked research workers and farmers; and in the reliance he placed on Cornell experts, and on other *American* experts as well. Perhaps it led him to have too much confidence in experts of any kind.

Meanwhile Dorothy's life (unlike Leonard's) went on much as it had before he became part of it. There were fewer dances and parties than before Willard's death, far fewer than when she was single. Her old friends from the cotillion days were not attending parties either. She was as active as ever socially, but in a different set. Her society now was made up of men and women who walked down Fifth Avenue with serious tread, intellectuals most of them with uphill work to do in a sad world not yet recovered from the war, and always, always there were the meetings of committees that behaved too informally to be quite counted as such. Kenneth Lindsay, a visitor from England, met her in 1922 when he led the Oxford Union debating team on its first tour of American universities, staying with her several times in 1922 and 1923. He intrigued, amused and interested her, and even made her feel a little less hostile to remarriage. Lindsay said that 1130 Fifth Avenue was a kind of conference centre for her causes. There could be three different meetings in progress simultaneously on three different floors. Miss Bogue, Dorothy's secretary, kept an appointments book for them. There were regulars, like the board of *The New Republic*, which met there every Friday. Dorothy never made an outside engagement for a Friday. She was absorbed in the events of the week and how to reflect them and comment on them in next week's paper. Herbert Croly would preside after dinner and the other editors would sit around to throw out their opinions and listen to hers. Her sense of almost personal responsibility for what was going wrong in the world, or at any rate in the United States, was keener than ever after Willard's death.

If her close friend, Theodore Roosevelt, had not died in 1919 he might have been nominated in 1920. As it was, the Republican candidate was Warren G. Harding. Instead of Wilson, the professor from Princeton, the newspaperman from Ohio. With such a man the League of Nations stood no chance. His 'return to normalcy' had no place for it.[28] A dreadful disappointment. But the fact that she and those who thought likewise could not get all they wanted – nothing like – did not deter them from striving for more limited and perhaps attainable goals. The new President at least called a Conference in Washington on Limitation of Armaments in 1921 to end naval competition between Britain, Japan and the United States. It had some success. Dorothy was one of six people emphatically in favour of disarmament who were elected by a coalition of one hundred women's organisations to attend the conference, presumably as observers. Two of the others were her close friend, Ruth Morgan, who although a Republican was with the Hoover minority in supporting the League; and John Dewey, the educationalist whose lectures in psychology Dorothy had attended. She sent detailed reports to Leonard on the preparations for the conference. It made Leonard call her a stateswoman.

The isolationism which kept America out of the League was allied with xenophobia. The isolationists put it about that slick British propagandists and French munition makers, Uncle Shylocks all, had lured American doughboys into the slaughterhouse on the Western Front. They were no more trustworthy in peace than they had been in war. The wartime hostility to Germans was carried over and magnified into a bitter intolerance towards all 'Reds'. The Russian Revolution polarised the politics of America as of the world. Liberals like Dorothy were almost as much under attack as labour leaders. She and her friends were forced to the 'left' by being classed 'pink-tea Bolsheviki'[29] if not communists. Anyone who could be called a communist, anarchist or socialist was fair game for any chief of police. Two particularly famous ones, labelled anarchists,

Nicola Sacco and Bartolomeo Vanzetti, were framed for allegedly killing a postmaster in Massachusetts. Dorothy was almost alone from her class in supporting them through their long legal fight – the Dreyfus case of America – which ended in their electrocution.

President Harding said he was only on one side, the side of business. He cleaved to the McKinley principle, 'less government in business and more business in government'.[30] Calvin Coolidge, Vice-President and then President, spoke for him as well as himself when he said that 'the business of America is business'[31] with far less protest than nearly forty years later greeted the statement that what was good for General Motors was good for America. Dorothy was on the side of labour. It was despite her stand rather than because of it that she was elected President of the newly formed Association of Junior Leagues of America.

Her heart was specially with the Women's Trade Union League. She had been a supporter before the war; she became even warmer now that all trade unions, for women even more than men, were seen by bigots as the agents of Moscow. The League was a militant group set up 'to aid women workers in their efforts to organize . . . and to secure better conditions'[32] by organising strikes and defending strikers who were arrested. Its leaders were socialists who would have been recognised as such even in Europe. Dorothy's particular friend was the most prominent amongst them, Rose Schneiderman. She says in her autobiography that Dorothy was a devoted supporter. In 1920 Rose stood as candidate for the US Senate for the newly formed New York Labor Party. 'After the election, I discovered that Mrs Willard D. Straight had contributed a thousand dollars towards my campaign.'[33] Joseph Lash, in his biography of Eleanor and Franklin Roosevelt, reports that in 1922 Rose 'first met Eleanor at a tea given by Mrs Willard Straight to interest her friends in purchasing a home for the League'.[34] Dorothy put up $20,000 herself and with money given by Eleanor and others the League was able to buy a five-storey brownstone building at 247 Lexington Avenue. In that same year Dorothy was made a life member of the League. It was a time when for many liberals being rich was almost automatically disgraceful. Dorothy was the exception for intellectuals like Walter Lippmann, Felix Frankfurter, Roger Baldwin, the civil rights leader, the woman who married him, Evelyn Preston, and (later) Harold Laski, as well as for labour leaders like Rose Schneiderman.

There seemed to be more hope in England than in America. Seebohm Rowntree, who stayed with her, businessman though he was, was not like Calvin Coolidge at all. She wrote to Leonard:[35]

> We want to establish some labor fellowships that will enable our
> women to go to England and work with the labor movement there,

and vice versa, so that the women leaders in both countries will have opportunities of contact.

Looking back on these years Dorothy wrote:[36]

At this time an ominous crisis had arisen in the struggle between the great industrial companies, such as the Steel Trust, and the trade unions, and a situation arose in which I felt called upon to support the workers who, to my mind, were being unjustly exploited. The cruel intolerance of this post-war period challenged me to withstand the terrifying wave of fear and prejudice that seemed about to crush all the liberal movements in which I believed. And thus I became a target for attack by the entrenched interests of the right wing. Not being by nature a fighter I found this struggle to maintain my integrity extremely hard and exhausting.

Her staff became increasingly worried that she was doing too much. 'Never a moment to herself', 'Trying to kill herself', they said.

It was not, of course, uninterrupted good works. There were even men in her life besides Leonard. Kenneth Lindsay for one was good-looking, clever, amusing, and as much interested in workers' education as she was. On the evenings they spent in Fifth Avenue, or the weekends in Westbury, it became clear that they had a lot in common. Lindsay made her more lively. Dorothy wrote to Leonard about him:[37]

I spent many hours in his room reading and talking to him. He is a bit of a genius, that lad – and his future is gleaming with possibilities. . . . I love him dearly.

Croly was closer to her, and for longer, than Lindsay. He and Dorothy saw a lot of each other not only at the Friday meetings of *The New Republic* staff but many times in between. She was not like the employer, nor he the employee. They were more friends engaged in a common enterprise. After Willard's death their relationship became much more intense, partly because she persuaded Herbert to write Willard's biography as a means of relieving their joint distress. Herbert had to consult her a great deal, and for this purpose stayed with her often and for long spells, with and without his wife, Louise, with whom Dorothy was also very friendly. The tone of his letters grew gradually warmer:[38]

I have read your letter many times and with a more poignant sense of wonder and thankfulness every time. It was beautiful of you to have thought it and to have written it. That you should feel as you do moves me beyond any thing which has happened to me since I was a very young man.

Dorothy's responses to his letters (if she could read his microscopic handwriting at all) have not been preserved. She obviously cannot have been chilly if he persevered for so long. It may have been one of the 'noble relationships' she needed during those years. Herbert was one of many who did not want her to leave America for England. His letters, once he had taken in the likelihood that she was going, show the strength of his opposition, both to England and to the man whose name he always misspelt:[39]

> I do not know whether or not you are still considering the possibility of not marrying. I cannot myself see more than one side to that question. If you love Elmhurst enough to marry him as I am sure you do, the difficulties are relatively of small importance. . . . But I myself would be profoundly sceptical of a subsequent plan of life which called for any but an exceedingly brief residence outside of this country. By this I mean a few months. . . . Perhaps I am not seeing straight but if you started to live for several years in England and if Elmhurst remains a British citizen the result would eventually be expatriation. You would become willy-nilly a British citizen; the associations and the interests of the children at their most susceptible period would become British, and it would be almost as difficult four years from now as it is at present to square accounts with your old life in this country.

Most of Dorothy's other friends also said the same.

When Leonard left Dorothy on Boston station in 1921 he was already committed. She was the woman for him, or would be if only he could overcome her scruples. For all his disappointment that he had not yet been able to, his heartsickness did not prevent him throwing himself into his new 'adventure', as he called it. India called him, as well as America; Tagore, the man, was as magnetic as Dorothy, the woman. There was also the link between them. It was not that Dorothy liked Tagore. She was put off by 'the woolliness of the poet's ideas and the phoney business of his dress and play acting'.[40] But she was again doing what she had done with Willard – Leonard had to go to Tagore and to the East to submit to his ordeals before he could wrest the fairy princess from her New York palace.

The money for the 'India project' was hers. When Tagore had been to see her in March he had not prevailed. When it came to opening her purse to Leonard that was a different matter. Disingenuously, she wrote to Leonard in June 1921:[41]

> When Tagore was here, I saw him two or three times, but through inadvertence on my part I let him get away without really doing

anything for him and it has worried me ever since. . . . Will you let me give you the legacy that would have been his? . . . It would be such fun to work it out in that way and so much more satisfactory to me than to hand it over bodily to Tagore.

In a letter a few weeks later she referred to India as a test:[42]

There's so much I want to say to you about your going to India. The more I think of it the more it seems to me absolutely right. I'm sure you can make your life count for more out there than you could anywhere else and it is men such as you that can make a real difference. But it's a real consecration on your part and I don't like to think of the many sacrifices involved. . . . It's a terrific test but a vital opportunity and I know you are equal to it.

She did not write nearly as often as he. Once he was in India he wrote almost every day. But when she did she urged him on:[43]

Oh Leonard! Your letters are full of trial and tribulation, of sacrifice and suffering, of joy and wonder and love. I have thought over them and thought over them and sometimes they nearly break my heart. The test of faith and courage that you are being put to is simply tremendous and I don't know how you face it sometimes without a weakening of the spirit. The obstacles, the discouragements seem so great, the ignorance, the poverty, the disease, so frustrating, so crushing, that you can hardly know where to begin. But I can see the power of your example and your own personality as the great force.

When Leonard arrived back in India in November 1921 the situation in the country was very different from when he had last been there. People were now intensely political, and if he and Tagore had not had a common attitude on the main issues Leonard could not have taken the job he did, an Englishman working for an Indian, or been accepted by those whom he directed, Indians working for an Englishman. The goodwill for the British which had marked the beginning of the war had long been dissipated. The campaign against 'the Turk' which Leonard had supported in Mesopotamia had split the Muslim community, and the fall of Kut-el-Amara in 1916, by showing the British as both bungling and weak, had broken a myth. The disillusion was nothing compared to what happened when the millions of Indian soldiers returned, to inflation and the same influenza epidemic which killed Willard.

The outcome was not for lack of trying by Lionel Curtis and the many others who produced the Montford (or Montagu-Chelmsford) reforms. On 20 August 1917 the wartime coalition government in Britain, through the mouth of Edwin Montagu, the new Secretary of State for India, declared itself in the House of Commons for the 'gradual development of self-governing institutions'.[44] The declaration marked a return to the outlook of Macaulay, of Gladstone who thought it had been a calamity that 'we have not been able to give to India the benefits and blessings of free institutions'[45] and of men like A. C. Hume who helped to bring the Indian National Congress into being in 1885. But the preparations for the new constitution were as slow as the reservation of so many powers to the Viceroy was infuriating. It was the same with the executive in the provincial 'dyarchies' (to use the Curtis term). The decision to go for self-government by stages rather than immediately antagonised all the new nationalists led, uncompromisingly, with great flair, by Mahatma Gandhi.

In the March of the year Leonard left America the new constitution had at last been inaugurated by the Duke of Connaught. But this mattered far less to Gandhi's followers than the simultaneous effort by the government, inspired in part by the same fear of the Russian Revolution which had sparked off reaction in America, to counter 'subversion'. The bitter incident which everyone still remembered was the 'Amritsar Massacre' two years before. Troops under General Dyer killed 379 people and wounded 1,200. The massacre was followed by public floggings and an order that in Amritsar all Indians passing a certain spot had to crawl on the ground. This oppression had a worse effect on Indo–British relations than anything since the Mutiny.[46] Tagore was so angered he wrote to Lord Chelmsford resigning his knighthood.[47] 'The very least I can do for my country is to take all consequences upon myself in giving voice to the protest of the millions of my countrymen, surprised into a dumb anguish of terror.'

Leonard could not have come to Santiniketan if Tagore had been either for the Government of India *or* wholly for Gandhi, which he was not despite his anger over the massacre. They were both middle-of-the-roaders. Leonard had seen quite enough of contemporary British officials to have little faith in them. Their air of superiority infuriated him; in 1921 'it was exceptional even to see an Englishman walking along Chowringee chatting with an Indian'.[48] He was also thoroughly critical of Evangelistic English missionaries who wrote off Hindus as widow-burners and heathens. He was firmly *for* Indian self-government.[49] At the same time, taking a long view, he trusted his fellow-countrymen enough to believe they would now act in the tradition of his English heroes in India – Warren Hastings as the governor who knew Bengali, Urdu and Persian and believed that without an understanding of Indian culture there could be no sound administration; the Sanskrit scholar Sir William Jones, grandfather Tagore's friend, who with Hastings's encouragement did so much to foster Indian culture; and William Carey, the Baptist scholar-missionary of the nineteenth century. Tagore had somewhat the same attitude: he was subject to frequent attacks in his own country because he said he admired the British character more than the Indian.

Tagore thus had more confidence in the British than Gandhi did and little confidence at all in Gandhi's kind of political action. He was more artist than politician, but a rare artist who believed in the value of science, which meant Western science, in a way Gandhi did not. A short time before Leonard's arrival the two of them, 'the two giants of modern India',[50] as they have been called, had a conference in Tagore's Calcutta home. Gandhi wanted to win over Tagore for his policy of non-violent non-co-operation with the Imperial power. Gandhi acknowledged the part Tagore had played nearly twenty years before in leading the campaign against Lord Curzon's decision to partition Bengal which drove a wedge between the two major religious communities. He argued that his Swaraj movement was the natural offspring of Tagore's earlier movement. Tagore told Leonard what he said in reply:[51]

> Gandhiji, the whole world is suffering today from the cult of a selfish and short-sighted nationalism. India has all down her history offered hospitality to the invader of whatever nation, creed or colour. I have come to believe that, as Indians, we not only have much to learn from the West but that we also have something to contribute. We dare not therefore shut the West out. But we still have to learn among ourselves how, through education, to collaborate and achieve a common understanding.

Many of his staff at Santiniketan were not as tolerant as their master: *they* were won over by Gandhi. The resulting crisis spread to Surul shortly after Leonard had taken up his post there. One of the militant students was Shotyen Bose. He asked Leonard for a full day's holiday for everyone to commemorate the anniversary of the massacre in Amritsar. Leonard agreed to that. More of a problem was their opposition to his and Tagore's wish to ask the District Board to repair the roads in and around the village; to the more fiery students this was a flagrant breach of Gandhi's policy of non co-operation with the authorities. C. F. Andrews, Tagore's close adviser at the time, was with the students. There were further demonstrations. Eventually Shotyen and three others were expelled by Leonard. Leonard reports how they were taken off in a lorry:[52]

> We took the shorter but much rougher road direct from Surul to Bolpur station. Unwittingly, by this decision we completely upset Shotyen's plan. He had taken for granted that we would travel via Santiniketan and that he could jump down there and start the patriotic demonstrations he had already arranged. As soon as we reached Bolpur Station Shotyen and two others jumped off saying

they had no intention at all of getting on to the train, and that they were going straight back to Santiniketan.

But they were intercepted on the instructions of the poet, who was in complete agreement with what Leonard had done.

Although the like stance they had on Indian politics was certainly a bond it was a negative one. The positive ties were of more importance. The first was their interest in the land, being both sons of landowners, in Tagore's case a zamindar on a vast scale but without the training for it that Leonard had. Tagore had come to England – including a school at Torquay in countryside he always liked[53] – for a general not an agricultural education. In the book I have already quoted Leonard called himself the Plowman, Tagore the Poet. But Tagore had a little bit of the Plowman in him too, and Leonard a little of the Poet.

One question had come to dominate Tagore's thinking: why do the peasants for whom he felt so much pity do so little for themselves? They could lift their families a little above poverty if only they would exert themselves. In 1901 he started a boarding-school at Santiniketan, mainly for the children of well-off parents, and in 1921 Visva-Bharati, a centre for study of the different cultures of the East. It included schools of Music, Art and Drama for adults. To Tagore education was nothing without the arts; he was poet, musician, dramatist and painter long before he was a teacher, even though he was customarily called Gurudev, revered teacher. Leonard said of him:[54]

> There was no aspect of human existence which did not exercise some
> fascination for him and around which he did not allow his mind and
> fertile imagination to play; and where, as a young man, I had been
> brought up in a world in which the secular and religious were
> separate, he insisted that in poetry, music, art and life they were one,
> and that there should be no dividing line.

Once education and the arts were established Tagore came back to his old question and decided to try to foster initiative in the neighbouring villages. Hence his offer to Leonard. He wanted someone to get it all going, the chosen place being the farm mentioned earlier outside the village of Surul, a mile or two from Santiniketan. He later gave the farm the name Sriniketan or Abode of Grace.

However much he fretted over Dorothy, Leonard enjoyed himself from the start. In December he was writing to his sister even more enthusiastically than he had from Cornell:[55]

> I'm happy as a king and have begun for the first time I reckon in
> twenty years to appreciate what life can be. School was Hell for ten
> years with overshadowed periods of Paradise regained during the

hols. Cambridge was haunted by examinations, the war was a perpetual nightmare and America hardly a feather bed, though the last few months were good. But here – well to start with, one of my ambitions in life has been realised, and I live in sandals, sockless, with either khaki trousers and khaki shirt or white flannels and a spotless white (or purple silk) shirt hanging out full length. Then I eat what I want and generally not too much, and, as you advise, look after myself. But all these are little points. In reality it is the charming people, the politeness, the kindness, the lack of hurry and fluster.

The anti-sahib was uppermost even though the sahib was still there in the confident dealings with the District Collector, the pleasure in drinking to the King with a local Rajah and the strong attachment to Baden-Powell's Scout principles, in theory and practice.

Surul and other nearby villages were in obvious decline, like so many in India. Irrigation used to be well looked after; by 1921 it was not. The tanks enclosing the village water supply were out of repair. Mixed crops once sustained a good diet; by then the attempt to specialise and grow some cash crops had lowered instead of raised the quality of agriculture. Firewood used to come from common grazing grounds and forests; by then there was almost none left, and soil erosion resulted from denudation. Rivers that once flowed freely had silted up. Handicraft manufacture which used to flourish had been destroyed by the competition from England. A rich cultural life had been fragmented.

Leonard's task was to try to start virtuous circles working. He moved to the farm, to a room built on the roof of its only substantial building, 'open', as he wrote to Dorothy, 'to the four winds, with a gorgeous view of the red rolling downs and the brown rice fields'.[56] The building was to house the Institute of Rural Reconstruction of which it was there and then decided that Leonard should be called Director. He brought with him eight older boys from Santiniketan.

It was through example he was to teach them, and through their example that the villagers were to learn. The first lesson was painful. The boys while at Santiniketan had been served by untouchable sweepers. Leonard shocked them by taking down his own latrine bucket and emptying it himself in a trench where in time it would add fertility to the soil. After a while the boys, overcoming their dread of caste-pollution, followed him in doing the same, and when the poet heard about it he also took his brass pot downstairs to empty. He congratulated Leonard on this and on many other things. He was almost as lavish as Dorothy in praise of anything he liked. Leonard does not say whether the practice spread to the villagers. I imagine not. But despite some backsliding when a caste sweeper was reintroduced by the boys and had to be banned by Leonard,[57] in time they became energetic collaborators, in general and not only over latrine buckets.

The buckets were symbolic of the spirit needed by Surul and the other villages and of Leonard's bearing. On another occasion he forgot that the degree to which you bowed your head depended upon the age of the people you were greeting. As at Laxton he did the wrong thing. He bowed quite low in passing to a group of girls who used to be his pupils. 'You forget that you are only saluting your pupils,' said his amused Bengali colleague.[58]

Leonard could not get going without money. Tagore had very little. Leonard cabled Dorothy for $25,000 almost as soon as he arrived. Without energetic helpers he could not have done anything either. Between them, along with some outside experts, they bored wells, constructed a new water tank, built a vermin-proof rice store, established a co-operative store and a weekly market. They tried to produce more food by growing more vegetables, by introducing poultry and better cattle and a dairy and by fencing and draining land. They also started up some rural craft industry.

A new ingredient was added as a result of a letter he wrote to Dorothy in January 1922, just before he moved to the room on the roof. He asked Dorothy quite categorically to marry him and to join him in India. She did not reply until 5 March. Marriage, she said, was out of the question. She wanted them to give each other love, comfort, co-operation and under-standing, but marriage, no. That was impossible. He should find someone else to marry, and to make it easy Dorothy despatched from New York a protégée of hers, Gretchen Green, who had some experience as an unqualified social worker. She meticulously and absurdly explained that she was providing him with a future wife who 'has a sort of glowing joy in simply working for other people' and who would help him with his noble work.[59] Leonard might have taken some hope from the fact that Dorothy's choice as the bride-to-be was distinctly plain.

After that brush-off there were no more letters from her for six months. The way was clear for Gretchen. She occupied the same little roof-room as Leonard – there was nowhere else – and played on his susceptibilities, including 'that most animal part'.[60] Apparently to no avail. It seems that Leonard resisted temptation both then and later, and was still a virgin in 1925 when he married. Leonard wrote repeatedly to tell Gretchen's donor, trying to arrange a marriage as deliberately as any Indian parent, that it was no good: he could never marry her, though he did appreciate the feminine touches she brought into his room and life. Leonard passed a test unique to him. Dorothy never sent a girl to Peking for Willard. But Gretchen added a new element to the village. She opened a dispensary, the first in what was to become a large network.[61]

After a year Leonard left the job, in February 1923. It was now for

Indians to carry it on, though with steady financial support from Dorothy until 1947. Leonard already regarded the experiment as successful:[62]

It is in fact through the children in our own neighbourhood that new life and hope have flooded the villages, which have been lost for two generations past in a slough of despair.... Out of the fruitless attempts of the unorganised adults to stem a village fire came the training of the boys as a Fire Brigade and with it drill, discipline and a sense of the utility of immediate obedience to a leader in case of emergency. Ninety per cent of the village was attacked with malaria, but through this need of life came the mapping of the village, its tanks, its dwellings, its pits and its drains, and then the digging of water channels – geography in fact with a vengeance. Not chemistry, not zoology, not bacteriology, not physiology – but the study of anopheles, the kerosining of tanks, the disinfection of wells, the registration of fever cases and the keeping of health records.

Leonard and Tagore had both suffered from conventional schooling and were correspondingly hopeful about what a school could do for children if only. ... The promise of Sriniketan gave them both the confidence to say if only what, and then to plan a really new school. When inviting Leonard to join him in preparing the 'prospectus' for a weekly boarding-school for village boys which he called Siksha-Satra (meaning Seat of Instruction) Tagore set out in general terms what he hoped for from it:[63]

Under our highly complex modern conditions, mechanical forces are organised with such efficiency that the materials produced grow far in advance of man's selective and assimilative capacity to simplify them into harmony with his nature and needs. Such an intemperate overgrowth of things, like the rank vegetation of the tropics, creates confinement for man. The nest is simple, it has an easy relationship with the sky; the cage is complex and costly, it is too much itself, excommunicating whatever lies outside. And modern man is busy building his cage, fast developing his parasitism on the monster, *Thing*, which he allows to envelop him on all sides. He is always occupied in adapting himself to its dead angularities, limits himself to its limitations, and merely becomes a part of it.

The counter was to create an atmosphere in which growth would be possible:[64]

Children have their active sub-conscious mind which, like the tree, has the power to gather its food from the surrounding atmosphere. For them the atmosphere is a great deal more important than rules and methods, building appliances, class teachings and text books. . . . But in our educational organisations we behave like miners, digging only for things substantial, through a laborious process of mechanical toil: and not like a tiller of the soil, whose work is in a perfect collaboration with Nature, in a passive relationship of sympathy with the atmosphere.

So with terms of reference which would flummox any Education Authority, the poet and the agriculturist sat down together to draw up a scheme for the new school. It opened in the same year as Dartington, and still continues. The agriculturist, in writing his part, spoke with the voice of Cornell, mixed up with that of Baden-Powell. He had much to say about the care and proper use of latrines, fire drill and control, cotton rug and dhurrie making, fabricating sun-dried mud bricks, making one-stringed instruments, soap making and poultry keeping. But sometimes the agriculturist seemed to speak with the same voice as the poet. Leonard never wrote better than when he was under Tagore's influence:[65]

> The aim, then, of the Siksha-Satra is, through experience in dealing with this overflowing abundance of child life, its charm and its simplicity, to provide the utmost liberty within surroundings that are filled with creative possibilities, with opportunities for the joy of play that is work – the work of exploration, and of work that is play – the reaping of a succession of novel experiences; to give the child that freedom of growth which the young tree demands for its tender shoot, that field for self-expansion in which all young life finds both training and happiness.

> Freedom for growth, experiment, enterprise and adventure, all are dependent upon Imagination, that greatest of gifts, that function of the mind upon which all progress depends. To release the Imagination, to give it wings, to 'open wide the mind's caged door', this is the most vital service that it is in the power of one human being to render to another, and one to which the Superintendent of the Siksha-Satra must pay constant and undivided attention. It is this gift of imaginative power which distinguishes man so markedly from the eating, preying, procreating animal, and which like the lamp of Aladdin endows him with the power to create a new world for himself after his own fashion.

> Life, to be life at all, has to be lived: and the parents' or professors' sins of repression and deprivation, of rod and ironbound rule, are visited upon the children unto the third and fourth generation.

The school was to be created with money they helped to raise, not just from Dorothy but from meetings at which Leonard spoke. The project attracted a great deal of attention in India. Some years after, Gandhi visited it and was so impressed that he decided it should be the model for an all-India revolution in primary education. Tagore jokingly volunteered to be his first Minister of Education. A member of the staff joined Gandhi and between the two of them they devised a system which generalised the practices of Siksha-Satra under the name of 'Basic Education'. This became the kernel of Gandhi's educational policy. The plan which Rabi and Leonard had drawn up therefore had an influence over the whole sub-continent; it was also to guide another experiment in England.

If a common political stance, a concern for rural reconstruction, an interest in education were three of the bonds between the two men, a fourth was of even greater importance. They both thought very well of Tagore. Tagore was vain; Leonard was admiring. Leonard had been disappointed in his own father but unable so far to find another man he could put in his place. He admired Somervell and, even more, Goldie, but he was never on as intimate terms with them as he was with Tagore after he gave up the Directorship of Sriniketan at Tagore's request. Leonard became his personal assistant and was with him a great deal, when he was not touring to make contacts for him in the Philippines, in China and Japan. They were to become closer still – and Leonard a member of the retinue Tagore liked to have with him when he was travelling – after Leonard's next visit to the USA.

Dorothy broke her six months' silence in December 1922. She apologised for the trouble she had caused by sending him a wife he did not want and promised to meet him in the following summer if he would come to America again. Silence fell again until the end of May 1923, after Leonard had landed in San Francisco. Then suddenly all was electric, all excitement. She telegraphed almost in the language of Borderland:

> Thankful to have you near. Please telegraph how you are and where I
> can reach you on your way across country. Shall I meet you in
> Chicago or await you here? Spare yourself for all those who love you.

It was as if she did not believe he would reappear: the telegram was sent too late to reach him. A slightly calmer letter written on 15 June did:

> I wanted to go out to Chicago to meet you – or anywhere else just in
> order to have an additional day with you – but I haven't known
> where to send you a word. Never mind, it's my fault, I'm afraid, and
> I'm paying the penalty now . . . for weeks and weeks I have been
> looking forward to having you back here at Westbury.

Despite the almost frantic beckoning Dorothy proceeded to do another disappearing act: she told him she was embarking from New York the day after he got there to be with Herbert Croly who was ill in Venice.

Leonard waited a month until she got back on 23 July. Then at last he had his chance. He went off with her to Woods Hole to stay until 11 August. The children were there and the usual stream of visitors passed through the house. But they found time to be on their own as well, sitting for hours on an old rock above the beach (they referred to it in letters afterwards as 'their' rock) or on the dock in the moonlight. Leonard took her out to sea quite often in a small sailing boat. Steering to the right of the red buoy and the left of the black became a private metaphor for the right course of conduct. He seized every chance he could to invent the private language which is always love's assistant. If he had been as imaginative as Willard he might have succeeded earlier.

After some days, emboldened by his reception, he proposed to her again. Again she refused, protesting that their commitment to good works, his in India, hers in America, must take precedence. Like an accountant of love, ticking off the headings on a balance sheet, she said they would openly admit and express their affection, friendship, even devotion for each other. But they must be sensible and never be overwhelemed by their feelings to the extent that they made excessive emotional demands on each other. Leonard was so upset by this that he did what he was expressly instructed not to do, let his feelings overwhelm him. He burst into tears and wept on Ruth Morgan's shoulder, Dorothy's being out of bounds.

To make matters worse, Dorothy did not keep to her own rules, which bewildered, embittered and yet gave him hope. After seeing him off on 11 August, not this time at Boston station but a pier in New York, she wrote that she was

> driven by a momentum that urges me to you, to you, irresistible and, I
> fear, relentless. But this time it is as if I were finding my own kingdom
> of heaven in finding you, even by a written word. But my hand
> trembles too much and I can't write with any stability. I shall have to
> compose myself first and come to you later. Anon. I'm afraid I'm
> 'waiting for my own true love'.

The proper letter which she promised followed on 14 August:

> I love to linger over these last weeks in my mind, that little spell of 19
> days which brought me perfect harmony. I think of it as a phrase of
> music. . . . You see, you sounded all the notes within me and you
> brought out melodies that I never knew were there: the response to
> birds and butterflies, rocks and moors and sea and our great brother
> the sun. . . . I love to think of you as brother – born to the wind and
> the sea and the sky and to all the creeping and flying things upon the
> earth; the blessed Francis in truth. I love to think of you, too, as the
> bringer of song, the gay and lyric Leonard who sings joy into my

heart. And I love the poet and the artist Leonard and the rhythmic Leonard on the tennis court, Leonard fleet of foot. And I love Leonard the mariner, and Leonard the lecturer, and the Leonard the friend of children, and Leonard the good companion of road and field and heath. And they are all mine, these Leonards, by virtue of the love I bear them, many in one, and all gathered up into Leonard, my beloved friend.

Leonard, though thankful, protested to her for continually picking him up and dashing him down. 'Do you think, Dorothy, that a man's heart is like a flute upon which a woman can play what tune she pleases?'[66] Even so, her letters made it easier to enjoy his family visit to Scotland:[67]

> I revelled in the open air, bracing, fiery with the wet weather and bracken under foot, the mountains and mists, the swollen amber coloured burns, the wheeling hawks, the grouse swinging round the hill tops with the wind, a hare doubling up its hind legs and giving its tail a wicked flick, the thrushes and wood pigeon and a snipe which zigzagged away from my feet out of sight, duck on the loch and the purple of the heather deepening in the evening light.

A few days after that, on 28 August, he said he would press his suit again and asked her to keep a 'little door open' for him. In response she once more closed it. There was no possibility of marriage. She felt bound to bring up her children in the USA. The difference in their ages was a gulf. She might not be able to bear him children – the same catalogue.

This further disappointment for Leonard brought on an attack of metaphors. He wrote on 3 September that he was steeling himself:

> It is just because our love has never been a slackening off, a loosing of armour, but always a tightening up and a buckling to of joints and straps, a dashing off into the fray or a standing by at the tiller, without the language, the gestures or the embraces that the world seems to recognise as true love.

Armour was apt: they both wore the armour of chastity. Dorothy made it amply and repeatedly clear she could not contemplate their becoming lovers. She implied in her letters that she did not think highly of this side of married life, except as a necessity for the procreation of children. Only when she had eventually decided to marry Leonard did she try to take herself in hand, reading Havelock Ellis in the hope of acquiring a less negative outlook to sex. There was still a year and a half to go before she had to put Ellis to the test.

Leonard seemed for some months to be suffering from shock:[68]

I can't see how else we could have trimmed our sails. I really can't. Nor, having taken a reef in, shall we say, and shortened sail before the storm of hard facts that the cyclone of Life has aroused, I suppose for our benefit, do I see that there is any other way of making harbour than as we are doing at present. What the harbour is, who knows? But I have faith enough to believe that our respective charts are as near the right ones as possible and that our compass is properly adjusted.

At the end of October her letters again ceased. Leonard did not know the reason until later. She was taken ill almost immediately after he left and got steadily worse. The doctors diagnosed thyroid trouble and advised a complete rest from her endless round of meetings, interviews, business meals, deciding whom to give money to and what to say to those she turned down, travelling, entertaining. She felt ill enough to comply. Very unusual. She was in and out of bed for over a year.

For Leonard it may have been a relief to get back to India and to work. From November to January he was with Tagore almost all the time, travelling around India, spreading abroad Sriniketan's need for funds. Leonard's admiration grew into something more, perhaps because he turned to Tagore to relieve his other disappointment. When he was leaving the service of the man who had (unlike his own father) entrusted him with running an 'estate' Leonard wrote to an old friend, Wyatt Rawson:[69]

> Said a sad goodbye last Monday – he's been a father to me – giving freedom and kindliness, and a strict disciplining as well as wholehearted sympathy when all but a very few had no faith or hope. I miss his beauty and stature.

On 7 December 1924, when he was temporarily separated from Tagore, Leonard wrote:

> But what a tyrant magician you are! It is rather now that 'my *brain* whirls and a drowsy numbness pains', for one touch from your magic wand and my imagination, an unsufficient sort of affair at any time, much pruned in its youth by experts in 'paidagogery', finds the windows of the cage open and its wings free. In the old days it tried to find satisfaction by ceaseless bodily activity, but India is a great and sometimes a masterful teacher, and slowly I think and hope a proper sense of reasoned detachment is making itself apparent.

In this Leonard was recreating the mood of an earlier letter he wrote to Tagore when he first arrived in the USA that summer. He had evidently taken Leonard to the river Padma which Tagore had so much loved in *his* youth:[70]

But why, oh why did the Creator bestow upon this fragile skeleton the nervous machinery for a Leviathan. I crave rest, I want again to float on the Padma in your boat and smoke my huqa and paint a little and perhaps most of all to find a Mother of the kind I never had, to love and be loved by, to weep upon, for my thoughts roll on and tear me to pieces.

The two of them twice became three, the first time with the addition of the beautiful girl who later became Lady Ranu Mookerjee. Tagore told Leonard (and often wrote) about the remarkable relationship that as an adolescent he had with his sister-in-law, who was of an age with him. Tagore's older brother was away at his business all day, leaving his young wife to share her leisure with the young poet. A few weeks after Tagore himself married, this sister-in-law died. After Tagore's wife herself died in her turn he had no comparable companionship with a woman until the 16-year-old Ranu arrived at Santiniketan. She brought back vividly the memories of his sister-in-law. He read and recited and sang to Ranu in the same way. She wrote to Leonard after Tagore's death:[71]

> There is some common bond between him and you and me and I know you will understand. All that you have written I remember very well indeed – all those quiet early afternoons in his house, he always made me sit on his knees and I used to hang on his neck – you sleeping in the small room next door.

What happened inside the triangle I do not know. Ranu may have used Leonard as a foil to tease Tagore. He responded jealously. Leonard presumably told him about Dorothy and he wrote:[72]

> Your marriage proposal has my hearty approval and blessings. It will take a huge load off my mind when it happens, for I have discovered that lately you have been paying an alarming amount of attention to a certain Brahmin maiden diverting her heart from its previous course.

One of Tagore's plays of the time, *Red Oleanders*, was based on the relationship of an old and a young man and a ravishing young girl. It was dedicated to Leonard.

The second time two became three was with Victoria Ocampo, the wealthy Argentine poetess, the 'very great beauty' whom Aldous Huxley met later.[73] Tagore had been invited to the centenary celebrations of Peru's independence in the autumn of 1924; its government paid the one-way fare for him and his secretary. When he and Leonard reached Buenos Aires Tagore suffered two setbacks: influenza and a letter from Romain Rolland warning him not on any account to get mixed up in the politics of Latin America. This made him unwilling to proceed, yet he felt he had a duty to do so. The dilemma, as on many other occasions, caused his 'psychological heart' (as Leonard called it)[74] to have palpitations and the doctors to advise him not to cross the Andes. Where then to go? They had no money either to stay or to return.

At this moment Victoria Ocampo arrived to rescue them. She had many gifts as well as beauty: wealth, intelligence and the utmost admiration for Tagore. She had studied in depth everything of Tagore's that had been translated into English, French or her own language of Spanish. She was delighted to find the idol accidentally incarnated in the flesh and at once threw herself at him. As she said later, 'I would have gladly torn my heart out to please him.'[75]

She carried the two of them off to a villa at San Isidro overlooking the River Plate, to stay until his health should recover, which unfortunately for her it had done, completely, as soon as it was decided not to go to Peru. Separated from her husband, she came to see them every day for two months and poured out her feelings for and to Tagore, or, if he would not listen, to Leonard. She wanted to be recognised as an artist, not just a charming woman. Tagore was readily attracted by the woman, less so by the intellect. The fact he could not or did not respond made her despair. He became even less welcoming when his jealousy of Leonard surfaced again as it had with Ranu. He wanted to return to India. He could see that Victoria and Leonard, who were of like ages, got on well together, and imagined more: that they wanted to delay his departure so they could have more time together. It was only when they were safely back on board ship to Italy, Victoria having paid for the tickets, that Tagore softened towards her. He bestowed on her a Sanskrit name, Vijaya, and wrote a new book of poems about her, about the beauty not just of herself but the pampas and the river, about gaucho horsemanship and the haunting sadness of their singing to the guitar.

He kept up a correspondence with her until his death. As late as 1940 he wrote, 'Often it comes to my mind, the picture of that riverside house, and the regret that in my absent-minded foolishness I had failed to accept fully the precious gift offered to me.'[76] Leonard also wrote to her regularly. She visited Dartington several times. What Dorothy thought of her is not recorded. Leonard sent a cable of protest to the Argentine Minister of Foreign Affairs when Victoria was imprisoned in 1953 by Perón's government.

The relationship with her, whatever else it did, also served to bring the two of them together after they sailed and was one of the many bonds which made Leonard a life member of Tagore's extended family. The nostalgic affection for Victoria washed over onto Leonard and no doubt the other way round as well. Later on Tagore wrote to Leonard about it:[77]

Dear Leonard, I have come to that stage of life when one gets fond of idly rummaging among the hoarded treasures of past days. Only the other day, when I was in that mood, suddenly and unaccountably came to my mind the Christmas morning in Argentina among flowering cactus beds, when you asked me to talk to you about something special for that occasion. The picture appeared to me so distant and yet so vividly near. The whole scene was exotic in character offering no associations with which we were familiar. The vision brought to me the memory of a happiness that made me feel almost sad, for it was of a kind that could no longer be repeated today. We two were of unequal age, but I was not aware of the difference for a moment, and our companionship was so utterly simple and intimate. I think you are the only one who closely came to know me when I was young and old at the same time, when my aspirations had the sureness of maturity and not having passed through the final buffetings of experience were youthful in their ferment of unbounded expectancy.

The letters suggest Leonard was moved by Tagore as by no one except Dorothy, with the advantage at that point that his feelings had been returned across the gap in age. Leonard may as a result have discovered new realms of feeling in himself and so gained a new maturity, which made just the difference in his final assault on New York. Dorothy certainly noticed:[78]

I can't help feeling that you have grown tremendously this past year, that you have more confidence and assurance and far greater inward resources . . . you are drawing nearer and nearer to the source of beauty and life and love and that God himself is filling your soul. If the poet has helped you along that journey I consider him just about the most valuable and fortunate man I know, for because of it you are going to give something great to the world.

Despite the new Leonard Dorothy did not come to the point right away. She was still ill. In that same letter she said:

Last year after you left I wrote rather intense and emotional letters, I'm afraid, and they must have confused and worried you. I wasn't well and I had been tremendously moved and stirred by you and all that emotion seemed to sweep me along. I needed you and I didn't hesitate to tell you so. But when I got to New York I was all right again and never after had such a sinking spell. You give me something that no one else gives me and an intellectual and spiritual bond such as ours is, I think, the rarest and most beautiful thing on earth. That's why I cling to you so, and need you – but I really don't want anything more and I know you don't.

It seemed dreadfully like the old story over again. But a bit later on, in August, all was different. Perhaps it was partly that Leonard had got rough with her about the touchy subject of her money immediately after his second visit to Woods Hole, where she was convalescing:[79]

Frankly I wonder whether you've ever sat down and totalled up the amount of harm you've managed to perpetuate with your wealth and tried to balance it with the achievements.

Dorothy replied on 19 August:

I have been able to release people from certain burdens so that they could follow their chosen path and give more freely their contribution to others. . . . I suppose I try to make it all an expression of love, though a miserably feeble one, I know. . . . I have always been on my guard against the danger of associating wealth with power. I mean, I have always been conscious of the terrific evil inherent in wealth when it is used for power and I have probably leaned over backwards in the effort to dissociate myself from controls.

Leonard had resolved 'As soon as I am able I'm going to cut myself off from your purse.'[80] In the same letter Dorothy, despite her expostulation about the good she sometimes did with her money, promised 'I do want you to know that if we ever should get married I would be quite ready to leave all the money behind, as it were, to be dispensed by a group of people over here, and you and I could start the great experiment in England empty-handed as you say.' She went on:

Last year if we had decided on marriage I should have been doing it from the wrong motive. A certain element of pity would have entered in. I knew that I had made you unhappy and the knowledge of that tore me right in two. And it was the same thing this year when X [Xenia, Gretchen Green] worked on my feelings and tried to make me feel sorry for you. Something rose up in me and choked the natural current of love and made it all seem impossible. Then when you came and I saw something new in you, something that represented your own triumph and spiritual victory, I knew that I could in fairness to you, marry you because I loved you, because I loved the pilgrim soul in you, and not because of any secondary reason.

The experiment in England which she mentioned in that letter and which Leonard had proposed was to matter for them in all kinds of ways, not least because it solved, or eased, the problem of the money. Leonard did not object to money if it was to be used not for him personally but for the experiment; she also could accept that. He spoke again about her money on 8 September:

> I am frightened of it, but on the other hand I'm driven to admit that, more especially when used to give children an opportunity and to stimulate educational advance, to make the world more beautiful and bring more of the daylight of happiness into the dark corners of childhood's imprisonment in the schoolroom, it may be a God-given gift and responsibility which we should only be shirking by handing it over to a trust.

Which is, strangely, just what they did do, with some of the money. The experiment was to be a school, and it gradually acquired a location. The subject comes into almost all their letters that autumn. On 18 September Leonard asked her quite specifically to join him in Europe when he returned there in the spring from his last trip with Tagore, to marry him and to help him to set going the experiment. On 28 September Dorothy at last tentatively accepted: not just marriage but England. She would have to find out first from her doctor whether she could have further children after her illness, and to consult the three children she already had. She wanted their plans kept secret from her friends in the USA for the time being. Then came the customary caution. They must reach a decision by next April whether to marry or to part. She no longer believed it was possible to go on as they had been doing. She warned him that she was likely to continue to vacillate:

> I have days of utter heartlessness when I don't seem to care about you at all. It was the same with Willard, and I came close to giving way right up to the end. Of course once we were married there were no more glacial periods, but they very nearly got the better of us during the preceding months. I want to tell you perfectly frankly now that I had a long glacial period last winter and also the previous winter (it seems almost climatic, doesn't it?) just as if the effect of your personality had worn off, almost as if I hadn't known you.

'The school' certainly helped to make her less vacillating than she otherwise would have been and to accept that her first life had died with the war and that she could contemplate starting another. 'The school' was a venture she could share in, of the same kind as many philanthropic ones she had supported before. She and Willard – Willard in his own family tradition – had long been interested in progressive education. Her children went to a progressive school, the Lincoln School, attached to Teachers College of Columbia University, and it would be a continuation for them if there were somewhere similar for them in England. That would reduce her guilt on their account. Then it was to be not in India but in the country she knew. Whereas she could not imagine living in the former country, the latter was almost a second home:[81]

> You know that I adore England and always have, since the early days when I stayed there so much with my sister. . . . I love the tradition of it, the ingrained culture, the freedom and the beauty, the combination of antiquity with perennial freshness and youth. . . . I shall feel rather like the man in Henry James' *Passionate Pilgrim*. Do you know him? There's no doubt that James subtly understood what it means for a certain type of American to be returning, as it were, to his home, England.

Leonard wrote to Dorothy about Siksha-Satra, of course, as he did about everything in India. Once he finally decided to leave – his work was done: the country did not suit his health – it was natural enough to take the idea with him. If it was something worthwhile for India it could be something worthwhile for England. The conception was general enough to take root anywhere. He wrote a draft of a letter about it in July or August 1924:

> The method of Surul is right, and if I had the energy and health I would dearly love to carry Surul ideas and spirit into England. It would be a school such as has not happened yet, drawing on India, America, China, again a concentration, again the fellowship of a few men of ideas and spirit.

Dorothy did ask him whether the school might not be in the USA, using Croly's argument that her children would not then have to be transplanted. Leonard did not respond; she did not press. She probably knew it had to be in England. His reassurance to her was that she would not be deserting America, for herself or her children:[82]

> We have each crossed the boundaries of nationalism and there is no picking up of one or dropping another country – no preferential treatment, I'm hoping. . . . Remember, let there be no idea of closing down on America for Beatrice and Whitney and Michael – it must and will always be the beloved home, as my Laxton home was to the age of 10, and they must have free and frequent access to the best it holds for them. Westbury and 1130 will be theirs, their homes, as they've always been won't they?

Leonard also wrote to her about the part of England where the school should be. He was quite clear about one thing – that it should be at a good distance from his parents. 'Whilst my mother and father would be alive it would be a fatal psychological mistake to consider the Barnsley neighbourhood, and the winter cold of the north would perish me to the bone.'[83] So it must needs be in the south, not too far from London or the coast. Dorset was the favourite to begin with; then he hardened on Devon. Why I do not know. He was with Tagore at the time and perhaps Tagore spoke of his fond memories of the Devon countryside when he had visited Torquay as a boy. Certainly Tagore wrote later to say how pleased he was that Devon had been the final choice. As to the kind of place, Leonard was looking for a building large enough for a school, and with surrounding land for the activities that were to be the essence of it – 'a farm, a garden, workshops, play grounds, woods and freedom'.[84] It all pointed to an estate, in Devon. Dorothy followed his train of thought and wrote to him when he was in Italy with Tagore,[85] 'Why don't you explore Devonshire now?'

The wedding was three months later, in April 1925. Leonard was now 31 and Dorothy 38. They were married not in Geneva but at home, in the garden at Westbury, according to the service of the Church of England. Brother Vic, who had followed Leonard on a course at Cornell, was best man. Payne was Dorothy's only close relative there, along with Willard's sister, a few close friends and Dorothy's large staff. Dorothy wore one of her wide-brimmed hats from under which she smiled shyly at the photographer. She was dressed in blue, her favourite colour for clothes and one of them for flowers. She fingered her pearl necklace throughout. Doing so exposed to view the bracelet round her arm, a present from Leonard in the summer of 1924. Leonard looked stolidly solemn, dressed in what the US newspapers called 'a gray business suit of English cut and pattern'. Dorothy omitted the still usual promise to obey. The press in the USA called it the marriage of 'ONE OF THE WORLD'S WEALTHIEST WOMEN' to 'SON OF ENGLISH CLERGYMAN'. They spent their honeymoon on Payne's private yacht in the Caribbean.

In 1920, when this chapter starts, Leonard was seeing Dorothy for the first time in New York. In 1925, when it ends, he is married to her. Few who knew them would have forecast the outcome; few who knew them well believed he would hold out or she give in.

Leonard hardly wavered in his determination at any time after the summer of 1921 when he first fell in love. He withstood subsequent rebuffs that would have put most men off completely. Most men, for that matter, if they were not just after her money, would have been deterred by just the characteristics that attracted Leonard. But, having been so wounded by the manner in which his mother had been treated by her lord and master, he wanted none of it. He was looking for someone with an independent mind and spirit much more common in America than England,[86] someone who would not be subservient to him or anyone else, an equal, of intelligence, and a partner for him in some common work. He wanted to be independent too, of course, in the same way that she did, but with the sort of independence that carried mutuality with it.

He therefore did not mind the dependence that the relationship entailed. However much Dorothy might deny it, her money was power, in personal as well as in impersonal relationships. It did not put him off, as it would lots of men who would have trouble in maintaining their masculine stance or vanity; it was something he welcomed because he had an inkling from Cornell of how it could be used. The aura her money lent her was also in her favour, as it had been for Willard too. After the Cosmopolitan Club it was her money that supported him in India and made it possible for him to run his own estate; her money which would fulfil a dream in England. She was throughout someone he could look up to. Leonard was prepared to look at himself in terms of the standard conventions about the behaviour of the two sexes and accept what he saw. He wrote to his brother, Richard, in June 1923, just when he was having one of his bad times with her:[87]

> She's magnificent. If I was 100% man she'd be too masculine for me: capable, vigorous, farsighted, a statesman in her way and one of those thoroughly international women that only America produces. But I'm not, and she sweeps me off my feet.

A reformer herself, she would not laugh or yawn at Leonard's hopes for human improvement; she would share them. He kept a copy of a letter he did not send her in July or August 1924 when the issue was still in the balance. Perhaps it sounded too unlike a love letter and he did not know which way he would go, receive love or settle for the noble friendship that had so far been all that was on offer:

> You happen to be the only woman in the world today who has shared so many of my own experiences; vital loss in the war, an attitude of pacifism, a real knowledge and sympathetic understanding of problems and countries the world around, a driving power to spend in causes and for people.

Leonard was as handsome a man as she was attractive a woman. Even if he did not have Willard's commanding brilliance and artistic gift, he had as much charm and enough energy to counter her melancholy. She did not have many handsome and eligible men paying court to her. Her contemporaries were married or dead. Also, being an Englishman was no disadvantage, especially since he was almost an American as well after being at Cornell. Like herself, Leonard had been away from home more than he was at it, over most of his life. They were both travellers, so far she by first class, he by second class. Moreover, in England she would not be quite so subject to the remaining criticism of her friends. Gertrude Whitney was told Elmhirst was 'quite a nice crank',[88] and many of her relatives and friends probably thought the same.

He started off with a signal advantage as Willard's messenger. This he added to by his ordeals in the Orient. On one of his ill-fated quests to Woods Hole, Dorothy, having rejected him yet again, gave Leonard some of Willard's clothes and a suitcase, and wrote:[89]

> There's a joy that comes to me always in the thought that it was Willard who brought you to me. For it was Cornell and his interest in the Cosmopolitan Club that led you to seek me out. . . . I can feel the fulness of his own joy in sharing ours.

His willingness to accept dependence upon her – she almost thrust her money at him after failing to give it to the dominating Tagore – must also have been in his favour. She had suffered too much from being dependent, on her mother, her stepmother, and Willard, all of whom had been torn away, and to become like that again could make her vulnerable to a repetition of the same kind of suffering. She was protecting herself by choosing, or being chosen by, someone who was not '100% man'.

This did not mean she felt safe. She went through the same cycle several times. She rejected Leonard and then awoke from the sleep of silence when he arrived back in America, like the fairy princess herself; as though he really had deserted her and she could only believe he had not when he was there, in person. Then further rejection and, for a short time after he had gone, repeated calls as if for him to return. The partings may have aroused some of the old feelings of loss which could be expressed positively – until it seemed that he really had gone, when she would retreat again into aloofness or silence.

Why should it have been different the third time round in 1924? A longer time had elapsed since Willard's death, much longer than the gap her father left before he married Edith. Leonard must have won growing admiration for his constancy, and, more decisive, he suddenly shone forth as a man more mature. Tagore had done his work.

Her long illness also played a part, giving her more time to ponder, weakening the ties with her American organisations and with some of her American friends who had tied her down, and generally making it seem less essential for her to remain in her own country. 'I realised then', she wrote much later, 'that I was not indispensable to my own country and that I would not feel guilty of desertion if I departed and joined Leonard in England.'[90]

Susan Hammond was the only one of Dorothy's close lifelong friends I saw who knew both her husbands well. She compared the two marriages:[91]

Willard came close to fulfilling the romantic dreams of her young life. He was a Sir Galahad – handsome, spirited, talented, gallant, kind and wise. He regarded her as womanly perfection, and pursued her with a knight's chivalry, and a good man's sincerity. . . . Dorothy was essentially a missionary at heart – she had to devote herself to good works, and in Leonard she found a devoted and sympathetic companion of the same persuasion. Leonard filled Dorothy's needs to perfection and she, in turn, was able to make his dreams come true. Marriage No. 1 was affluent, gay, happy, full, easy, interesting – and complete enough. Marriage No. 2 was self-denying, filled with generosity and consideration for others, serious, creative and completely satisfying.

When Leonard and Dorothy entered into their compact on the English experiment all would have been spoilt if they had tried to set down just what they had agreed. The vagueness of the concept which went with the word experiment was part of the excitement. But although they did not make their ideas explicit at the outset, and did not sweat too much over them after the launch, this does not mean they were without any. I therefore need to say something more about the notions they had before I can get them over the threshold and into Dartington itself. They brought into the experiment their individual capacities and their individual experiences; they also brought to it certain general ideas which they had obtained from the 'gene-pool' of such ideas in the societies they came from. To say the ideas are general is not to take away from their individuality, for Leonard and Dorothy were as much their own man and woman as anyone else in the choice of, and interpretation they put upon, the general ideas they adopted.

In one vital respect the definition of the experiment was not vague at all. It was to be a school. Given that they were not professionals irritated by some little detail of the curriculum or teaching method, this alone required them to entertain some notions about ways in which some rather large social improvements could be brought about. If they had wanted to start a model farm or a marvellous factory or a splendid research station they could have kept to a narrower vision. But a school, no. To create a school intended from its inception to be a departure from established practice is bound to be a radical step. If not to be like the run of schools, if, more, meant to be in good part their opposite, no founders could avoid facing up to some fundamental issues. It is not enough to decide that the new school is to be unlike ordinary schools. That decrees what the new school shall not be (a guide certainly), not what it shall. To formulate the positives means looking beyond education to its wider setting. Anyone perfectly well satisfied with society will obviously not want to reform education: education is playing its proper part in a happy scheme. But for anyone dissatisfied with it education may be seen as the means of making over society to its advantage. To hazard a new school therefore requires a compound of ideas – a rejection of both existing schools and existing society and a positive belief that a new kind of school will, through the new men and women it produces, alter society for the better or that society will just be better because the people are. The elements in the compound do not have to be described explicitly, nor the manner in which they are to be re-synthesised. Implicitly, they must be.

The experiment was all the more radical because the school was not seen as a self-contained educational institution, preparing children to become adults who would eventually help move society on to a better footing. Its essence was that it was not to be a school at all of the sort that most people would recognise. There were to be children in it, but it was not to be an institution of the book. Its classrooms were to be 'a farm, a garden, workshops, play grounds, woods and freedom', its main book the book of nature. As this had been opened up for Leonard by the dales of Derbyshire and by the waters of the Padma so should it be opened up for others by the rolling hills of Devonshire and the waters of the Dart. Quite how the farm and garden, forests and freedom were to be used for education could be left unstated. The intention to have them at all, not just as the setting for the school but as an essential part of it, meant there would have to be on hand much besides chalk and talk. This intention committed them to include in the experiment many of the features of a rounded society.

I must stress again that most of the design was left unsketched. They had only the lightest ideological baggage. Leonard, and much more Dorothy, were both in their different ways religious. But their religion was not the militant or articulate sort held by many other founders of new communities; the arts apart, it was certainly no foundation for a charter charged with the principles of the good life. They were both more securely in a secular tradition, and a pragmatic one at that, like most of the people who have passed through Dartington. In more than half a century there has never been any full statement of what Dartington is about. People have to leave it alone or, if they cannot show such forbearance, puzzle it out for themselves, each arriving at his own interpretation, as I am having to do in writing this memoir.

Mine is that in practice they had utopian hopes though without the rhetoric that often goes with them. I know that word, utopian, has an unfavourable connotation for many people, in as much as out of Dartington: utopias are unattainable and therefore crackpot. That is not my position, nor (I think) the Elmhirsts'. They derived their ideas not from the realm of what is but from the realm of what might be, and also went a little beyond what might be into what was probably unattainable, although still worth striving for. They were not so far from ordinary opinion as to believe in the perfectibility of man. But they did believe in his improvability, and about that they were perhaps more ambitious than most realists would say they had any right to be – even though they did not lay themselves open to one kind of challenge by being synthesisers in an intellectual sense like so many other founders of new communities.[92] They were not so much fountains as channels or conduits through which travelled a constant flow of ideas to find outlets in Dartington, not so much innovators as enablers. The originality of the place rested in the combination and recombination of ideas gathered from many different sources. If they had all come from England, Dartington would have been more of a single piece; or from America; or from India. Coming from all three countries and many others the place was more unusual.

James Madison said of his American Republic to an English visitor that it is 'useful in proving things before held impossible'.[93] Though he much preferred Jefferson to Madison, Leonard would have nodded his agreement, and perhaps Dorothy too despite her sad experience of American intolerance after the First World War. She was brought up in a mansion on Fifth Avenue. But her own ancestors from the *Mayflower* had established a kind of utopian community in the Massachusetts Bay Colony. Other such – Oneida, Amana, Bethel, Shakers, Rappites, Owenites, Brook Farm, followers of Fourier – had flourished there in the nineteenth century.[94] She was citizen of a country (and Leonard almost one by adoption) which had never thrown out the dreams which so many immigrants had of the earthly paradise. Even in this century the Hutterian Brethren and the Bruderhof have more than maintained themselves, and along with them some Skinnerite communities (whether or not members of the Federation of Egalitarian Communities) and communes estimated at one time to number as many as 3,000.[95] Even ordinary places sometimes have an apocalyptic flavour about them:[96]

> Drive through Jerusalem Corners, New York, or Promise City, Iowa; pass the freeway exits for Elysian Village and Arcadia in California; stop at 'Garden of Eatun' restaurant in Cozad, Nebraska.

Neither Dorothy nor Leonard ever visited Promise City in Iowa. But they had the spirit, as did the other Americans who flocked to Dartington. To transplant onto English soil ideas from any other country was to guarantee some originality, locally; transplant ideas from America and they would, coming from the circles in which they had moved, have a special tinge of ambition and hope, all the more so when crossed with those Leonard had gained from Tagore. This was especially true of this particular couple. They were not subject as much to the limitation, money, which makes most people modest in their ambitions. If what they wanted could be bought they could within reason have it, and therefore be ambitious without being impractical.

Leonard was more explicit about the ways in which the attainment of goals might be measured than about their nature. But they were there clearly enough. If they had the impress of American experience upon them, and the characteristic cast given by the 1920s, the hopes were those which have inspired many reform movements at many different periods and in many different countries since the Age of Enlightenment. The five which have had the most influence on Dartington can for shorthand be characterised in this way — the educational myth, the cultural myth, the arcadian myth, the humanist myth and the scientific myth. In using the word myth I do not mean exercises of the imagination to account for what has happened in the past but for what might happen in the future, going beyond the realistically attainable.

Mankind can be liberated through education.

A new flowering of the arts can transform a society impoverished by industrialisation and secularisation.

A society which combines the best of town and country combines the best of both worlds.

A pervasive concern for the individual human being and his right to self-determination can be combined with the efficient operation of agriculture and industry.

The scientific spirit can be a continuous spur to progress.

On this last myth Leonard was, though speaking more of the social than the natural sciences, in a grand tradition when he wrote about Dartington some time later, in 1934:

> Another Utopia, you will say. Perhaps, but with this difference: that economics and psychology have begun to offer us yardsticks of measurement, clumsy as yet, that the old Utopias never possessed, yardsticks that we can apply to experiments out of the past like Robert Owen's or Brigham Young's, in order to check on our ventures. When they broke down it was generally for one of these reasons: they disregarded sound economics, they followed some ethical or theoretical principle too rigidly, or they attempted to isolate themselves too completely from the social and economic world around them.

He was going better than the *old* utopias by putting his faith in the methods of science.

The five myths have shaped the structure of the rest of the book, each of them being the subject of its own chapters. The setting has been described in the next chapter, and then comes education in Chapters 6 and 7; the arts in Chapters 8 and 9; arcady in Chapter 10, the scientific myth in Chapter 11 and the humanist one in Chapter 12. I have generally given much more space to the earlier than to the later years of their period at Dartington, since the earlier were the more formative, in which their influence was greater.

The underlying hope was not that one or other of the myths might be realised but that they all would be realised together in one place in an environment of mutual support. New men would not be evolved except through the reform of education; they would not be able to fulfil themselves and express their feelings without the arts; they would not be whole without the beauty of nature near at hand to nourish them; and all would fail unless based securely on the foundation of a sound economy which did not sacrifice the individual to the machine or the organisation, and which was guided by science.

I am not suggesting that Leonard's and Dorothy's conception contained all, or even most, of the features which have characterised many more full-blooded utopian communities, from those of the Shakers to the Kibbutzim. They were not committed to the replacement of individual material rewards by more collective motivations or to the sharing out of property in an egalitarian manner and its replacement by collective ownership. After their early short-lived debate about whether to give away all the money, they held on to the control of Dorothy's fortune, although making a part of it into the Dartington Hall Trust, and enjoyed a standard of life so much higher than anyone else's in the place as to be on a different plane. They were not committed to the replacement of the individual family by larger groupings in which sexual relationships would be more collective although 'free love' played its part at Dartington. They were not committed to the organisation of work as a democracy, with members choosing their managers and the work they preferred to do from one period of their lives to another. They were not committed to the reintroduction of symbolic ritual into the collective life unless through the arts. There was nothing like the Shaker ceremonies at Dartington.[97]

But in four vital respects they were, by positing a school allied to a farm, workshops and the rest, following the same road as other utopian communities. The link between utopianism and education is an old story:[98]

> The real by-products of nearly all the English communities have been new departments of and new departures in education. The Quakers and Moravians have left an indelible legacy of experiment and tolerance. Lee was an instigator of Charity Schools; Owen a pioneer of infant schools; Greaves and Minter Morgan explorers of the school as a centre of socialisation.

Secondly, the setting they chose was, like the others, rural. Utopias do not seem to sit easily in cities. Thirdly, the others are not called communities for nothing; nor, on many occasions, was Dartington. The common enemy is the series of specialised institutions developed to take the place of the pre-industrial family which in its community setting at one and the same time performed the functions of agricultural production, of a handicraft factory, of a school, a church and a police force.[99] Specialisation has also been fragmentation and given rise to the alienation or isolation of individuals about which so many complain. Without having to be self-sufficient – Leonard was firmly against that – the community was seen as the agent of reintegration, the means by which the people who compose it could take collective responsibility for bringing together many different aspects of their lives. School, arts, workshop, farm, forestry would be organised separately but within the matrix of a larger community to which they all belonged, a community which would also be (in Leonard's words) a 'fellowship of a few men of ideas and spirit' shaped by all its members on the democratic model proper to a project which started in America.

In a fourth respect, too, Dartington was the same as other utopian communities. It was a microcosm, containing in it many of the elements of the great society, but in miniature:

> To see a World in a Grain of Sand,
>   And a Heaven in a Wild Flower,
> Hold Infinity in the palm of your hand,
>   And Eternity in an hour.

'From one point of view', said Leonard, 'in everything we have attempted at Dartington we have endeavoured to secure that element of universality which would make such discoveries as we made there be applicable, in principle at any rate, to any other part of the globe.'[100] To make over the small into something better might in its turn lead to making over the big into something better. You did not have to be a visionary, in the 1920s any more than at any other time, to recognise, the world being in its customary sorry state, that something better was needed.

CHAPTER 5

THE ENGLISH EXPERIMENT

Heresy-hunting is, with quite responsible
members of the leisured class, a recognized
form of British sport, and is organized
mainly around tea-tables in the country and
dinner-tables in London.

Faith and Works, 1937

The 'English experiment' was bound to be shaped by the place they chose
for it, or rather that Leonard chose. He was the Englishman, actually
coming home after ten years' absence: the American was only reassuring
him when she said England was *like* coming home. They had narrowed the
search to Devon.

Leonard went to the country's swankiest estate agent of the time,
Knight, Frank & Rutley. He took delight all his life thereafter in em-
broidering his exchange with the dapper young man behind the desk:[1]

'Well, sir, what can I do for you?'
'I want a place.'
'What kind of place? Hunting, shooting, fishing, golf?'
'No.'
'Then how many bedrooms?'
'I've no idea.'
'What then do you want, sir?'
'It must be beautiful, we're starting a school. We expect to make
farming pay, it must have a reasonably productive soil and climate,
and as much variety as possible, woods, forest, orchards, etc. and if
you can give me all those, then historical associations thrown in. Yes,
and in Devon, Dorset or Somerset.'

From the forty-eight estates offered him in the West Country he made
straight away for those in Devon.

On Monday 2 March 1925, he bought himself a Talbot with a dicky seat, a driving licence and a driving lesson. He had never driven anything before except the Ford truck between Surul and Bolpur, and he never mastered the art, although he got nearer to it than Dorothy. Accompanied by his sister Irene, who could be relied on to be more biddable than the wife the poultry professor had told him not to take with him, he set off on the Tuesday morning, with a driver from the Talbot garage to take them out to the suburbs through the terrifying streets of London. By Tuesday night at 9 p.m. they were in Exeter, on Wednesday at Marley House near South Brent. Its Georgian mansion and 'pleasure grounds' (to use the estate agent's term) were on offer for £5,500, or, together with a working estate of 1,600 acres, for £38,000. Judging the stucco house dull, he turned back to find the next on the list. They could find no entrance to it anywhere. The Dartington Hall offered by Knight, Frank & Rutley, if it existed at all, was well hidden. It is looped around by the river Dart and is all on one side of the main road, with the Hall at the top of a hill in the middle of the loop, the village of Dartington at the bottom, on the main road from Totnes to Plymouth and Buckfastleigh. Geography creates between the Hall and Dartington village a sense of distance which has persisted strongly even into the age of the car; and still more between the Hall and everything beyond. Within the river's loop people could the more readily feel themselves a separate community and their neighbours regard them like that as well. The sense of distance was, if anything, increased when the direct road through the garden to the front door of the Hall was closed to cars.

At last Leonard found the way in. He crept in bottom gear along a little cutting over a brook, and then up the hill and to his first view of the courtyard. It was like falling in love at first sight: he knew he need look no further. On his return to London he wrote to Dorothy on the Friday:[2]

> In we went and up and down some wonderful hills till we pulled up in a veritable fairy land – in winter too – what it would be like in spring or summer or autumn I dare not imagine. I wanted to kneel and worship the beauty of it all and every fresh vista only seemed the more to recommend the handiwork of nature joined with the reverent hand of generations of men . . . unlimited farm buildings with roofs and windows and doors like a fairy land, and such farmer folk, and the garden and trees you must see for yourself, the orchards, the river and the boathouse and all the nine-tenths that remain unexplored . . . and the most ideal place for a children's growing ground I ever saw, with room to spread, and rooms to spare and be left empty if not wanted at the outset, and a thousand other delights. I'm sorry, I've dreamt of it ever since as a fit home for you and the children and I've pictured you there – the squire's

wife, and I've found local possibilities of all kinds and part of my heart remains there. But I've done nothing definite yet – merely paved the way so that at a moment's notice we can set the wheels in motion.

He did not comment on what Knight, Frank & Rutley considered a great asset of the place – 'Hunting with the South Devon and Dartmoor Foxhounds, and the Dartmoor Otter Hounds'.[3]

One charm was age. If Dorothy was to be wife to a squire, let him not be a petty one. He was captivated by his 'historical associations'; they released his imagination. Just as he pointed to the grooves in the stone door of the banqueting hall where generations of archers sharpened their arrows before departing for the chase, or the way the original master mason picked out the best features of New College or Winchester College to emulate at Dartington, so he would throughout his life signal whole or part invention by saying 'It is not generally known that . . .'. Dorothy's stock response was to smile and murmur 'Are you really sure, Jerry?' – that being the name her children had given him. On this occasion, at first glimpse, he thought he saw the relics of a Saxon keep from which the Danes must have been held in their attack on Devon. He got it wrong.

The agents' particulars were a clue to the history, and would have predisposed him to like what he saw before he trundled over the brook. This 'ancient and historic demesne'[4] was the property of Arthur Melville Champernowne, Esq. He was, if a petty squire with a purely local influence, from an old family which had owned Dartington Hall since 1559. The buildings, even though they did not go back to the Saxons, went back to the late fourteenth century, and when Leonard discovered the truth it was richer even than his imagination. The manor house at Dartington had been built by the half-brother of a king. The founder was John Holand, Earl of Huntingdon and Duke of Exeter – one of the rooms on the plan of the house was called the Duke's Room. Holand was a famous jouster whose skill was frequently referred to by Froissart; the sunken garden that Leonard saw was evidently a tiltyard where Holand could practise, watched in the lists by spectators sitting on the terraces.[5] John Harvey, who wrote dozens of letters to Leonard about the buildings, found in the Public Record Office a detailed inventory of the contents of Dartington in 1399. He says, 'The two jousting saddles and other equipment go a long way to support the Tiltyard as an original work of John Holand's.'[6]

Holand's half-brother, Richard II, commands general distaste from historians. Leonard would not have it at all. The others had got it wrong; eventually justice would be done to that 'sensitive soul'[7] whom 'his blood-thirsty uncles turned into a nervous wreck'.[8] 'I still await a fair appreciation of Richard II. He seems to me to have been the first King of England since Alfred the Great to value peace for its own sake and to have preferred the pursuit of the Arts to empire building and annual forays, mainly for plunder.'[9] To couple him with Alfred in the same sentence was the highest commendation Leonard could give.

The association with King Richard could be all the closer because on the vault of the porch tower was, and is, his badge, he having given the manor to Holand. The royal badge, shown in Plate 17, depicted a graceful white hart lying on a red rose. This later became the symbol of the House of Lancaster in the wars of the red rose against the white rose of York. Though a Yorkshireman, Leonard chose Richard's white hart as the symbol of the modern Dartington. It now helps to sell a whole range of products from Dartington Glass to Dartington Textiles, from Dartington Furniture to Dartington Pottery. There is also a White Hart Club and a White Hart Dining Room in the space which was the kitchen of the original manor. The mother whom Richard and Holand had in common was Joan, the 'Fair Maid of Kent', wife first to Sir Thomas Holand and then to the Black Prince, Edward Prince of Wales. Leonard grasped her too and spoke of her with affection for many years to come:[10]

> I cannot help thinking that the Fair Maid of Kent (who was in intimate touch with all the millionaires of the day and who ran the Court and with whom her brothers-in-law seem for the most part to have been in love) had a hand in the planning of Dartington with her son John Holand. . . . There must have been a lot of discussion around the Court about building and the planning of buildings and how to civilise these terrible Norman and Plantagenet castles of earlier days.

Even with such associations the ruins – the Great Hall with no roof or glass in the windows, the kitchen block fallen down, the porch tower nearing collapse – would most emphatically have held no advantage for most people. Leonard was different. Ruins could be restored. He said later, 'I had discussed this with my future wife. I knew her resources were such that I need not be frightened.'[11]

To other people who knew that the estate had been running down for centuries, and almost to the point of catastrophe since 1921 when the Champernownes moved out and left the house empty, the sight was a sad one.[12] Long gone were the days when estates like this had been self-sufficient at a decent standard, with their own food and their supply of wood for burning, their own sawmill and their own cider press. The Champernowne family had relied solely on rents and these had been falling for many years, leaving less money for maintenance. Mrs Crook was the wife of the tenant farmer who lived in the courtyard and used for his farm the buildings which are now the theatre, college library and college office.

She remembers hearing the rats scampering around at night in the rats' 'private house', the neglected gardens, the fallen ceilings. Only the trees were looked after with any care. They could be turned into money. Not long before Leonard drove up on that first visit one of the foresters, George Miller, was killed by a tree blown down in a gale. It was on the edge of the garden. Frank Crook went off to Totnes on his motorbike and sidecar to fetch a doctor; he was too late.[13] Mr Champernowne had with Mr Miller's help felled and sold a lot of timber shortly before Leonard came on the scene.

Mrs Crook was the first person Leonard spoke to. He knocked at her door, announced at that point even before he had seen any of the other forty-six estates on his list that he was thinking of buying the Hall, but first had to contact a lady in the USA about it. Could he and Irene have a cup of tea? Mrs Crook set out Devonshire cream and home-made cakes for them in a room looking over the farmyard.[14] They did not see the same things. Where through the window Mrs Crook saw dereliction, Leonard saw opportunity, to put the roofs back, to clear away the brambles, to restore everything to its former indubitable state of magnificence. That afternoon a large element was therefore added to the English experiment – restoration of ancient buildings.

Just over a week later, after securing an option on the property, Leonard left for New York and the wedding described in the last chapter; he was full of the place where his dream could be brought to life. How would Dorothy take it? She had enjoyed sitting in a tent in the rainy glen at Cornell. Would she, the grand lady from Fifth Avenue, the friend of Presidents and Mayors, writers and reformers, Junior League President, be able to see herself as Leonard saw her, a squire's wife in a rambling, almost derelict house in Devon? When they heard about it some of her American friends went further than Croly; they prophesied disaster.

The final answer had to wait her inspection. She and Leonard boarded the White Star Line's S.S. *Majestic* on 20 May; the world's largest liner, it was soon speeding towards Dartington doing at best 25 knots and clocking 578 miles in the day. On Friday 29 May Irene and brother Richard met them at Southampton. By Friday night they were in Exeter again. Here is the entry in her mauve leather diary with its brass lock for the Saturday when she saw Dartington and Totnes, the nearest town, for the first time:[15]

> Sat. Exeter. To Totnes by car – thence Dartington – all morning in the place. Too heavenly. Lunch at Seymour Hotel. Back to Dartington – interior difficult! Tea Elizabeth Tea Room.

On the following day they both attended the service in Exeter Cathedral and went for a walk before lunch. When Dorothy came back she 'wept idiotically'.[16] The next few weeks were spent in and out of Dartington, with the estate agents in London, with Leonard's solicitor uncle from York, with Pom who negotiated the purchase of the estate for £30,000. She acted as if the decision were already taken, as it had been, really, when Dorothy made up her mind to marry and move to England. The detail – for instance, where the experiment was to be – could from then on be left to Leonard.

The next year was chaotic. They had no home. They could not move into the Hall along with the rats. There was nothing to move into. They started off, in June, by staying at the Seymour Hotel in Totnes, but were never there for many days at a stretch. They had to visit Leonard's parents for one thing, much to Leonard's terror, according to Irene. He was afraid his Fairy Godmother would be put off by his parents and they by her. When it came to the point of going through the front door of 'Elmhirst' with her he could not make himself step over the threshold. He stayed outside. She entered on her own and introduced herself as their new daughter-in-law. Irene, who was there on the inside of the house, said her parents were soon 'eating out of her hand'.[17]

In October they rented a dull Victorian house in Totnes called 'Elmsleigh' and left the hotel behind. But they were still very much on the move, and though married only a few months and Dorothy pregnant, often apart. Leonard went to see old friends or relations on his own, Dorothy to visit a school with Kenneth Lindsay, or to buy furniture in antique shops. In the middle of the month she was off to America. Her three children had stayed there until Dartington could be made ready for them. Michael Straight remembers Dorothy at Westbury taking his hand into her bed and placing it on her bare belly so that he could feel the baby move within her – an awesome experience for a 10-year-old who had seen little of his mother. While she was in New York Leonard toured Denmark with brother Richard and Roger Morel (soon to be employed at Dartington) and then instead of returning to Devonshire sailed after her to America. On 14 December they were together again at Cornell for the formal dedication of Willard Straight Hall, the product of the double marriage.

Being married had not much changed the pattern of their lives, except that they minded more being apart. Dorothy did anyway, when she was on her own at Dartington. She wrote to Leonard on most days he was away to say she was missing him and feeling lost. She made the best of the Dartington village sports day and walks on her own around Totnes:[18]

> I have explored Totnes the last two days, seeing the Norman castle,
> the Guildhall and a beautiful old Gothic doorway in a little side street.

> I have also found a glorious restaurant where you can get duck and
> chicken and delectable loganberry tart. I had lunch there yesterday.
> Isn't that enterprising!

She was not used to carrying money with her. Miss Bogue had done that
for her in America, like a royal purse-bearer. She bought things in some
Totnes shops and forgot to pay.[19]

She could not pretend she liked being on her own, homesick as she
was for America and for her American friends. Her daughter Beatrice told
me 'I think that mother was infinitely homesick for America where our real
friends were'.[20] She had only her maid, Louisa, and after a time, for all her
love of her mistress, she could not stand the loneliness and returned to
America.

Above all she wanted Leonard:[21]

> Oh Jerry, I long for you so. I had a quaint dream about you last night.
> You were going about naked and looking positively angelic, and I was
> trying to persuade some man that your legs were round and beautiful.
> You were laughing merrily and it was apparently all great fun. I think
> of it now with something of a pang, for that intense longing of
> pre-marriage days has returned upon me. In those days it was
> agonized by uncertainties and dreads of one sort or another; now I'm
> free of those, but the need itself seems stronger than ever. However, I
> rejoice really in such bondage – in the knowledge of the terrific pull
> you can exert.

Only once did Leonard reply with anything other than assurance. He said
he felt like Lady Mary Wortley Montagu, 'perfectly unacquainted with a
proper matrimonial style'.[22] Dorothy replied by return of post:[23]

> And now you speak of being 'wholly unsatisfactory'. Jerry, how can
> you! You surely have some conception of what you have been doing
> for me. I'll quote you a letter from Ruth which came this morning.
> 'Evelyn says she has never seen you so gay, so lovely or so happy. . . .'
> So there, Jerry, if you can't see how happy I am, you'll have to rely on
> the eyesight of others . . . your sensitiveness to beauty is like the
> sensitiveness of my body to yours . . . just as our bodies are finding a
> more perfect adjustment so our wills and minds and understanding
> will also.

After their return from America in January 1926 they had two more
months based in Totnes before Dorothy left for London, to await the birth
of their first child. She stayed for a fortnight at the Royal Palace Hotel in
Kensington to be near nursing home and doctor. She shopped for her new
home, interviewed domestic staff and wrote to Leonard:[24]

I'm glad Vic can't see the bathroom here, for he would rapidly lose all the respect he would have for me over the £2 easy chairs. I walked into Floris the other day – the perfumers' in Jermyn St – and decided it was the moment for a cosmetic debauch. I also persuaded myself that it was a good opportunity to try out different bath crystals, perfumes, soaps, powders, etc. for Dartington. Well – all I can say is, that when next we have a joint bath here you will think you are lying on a bank of wild thyme.

Ruth was born on 28 March. Leonard was at the nursing home for the birth but was turned out of the room at the end. They were both delighted with the baby. He immediately sent the news to Yorkshire. 'The baby is really handsome, of course, and full of beans.'[25] But Dorothy was in the nursing home for a month. She was not long back in Devon again before at last, in May, they moved onto their own property, into the newly acquired Old Parsonage which, bought from the Church, was in much better repair than the Hall. Her other children had all arrived from America by June.

Their second child, Bill, was born three years later, on 26 February 1929, also in a London nursing home.

Given all their moving about in the first year, how did they accomplish anything on their new estate? Leonard was very active when he was there, planning, superintending, hiring, instituting. He also called in the help of people he could trust, his three brothers, Pom, Vic and Richard. They too had a feel for the countryside ingrained in them, and the same wish to escape confinement with their parents. Marvelling equally at the sudden change in the family fortunes – it was as if the whole family had married into the Whitney money – they were all summoned to the scene, as in medieval times a man would have called upon his brothers. They arrived very soon after the decision to purchase was made, to cut down trees, clear undergrowth and mull over the detailed plans for rebuilding.

Willie was, as I said before, originally to be the solicitor of the family. When he was killed Pom took his place – the word, Pom, being for some reason as near as he could get when very young to saying 'boy'. After leaving Winchester he was articled in his uncle's firm in York. He was the stockiest of the family, always eager and energetic, a great cricketer as well as a reliable lawyer. He was the instigator of the first cricket team at Dartington and the first pitch. He became the closest of all Leonard's brothers. Amongst many other things, he was, along with Fred Gwatkin from the London firm of McKenna & Co., legal adviser to Dartington. Appointed one of the first Trustees in 1932, he remained one until 1980 when he became the first Trustee Emeritus.

Parallel to Dartington, he also ran the family estate at Barnsley alongside his legal practice, graduating from being his father's assistant to becoming estate manager. His father did not leave Leonard any money but when he died in 1948 he did bequeath him, as the eldest surviving son, all the 600-acre Elmhirst estate. Leonard, with the agreement of Bill, his son, and all his brothers, gave the property to Pom, including Houndhill which had once been part of the Elmhirst estate and which Leonard bought back. Pom in his turn gave the property to his eldest son, Richard, in 1967. There was friendly competition between Pom's farm and the Dartington ones for a half century. To Pom Leonard was more than a benefactor:[26]

> From childhood onward Leonard was always my hero. He was the leader, the older brother. I have always enjoyed his gift of having ideas, of creating adventures. . . . To me he was a man worth following wherever he went.

Pom and his always sensible, always warm-hearted wife, Gwen, were closer to Leonard than kin.

Richard and Vic were both employees at Dartington. Some time after he had been to Denmark with Leonard, Richard went off to Cornell for a poultry course to prepare himself to run the Dartington Poultry Department. He was the dashing captain of the Dartington Cricket XI as long as he was there, and if anything even more stylish than Leonard in his choice of clothes, whether white flannels or what seemed then actually to be *smart* brown breeches or plus fours. He had been an officer in the Coldstreams, and looked the part when, as he stood by the wicket to bowl, he paused for a commanding moment to survey the field before signalling one man to come closer from long leg, another to fall back to mid-on.

Vic was different again. He was the calmest of the brothers, at least outwardly, if slowness in movement suggests calm. He had an even more bushy moustache than Leonard's, presumably first grown when he was a Second Lieutenant in the York and Lancaster Regiment. If a small child spoke to him he would lean right down to listen gravely to what he or she said. He was more the listener than any of his other brothers. In the autumn of 1925 Vic returned from a year's brush with the magic of Cornell and Leonard's new money. For the rest of that year and into 1926, whenever Leonard and Dorothy were away, Vic was left in charge. He was in effect estate steward.

There was a great deal for Vic to look after. Wholesale reconstruction of the main buildings would have to wait – the banqueting hall, the tower block and the enormous medieval kitchen. The first tasks were to renovate and modernise the dwelling house so that the Elmhirsts could move in as quickly as possible, convert a stable building into the first boarding-house for the school and put up some new houses for staff and children. Sir Henry

Tanner, a London architect, drew up the plans for restoring what had been the Champernowne's private house, wrongly named then and forever, since it was never private. His deputy recommended Albert Fincham as clerk of works. Already 70, he looked almost a caricature of the Victorian artisan; he was also one of the most skilled and diligent workmen ever employed at Dartington. Quite early on, Mr Fincham persuaded Leonard that the work would be better done by direct labour than by outside contractors. So early in 1927 an Engineering and Building Department was set up with its own Dartington workforce. To judge by the number of buildings it apparently needed the English experiment was to be on a sizeable scale.

The Engineering and Building Department eventually became, in Staverton Contractors Ltd, one of the largest building companies in the west of England. Mr Fincham was responsible for that, and much else at Dartington, even though he was there for only eighteen months. Dorothy was captivated by his courtliness, his liveliness and his delight in all the good building being done:[27]

> Mr Fincham was more adorable than ever this morning. We discovered so many building sites that you will find it hard to restrain us from plunging straight into a village. When I first mentioned cottages he actually looked up and showed a quiver of excitement: 'Will you let me design them for you?' What could I say. I succumbed completely.

Fincham did design them, as he also did the new Barton farmhouse. Two pairs of staff cottages stand near the Hall as a memorial to him. The picturesque stone walls and Delabole slate roofs were so costly that nothing of the kind was ever built again, even at Dartington.

Mr Fincham began the restoration of most of the East and part of the South and West wings of the courtyard. He was craftsman as well as clerk of works.[28] He set a standard. The only good builders for Dartington in the next fifty years would be people who had the same pride in workmanship. The next man after Fincham, the architect William Weir, had it as well.

The monumental task they did not dare tackle right at the beginning was to rebuild the walls and reroof the two largest buildings of all, Holand's 70-foot-long banqueting hall and his almost equally large kitchen. For this a specialist was needed. Lord Sandwich (whom Leonard knew through their common interest in experimental education) recommended Weir as architect. Restoration of medieval buildings had been his occupation. He had done much work for the Society for the Protection of Ancient Buildings which William Morris had started.

His first task when he came to Dartington in 1926 was to save the porch tower and the rooms adjoining it. He moved from there to the East

Wing and further work in the private house before the time came for the hall. Leonard was as fascinated as Weir by the problem of the roof. The intention was to restore the past unless there was strong reason not to. No reliable drawings came to light until later. Mr Champernowne would not let the newcomers see any of the old papers he had. To go by, there was only the precious outline traced in the plaster of the high wall above the dais which is shown in Plate 15. Coupled with the corbels, the trace showed the shape of the beams which had been there until 1813 when the roof was removed, because it was in a dangerous state and too expensive to repair. From this evidence Weir could draw for Leonard a hammer-beam roof like that in Westminster Hall and in some ways like that in New College, Oxford. The two connections were almost equally agreeable. The same Richard II had a hand in the former, built in its permanent form a little after Dartington. 'His reconstruction of the great hall at the Palace of Westminster between 1394 and 1401 is one of the outstanding achievements of the Gothic world.'[29] William of Wykeham was as good a companion – a great educator as well as a great builder in both New College and Winchester College.

Leonard, loving the game of being a detective into history, for the rest of his life looked for signs in other famous buildings of the artistry of the same master mason who had built Dartington. He visited all the other hammer-beams. He also loved being by Weir's side as Weir chose the iron studs, hinges, bolts and latches for the doors, walked through the Dartington woods to select oak branches of the right rounded shapes for the roof trusses, or took the spokeshave from the carpenter to show him just how a medieval craftsman would finish off the chamfers on the oak beams. Over a period of seven years as architect no detail was too tiny for him. Bob Hening, his successor as long-term Dartington architect, appreciates the concern he showed for detail, like the occasional ridge tiles in the courtyard: they are raised to allow a minimum circulation of air around roof timbers otherwise sealed in and prone to dry rot; they are even covered with wire netting to keep out birds. Weir also encouraged his stonemasons to set each rough hewn stone in the hall with the merest inclination to the outside so that retained moisture would be more likely to find a way out than a way in.[30] In the wet Devon climate the local rather porous stone was always liable to let damp in.

Services were needed for the new buildings. So low had rents fallen along with local farm prices – milk down to 7d. a gallon, cream to 8d. a pound at High Beara Farm, Landscove, near Totnes[31] – that the Champernownes had hardly been able to afford any of the new amenities of the twentieth century. Dorothy could not be expected to live like a Devon peasant pondering the price of milk through the broken pane of a damp room. For an American a reliable supply of electricity was essential. But there was no public authority to supply it to a place so remote, or many other services as essential. So Dartington had to make a move towards self-sufficiency.

Wiring the house started in October 1925. Five electricians – Jack Collingbourne, Sid Austin, Sid Collingbourne, Jack Gallon and Vic Cannon – came from London to do it and then to install an old 25·h.p. paraffin engine to generate the current. They stayed on as permanent, key members of the staff. The engine was only second-hand because Leonard had decided to construct a hydroelectric station to serve the estate on the river Dart at Staverton Town Mills. It was not formally opened until 1930 when Ruth, then aged 4, performed the ceremony.

The estate was also without mains water. So mains were laid, a reservoir built and pumping engines installed. Sewage works had to be built to replace earth closets. A Dartington fire brigade was formed. The old thoroughfares were modernised and new roads built, estate refuse collection organised and an estate transport service started. Dartington became a local state.

In September 1926 the first stage of the building work was complete, the private house ready to move into. What sort of household was it to be? This was as much Dorothy's province as buildings and services were Leonard's.

Dorothy took for granted that her new establishment would be like her old ones in New York City and on Long Island, which themselves borrowed much from England, including their butlers. Her new English household, the third, should be run on the same pattern and of course subject to the same strict economy. Dorothy wrote to Miss Bogue a few weeks after moving into the Hall:[32]

> In order to keep within our financial limits for this year we are going to require retrenchment. Here at Dartington we are all operating on a careful monthly budget, which means the Household as well as the Building, Forestry, Farm and School Departments. I asked Mr Gorton to do the same thing in New York. He is going to ask Mrs James to prepare a monthly Budget on the basis of a certain allowance for food for persons in the house, just as we do here. He is also going to ask Pembroke to do the same thing for Westbury.

There was no thought of securing retrenchment by cutting down the number of homes, though she did sell her house at 1130 Fifth Avenue and instead bought a large apartment at 1172 Park Avenue. Her American staff did their best to drive away the wicked idea of major economies being made in her American establishment by insisting at every conceivable opportunity that she was only 'visiting' England. Even Leonard, aware as he was of the criticism of him coming from America and aware too of Dorothy's homesickness, seems to have fanned the same hope. On 17 February 1927 he was writing to Miss Bogue:

> By that time[the Spring], the biggest part of the work should be established, and though there is a great deal to be done yet, I think the foundations are laid in such a way that after a certain period, the school ought to be able to run right ahead. I know there are many who think Mrs Elmhirst has been decoyed, trapped and inveigled away from her natural home. All I can do is depend on those of her friends who understand her . . . neither she nor I have the slightest intention of doing what some of her friends accuse us of, getting out of touch with things across the water.

Miss Bogue was not to be comforted so easily:[33]

> The fact that you and she have bought a place in England, have started a school there, have been away from America for some time, and have sold the house here, all *seem* to point to Mrs Elmhirst's leaving America for a long sojourn abroad. I have always combated this rumour when it comes to me, personally, but even though I do refute it, there are many people who seem to know much better than I do, so I have gotten in the habit of paying little attention to what they say as I feel their remarks arise from ignorance and are not worth consideration.

It was an odd relationship, although no more so than many others Dorothy had with her dependants. Miss Bogue had two and a half large homes (the 'camp' she had rights to in the Adirondacks being counted as a half) all waiting for Dorothy; she was imploring her to visit them and to justify her existence and theirs. Yet on 3 February 1931 Dorothy wrote to Miss Bogue saying 'Would it be convenient for you to have us over for the month of June?' She was not being mischievous. It was her way of denying the cash nexus. Like some other very rich people she could not concede that people worked for money. She insisted that porters, chauffeurs, maids, secretaries served her out of graciousness and kindness and that they should be given their reward in thanks and gratitude. The make-believe then became real. Many of them did serve her not just for the money.

I remember Miss Bogue in 1931 meeting the S.S. *Majestic* at its Manhattan terminal with Dorothy's own Packard driven by the New York chauffeur to back her up, and, as if that was not enough, a hired 16-cylinder Cadillac as well for 'the boys'. It enthralled me by being able to start in top gear – a one-gear car. She fussed and looked delighted and offended all at once, especially the last when later that same night she stood on the platform and saw us go off without her from Grand Central Station in Harry's same private car on the train to Raquette Lake in the Adirondacks where Dorothy had the use of a luxury house incongruously called a 'camp'. On the strength of Dorothy's cheque-book she showered me with presents, which appeared to come not from Dorothy but from her.

Miss Bogue was the steward of a branch which she hoped would be restored to its proper state of headquarters. She cannot have been too pleased about the size of the household at Dartington: *it* did not look like a branch. Retrenchment or no, the new household at the Hall turned out to be on the same scale as Dorothy's other ones in America. The house opened with a staff of over twenty to run it, many of them recruited from the Regina Employment Bureau of Duke Street, Grosvenor Square, known at Dartington even then as the Vagina Bureau. They were headed by Walter Thomas, the butler, trained in the same kind of household. Leonard and Vic made mild remonstrances about its size. But Leonard knew Dorothy, used to this style of life, would without it feel even more lost in a foreign country. Living in pinched circumstances, tumbledown buildings, ruined courtyard, wild overgrown garden, could be altogether too much without proper compensation.

Thomas had started in the employ of the Marquess of Bute who owned Cardiff Castle. Tommy (if anyone dared even at Dartington to be so intimate) was well over six foot. He had entered service with the Marquess as one of eight footmen, each pair, who presumably stood and moved together, the same height. He nearly always wore a black coat, waistcoat and striped trousers, except when he was polishing silver, which was quite often, and then a green baize apron was produced for the ceremony; or polishing glasses, when he wore a white one. Whenever the family was away he would shut himself up for several weeks to give the silver a complete going over, rubbing away with rouge and thumb. He also wore on ordinary occasions the grave expression of an undertaker, and when he smiled, as he did sometimes, the slightly wry smile had to battle with the lines of gravity before it twinkled through. He served everyone at table, duke and commoner, artist and politician, saint and scrounger, as though they were of equal importance, although he would sometimes whisper instructions to people who were obviously flummoxed by what to do at the various crisis points in a meal with the elaborate pattern of knives and forks of different shapes and sizes which he had laid before them.

Whatever farmworkers were paid – their wages being higher than on neighbouring farms – the household staff were certainly not treated generously. Dorothy settled their wages: she was almost tight-fisted. She quibbled over what Thomas was to get. He wrote to 'Madam' from the Isle of Wight – 'Regards wages I ask £125 inclusive a year, which I have been receiving in my last situation', while 'I beg to remain, Madam, Yours Most

Obediently, Walter Thomas'.[34] Evidently Dorothy would not agree to as much as that. Eleven days later he wrote to her secretary that 'Regards wages I have thought it over and will accept £120 which I hope Mrs Elmhirst will agree to pay'.[35]

Another important member of the staff came a few months after Thomas. Emily had been a sewing maid at Ludgrove School, a preparatory school for Eton bursting with young earls and marquesses. She had to stand out for some time before Dorothy agreed to pay her as much as £24 p.a., which was less than she had been earning at the school. Emily arrived at the house on a winter's night. The taxi broke down before it could cross the brook. She had to walk up the hill. When she knocked at the front door of the house in complete darkness, and knocked and knocked again:[36]

> someone came to the door with a candle and candlestick held high. I thought 'God, what is this?' It was Thomas.

Emily eventually married him, the man whom she thought of as the one who 'kept up the standards'[37] of the establishment, who 'managed the atmosphere'.[38]

Another department of the house was headed by Marjorie Hutchinson, later Fogden, who marvellously combined being secretary to both Dorothy and Leonard, and has since then held a whole series of crucial jobs at Dartington.

Dorothy Carter was the young housekeeper although she did not ordinarily get the title to go with the job. She changed her first name to Paula to avoid the confusion with the older Dorothy. She was both in the front of the house, a friend of the Elmhirsts who managed to get from them the information about their visits and visitors which the servants could not easily get, and also sufficiently one of the servants to be accepted by them too. Later on, after she married Roger Morel, she became a dancer, an actress, the librarian, the wardrobe mistress for the Arts College and prime mover in amateur dramatics on the estate right through almost until the 1980s. She is now looking after the flowers in the Hall.

The other staff were:

Footmen	Footman (William) and assistant (Herbert).
Kitchen staff	Cook and two kitchen maids. The cook was by convention always called Mrs although she was usually a spinster.
Housemaids	Four, headed after a time by Emily, plus a family in the village, the Gribbles, to whom a chauffeur took the laundry every day. They all four wore aprons in the morning but, to show that Dartington was different, their own dresses in the afternoon.

	Dorothy herself would change her clothes three times a day.
Nursery	Nurse Lamb and a nursery maid.
Chauffeurs	Two chauffeurs, plus a handyman who had his time cut out washing Dorothy and Leonard's own cars and those for the estate, including what were almost the only American cars in Devon, huge cars too, a Buick, a La Salle and a De Soto.
Gardeners	Mr Woods, recommended by Seebohm Rowntree, plus two others. They sent up vegetables to the kitchen every day, and fruit in season, as the Barton Farm sent milk, eggs and butter. Dorothy would not allow margarine to enter the house.
Maintenance	George Perry, cabinet maker, always genial in his white apron, his pencil behind his ear, was responsible for the maintenance and repair of the furniture and for many odd jobs including (much later on) teaching Dorothy's last son carpentry.
Photographer	George Bennett who took pictures and showed films on his always-breaking-down projector. He had been Willard's batman in France.

The hierarchy was strict. Thomas had his two smaller but senior assistants on each side of him when the whole staff sat down to their meals in the staff dining room. Free meals, and for many of them free board and free clothes, were an addition to the meagre wage. Thomas had two complete suits a year free from a tailor in Totnes, and the footman one, together with tips from guests. The maids had the perks they customarily received in big houses. When people had breakfast in bed the convention was that the maids should pocket the fruit, but the unused butter and marmalade had to be thrown away on the grounds that, unlike the fruit protected by its skin, they had been soiled by being in a bedroom. Not only did the household staff eat free in the Hall; in one or other dining-room in the courtyard so did all the other people then employed. Everyone (including the children in the school) was a member of the household, as garden and farm were part of the household economy.

Thomas was supported by others trained in aristocratic houses. Dick Rushton, who became the permanent chauffeur, had been for eight years with the Duke of Portland, 'been with' as the phrase went, rather than 'worked for'. He remained a great support to the Elmhirsts, and particularly to Dorothy, throughout their lives. Ada Osborne, who was housekeeper after Paula Morel, had worked for the Pagets. Johnny Johnson, head gardener of a later era, had been apprenticed on the Earl of Liverpool's

12 Dorothy drawn by Willard, probably 1912

13 Dartington Hall, entrance to the courtyard, *c.* 1925

14 Dartington Hall, entrance to the restored courtyard

estate and was gardener to the Earl of Yarborough before Dartington. Inside the house the routines were much like those of other propertied families.

The household staff were up at 6.30 in the morning, with candles to light them in the dark of winter before the electricity engine came on. Their first task was to see to the heating. Thomas, William and Herbert stoked the big boilers with coke, which did little more than take the chill off the air. Hence the fires. The men carried the logs, the women laid and lit them, room by room, through the whole house. In the different bedrooms who lit the fire depended upon who did the calling. It was maids for women and couples and men for men; whoever it was re-laid and lit the fire. The guests all had morning tea – Leonard and Dorothy didn't. *They* were called at 7.30. Their bath was run off while their bedroom fire was being lit. They came down prompt at 8 for breakfast, picking up, as they passed the big marble table, letters from the pile that had usually been delivered by the postman before then. From 8.30 to 9 they would sit by the fire in the Music Room (as their dining-room was called) and read the papers or more letters before the dictation session began. They were always called either by Emily or the second maid who worked in the 'front' of the house. The third and fourth maids worked in the back of the house, cleaning the rooms of the staff, the staff dining-room and the kitchen. The servants needed servants. The staff had their breakfast 'as soon as the dining-room had gone in'.[39] They often had to be quick so that they could get back to finish off the front rooms before Dorothy and Leonard reappeared.

Dartington was again a great household as it had been in Holand's time, without the knights, the archers and the huntsmen but with a strange brilliance of its own.

The manner in which the children were brought up was the same as in America. Dorothy's early years were spent in a nursery, and so were those of Whitney, Beatrice and Michael. Leonard remonstrated with her in 1923 after one of his visits to Woods Hole. Dorothy promised to reform:[40]

> And thank you, too, for telling me to spend more time with the children. I need to be reminded of that, I'm afraid, for I let other people and other interests come first and disregard too easily the need of the children. I'm going to do as you say, next winter – take Whitney to the opera every other Saturday afternoon – and I'm going to make the late afternoon hours theirs and theirs only. Because I shall always feel you urging me on to this it will be easier to refuse the other demands. It's good of you to help me thus – no one else ever does – and it's always you who point the way for me. Thank you.

Good intentions did not take her, or Leonard, all that far. Ruth and Bill spent most of their time in their own quarters at the Hall with their nanny, Miss Jefferies, who was always obsessed with protecting all her charges, and especially Bill, from any infection. Known as Da, this being what Bill called her, she had Jean Bolt to assist her as her nursery maid. They all had breakfast together in the nursery, and not, until they were older, downstairs with their parents. One or other maid took it upstairs on trays. The dishes were reheated on the trivet on the nursery fire or on the hotplate.

They were alone up there in the evenings as well. Sybil Crook, the daughter of the farmer whom Leonard kept on, crept into the private house every night, tiptoeing past the butler's pantry where the frightening Thomas was on guard and up the main staircase to the top floor. Ruth and Bill were in nightdress and pyjamas. Sybil sat on the floor, was given a cup of Horlicks and a biscuit and allowed to listen to Da read a bedtime story, Winnie-the-Pooh, say. Sybil and other local children also climbed with the two new young Elmhirsts up and down Mr Weir's scaffolding and ran round on the planks in the great hall whenever Da was out of the way.[41]

Except on the holidays the family spent together – one of the advantages of travel was that you could feel more at home when away from it because there were not the usual distractions – Dorothy and Leonard saw very little of their children. Leonard had been different in his family of origin. Brother Richard could not understand the change:[42]

> Leonard was wonderful with his younger brothers and hopeless with his own children. They were left to a paid Nanny. They were supposed to go up to the nursery between six and six thirty to be with their children. But you know what Dartington is, something always came up which prevented them doing it. At mealtimes there was rarely a meal without a guest there to whom Leonard and Dorothy had to give their time. Leonard was always perfectly at home with other people's children, not his own.

Dorothy was also, as I have said before, liable to be more solicitous about other people's children than her own. She had no hesitation about giving Whitney's favourite toys to Bobby Sanborn. When a grown man Whitney in a terrible scene upbraided her for this unforgivable act. She also did this later on with Bill's favourite teddybear. Her attitude was that objects like that could always be replaced with new ones. Michael was saddled with me as his companion whenever he went off to America for holidays in the early 1930s. Bill and Ruth were brought up with Dorcas Edwards and Eloise Elmhirst. Dorcas's mother had been abandoned by her husband and Dorcas was befriended by Dorothy. Eloise was the daughter of Leonard's brother, Richard, whose marriage to Louise Soelberg had broken down. Michael says that one of the disadvantages of the Hall as a home was that Whitney, Beatrice and he never knew who might be in their bed.

The extent to which tradition was being followed was demonstrated by one of the great pre-war events – the marriage of Whitney, by then a well-known racing driver, to Lady Daphne Finch Hatton, daughter of the Earl and Countess of Winchilsea and Nottingham. This did not happen until a good deal later, in 1935, but it is very much in keeping with the kind of state Dorothy maintained from the start. The wedding is still one of the great folk-memories of Dartington, showing how 'rural' the local people were, if not the newcomers.

St Margaret's, Westminster, the home of fashionable weddings, was beautifully decorated with the same sort of flowers that Dorothy had for her debut in New York in 1906. The gentlemen wore morning dress, the ladies (including Dorothy) narrow-skirted summer dresses reaching to mid-calf or ankle, with wide-brimmed hats decked with ostrich feathers or large ribbons. Some of the women had fashionable dead foxes around their necks. The church was almost full when a group of men in heavy boots and obviously Sunday-best suits, clutching large bowler hats and accompanied by their wives, clattered in. The Dartington contingent had arrived.

It was quite a change for an American plutocrat marrying into the English aristocracy to be able to match the feudal retainers of the other side with some of his own. Ann Collingbourne told me that:[43]

> They said that Whitney's in-laws were sending their staff, gardeners and other staff, and Whitney wanted the same number of people from our staff, so to speak, and we had to look at the service and estimate how many people. Seven years and over was decided because the numbers wouldn't have allowed for six years and over.

The wedding was not what made the main impact on the group from Dartington. They were more impressed by London, which few of them had ever been able to travel to before and some would never see again.

Seventy-three of them travelled overnight on the long trip.[44] In one coach was Bob Crook, always called Blaster Crook by Leonard, who was in charge of the gangs of twenty or so men who laid drains; he used dynamite to blow up any obstacles. He clutched a large brown paper parcel under his arm and refused to be parted from it on the coach, saying it was far too important to put on the rack. After two stops for breakfast, at Salisbury at 6.0 a.m. and Basingstoke at 8.30, the coach approached Slough. Bob Crook asked how far it was to London. On being told, he said it was time for him to be sorting himself out. He unwrapped his parcel and mumbled and swore to himself. Then everything went quiet and he said, 'That'll have to do.' He had donned a big black bowler hat and wriggled into a 'dicky front', a stiffly starched shirt front. Unfortunately, refusing to stay in place, it kept on slipping up from his waist. He was rescued by a companion, who fastened a piece of twine round his stomach and secured him fore and aft. Another member of the party also wore a very large bowler hat which had been in the family for over seventy years and came forth only for such special occasions. He had stuffed three or four pages of the *Daily Herald* inside but it still kept falling down over his ears.

The party stayed at the Russell Hotel. First, they had to reach it. The coach parked on the opposite side of a road busy with traffic. Herbert Pickford, a mason, refused help from George Honeywill, the plumber, who knew London from holidays spent there. Herbert clutched his Woolworth attaché case under his arm, held his trilby hat on with his other hand and rushed headlong across the road in one dart. Reunited with George on the opposite pavement, he told him, 'George, I'd rather do a hard day's work than cross that road again.'

Dinner at the hotel was a confusing meal, with incomprehensible menus and a large array of knives and forks and no Thomas to understand them. One man, inevitably, ordered 'Zider'. Another refused to use the lift to reach his third floor room, trusting only his own legs to carry him up the stairs. Bob Crook did not trust the hotel staff to look after his boots. He refused to add them to the row lined up in the corridor outside the bedrooms and said he would clean them himself with his handkerchief. Someone discovered that if he picked up the phone room service was at the other end. He ordered a couple of brandies first thing in the morning and invited the waitress to sit on the edge of the bed and talk to him. At breakfast, one old man recounted how he had been unable to blow out the light the previous night and how it had then gone out suddenly. He must unwittingly have touched the electric switch.

Nothing I have said yet accounts for the hostility felt towards the new Dartington. The Elmhirsts liked Devon; Devon did not like the Elmhirsts. This was not Leonard's doing so much as Dorothy's. He was conscious of being the country gentleman, and other people thought they could perfectly well recognise the genuine article, at any rate until they heard him expound his ideas. He could for the first time afford a Savile Row tailor and handmade shoes. No more did he have to mend his own socks. Well groomed, from the neat tie down to the mirror-bright shoes that were Thomas's special care, always courteous, avoiding overt display of feeling as firmly as anyone else who had been through a public school, proud of his descent from a long-established if small landowning family, he looked and acted the part. If he had only shared the beliefs as well as the manners of the gentry he would soon have been accepted by his fellow lords of other manors.

Dorothy was the trouble. Some people thought the name should be £lmhirst. She had too much money altogether, to spend on a household probably the biggest in Devon, on dresses that were so discreet they looked as expensive as her pearls and, worse, to throw away on all sorts of daft schemes. Her reserve was also against her. There was no doubt about her being a grand lady, who had been deferred to all her life. Her shyness made it the more difficult to take. She did not unbend at all easily in a way that would make others feel at home. She was liable to give a slight sideways nod of the head when talking to, or being talked at by, people she was not particularly interested in.

Being American was also against her. The United States was not popular in England in the 1920s. The war was still fresh in the memory. Among the dead were men from Dartington as from every other village and town in Devon:[45]

> At Upton Pyne, in the empty sunlight, where hardly a young man is to be seen today, the cross outside the churchyard gate records the names of sixteen men killed from this small parish alone. Hardly a family escaped. And so it was, to a greater or lesser degree, in every village.

Some thought the county and country would never recover. Perhaps they have not. Leonard would often think of his two brothers and the many others from St Anselm's, Repton, Cambridge and Barnsley who had been slaughtered.

Many people bristled whenever Americans who had entered the war so late, too late to help their own dead relatives and friends, bragged about what they had done. 'Brag' was a word commonly associated with the Yanks. Or they laughed, not altogether good-humouredly, when in a local cricket match at Staverton Professor Roehl from Cornell swung his bat as if it were a baseball bat and both Michael and Whitney were bowled out for ducks at a game they had never played before. At one local fête where Whitney went in for a motor cycle race with his Norton the local grandee said in her opening address, 'If there's one thing I can't stand, it's Americans.' [46] Dorothy, of course, did not brag. Perhaps it would have comforted her detractors if she had. She did not conform to anyone's stereotype of the American or of the millionaire; all the same, she was both.

Riches might have been forgiven before long. The American origin might have been also. If only the new squire and his wife had conformed. This they most emphatically did not do. They did not, to mention their first sin, subscribe to the gentry's passion for sport which was certainly no less marked in Devon than it had been in Yorkshire. It was all horses, riding on the moor almost every day, attending point-to-point races, hunting all the winter. The Hall lay in the territory of the South Devon Hunt whose kennels were in Dartington village. The baying of the hounds kept awake generations of children at the school. Christine Raikes, a neighbour and later a friend, described the Devon cult:[47]

> The conversation usually revolved round horses and their achievements in special circumstances such as galloping over the bogs, jumping the walls or running in point-to-point races – with a good many people this would result in a boasting match. 'Why did you refuse that wall? My horse went over alright' – 'So you came down in Black Lane' (a bad boggy area) – '*I* was alright on my pony but of course she is *very* clever.'
>
> There were fat old ladies hitched on to side saddles talking over technicalities and the 'with it' ones being very snorty to them – the same kind, both male and female, would yell at people if they were in the way or doing the wrong thing.

Shooting was popular too. Landowners arranged large shooting parties of the kind Leonard's father would have loved. Other pastimes were country walks, picnics in pony-carriages or, occasionally, motorcars. Tennis parties were regular features of each summer and there were tennis clubs at Ashburton, Chudleigh and Newton Abbot. There were puppy-judging parties, and in May the Devon County Show was a meeting place for all the county families. Daughters accompanied by their mothers went to whist drives and dances. They wrote down the names of their partners for each dance, using a pencil with a tassel which hung from the card.

From all these delights the new owners of Dartington excluded themselves. They went one worse than that – they refused permission for the hunts to ride over their land. When they made heresy plain, in this public manner, it was taken by some as a declaration of civil war.

Before this dreadful news some members of county families had done what was then customary: turned up without appointment to leave their cards. Thomas knew all about that from the Marquess of Bute. He had a well-polished silver salver in the hall of the Hall to receive them. The card was an invitation to call. Dorothy should have responded by getting in her trap, or if she had none, her car, and drinking cups of tea out of the special china old families kept for such ceremonial occasions. Instead, the cards were liable to pile up on top of each other.

This was in spite of Dorothy doing her best. She knew as well as Thomas what the custom was; she did not want to flout it. But she had so little time. There was so much to do. So not everyone who left a card was called on. She tried to make amends later by inviting to tea some of those who had in effect invited her. This was not the correct protocol. Mrs

Jervoise-Smith, the head of a local landed family, replied in the third person saying that, since obviously Mrs Elmhirst was not desirous of making the acquaintance of her neighbours, Mrs Jervoise-Smith could not accept an invitation to tea. Mrs Jervoise-Smith made her cow woman go and stay in the house with her to keep her company but she had to bring her own sheets instead of using any of the vast stock of family sheets.[48]

Clergy and gentry were very closely allied. The Rev. J. S. Martin, the local rector and a relative of the Champernownes, was expecting the new squire to behave as the old had done. He was looking forward to welcoming him to his church on the main road. Leonard and Dorothy would surely set a necessary example to the villagers and to the newcomers being brought in by them. So much the greater the disappointment when they did not. They did not come to church, except most infrequently. Mr Martin felt slighted personally and on behalf of his church mortally offended.

The rector became openly hostile. As Leonard put it, the devil seemed to Martin to have moved his headquarters from Moscow to Dartington. To accuse someone of being a socialist, let alone a communist, was almost to cry treason. This was to go as far as you could in a county like Devon where even the newly arisen Labour Party, which had actually formed a government in 1924, was anathema. In another part of the county a lady was so opposed that 'when one of the gardeners voted Labour she insisted on pulling the blinds of the sitting-room to show her disapproval while he weeded the path outside'.[49] The rector read in the *Morning Post* that a new society had been formed called the World Revolution Society. He decided Dartington was a shelter for it, a means of getting control of children at an early age, without the aid of religion.

The letter he wrote to Leonard later on showed his attitude:[50]

My wife saw Mrs Hill who said that she and Olive Matthews were wheeling Mrs Matthews up the hill – on Thursday I believe – when they saw the young man Bowden without any clothing at all by the gate into the nursery.

She learnt also another thing. On a recent Sunday when all the ringers were out in the road by the Church there came up the road a young man with a young woman, thought to be in her twenties, very fully developed, wearing nothing but the scantiest pair of drawers, such as an acrobat might wear over his skin tights.

One cannot get rid of the Fall of Man by going about naked. On the contrary such behaviour promoted the effect of the Fall.

Martin's successor, the Rev. R. A. Edwards, became a mediator between parish and Hall, and attempted to pinpoint some of the sources of tension by going back over history in a Report to the Bishop of Exeter, a copy of which he sent to Leonard:[51]

> Every failure was noted; new buildings were classed as ugly, and for years many old inhabitants never even went to look at the restored Great Hall; every unpaid account left with a Totnes tradesman was added up and magnified; every piece of individual misbehaviour became a major scandal and tales that were complete lies were freely believed and put into circulation; every mistake made in the urgent haste of getting the idea into being was built up into a piece of calculated wickedness . . . rumours of what was going on spread all over England, and at different times various different authorities, including the police (who for some six months actually put a man in, and paid his fees, as a student in the Gardens Department), were asked to make enquiries about it. The fundamental reason for it all was that the whole thing was utterly new and mysterious.

The gentry were against them, the clergy were against them, the local farmers were against them. They had all been hit by the post-war agricultural depression, their labourers even more so. The Devonshire County Report for the 1919 Committee on Wages and Conditions in Agriculture summarised their seven chief complaints:[52]

> (1) bad housing; (2) abominably long hours; (3) days of labour without intermission; (4) low wages; (5) indifferent food; (6) lacking good boots and stout clothing and (7) the lack of hope for better circumstances.

By 1926 things were worse. Not a farmer in the district paid the legal minimum wage, 32s. 6d. (162½p), in 1925 in Devon. The tenant of High Beara Farm paid his workers 23s. a week in 1928.[53] On the Dartington farm, shortly before the Elmhirsts arrived, the wages were only 15s. a week, which was not much even when allowance was made for rent-free houses, free milk and cider, free manure for gardens, free potatoes from farm land and (unlike Laxton) the right to catch rabbits.

Something had to be done to try to raise the standard of living. A decision had to be made about wages and it was this which roused the antagonism. The agricultural minimum wage, although laid down by a government tribunal, was just an aspiration in Devon. There were no trade unions or other bodies to enforce it. The General Strike of 1926, although it made the middle classes of Devon and elsewhere fear the country was on the verge of revolution, hardly touched farm labourers. Unless told about it by the people who bought the *Morning Post* they were quite isolated from the wider world until broadcasting and the luxury of a daily paper brought the news into their cottages.

The Elmhirsts decided to pay the legal minimum wage on the Dartington farms. Thereby, Leonard set a standard to which few others could, or if they could would, conform. He did not do it with the backing of Mr Crook who had to confront the bitterness of his fellow farmers when he met them at Totnes or Newton Abbot markets. What *were* those new people doing? Couldn't he stop them ruining every farmer around by making their labourers discontented? What was wrong with 15s. a week? It was all very well for 'them' with their American money. 'They' could afford such ridiculous wages. 'We' could not. Stories about the new squire that he thought were against the farmers they thought were against him. Visiting a local farmer he pointed out that by any standards, not just Cornell's, his milk pails were filthy. The farmer dipped his own dirty hands into the milk and let it drop back into the pail. No need for clean pails, he explained. 'Ur clanes ursel.'[54]

Not only were the farmers opposed. Many of the people in the village of Dartington were also. The village did not have physical cohesion. It was (and is) not a clustered village but a collection of hamlets – Staple, Week, Cott – added to later by the new hamlets the Elmhirsts built at Broom Park and Huxhams Cross. Amongst its 120 or so families the ones in paid jobs worked on farms, in quarries, in shops in Totnes or in domestic service. But whichever hamlet they lived in or whatever job they had, hardly one of them had a good word to say for the new people at the Hall.

This was in keeping with geography and tradition. The Champernownes had not been popular either. When Mrs Champernowne paid a call in the village she came on horseback, rode her horse across people's lawns and rapped on the door with a whip.[55] The Elmhirsts were not like that. They were alarming all the same, with all the 'foreigners' they were bringing in to join the American in the big house, and all their strange goings on, much exaggerated as these were in the telling. Even the labourers whose wages had been raised and the other people who got jobs on the new estate were much more on the side of 'Us' than of 'Them'. Outside the workplace the lives of the people in the village and at the Hall remained very much separate for many years, the villagers going to church and Women's Institute, the Hall not; the villagers having their parish council and village hall and the Hall its grandly restored buildings; the village having one cricket team and the Hall another. Fading of the hostility had to wait at least until King George V's Silver Jubilee in 1935. The celebrations were at the Hall and the Elmhirsts sent their cars to pick people up from outlying places. Another King inspired people, for a time.

The idea of the English experiment had brought the Elmhirsts together, in America, and brought them to England. The first step towards actuality, for people not given to drawing up detailed plans about anything, had been to find a place where it could happen. Perhaps guided by Tagore's hand, the pin was stuck into the map at Dartington and thereby a new dimension added. Dartington Hall had once been the seat of a Plantagenet. There was beauty in the ruins, more beauty still in the promise they offered for the future if they could be restored to their past grandeur. The new notion of restoring the past was therefore introduced into the experiment, the past being represented not just by the buildings but by the many-sided, manorial estate of which the buildings were the centre. Practically all utopias have gilded the past. There is nearly always an underlying supposition that there was once a Golden Age and all that is needed to make the future brighter is to return to that Age, in a suitable modern form.

The place Leonard chose also shaped the nature of the experiment by introducing an abiding contradiction into it, and especially into the expression given to the fourth utopian myth which I identified in the last chapter. On the one hand he and Dorothy believed in the overriding value of the individual and, with that, in the virtues of democracy. They wanted Dartington to be not just a reflection of a hierarchical Devon society but a self-governing community whose members would take their own decisions for themselves, instead of having them taken for them by the founders or their successors. They were in the tradition of America. On the other hand they were led by the character of the place to act the feudal lord and lady. Dorothy's money had assigned something of that role to her in America, but without the English kind of landed estate to go with it. Leonard had been much influenced by Tagore, the guru, the aristocrat in a large house in the midst of his villagers, enjoying a living standard which was thrown into relief by the squalor and poverty that surrounded him. In selecting Dartington as their seat they were behaving as they had been taught they should, but with a new twist to it that was characteristically English. Dorothy had not been the Duchess of Fifth Avenue nor Leonard the Duke of Santiniketan. Now they were in the tradition of England, in a physical setting devised for the Duke and Duchess of Exeter.

If Dartington had no more than the flavour of hierarchy it would soon have won acceptance from local people. The county was hierarchical too, and if the Elmhirsts had been true to type as lord and lady of the manor they would have before long been welcomed on almost all sides. But they were not. Feudal they might be; they were also not just advocates of democracy but outrageously new-fangled in other ways as well. Initial puzzlement hardened into hostility, on both sides. Gentry, clergy, farmers, working people turned against the newcomers, and after a time the newcomers hardly bothered to avoid offending local susceptibilities. The experimenters could be more original as a result and benefit too from a heightened sense of solidarity on the inside because there was so much antagonism to them from the outside. Dorothy wrote to one of her

American friends in 1927, 'I am afraid we see very little of the neighbours, but for the time being we are concentrating on building up a community life among ourselves.'[56]

CHAPTER 6

TO THE
TOTNES STATION

—◦◯◦—

There will also be an electric installation,
which will enable students to gain some
idea of the use and theory of electricity.

Prospectus, 1926

On the afternoon of Friday 24 September 1926 the principal chauffeur drove Dorothy and Leonard in the new Buick down the hill to Totnes station to meet the first 'school train'. The initial six pupils (other than Dorothy's own three children) arrived that day. Four boys, two girls.

This was the day already notified to the parents, the standard time for the start of an academic year in Britain. But despite all the overtime Leonard and Vic had persuaded the men to do, the buildings were not ready. The General Strike had delayed the arrival of materials and furniture. The national coal strike was still dragging on and continuing to slow everything down. The barn and shippon on one side of the courtyard had not yet been finished for the boys; they had to lodge temporarily in the Old Parsonage, which Leonard and Dorothy had just moved out of, and come up to the 'school' by day to play on the building sites and collect cigarette cards from the workmen. Nor was the 'girls' cottage' ready. They had to put up in the private house. This was the first and last time boys and girls were a mile apart.

The delay was not due to any obscurity in the instructions to the architect. Dorothy left it all to Leonard, and he was quite clear what he wanted: to restore the East Wing and divide it into single rooms. At Repton, he said, his looks protected him from sexual advances by the older boys, let alone from being turned into a 'school tart' or (one rung down) a 'house reliever'.[1] But feeling acutely conscious of being watched by the other boys for signs of the greatest sin, nonconformity, he hated dormitories and longed for the privacy of a bedroom of his own. 'If it's boarding, then a room for every child without question; you give every plant you want to grow a pot of its own, you don't stick two plants in one pot.'[2] Dorothy was surprised by his vehemence. She took it for granted her children would have their own rooms as they did in most American boarding-schools anyway.

If the building was for a school, generously appointed, what was the school for? Since this was not to be like other schools they had to be explicit. They could not get by with platitudes about 'homely food' and 'plenty of fresh air' like conventional schools. Unless they could tell parents what sort of place they were being asked to send their children to they might not have anyone to meet at Totnes station. Leonard wanted at one time to ban the word 'school' completely, but even a non-school would need a Prospectus. Eton had one, Dartington was to have one too – or if not a Prospectus, a Counter-Prospectus or Non-Prospectus. In the event they had two printed. *Outline of an Educational Experiment* was written mainly by Leonard, the *Prospectus* also by Leonard with the same material but with the help of Wyatt Rawson, who appears later in this chapter. The picture of Dorothy reproduced as Plate 18 shows her, according to Leonard, typing his version while sitting in the sun on a low wall under the Luccombe Oak. The summer of 1926 was a fine one. Many of the meetings to discuss what to do when the pupils arrived were held on the lawn.

What then to say? Leonard had one good negative rule to guide him:[3]

New and experimental schools are generally started by people who have been miserable at school themselves. . . . The school my wife and I started . . . was in some measure therefore an expression of protest against the system at Repton, under which I suffered sufficiently to have retained bitter and even cruel memories.

Therefore no corporal punishment, indeed no punishment at all; no prefects; no uniforms; no Officers' Training Corps; no segregation of the sexes; no compulsory games, compulsory religion or compulsory anything else; no more Latin, no more Greek; no competition; no jingoism.

Leonard was not alone in reacting so strongly against what he had been familiar with. There were many as yet unknown allies. As L. C. B. Seaman said in his history of the period between the wars:[4]

The predominantly left-wing intellectuals of the thirties regularly asserted of their old schools that they were brutalizing, that they encouraged excessive athleticism, a dubiously complacent form of Christianity, an unthinking patriotism and were narrowly class-conscious.

Esmond Romilly, who later married Jessica Mitford, was one of these intellectuals. After being expelled from Wellington he edited a specifically anti-public-school magazine called *Out of Bounds* with verbal and financial support from Bernard Shaw.

In the previous decade three books had achieved some notoriety for their frankness about homosexual practices at public schools. Alec Waugh, very happy at Sherborne, as well as very critical, made only restrained references to them.[5] Robert Graves from Charterhouse was more open, less happy and even more critical.[6] Ernest Raymond went much further in *Tell England*.[7] He told England, including Leonard and Dorothy and many of the people recruited by Dartington, how powerful and nauseating the mix could be between cricket, beating, homosexuality and masochism. The suggestively named Doe got the greatest thrill he'd ever had when he was savagely beaten on his bottom by the handsome young master, Radley, who was also hitting the ball so well for his county cricket team. Here was the detail people needed, not just about sex but about all the other public-school practices Leonard loathed.

Mr Seaman put his finger on an important point when he spoke of ex- and also anti- public-school left-wingers. Not even Leonard, the Englishman, appeared to know that he and Dorothy were in an English tradition which has persisted on the fringes of socialism for at least a century.[8] Its adherents have sometimes been called 'the middle-class beard-and-sandals brigade' or written off, as Orwell wrote them off in *The Road to Wigan Pier*, as 'all that dreary tribe of high-minded women and sandal-wearers and bearded fruit-juice drinkers who come flocking towards the smell of "progress" like bluebottles to a dead cat'.[9] Orwell thought the tribe could be the death of socialism:[10]

> It could help enormously, for instance, if the smell of crankishness which still clings to the Socialist movement could be dispelled. If only the sandals and the pistachio-coloured shirts could be put in a pile and burnt, and every vegetarian, teetotaller and creeping Jesus sent home to Welwyn Garden City to do his yoga exercises quietly!

They had not always been so derided. In the 1880s, before Orwell was born, they shone forth in the Fellowship of the New Life, a notably high-minded body 'devoted to purifying cupidity in society by the labours of reformed and redeemed individuals who, through a self-supporting life based on manual work in communities, through education and religious communism and steadfast attention to social change, could reconstruct society'.[11] The Fabian Society was a breakaway from it. Before that the Fellowship had brought together people like Edward Peace (the secretary of the new Fabian Society) and Frank Podmore, who gave the Fabians their name. Both of them, and many of the other members, were as interested in psychical research as in pacifism and socialism. Others fancied the occult along with politics or embraced a very English mixture of agnosticism and pantheism. Their common attributes did not end there. They often marked themselves out by their appearance: beards, when beards were not common; long hair, when that was not either; clothing – the sandals already mentioned, homespun knickerbockers or long woollen shirts in plain colours.

Long or short, clothing had to allow 'freedom of movement for the limbs'. This led on to Isadora Duncan, Martha Graham and 'modern' dance in general. Eating was as important as dressing. Vegetarianism and other sorts of dietary discipline were one of the hallmarks. Simple-lifers with plenty of money also went in for Heal's and other plain but expensive furniture, hand-made pottery, log-fires and bicycles.

The 'new woman', from Ibsen's heroines in the last century to Vera Brittain in the decade in which Dartington was founded, has always been much to the fore, together with the practice of more sexual freedom than convention allowed. So has an interest in the crafts and folk songs and in the preservation of everything old, especially buildings. William Morris was quintessential: as well as a conservationist he was a founder of the Socialist League, a designer, a novelist and a poet. Since they first sprang up garden cities have been one of the most influential expressions of the tradition. Armytage caricatured a 'typical garden citizen' as[12]

> Clad in knickerbockers and, of course, sandals, a vegetarian and a member of the Theosophical Society, who kept two tortoises 'which he polishes periodically with the best Lucca oil'. Over his mantelpiece was a large photo of Madame Blavatsky and on his library shelves were *Isis Unveiled* and the works of William Morris, H. G. Wells and Tolstoy.

Today the photograph would be of Aurobindo, the Maharishi or whoever is Top of the Guru charts this week.

Another prominent characteristic has been the belief in 'progressive education'. The new brand of schools started out from the same Fellowship of the New Life. One of its principal tenets was that 'All schools ought to be communities, miniature commonwealths or states, as they were in the Middle Ages'.[13] Abbotsholme and Bedales, two of the earliest progressive schools, sprang direct from the Fellowship. Unless such schools had already existed, and much more important, unless sizeable numbers of supporters for them had been there already, the Dartington school would not have had much of a chance. Dorothy and Leonard did not know it at the time, but just by setting up their experiment and sending out the right signals into the fog always hanging over England they were in time almost bound to attract the adherents of an English utopian tradition to mix with their more American one. The signals went to high-minded middle-class parents who would not send their sons to a State school because it made religion compulsory or to a public school because it made military training compulsory as well. Dorothy did not wear a dirndl skirt nor Leonard a beard. In their own life style they were the very opposite of Bohemians: they were not sun-lovers, naturists, vegetarians or youth hostellers. They ate white bread. They were never seen naked in public. All the same, they were to be a magnet for the devotees of naked bodies and cabbage juice.

If they had known more about progressive schools they presumably would, before the trip to the Totnes station, have visited some of the twenty-one of them described a few years later in Trevor Blewitt's book on the subject.[14] Perhaps they would have been influenced by them. As it was, they saw, together or separately, an odd bunch, Oundle, Dauntsey's, Sidcot and Ackworth; and do not appear to have learnt anything from them, not even from Sanderson's Oundle.[15] Leonard talked about the inspiration of more exotic-sounding schools in more distant places – like the Travel School of Bogotá in Colombia which was organised around agricultural work. He had heard of it when in Argentina with Tagore – a man came into the house by chance who had been there. Another school in the Philippines – the Munos School – Leonard had actually visited.[16] The first *Prospectus* featured them both as models for Devon. At least Leonard could be pretty sure that no one in England would have heard of them.

Another school he visited twice, and was impressed by, was Daddy George's Junior Republic.[17] It happened to be very close to Cornell. The second time he was in the company of Wyatt Rawson. Maybe it was not specifically mentioned in the *Prospectus* because its pupils (citizens as they were called) were all juvenile delinquents. The school had its own elected legislature, judges and prison. No one got any food unless he worked and earned money in the bakery, the printing house, the hotel, the dairy or on the farm which made up the economy of the Republic. It was copied in England with a more appropriate name. Republic would have stood no chance. The school was called the Little Commonwealth or sometimes Homer Lane's Little Commonwealth after its head. Lane's most famous saying about children was simply that he was 'on their side', implying that ordinary teachers were not. The school was set up on an estate in Dorset, not so unlike Dartington, belonging to Lord Sandwich, one of the very few English people whose advice Leonard sought, and not just about architects. He first went to stay with him in 1923 at Hinchingbrooke. There was a special bond. Lady Sandwich, Alberta Sturges, was an American. The Commonwealth was closed down soon after it opened by a scandal about Lane's relationship to one of his girl pupils. This scandal and its drastic consequence were often talked about at Dartington during the

1920s and 1930s. Critics of the school were always ready to warn that at any moment unless this and that was done one of His Majesty's Inspectors of Education would march in, take fright at the sight of the naked boys and girls and close the school.

An even greater influence from America was the Lincoln School,[18] despite not being mentioned in the Prospectus. Dorothy believed in its principles. She even took the trouble to attend a course of lectures in the autumn of 1921 at her own New School for Social Research. They were given by John Dewey,[19] the inspiration behind Lincoln and many other schools.[20]

Dewey was recognisable in the first Dartington manifesto; more so if not mentioned by name was the man behind him as well as behind Pestalozzi, Froebel, Herbart, Neill and a thousand other progressive educators – I mean Rousseau, particularly in his *Émile*. In 1762 Rousseau was doing his best in *The Social Contract* to undermine the state by calling in question its absolute right to demand obedience from any citizen. Did the individual exist for the sake of society; or society for the sake of the individual? There could according to him be only one answer.

In *Émile* he asked an equally fundamental and linked question – how in practice does society succeed in enslaving the individual? Simply by bringing its full weight to bear on children while they are still impressionable, by implanting in them, so deep they do not know it's there, a lively fear of authority. Individuality is destroyed for the sake of the mass, the very purpose of orthodox education being to make children into thorough conformists without their knowing it.[21] The demands of adult society are therefore the imperatives handed to educators. The children of today must be moulded into the obedient subjects of tomorrow.

That orthodox view of the purpose of education had always been strongly supported by the doctrine of original sin. If children are little monsters of course they have to be tamed. To carry conviction Rousseau had to combat that notion, widely accepted despite the teaching of Jesus that older people must become as little children if they are to enter the kingdom of heaven. Rousseau was with Jesus. He believed in original virtue. 'Everything is good as it comes from the hands of the Maker of the world but degenerates once it gets into the hands of man.'[22] Most of today's ecologists would agree, and almost all progressive educators. Rousseau repeatedly contrasts the goodness of the natural man, the child as made by nature, with the badness of man-made institutions. A choice has to be made between making a man and making a citizen. Rousseau, Dewey and the Elmhirsts had no hesitation about which mattered more.

Their common concern was not with what the child is to become but with what the child is. The high mortality of children in Rousseau's time clinched his argument:[23]

> Of all the children born a bare half survive at adolescence, and it is improbable that your pupil will reach manhood. In view of this, what are we to think of the barbarous education which sacrifices the present to an uncertain future and makes the child miserable in order to prepare him for a remote happiness which he will probably not live to enjoy?

Leonard and Dorothy could not follow him by saying that most of the children who came to their school would presumably die before leaving it. But this did not detract from the belief they had in Rousseau's main conclusion. Children are not (they thought) of value because one day they will become adults carrying on the work of society but in their own right, here and now in this living present. What 7-year-olds or 14-year-olds do with any day in their lives matters on that day just as much as what any adult does – matters more, say those with a proper reverence for the child. 'For us it is vital', said the *Outline*, 'that education be conceived of as life, and not merely as a preparation for life.' If any one sentence held the key to the initial experiment, this was it.

From it follow the four main principles behind the school.

(1) *Curriculum should flow from children's own interests.* If the purpose of a school is to prepare the child for adult life, and particularly for a job, almost any curriculum can be made acceptable, the teaching of almost anything justified. Latin, Greek, Hebrew or even Sanskrit have been, quite rightly, on the grounds that each can prove a good training on the royal road to a richly furnished and smoothly turning adult mind – this despite the awkward fact that it is impossible to demonstrate with assurance over a period of say twenty years that the acquisition of some particular knowledge or aptitude at the age of 8 has left any residue at the age of 28. Whatever the curriculum, it is ordinarily determined by adults thinking of adult needs. But once think of school as life rather than preparation for it and the centre of gravity shifts from teacher and textbook (in the words of Dewey this time)[24] to 'the immediate instincts and activities of the child himself'.[25] Dewey was as much of an adherent of a 'child-centred' education as Rousseau.

The reason most classrooms are so dead, so lacking in motivation, is that children are taught subjects which interest them hardly at all: they are drilled from the age of 5 to 18 in the absorption of facts and other people's opinions about a ready-made universe of knowledge chopped up into arithmetic, geography, history, physics or biology. So dull is it for the great majority of children that they have to be regimented into learning not just by the superior force of adults with their endless discipline (as women like Leonard's mother have been regimented by the superior force of men) but by transferring from the adult world into the school a simulacrum of its standard system of competition – punishments for those who fail to absorb dead knowledge, rewards for those who succeed. These rivalries introduced into the classroom and on to the playing-field become the teacher's chief aid in enforcing discipline. No matter if the child's spirit is broken on the wheel of geography or biology – all the better, some may think, because if the spirit is gone what is left is the conformity society must have.

(2) *Learning by doing*. Proceed from the child's instincts and interests and traditional academic subjects taught in traditional ways have to give way to other pursuits which children *are* interested in. They want to make things with their hands and see the results of their labours; they want to express their feelings about the marvellous world they are growing up in, and the strange people in it; they want to play and jump and run. These then are what children *should* do. Since they like manual better than mental work let them do it. The emphasis is a common one. Rousseau: 'Of all the occupations in which man can earn a living, manual work comes nearest to the state of nature.'[26] Dewey: 'We must conceive of work in wood and metal, of weaving, sewing and cooking, as methods of living and learning, not as distinct studies . . . as instrumentalities through which the school itself shall be made a genuine form of active community life, instead of a place set apart in which to learn lessons.'[27] Dartington *Outline*: 'Handicraft will be regarded as of vital importance, involving as it does that close co-operation of hand and brain which makes co-ordinated growth possible. In this way the child will have natural access to the world of form, colour and line in the handling of stone, wood, clay and textiles.'

The new school was not to have ordinary workshops for such activities. The estate was to be the school's common workshop. With such a large outdoor classroom (this being the way the estate was at first visualised) every child should be able to work on a useful project in one or other of the twelve departments attached to the school.[28] In the Garden Department, for example, 'All students who intend to grow vegetables or fruit, or to keep bees, will work in this department, as will also those who shew a taste for landscape gardening or botanical science.' In the Building Department 'Students will assist from the start in the erection of stock shelters or garden huts on sites near their own field projects.' 'The Workshop Department will be concerned with the repair and simple construction work needed for the farm and garden.' Clearly a rich life, with one and a half departments to each pupil in the opening term. All the full-time workers in the departments were to belong to the permanent staff of the school. To Leonard it all made sense because he had learnt more on his family estate than ever in any conventional classroom. He got poor marks in his degrees at Cambridge and Cornell; he got good marks from any sophisticate who saw him cut down a tree and could appreciate the stump flat to the ground. 'For me', said Leonard to Edward Lindeman, 'everyone was to go to school by being on the Estate. It was through the Estate and the men on it that I saw part of my own contribution coming.'[29] Leonard had learnt by doing more than from books; and so was it to be for others.

On one point of detail: since the children were to work in the departments, caring for livestock and garden and field crops, they would not all be able to have holidays at the same time. Holidays would have to be staggered.

Leonard and Dorothy also played with one far-reaching notion, not made quite explicit, which went beyond anything envisaged by Rousseau or Dewey or any other educationist that I know of before that – the notion that the children were through their work in gardens and other departments to be self-sufficient, if not on their own then in conjunction with the adults on the estate. The school, said the *Outline*,

> must in fact be a little world in itself, carrying on in a real, if
> elementary and simple way, the activities of the great world around it.
> ... Like the village community of earlier times, which was in many
> respects self-sufficing, the school community of today must engage in
> many practical enterprises.

Leonard wrote to Lindeman in January 1925 that it was his hope to 'win our own material independence in as small groups as we can by innumerable experiments, using children as the best of pioneers and experimenters'.[30]

Nearly a whole page of the *Outline* was given over to an account of how it might all work in one department, on a poultry project, this being just one of the many 'projects' on which the children were going to spend their time. They would learn about building by putting up *well-ventilated* quarters for the hens, about the science of nutrition from devising a balanced ration, about the interpretation of statistics from the keeping of accounts and about commerce from finding markets for their feathers and manure. Was it after all to be only a hen-centred education? The plan sounded improbable; but I myself actually carried it into practice when I arrived as a pupil, though I'm afraid without learning anything about nutrition or statistics, let alone finding any markets for the precious feathers or manure.

(3) *Adults should be friends, not authority figures.* When neither work had to be done nor games played unless children wanted to, adults did not need to be invested with any special authority. Prefects were likewise

unnecessary. Adults could be thought of as friends and counsellors, not masters. They were known at Dartington as Seniors and the children as Juniors, as though all were pupils who just happened to be of different ages. One thing they were *not* allowed to do on either side: call each other by their surnames, let alone make the dreadful mistake of saying Mr and Mrs, or still more horrifying, Sir. Instead, it was Dorothy and Jerry (for Leonard), Pop for John Wales, Vic for Victor Elmhirst, Lottie for Mrs Hayden. Thomas, the butler, and Rushton, the chauffeur, were the only men in the place to preserve the surname intact.

(4) *The school a self-governing commonwealth*. Harking back to Lionel Curtis as well as Daddy George, one of the chief hopes for the school was that it would become a 'self-governing commonwealth'.[31] In a genuine democracy children were to learn the arts of self-government and co-operative enterprise not through being told about them but by practising them. They were to be involved actively, decision-makers as well as craftsmen, in all the collective activities of the community. Discipline was, as in the Junior Republic and the Little Commonwealth, to be 'enforced by the students' own Court and Judge'.[32]

These principles belonged to the true gospel, at least as it would be interpreted in the twentieth century. The Elmhirsts added some innovations that would have been too much for Rousseau. The first was co-education. The advice for Émile was quite different when it came to his sister, Sophie. Contradicting his doctrine of child-centredness, Rousseau insisted that in the education of girls the requirements of adult society should prevail. He was in favour only of a boy-centred education. Darting-ton was more consistent in inviting girls as well as boys to join the commonwealth. They were not (according to the first plan) to live together – that would perhaps have seemed too revolutionary a break from Repton. The *Prospectus* called for a 'Girls' Department' which apparently did not mean much more than a cottage for girls to live in as there was to be a building for boys. Otherwise, the two sexes were to have the same regime. 'A normal life is not to be secured merely by mixing boys and girls in the classroom or on the playground, but through compan-ionship in action, in self-government as well as in recreation.'[33]

But the biggest surprise, disappointment too, to any reincarnate Rousseau would not have been that but the attribution in print of the whole idea not to him but to another giant from the wrong side of the Channel, Baden-Powell. To Leonard he was not Bathing-Towel, or the man who hounded the blacks out of Mafeking to their death;[34] to Leonard he was not just the hero who had withstood a long siege but a far-sighted educationist whose precepts he had tried to apply at Sriniketan. The *Prospectus* sums up the whole manifesto in a fine downbeat English manner. 'These plans, as a keen scout or guide will notice, do little more than adapt the principles of Scouting to the academic work of the School.' Scoutmaster Leonard also declared that all students would be members of a Fire Brigade, 'drilled and trained to meet emergencies in case of fire or accident'.[35]

The fault of the *Outline* and the *Prospectus* was the same as Rousseau's: with the exception of the feathers and manure, and the Fire Brigade, they were rather lofty, rather philosophical. This did not matter to Rousseau. Émile was an imaginary boy taught by an imaginary tutor. In a one-to-one relationship the practicalities did not have to be rehearsed; they were all the better for being left to imagination. For an actual school that was impossible, even if it had only nine pupils and even though it was in many ways not unlike the *Émile* household, Leonard's home when under the sway of the governesses, or the home school that Dorothy had attended in her father's mansion. All manner of detailed preparations had to be made – a sawmill erected so that timber from the estate could be sawn up for use in the reconstruction of the courtyard buildings, greenhouses which the Champernownes had not used for decades fitted with new glass, a craft workshop established for the school/estate. Dorothy had to order beds and tables from Heal's and Leonard tools from New York. Mr Gorton, Dorothy's agent in New York, got more and more puzzled by what was happening in the Devon school. Rather later on Leonard asked him to buy a 'hand squirt for spraying cows in summertime with a kind of disinfectant that keeps off flies',[36] 'an electrician's brace and bits for use in electric wiring. Also a gummed tape machine for binding packages. A radio for Whitney.'[37]

As well as gather materials for the school they had to staff the twelve departments, or rather the only ones they could get going in time, the Garden Department, the Farm Department, the Forestry Department, the Building Department and the crucial Accounts Department where mathematics was to be taught as well as 'weights and measures, decimals and fractions, the elements of geometry, and an elementary knowledge of algebra, wherever it is of practical value'.[38] That doubting of algebra was typical. Although the employees of all these departments were considered to be teachers, Leonard and Dorothy thought there also ought to be a few people on the staff of the school who did nothing else besides teach. They played safe to that extent.

There was no thought of advertising for teachers of any sort; they would not have known quite how to frame the advertisement. How much more natural to consider the friends whom they knew at first hand who could qualify for the 'fellowship of a few men of ideas and spirit'. The first Leonard turned to was the Wyatt Rawson I have already mentioned. A fellow-undergraduate at Trinity, he was one of the few friends from there whom Leonard had kept up with. Like Leonard, he had spent a period in America, in his case as an Instructor at Brown University:[39]

> Rawson, my old Cambridge friend, is as thorough an introvert as he could be, very feminine by nature, a dealer in individuals, filled with suspicion over people operating in groups, and therefore on occasion quite antisocial in both word and deed. He is right most of the time, even when he laughs at what he calls my 'idealism'. . . . I could engage myself to Rawson for life quite easily. He plays on the piano the things that I most like and in the way I most like them played. We went over all our favourite folk tunes last night. He rarely hands out approval of any kind. He can always see the weak spot in any of my opinions and does not hesitate to offer a rebuke. Such a friend is to me of a value beyond rubies.

As soon as Dorothy said yes to Dartington Leonard asked Wyatt if he would also say yes to him, leave his brother's preparatory school at Cockfosters and join him in the new adventure. Wyatt had no hesitation about accepting. He took seriously the unity of the school and estate. He himself found new recruits in Rex Gardner, a sandalled man in a corduroy jacket, who was put in charge of the estate craft workshop and 'Doc' Watson, a former Scoutmaster (an obvious asset that) who was appointed Dartington's first Secretary/Accountant. He also began the school day at 7 a.m. by blowing on a whistle and shouting 'Rise and Shine' in the school corridor, which was a trifle *too* scoutmasterish for some. As for Wyatt, he was everywhere. Before long he was calling on the Juniors to relate their dreams to him, and then with the tools he had newly fashioned out of Freud, he would 'analyse' them. 'You dreamed you were chased by a snake? Aha!'[40]

Next to be recruited was Marjorie Wise, once again bringing experience from America. An Englishwoman, she got her AB from Columbia University before returning to England. Recommended to Dorothy by a lecturer they both knew at Teachers College, she at once agreed to leave her post as a teacher at Clapham High School and come to Dartington. Mr Rawson and Miss Wise were joined by Vic, who gave up most of the other things he was doing to come on to the school staff, and these three by John Wales, the first recruit with no American connections. With an Agricultural Diploma from Reading University, he was more an agriculturist than a teacher. He had not been able to live on a cowman's wage. Luckily for him his father and Wyatt were both customers at Mayhew's second-hand bookshop in Charing Cross Road in London. Mr Mayhew passed on Wyatt's name to John who wrote asking if there was a job at Dartington. When he first arrived Dorothy hurried to the front door and greeted him with great warmth while at the same time nervously fingering the custom-ary pearls.[41] Each new member of staff was an anxiety. Taken on as librarian, he turned out to be a gifted teacher (and later writer) as well as administrator.

So many people came from America it was like colonisation in reverse. Professor Lindeman came from the New School of Social Work in New York to advise on everything; Professor Heuser from Cornell to design the poultry unit; Professor Roehl from the same place to set up a workshop where children could learn the manual skills they would need on an estate like Dartington; Clarice Evans from Teachers College to teach science; Dr and Mrs Bonser, again from Teachers College, to prepare the fateful report that is part of the story to come; and later on, Miss Winifred Harley, another Englishwoman who had been in a school in Detroit, to take charge of a new Nursery School which would be for Ruth and Bill, children of the second marriage, what the rest of the school was intended to be for Whitney, Beatrice and Michael. The key figure of the period after 1931 was, as we shall see, also an Englishman from America, Bill Curry.

America was not only where Dorothy's friends and connections were but Leonard's too. He had been out of England for most of the ten years since 1915. But they did not intend to rely just on Americans or Anglo-Americans. 'Recourse', said the *Outline*, 'will frequently be had to visitors whose services will be engaged as the need arises to stimulate and advise in special fields where a whole-time expert would be out of the question.' Such people began to come even without invitation. Stories about the extraordinary American millionairess married to an Englishman and her nudist school in Devon (almost as delightfully shocking as, say, a nudists' camp in Windsor Great Park) began to circulate in London and elsewhere. T. E. Lawrence raced over from Dorset at over 100 m.p.h. on his Brough Superior motorbike and left it propped up by the front door. Michael used to sit on it making motor-cycle noises to himself while Lawrence was eating Thomas's cucumber sandwiches. Bernard Shaw arrived with Lady Astor, the MP for one of the Plymouth constituencies, who thought the children she'd heard threw food at each other would make him laugh. I was in the dining-room, guzzling, when they looked hopefully around the door, but I was too keen on the food to throw it at anyone, and the other children disappointed them too. We had clothes on and ate with spoons. Another frequent visitor in the 1920s and after, up till the end of the war, was H. N. Brailsford, the socialist writer. The Elmhirsts had 'recourse' to him in the same sort of way they had to various professors from Cornell. Brailsford stayed at Dartington for six weeks during the autumn term of 1928. He gave an evening class for Seniors on 'current affairs' and taught some of the older Juniors as well. Then and later, on many occasions, he came with his friend, Clare Leighton, the wood engraver (the domestic staff hesitated about putting them into one room), whom he married in 1931.

By then Dorothy had fully reverted to her previous custom of the country-house weekend. It kept her in touch with her American friends when they came to Europe and, if not friends, with the sort of worldly and artistic people who had been as much part of her life before she married Leonard as they had been of her father's and Willard's. She prided herself on keeping open house; this had in previous ages been 'an essential part of the image of a great man'.[42] In America the weekend party would be collected from different parts of New York City by Matthew Hammill, Dorothy's chauffeur, and driven over the Triboro Bridge to Long Island. In England the party would leave Paddington on one of the Great Western Railways's fast trains on Friday evening and be met at Newton Abbot by one of Dorothy's English chauffeurs and taken to Leonard's study for refreshment and the beginning of a conversation which was to continue for the next two days over the silver coffeepots and the log fires, through the many rooms smelling of wood smoke and lilies of the valley, over the pheasant and peaches for dinner and the wafer-thin white sandwiches served for afternoon tea. The bedrooms were well stocked with copies of *Country Life*, the *New Statesman*, *Harper's* and *The New Republic* and the latest books from both countries. No one had to get up for breakfast unless he or she wanted to. Washing was taken away after breakfast to be done in the day. Some regulars brought down sackfuls of soiled clothing for the sake of the free laundry. On Saturday there was a choice between walking around the gardens, bird-watching on the cliffs between Torquay and Plymouth or on Dartmoor, sight-seeing, or visiting 'The Chalet', the house the Elmhirsts bought at Portwrinkle in Cornwall for a quiet retreat.

There was constant coming and going between people from the school/estate and the visitors. The accountants or foresters or farmers who came up to see Leonard were introduced to the guests and talked shop or art (if that wasn't shop) over their cups of coffee. Once the old buildings were restored the household was as like as any could be in the twentieth century to that of Gaston le Foix described by Leonard's beloved Froissart:[43]

> There was seen in his hall, chamber and court, knights and squires of honour going up and down, and talking of arms and of armours; all honour there was found, all manner of tidings of every realm and country there might be heard, for out of every country there was resort, for valiantness of this earl.

As befits a household with a co-educational school interpenetrating it there was much less segregation of the sexes than usual in most large households of the day. Leonard and Pom when he was there would delight in the kind of stories told in broad Yorkshire accents which would in other houses be kept for male gatherings. Not all the women found it easy to laugh unaffectedly at Leonard's Uncle Charles:[44]

> The Elmhirsts [Leonard would say] once owned the best beats on Broomhead Moor and used to set off with guns, dogs, gamebags in the wagonette and on horseback on 11th August from Elmhirst to the Wigtwizzle Inn. Our Uncle Charles was always one of the party up to the turn of the century and on one evening was seen by the landlady to take a drink of Epsom salts before retiring. 'What are you drinking, Mester Charles?' she said. 'Just a dose to clear my eye', says Charles. 'Yer doan't want to use that gut rot,' says she. 'Yer want ter swallow this lead ball' – reaching it down from the mantelpiece – 'it's bin thruff and thruff me and my mester many a time.'

At Dartington there was no special smoking-room for males – Leonard did not smoke except for the occasional Corona Corona taken tenderly out of its sandalwood box – no gun room and the billard room was turned into a servants' hall not long after they arrived.

Much had been done by September 1926; much remained to be done. To put the finishing touches a meeting was called for the staff of school and estate. Reliance was again placed upon one of those welcome visiting experts, old admirer of Dorothy and a member of her New York Committee of Friends which administered grants on her behalf in the USA. Lindeman was invited to act as Chairman. The record of the meeting has been preserved.[45]

The most important decision was to dispense with a headmaster. No one, Mr Rawson said, was good enough to be allowed uncontrolled authority over a child. Better to have rotating Chairmen, drawn from different members of the staff in turn, and majority control. Leonard agreed: a combined intelligence was better than the authority of one. Then followed a remark quite as revealing as the 'decision' itself, made by Mr Woods, the head gardener, who was to play an important role in the next years. He said, 'I feel we know what Mr Elmhirst wants.' If the meeting had declared itself against a headmaster there was no doubt who was in command. The Dartington contradiction had not been resolved. For all the talk of the school being a self-governing commonwealth, Leonard and Dorothy were acknowledged master and mistress, all the more securely ensconced because, despite being different in so many ways, they succeeded in maintaining their own unity in all the minor and major crises of

Dartington. Hundreds of attempts were made by embattled individuals and factions to divide them. All failed.

There was also discussion at the meeting about the project method and how it could be used to get the utmost, educationally, out of manual work on the estate. Mr Woods had already had some experience with it, even before the first term began. He had looked after Michael Straight's gardening and described how he had tried to allow Michael's interests to express themselves. This was his puzzled report on one conversation:

Mr W.:   Michael, what would you like to grow?
M.:   Anything.
Mr W.:   Celery?
M.:   Yes.
Mr W.:   Cauliflower, lettuce, peas?
M.:   Yes. But can't I grow flowers too?
Mr W.:   They won't have the same commercial value.
M.:   I would like to show them to Mother.

Then Vic asked him, rather bizarrely even for Dartington,

Vic: Would you allow Michael to grow bananas?
Mr W.:   Only if he insists.

Mr Woods added that Michael's interest had waned once all the ground had been planted. 'He is not so interested in weeding.'

On the opening day of the first term the Juniors hardly had time to look round the buildings before being plunged straight into their first exercise in self-government. The fire was lit in the library. The children sat on the floor and were asked to choose their advisers from among the Seniors. It was not easy. Apart from Dorothy's three children who had met everyone, the others did not know who the strange adults were.

For all the confusion there was an air of excitement in the house. Ruth Morgan was staying too and that night, according to the diary Dorothy kept, she asked Leonard what it was like to have a school on the premises. 'I feel merely', said Leonard, 'as if our family had been enlarged.'[46] This was how he hoped it would be. 'I want the thing', he wrote to Wyatt on 8 February 1925, 'to grow quite naturally out of our own home life and never to mention the word school from the start.' He had regretfully given way over the word. No one could think of a better. He had not given way about the new home he wanted to make for his step-children and, now, their fellow Juniors.

But Saturday saw a set-back for self-government. Whitney, the most outspoken Junior by far, uttered a heresy. 'We are having too many meetings.'[47] He got his way, for a short time. There was no general meeting at all on Sunday morning to decide what to do; each child decided individually. All but two went to church. The *Outline* and *Prospectus* had said very little either for or against church-going. It was up to the children. So they went that first Sunday but found the service, especially the sermon, too boring. Few ever went again.

On Sunday afternoon Whitney had to give in. There *was* a meeting after lunch. After a long discussion the children decided that Sunday afternoon should be a free time and that a special song should be learnt for the following Sunday. That evening, on the first of thousands of such occasions, Ruth Morgan talked about the League of Nations, particularly the effects of the admission of Germany and the problems of settling Greek refugees. Whitney showed his distaste, and independence, by lying full length on the floor throughout the talk, his feet pointing away from Miss Morgan.[48] At another meeting a morning was spent debating whether the Totnes barber should be driven up to the Hall once a fortnight to cut the boys' hair or whether the boys should be driven down to the scissors.[49]

What was done day by day to fulfil those hopes in the *Outline* and the *Prospectus*? I know only what Dorothy wrote in the daily diary she kept for a month or two or from her letters to friends in America. She and Leonard were clearly at the heart of everything. She was responsible for one of the first 'projects' for the girls, the furnishing of their cottage. They were, under her guidance, to choose the furniture and, with money she gave them, to pay for it as well as sending off neatly written letters in reply to those from suppliers addressing the 12-year-old Beatrice as 'Dear Madam'. They obviously needed bank accounts to put Dorothy's money into and take it out of. The chauffeur took Dorothy and three girls to the National Provincial Bank in Totnes first thing after breakfast on Monday morning:[50]

> I introduced each girl to Mr Joy and explained the purpose of the account. At first he was inclined to think that no minor had the power to draw cheques . . . but after looking up the law he announced that it would be quite legitimate and legal. . . . At the jeweller's, where I met Whitney, Michael and Oliver, I was asked to help them select their watches. As Louis' watch was to cost 10/- Whitney and Michael refused to get more expensive watches, though it was evident they would have liked to buy the kind of watch that Keith has.

The shopkeepers of Totnes could hardly believe their sudden good fortune. Many others besides Mr Joy watched Dorothy as if she were too good to be true.

Leonard was in charge of a class of a somewhat more ordinary sort, history. For the project work he took his Juniors on a series of trips; twice to prehistoric caves, in Torquay and near Buckfastleigh, to get some impressions of the way early man lived; and once to Dartmoor to see the first hut circles built by early men when they moved from the caves to the uplands. Leonard's plan was to divide his class into groups, some specialising in geology, others in anthropology, others in art and craft. 'I believe', wrote Dorothy to Susie Hammond, 'it is the ideal way to gain an understanding of the development of man, and if you could see the eagerness of the children you would feel they were all embarked on a true "Research Magnificent".'[51] Leonard also read a lot to the children in the evenings, for instance bits of Froissart and Chaucer – the tale of the Prioress.[52]

But the problems of self-government would not go away. Whitney was often at a loose end and if he did not know what he wanted to do the Seniors had to think of something for him. They suggested he should accompany Leonard each morning on his regular tours of the estate, taking notes. Other children also had too little initiative. Dorothy was adviser to Keith Ponsford:[53]

> I find great difficulty [she wrote] in getting him to initiate any suggestions. He practically never volunteers a remark on his own, and his mental indefiniteness is baffling. I haven't yet been able to get a clear answer from him on anything when it means a choice.

And Vic said, 'I'm puzzled to know what to do when Keith comes up and kicks me in the shins.'[54] Keith had an obsession with shins. Some of the women on the staff wanted to turn and run when they saw his boots stamping towards them.

The staff could not fail to recognise that some of the other children were also pretty rum. The project for one of the other boys was to help Frank Crook make cider. The press was inside a barn, operated by a horse which walked around in circles pushing the bar attached to the press. One day Leonard entered the barn to find the boy laying into the horse with a stick to make it trot and then running around after it, beating it mercilessly. His project had to be changed at once, his craving for mangling the horse over-ruled.[55]

Several of the children, used to single-sex schools, were put out by the co-education. In the first term in their separate quarters this was not so noticeable, but in the second the boys moved into their new rooms. As one of the girls noted:[56]

> The boys having moved up into their quarters we saw more of them and began to fall for some boys, and hate others. There was a bust up and we got into bad ways and took interest in vulgar jokes. Things got so bad by the end of the term that we had a big meeting, and decided we got to pull up otherwise the girls department would have to close.

> In the meeting Jerry talked about sex feelings and we learnt of things
> that we had no idea of before. After the meeting we began to realise
> what a wonderful thing nature is. And now we are natural.

One talk did not settle all the anxieties. There was evidently a need for
'instruction' which could fall only to the Seniors to impart. Some were
distinctly uneasy. In a memorandum circulated around the staff, Vic urged
that sexual instruction should be approached through botany and 'be
given in the morning and not at night'.

Dorothy had started Question Club for the Juniors and continued for
many years to run it; any issue could be raised there. She reassured Vic:[57]

> What I have been doing, and what I imagine you have been doing too,
> is to answer in a perfectly straightforward way the questions about
> sex that arise in children's minds. Now, from my experience with
> Question Club, I can speak with absolute certainty on one point, and
> that is that children are naturally interested in the whole subject. . . .
> He [one of the boys] said, 'Will you tell us about a girl's periods?' Ever
> since that time they have brought up questions of this kind and many
> others, and after seeing the performance of *Anna Christie* they asked
> at the subsequent meeting what a prostitute was. We have, of course,
> discussed 'babies' by the hour, and the older group have asked me,
> just as Kit asked you, whether there is any way of preventing
> conception. It seems a perfectly typical and inevitable question, and I
> answered it, I imagine, very much as you did.

The frankness of the Question Club did not stop Jack Sayce, one of the
boys, setting up a competitor to it in a secret Kissing Club. He paired off
the boys and girls and directed them to meet in the woods and do their
thing under Jack's tuition. It did not remain secret for long. The Juniors
were all called together for a speech from Leonard, who said he had not
kissed Dorothy until they were married. The Kissing Club was
disbanded.[58]

Leonard was not the only one who took the Juniors on expeditions.
Dorothy did too.[59] On 24 June 1927 she set out in the Buick station wagon
with eleven others to catch the boat from Ilfracombe to Swansea and from
there go by train to Llanwrtyd Wells and the start of the school walking
tour. On the first leg they walked seven miles, on the second eleven and so
on for two weeks.

On 28 June they stayed in the Goat Hotel at Bala. There was an eclipse
the following morning:

> Up at 5 to see eclipse in pouring rain. Tramped up hill back of town
> and waited and waited. At 6.32 a weird, blue, grey darkness spread

over earth. The kids piped nervously. . . . Caught 11.30 train on narrow gauge up to Festiniog. Lunched on sandwiches and tea. Had delightful time with 2 miners on train who sang to us.

On 30 June they walked twenty-three miles through continuous rain. Dorothy kept a detailed account of the money she spent – 9s. 3d. on one day, for instance, made up of 6d. for sandwiches, 1s. 9d. for tea, 2s. for supper, 5s. for bed and breakfast. Miss Bogue was far away.

At Dartington there were other problems besides sex: for instance, the perennial one of bedtimes. The report on the first term claimed that on this issue at least good sense had prevailed:[60]

> A series of late evenings spent on practical jokes, and one impromptu bedroom feast to which Miss Wise put an end at midnight, led them to realise that late nights and dissipation must be paid for by tired mornings and a long process of tiresome and unnecessary cleaning up.

Safety was another issue. Lime was mishandled. There was a risk of fire. Scaffolding was dangerous. At some point a loaded gun was left in a public room. So a general meeting was called to which everyone came from estate and school. It was agreed that dangers should be divided into two classes, red and pink. The Juniors decided into which category any particular danger should go, and the consequent seriousness with which it was regarded. Sliding down banisters was pink; riding without brakes red.[61] This was followed by a set of Swimming Rules. No one was to go swimming without at least one Senior Swimmer in the party, a test for a Senior Swimmer being 'able to carry either Fish or Beatrice across the river'. The penalties for breaking the rules which could be 'inflicted by a Senior or Mark or Whitney' were

> 1st time – No swimming for a week
> 2nd time – No swimming for a fortnight
> 3rd time – No swimming for a month

Rules of a sort multiplied, some of them with the sanction of the General Meeting of all Juniors and Seniors. But the rules are not what people remember. To very few of the children – either in that first year or in the few that followed – did it seem like a school. As well as the projects to do with the rebuilding, which was going along at a great pace, and with the operation of the estate, there must have been some ordinary classes, without visits to prehistoric caves. But they are not remembered. In retrospect it does seem like the large extended family Leonard wanted it to be, made up of the people on an estate and in a school which were not yet fully differentiated from each other. Seniors did not go home at 4 or 6 or 8.

They were always around. Their weddings were affairs for the whole of the community to engage in, as when John Wales, Vic and then Richard were married. In early photographs like the one reproduced as Plate 19 doctors and horsemen, turners and butlers, teachers and children were all together.

It all held together as well as it did partly because the instigators maintained an element of formal structure which created a counterpoint to the general informality. Every evening, whether there were visitors or not in this little state, there was almost a state occasion to which nearly all the Seniors came. They changed into evening clothes for the dinner, and usually sat in the same places, Peggy Wales, for instance, being next to Vic. Thomas waited on them. The table was laid with silver and glass. The meal started with soup and ended with the decanter of port being passed around; the talk was about the exciting affairs of the day, such as Keith's liking for shins or Jack's for kissing.

Sometimes children were at table as well. On Question Club evening, instead of discussing where babies came from or where the League of Nations was going to, the Juniors would sometimes make apple-pie beds for Leonard and hang around the house, talking to Dorothy about which dress she was to wear for dinner. Ann King-Hall and Pauline Hunter remember dressing up in some of Ann's mother's gowns and going to show Dorothy how they looked. They were invited to stay to dinner and eat strawberries, in January.

After the port came the activities. Another letter from Dorothy describes some of them:[62]

> Our evenings have become delightfully social. On Mondays we all get together to sew, staff and children, often to the accompaniment of song or the gramophone. On Tuesdays we have a Dancing Class, composed of Seniors, the older Juniors, the gardener's children, the maids of our household, and our second man. It is a most wonderful and unique affair, about thirty of us in all. We are learning the charleston, the tango, and all the latest tricks of the trade, and even Whitney has decided that we are thoroughly up to date. On Wednesday we used to have chorus singing, but recently science has encroached on art, and Mr Heuser (our poultry expert from Cornell) has been dissecting chickens and giving the most thrilling demonstrations in physiology and biology. . . . For the discussions we all gather around the fire on the floor and thrash out some subject like the meaning of drudgery, or the consequences of punishment, or what religion means to us individually. . . . Last week Leonard read aloud a sketch of the life of Buddha.

15 Dartington Hall, the ruins of
the Great Hall, showing the marks
of the beams

16 White Hart boss, entrance
porch to the Great Hall

17 The restored Great Hall

18 Dorothy in the garden at Dartington, 1926, reportedly typing the first *Prospectus* of the school

19 The Dartington estate and school, 1927. Dorothy is seated in the second row from the front, fifth along from the left, with Leonard next to her. He wrote the names of some of the people on the original photograph

The first year went smoothly enough, with few children around and plenty of grown-ups. In the second year came the first serious conflict. It was about the basic question of authority which has been under dispute so continuously throughout the history of the school. At the early Lindeman meeting Leonard said he was against having a single headmaster and he had stuck to it. He also said he was in favour of a democracy, and some of the staff took him literally. So far Mr Rawson had been as near to being head as anyone in the school, relied upon by Leonard in every situation, with Miss Wise his chief partner. They were the two with previous training or experience in education, both intellectuals, and perhaps resented as such by others. Also, they were seen kissing in the garden, and some of the staff thought this even more outrageous than the Juniors' Kissing Club, even though they were both single.

The school staff met to consider this shocking event when Leonard and Dorothy were away. They were often in America, India or elsewhere, both then and afterwards; when they were, Question Club and history classes had to be temporarily suspended. On this occasion it was decided by a majority vote to sack Mr Rawson and Miss Wise, and to appoint Mr Woods, the gardener, as Chairman of the Education Committee, on paper the supreme policy-making body of the estate. Mr Woods may have thought this would be what Mr Elmhirst wanted. If so this time he was wrong. Leonard and Dorothy did not want that at all; they were deeply shocked. How could they manage without the two key people, or the school without its only experienced teachers? If this was what 'democracy' meant, it could not be accepted. On his return Leonard called another, fuller, meeting of the staff, and persuaded them to rescind the decision. The others knew well enough where their salaries were coming from. Mr Rawson and Miss Wise stayed on. From that time on it became increasingly clear that there would need at some stage to be a head.

This crisis was particularly trying for Dorothy because it coincided with one in her own life. She was pregnant again and looking forward with great excitement to having a boy this time. She and Leonard (hoping for contraries) had given the foetus the name of Joan:[63]

6 March 1927   Those dreaded pains commenced about 1 and ran along at intervals of 2 minutes and less until about 4 when I felt something snap inside. The bag had broken. . . . What a day of hope and dread following hard on each other's heels back and forth. And through all the uncertainty the sounds of spring through the window.

7 March   Joan slipped away this morning, so gently that I didn't know she had gone. It was hard to believe at

first because there was no pain, no sign. Then I asked Maude for a sight of Joan. She brought her to me in the little soap dish – so lovely, so perfect, about 4 inches long and wonderfully formed – one arm up to her head, the other at her side – her tiny form quite red and soft but complete and unblemished – her eyes open and such a vigorous head and chest.

8 March   J. (Jerry = Leonard) came in before lunch to find me weeping. I could only see it all as the bitter experience of gaining and losing the most cherished prize, all in a moment of time. . . . Then J. showed me my own weakness and, incidentally, his strength. 'Don't let yourself want things so intensely. The wind blows where it listeth. Seek ye first the Kingdom. Be yourself, don't always strive for results, for action. Learn to become yourself.'

9 March   My bed is in window. J. came up last night while others were dancing and lay on my bed in moonlight. . . . Jerry went on to talk of his youth – how when he was 4 he wrote hymns and sang them and begged that his tulip be placed on the altar.

10 March   Last night we talked again. To my question whether his attitude was a fatalistic one J. answered that it was the meaning to him of losing one's life to find it.

On top of these troubles the constant sniping from outside sometimes caused upsets as well as enhancing solidarity. One of the few locals who had some influence over them was Dr S. R. Williams, the school doctor, even though on many matters he shared and voiced the opinions of the gentry. Dorothy and Leonard asked him to make a report on the development of the school.[64] He had previously recommended there should be a compulsory rest for half an hour for all children before the midday and evening meals, and also that the staff should have their meals separately. He was delighted that his second suggestion had been acted upon: it had been accepted because 'It is a Rule' and people, especially children, need Rules. His regret was that the very social activities which Dorothy and everybody else took such delight in, 'Question Clubs, Sing-Songs, and so forth have been allowed to take the place of the quiet reading which I advocated'.

He went on to draw attention to the fatigue which he noticed, or thought he noticed, amongst many of the children. He put it down again to the lack of Rules.

> Nearly all children are confirmed ritualists – they love routines more than freedom. The reason is that an ordered life is easier, the child has more energy and leisure to devote to the important things it wants to do. Breaking through the routine may add an occasional spice to life, but that is all. I do not think that freedom has had a good influence on your children in some respects. . . . Collectively, they do not compare well with a similar number of similar age from an Elementary School. For instance, I came down once to give them a lesson in First Aid. I arrived at the appointed time. Ten minutes later several noisy Juniors, rather dirty, came in without any apology or adequate excuse for being late. I retired.

He ended by paying a tribute to the splendid work of Maude (the Matron) and also of Whitney who had apparently got over the hostility he showed at the start of the first term. 'The sense of responsibility shown by Whitney during the first year was quite remarkable and the admirable way in which he set the pace beyond praise.'

Dr Williams may have added to the unease felt by some people on the inside, but the views on education of a country doctor hardly commanded any great sympathy. The next people from outside to be invited to 'inspect' the school, in that same academic year, carried more weight. Dr and Mrs Bonser from Teachers College in New York, one of them the co-author of a book on *Industrial Arts for Elementary Schools*, wrote the most important document in the early history after the *Outline* and the *Prospectus* – the Bonser Report as it came to be known.[65] Here was an account by professionals from one of the institutions which had contributed most to the original idea – unfortunately there was no parallel team from Bengal.

Much of it was a restatement of the 'philosophy' of education which they assumed they shared with the founders and with the staff, and which they thought no less sound because it had not yet been fully applied anywhere, not even at Lincoln School. The central belief (as they put it) was that the unfolding of forces within children could be effectively promoted by an interaction with their natural and social environment different from that customary in ordinary schools, a setting more like the adult world than a school. Given a rich environment, the child·could grow by responding to opportunities rather than through subjection to any personal, conscious coercion. The child would have to adjust himself to natural and social forces because these exerted a coercion which could not be resisted; he could do this without yielding the control of his personality to that of another.

For the achievement of such a happy state two conditions had to be satisfied. The first, the presence of a rich environment, the Bonsers thought the estate satisfied to the full. 'For the testing of this philosophy of education a more hopeful and satisfying environment could scarcely be imagined.' The second condition, and here came the rub, was the right kind of teachers. They were not just part of the immediate environment themselves; they were also the middlemen between the children and all the other elements in the environment, helping to make use each for his or her own growth of what was there. But some of the teachers at Dartington did not yet know, in practical terms, how to fulfil this vital educational role. The rest of the Report was mainly devoted to suggestions, put forward with as much tact as any official Inspector, about ways to improve their performance.

The Bonser Report was in part a restatement from New York of the original Siksha-Satra doctrine, a plea once again for ending the separation between 'life', particularly the 'work' which was part of it, and 'education'. It also attempted to formulate what would be needed if teachers were to bridge the gap and so focused on the need for more professionalism in the school.

The staff voted on the urgency with which a number of issues arising out of the report should be tackled; those to do with the estate came last. Underlying all the controversy about such questions as 'how can self-discipline be secured?' was another, even more fundamental, about skill. The Bonsers had demonstrated some expertise themselves and this made all the more telling their criticism of its lack amongst the teachers. Where was the training, where the experience? Almost everyone knew the answer. The report was a special blow to Leonard and Dorothy. They had been told, implicitly, that despite their enthusiastic work as advisers and history teachers, they were not competent. They did not dispute it.

The next chapter in the story of the school, according to one way of looking at it, did not start until 1931. According to another, it started with the Bonser Report. It was after that that the decision to seek a headmaster was made. The attempt to vote out Miss Wise and Mr Rawson played its part. So did the latter's own departure towards the end of 1928 for London and a leading position in the New Education Fellowship. If any head had been appointed from the existing staff he would have been the obvious choice.

One cannot say that the next two or three years constituted an interregnum in the school. There had not been a King before, at least in name. It was more a pre-regnum, waiting for the King. In September 1928 John Wales and Vic were appointed joint acting heads, Marjorie Wise concentrating on the survey which led to a book about schools in the State system.[66] The new appointments were not intended to be permanent and, whenever it was suggested they should be, John Wales firmly countered it. He thought he needed more training; untrained as he was, he did not consider himself fit for the post. The reason the temporary lasted as long as three years was simply that it took nearly a year to get through the process of advertising – used this time – and when Bill Curry was selected from the short-list he had to give a good part of a year's notice to the Oak Lane Country Day School of which he had been Principal, a school created in 1916 to apply Dewey's ideas in Philadelphia.

Dartington did not stand still just because the search was on for a proper headmaster. A little nursery school was, for instance, started in 1929 in a Playhouse in the garden. This was primarily for Ruth but ten other children joined her. Miss Jefferies was in charge. Ruth said, 'We had little gardens or plots there where we sowed annuals. There were also fowls, and at one side swings and roundabouts.'[67] Out of that came a plan for a real Nursery School. A large new building was put up for the purpose at Aller Park and Miss Harley came from the Merrill-Palmer School in Detroit to be the head. Leonard and Dorothy paid close attention to the detail. While Miss Harley was still in Detroit Leonard wrote to her that 'Dorothy and I have been over the lighting fixtures this morning, and are allowing for more plugs right through the building'.[68] This school was intended to be very 'scientific', based on the 'scientific' study of young children, and with a diet for the children derived directly from the 'scientific' study of nutrition. Bill went to Aller Park when it was opened in 1931. He was 2.

The main school was getting steadily better known. The number of pupils went up, to twenty-five, in September 1929. A new and bigger prospectus had been printed earlier that year. There was now a structure to the school which would have been recognisable to Somervell if not to the Cossack. The Junior School was for children of 8 up to 13, the same age that children moved from prep to public school in the English middle classes generally. 'This, the normal preparatory school stage, was taken as the period for granting the widest possible range of opportunity, especially in those practical activities which appeal most naturally to children of this age.' The Senior School (13 to 18) was said to have an 'Academic Side' for 'those boys and girls who wish to enter for such examinations as School or Higher Certificate, or who plan a definite professional career which will entail passing into a university'. Siksha-Satra was being replaced by something more orthodox.

That is, however, not how it seemed to me or several of the other children who arrived that September. For those who had been at orthodox schools the difference seemed immense, especially in the behaviour of the adults. When she heard she had a baby half-brother Pauline Church sat on Vic's lap for the best part of two days until she began to recover. Ernest Gruenberg was taking so much pleasure in learning pottery from Bernard and David Leach that he almost decided to take that up instead of psychology. Dougie Hart was finding the first adults in his life who were 'on his side'. As for me, the murderous feelings I had before were leaving me because I was happy. The adults may have been suffering from doubt and anxiety. To us it seemed that the little world Dorothy and Leonard had created was not far short of a children's paradise.

Just turned 14, I arrived in September 1929. It was my fifth main school, after two preparatory boarding-schools and two State day schools, in London and Australia. I may have been unlucky but, if I was, so were many other children. These schools were not so categorical about their philosophies as they were about the multitudinous rules which they superimposed upon us with varying degrees of savagery. The geography master at the London elementary school, standing like a Cyclops, took delight in superimposing the edge of his ruler on the outstretched knuckles of any 7-year-olds who failed to remember the name of the river on whose banks Rome was alleged to stand. I can remember seeing the little smile playing on his lips a second before I felt the pain splitting through my hands.

At my first prep school the senior master was a tyrant corrupted by his own almost absolute power. He forced boys who broke his rules, or showed any spirit of defiance, to fall into the rear of the daily crocodile walks through the city with their coats turned inside out as a sign of disgrace. On punishment nights the wrongdoers had to strip naked in the Scout Room (definitely *not* run on Leonard's principles) in the middle of a circle of watching boys and submit to being flogged by him with a buckled Scout belt. His terrified courtiers among the pupils were even more odious than he. I vowed then at the age of 9 that I would murder him when I became a man if I ever met him again. So far, I haven't. Perhaps a fellow-sufferer has forestalled me. To all four schools Dartington was a complete contrast. I was bullied there by other boys – especially by one who called me 'Belly' and always dug me painfully in the stomach as he passed me and, when I protested, laughed and said, 'Can't you take a joke?' But never by any of the 'teachers'. They were not only grown-up; they were friendly.

I am not sure whether or not the story is apocryphal of the small Dartington girl who said, 'Oh dear, do I have to do what I want to do all over again today?' At any rate her spirit was not mine. For the nine previous years my schooling had been minced together into 45-minute parcels labelled Latin, Scripture, Arithmetic. I got the smell of something different when I visited Dartington the term before my admission and found one big boy – Whitney, I learnt later – on his back under a Model T Ford in the middle of the morning. He gave me a ride in it, reversing at speed up perilously steep fields as though that was what the Ford was made for, and determined me to get to that 'school' if I could, despite my worries about there being no compulsory games. Of that compulsion I approved. The headmaster of my prep school had said to my startled mother when she asked his advice about my long-term future, 'With practice, your son might make a good wicket-keeper.' To develop that signal talent he advised I should be sent further down the river Dart, to the Dartmouth Royal Naval College.

The Model T won, and when I did arrive, instead of attending classes regularly as I had for the previous eight years, I went into partnership with another boy to buy and sell motorcycles. We kept one of the best for two years, perhaps because of its name – a 1920 Triumph costing thirty shillings which ran on free paraffin from the Boiler House – and must have ridden it a thousand times up and down the private road by the river, trying to clip another second off our own record. Later on, I contracted with the dance teacher, Margaret Barr (who will reappear in chapter 9) to take part as an unenthusiastic, ungainly member of her troupe in one of her epic dances, *The People*, if in return I could drive her Morris Cowley once up and down the drive and listen to the sweet hum of its engine for each rehearsal I attended. 'Regular opportunity for music, singing and every creative activity', said the *Outline* – perhaps not quite what was intended. But until my partner and I tired of motorcycles it meant days spent with the wind whistling in our hair instead of Latin and Greek through and out of our ears. Twice a week I deserted the Triumph for an ordinary push-cycle – a red Hercules with racing handlebars given to me and the other poor boys by Beatrice – and pedalled at breakneck pace to the cinema in Paignton or Torquay.

The ostensible reason for my being at Dartington was not the Ford or the Morris Cowley but the readiness of my grandfather in Australia to pay for my continued education provided it was strictly vocational, for fruit-farming. He wanted me to go to Tasmania, and this was the only school anyone knew of where I could learn the trade. He was the only relative with any money. My father was a largely unemployed violinist.

I became an apprentice in the orchards and, when I was not fiddling with carburettors, 'life' was picking up and bagging apples for cider-making. I had an exercise book in which I drew pictures of trees, with all the branches cut through with lines to show where they should be pruned, looking like a manual of acupuncture. That lasted six months, until Tasmania faded as an ambition and my grandfather refused to pay any more. But I was able to stay on. I got a scholarship, or perhaps I should say a motorbikeship.

Fruit was followed by poultry. A group of boys and girls set up a tiny poultry co-operative called Darfowls, with me as Secretary. We entered into a formal lease (learning law too from the poultry project?) with Mr Elmhirst for the ground on which the hen-house stood. It was strange to see Leonard called that in the lease. The eggs were candled and sold to the school kitchen at whatever the market price was that week in Totnes. At the end of a year's work, supervised by a real poultryman, each member of the co-operative got a dividend of four shillings. Apart from some book-keeping I learnt I could no more hope to be a good farmer of poultry than I could of fruit: I could candle splendidly; but I could not bear to wring the chickens' necks, although I tried and tried to bring myself and the hen to the crunch. From poultry I progressed to the architect's office to learn draughtsmanship, designing one paper house after another; and always there was what was later called 'Useful Work', felling and thinning trees in the wood for whose care the school was responsible on Gallow's Hill.[69] The little world had a great deal of variety given to it by practitioners who were not so much teachers as doers. I learnt a vital negative lesson, about things I was *not* capable of doing. I could not wring a neck, I could not dance, I could not design a house, I could not grow fruit, I could not make money from hens, I could not stand next to a naked girl of my own age in a shower without being startled; the beginning, I realised, of a much longer list.

For the three previous years there had, for me, been Chapel twice a day, which meant trying like everyone else to avoid the row of chairs in front of the headmaster's wife who viciously tweaked the ears of any boy whose attention seemed to be wandering from her very demanding God. The absence of Chapel made me a little uneasy at first. Where had God gone? And God's wife? Was there no one waiting to dig her nails into the lobes of my ears? I was so shocked that even on Armistice Day there was to be no service, no singing of 'The Recessional', that at five to eleven on 11 November 1929 I went off to my room and, hoping no one would come in, knelt down by my bed to pray for ten minutes before having another go at breaking the track record on the Triumph. On 11 November 1930 there was not even a one-boy ceremony.

About a matter even more vital to me there was nothing in any of the prospectuses. My other boarding-schools had *claimed* to provide 'whole-some food' or something like that calculated to pacify anxious mothers and enrage their even more anxious children. In fact, for most of my childhood, I seemed, looking back on it, to have been almost permanently hungry, either at home, where there was at some periods little money to buy food with, or, far more, at school. At the first prep school both breakfast, the first, and tea, the last meal, consisted, year in, year out, except when a parent came to a meal, of the same bread and black treacle, and not enough of that. At the second my obsession with my stomach receded only for two or three hours once a week on a Wednesday when the turn came for really filling suet pudding with golden syrup. Sometimes there were actually second helpings, on the principle of first come, first served, so I used to swallow the whole lot in about five seconds and race for the queue. Both schools were run by the kind of headmaster's wife who recommended a certain kind of cheese to another on the ground that boys did not like it and so ate very little of it.

By contrast here I was in a Ginger Bread House. I never felt hungry for four years. And what food! Apple sauce in great bowls for breakfast, piles of cornflakes and giant jugs of milk. Roast beef without gristle, crisp Yorkshire Pudding. Bean shoots from China. When visitors came to a meal at one of my old schools there was a special spread to impress them. At Dartington it was always visitors' day. There we were at the tables eating strawberries and cream. I can remember no sense of guilt that I was eating like this while most people in the world were not even as well off as I had been on bread and treacle. Before I had always longed for the end of the term.

> This time next week where shall I be
> Out of the gates of misery.
> No more Latin, no more French.
> No more sitting on a hard board bench.

Now it was the other way round: I longed for the end of the holidays. Then I could get down again to the wondrous slog of eating my way through three solid meals a day, every day, until at last I was convinced at the very seat of my emotions that the Devonshire cream was not a Devonshire dream. No wonder I was nicknamed 'Belly'.

I can hardly remember a rainy day, and in Devon, for the first two years after the Wall Street Crash, with Ramsay MacDonald as Prime Minister. In recounting my move from the kind of schools which Dartington was reacting against as much as I was myself I have again declared my bias.

By the time I arrived the relationships between children, and between adults and children, had a recognisable character to them. Newcomers behaved according to the conventions that had been established – they were almost exaggeratedly at ease, they delighted in the relative absence of rules, they talked a lot. Children accepted adults and adults children as people not greatly divided by age. Sexuality was throbbing in the air. Pupils did not work very hard. A tradition had been created.

To some people the outcome was rather miraculous. Hardly any hard-headed and knowledgeable observer visiting the 'school' in that first autumn term of 1926 would have prophesied a long life. Being in the tradition of Rousseau (whether or not acknowledged) was dire enough. Any reformer who wishes to cut cleanly through the thousand ties which bind orthodox schools to the society for which they are 'preparing' children is also setting himself adrift. Being child-centred does not in itself tell anyone what to do. The observer of Dartington would surely have predicted that the sort of adults, and children, such a school would attract would bring on its downfall. If it did not fall for the same reasons as the Little Commonwealth, internal rows would kill it off before many years had passed.

But the 'little world' did not collapse. The money helped. So did the lack of zealotry. At no time were Dorothy and Leonard so carried away with enthusiasm, intoxicating as it sometimes was, that they closed their minds. The school never became a community of people so committed that they could no longer see what they were doing with any objectivity. Visitors came of their own accord, as well as when invited, and not all of them were sycophants. The two founders may have been utopian but they were also pragmatic and chose at least some others who were as well. Rousseau *was* cross-bred with Baden-Powell.

CHAPTER 7

MICROCOSM

⟶∘◉∘⟵

Similarly, a student who, in order to pursue
some definite profession of his own choosing,
is considered by the Staff to have the
requisite intellectual equipment, will be
given the instruction necessary to enable
him to pass any special examination.

Prospectus, 1926

By the end of the 1920s the school already had a tradition of its own which
no one except a determined headmaster could alter. W. B. Curry was
determined. He had the power and he used it if not to destroy then
certainly to modify the tradition, even if like other new heads he had to
contend with the united resistance of the existing pupils. In Liberty Hall we
might be, but as conservative as any other children: it was thus when Hu
and Lois Child arrived as the second heads twenty-six years later. In 1931
we did not like being moved out of our courtyard into the unfriendly new
building at Foxhole. We did not like school numbers being enlarged. We
did not like the loss of any of the freedoms which time over the last year or
two had for us sufficiently hallowed. I was especially incensed by the
upstart's outrageous decision to ban firearms and motor-driven vehicles,
including my beautiful Triumph. Demonstrators sat on the roof of the
school – forbidden in itself – and threw pillows and food down onto the
ground in front of the new head's study. He was dared to come up and get
us down, which he very sensibly did not attempt. The revolution lasted till
supper time.

Dorothy and Leonard did not approve of the demonstration. They
had gone to much trouble to find Curry. In response to the advertisement
came many applicants and the then Education Committee interviewed the
most hopeful-sounding. No one was quite right. All the candidates on the

short-list were professionals without a doubt but professionals who had been teachers before only at orthodox schools. Although they naturally professed the most heartfelt sympathy for the new school that the Elmhirsts had started, could they really be trusted? With all those children to be responsible for, many of whom had been part of their home during the period when home and school had been one, how awful to make a mistake. Much safer to find a man who had successfully run a school not too unlike Dartington. Chance came to their aid. Margaret Isherwood had been recommended to Dorothy by the Froebel College in London as a suitable person to head the girls' section in succession to Marjorie Wise. She was herself teaching at the Oak Lane Country Day School in Phila-delphia. Her sister, Ena, was married to Bill Curry, its headmaster. Margaret came to Dartington in 1929 to be interviewed. She told Dorothy and Leonard about Bill. The next time they sailed to America Dorothy and Leonard went to Oak Lane. They liked the school and liked Bill well enough to invite him to visit Dartington.

He could not come until the Easter vacation in 1930, after the end of his term, so he could not see Dartington school in action – just as well, some of the Seniors probably thought – but he could talk to the Elmhirsts and the other staff. Rather strangely, Tagore was staying there at the same time. Bill was wary of this awesome figure, Ena not. She liked his great blue cloak. On a walk with her in the garden he advocated compulsory 'night education' for everyone. All children should be got up from bed and taken out of doors at night to accustom them to darkness and all the creatures that slither through it.[1] Bill also let flow with his views on education, and the Elmhirsts were again impressed. They waited for the next meeting of the Education Committee and after that Leonard sent off the formal offer, not of the headship but the grander job which would accord with the original vision of a school and estate bound together into one large educational enterprise: 'Director of Education to the Social and Educa-tional Experiment now being carried out at Dartington Hall, Totnes.' In the same letter[2] Leonard said he would get a salary of £1,000 a year to start with, higher than any other Experimenter.

Bill asked for a proper legal agreement. Fred Gwatkin, their solicitor, was about to be appointed a Trustee. He drew up the contract. The new Trust was set up in March 1931. The contract, while appointing Bill as Administrative Head of the school, required him to conform to the reasonable instructions of the Trustees. Bill showed his mettle by a cable sent to Dartington on 17 February 1931: 'Deeply shocked by proposed agreement which departs both from the spirit and the letter of our discussion and my letter of Nov. 4th. Articles 2, 3, 4 and 7 are quite unacceptable. Must withdraw unless agreement embodies original condi-tions of freedom from interference by Trustees in all matters of educational administration.' He was determined to put the founders in their place; he succeeded. They surrendered, even though it meant they were to be no longer Seniors at all, let alone the most Senior Seniors of all. The new head was not, like Mr Woods, going to find out what Mr Elmhirst wanted; he was going to tell him and Dorothy what *he* wanted.

Neither of them was put off. Once having formed a view about him they stuck to it. Discount the customary exaggeration in Dorothy's letter to Miss Bogue, and it was still a glowing report:[3]

> The advent of the Curry's [sic] has been the beginning of a new era at Dartington. He is not only a great educator but an extraordinarily fine human being – and so is she. He speaks and acts with the authority that grows out of real knowledge and wisdom, and in so young a man that kind of maturity is rarely found. He can be as young and gay as the youngest children and they regard him without a vestige of fear and yet with the deepest respect. Beatrice so often says to me, 'He *is* a peach', and Michael says, 'Mr Curry is so *extraordinarily* nice'. . . . Leonard and I simply don't know how to thank our stars for him – somehow he came, almost out of the blue, and is going to live in a celestial house with wings.

Leonard spoke later in the same vein:[4]

> Oh, at that time in history, whether in America or England, I don't think there was in the school world another mind as creative or as positive or as courageous as Curry's.

Curry's first asset was the personality Dorothy found so attractive. Watching him, a short and rather round man with a bald head and big pipe talking to children especially, as Plate 26 shows him, or to the lesser number of adults he got on with, it was difficult not to like him. He so obviously enjoyed other people. He talked so well. He laughed so much, sometimes deep, sometimes high, at his own jokes even more loud and long than at other people's. His laugh became as much a party piece as the jokes it accompanied, like the various stories Bill embroidered about the parson arriving at the Hall. In one the parson complained about being met by a naked butler – but how, if he was naked, could he know he was a butler? asked Bill. In another the parson was greeted not by a naked butler, but by a naked teenage girl. 'My God,' gasped the astonished visitor. 'There is no God,' she replied, slamming the door.

For anyone not jealous, the passion of a small man for large cars – he owned at various times two vintage Rolls-Royces, a Bentley, an Auburn and the Hispano Suiza used in the film *The Third Man* – could not be held against him. Nor his blossoming out in the new school prospectus as 'William Burnlee Curry, MA Cambridge; BSc London. Sometime Senior

Scholar of Trinity College, Cambridge. Formerly Headmaster of the Oak Lane Country Day School, Philadelphia, USA.'

Another asset was by now very much standard: his Anglo-American background, the Anglo bit of it almost as good as the American. Born in 1900 at Jarrow, the eldest son of a grocer whom he did not get on with and a mother who worshipped him, he won from his grammar school a scholarship to Leonard's and Wyatt's old college. Being a physicist was also in his favour for people who knew nothing of science and so were in awe of it; so was his having taught at Greshams and then, with Ena, at the best known progressive school in Britain, Bedales, while Badley was headmaster.

His experience in America was more to the point, for the school, than Wyatt's at Brown University or for that matter, in the world of education, than Leonard's at Cornell. The Oak Lane School, where he started as science teacher, although not quite Lincoln, was also a 'progressive day school', on the John Dewey model. It was financed by wealthy Jewish parents. Without them it could not have survived nor he been appointed head in 1927. Without them, and in particular Leopold Stokowski, the conductor of the Philadelphia Symphony Orchestra, Ena would not have been able to build a fine new nursery school attached to Oak Lane. It was designed by a friend of Stokowski, a rising Philadelphia architect called William Lescaze who was later to achieve some fame internationally with his skyscraper for the Philadelphia Saving Fund Society and, locally, in Devon. The parents also had their drawbacks. They brought on the departure of their English head. Although more or less ignorant of education (he would say) they pressed their views with infuriating persistence on ordinary teachers and, worse still, on him, the head. Far better, he thought, a boarding-school with parents far, far away, provided, of course, that trustees on the spot did not do duty for parents who were not, by interfering in his own professional domain.

But Curry only got the job, on his own terms, because he was in agreement with so much of what the founders thought and did. He made it clear, with finesse, that he was as much 'on the side' of children as he was often not on the side of their parents. The mentor whom he liked to quote, and with whom he became a fast friend, was Bertrand Russell – Bertie, as Curry called him. So often was Bertie brought forth in support that the saying in the school in the 1930s was, 'There is no God but Russell and Curry is his prophet.'[5] To Russell fell the honour of being quoted in favour of child-centredness, rather than Rousseau or Dewey:[6]

> The man who has reverence will not think it his duty to 'mould' the young. He feels in all that lives, and most of all in children, something sacred, indefinable, unlimited, something individual and strangely

precious, the growing principle of life, an embodied fragment of the dumb striving of the world.

Curry's further virtue was that he saw more clearly than anyone since 1925 that reverence for children and its consequence, freedom for their personalities to unfold in accord with their natures, were not in themselves enough. That was a negative view of education. Is there no life after school? If all that was necessary to produce perfect children, and hence perfect human beings, was to leave them alone and glory in the splendour of their growth, why go to the trouble of having schools at all?[7]

> The principle of liberty, while important in education, is essentially a negative principle. Liberty is important because it is the condition of the achievement of many good ends, but it is not an end in itself.

Curry did not want to make the choice Rousseau and the Elmhirsts made, between making a man and making a citizen. He wanted the citizen as well as the man. We have schools, Curry kept saying, because we want children to learn to live in society, first in a small society with each other, and second, by extension, in the great society with strangers. It is not only the child in the present day who matters; he or she also needs to be prepared to become a good citizen in the future. But of what sort of society? Not just a conformist to what is but a creator of what could be. And so he posed the great question, what sort of alternative society are children to be prepared for? His question had not been asked in the first prospectuses.

By way of answer Curry picked up from Russell a line of argument very appealing in the 1920s and 1930s. Dorothy and Leonard had both been caught up in the horrors of the war. Their own memories and others were being sharpened by plays like *Journey's End* and the growing number of books being published in the early 1930s in the vein of Remarque's *All Quiet on the Western Front*. They became even more passionate in their wish than they had been that mankind should learn from the terrible mistakes which had led to the deaths of Willard and Willie. Their hopes, like those of Ruth Morgan and Goldie, had been placed in the League of Nations. Here was a body to which nations would according to the rule of law submit their disputes for third party judgment instead of trying to settle them by force. Would it succeed? The question was given an edge of desperation by the emergence of Hitler. His rise coincided with that of Curry. Like most ardent supporters of the League of Nations the Elmhirsts also believed that Germany had been unjustly treated at Versailles by Lloyd George and Clemenceau when they outwitted the President whom Willard was about to help when he died. Reparations had been too heavy; too much territory, in the Saar, Sudentenland and East Prussia, had been annexed by the victors.

In so far as Hitler wanted to redress the wrongs done by the Diktat of Versailles he therefore found much sympathy at Dartington, though not elsewhere in Devon. Dartington opinion did not change very much between 1931 and 1938 when the school staff sent a letter signed by all of them to the *Torbay Herald* (of all the influential journals in the world) asking that Hitler's just grievances over Versailles should be remedied. The signatories were mostly pacifists. Some rather miraculously combined being pacifist and communist at the same time, or at least used the two labels at once. But Hitler was not at all an appealing victim for Dartingtonians, or almost anyone else in Britain, to sympathise with. The more damage he did once he was in power, from the Reichstag Trial to the first Pogroms, the more frightening he became and the more wracked the Elmhirsts and the rest of us became by the dilemma – could we still sympathise with the German demand for justice now that Hitler was its champion? They too, if they had been active members of the Labour Party, could have been told, as George Lansbury was told by Ernest Bevin at the 1935 Party Conference, to keep our bleeding consciences to ourselves.

In enunciating the policy for the school, Curry's starting-point was the self-evident fact that people did not resist war but delighted in it. 'When war breaks out the crowds in the streets are not funereal. For the most part they are wildly elated.'[8] People backed their own country whatever happened and whatever it did, right or wrong, and then were ready to prove their unthinking loyalty by committing any atrocity asked of them. In the first book he wrote at Dartington, *The School and a Changing Civilisation*, Curry was already advancing the arguments he so much developed when at the other end of the decade he became one of the leaders of Federal Union:[9]

> If some morning one read in the newspaper that a man had stuck a bayonet into the stomachs of six other men, turned it round, and pulled it out again, kicking the men off if necessary, one would infer that this was the act of a dangerous villain, and one would expect him to be punished for a singularly brutal crime. The same act committed in war time, against men no more deserving of maltreatment, may become a normal part of one's duty. Compassion, sensitiveness, and horror of cruelty cease to be virtues, and become vices likely to hinder the march towards victory.[10]

How is such callousness induced? Curry's answer was crisp and confident: by the orthodox school, the seedbed of all the sins which men are only too eager to commit on behalf of their own herd. Although he had been to a grammar school himself he too, like Leonard, was thinking far more of public schools. Public schools were flourishing. They were schools which boasted of their Officers' Training Corps, they were schools where there was a considerable worship of 'good form'. They fostered an unreasoning loyalty to themselves and, from there, by an easy transition, to King and Country. 'Loyalty, which means supporting your herd against the other herd, becomes the most fundamental of the virtues.'[11] Worse still, they relied on violence to secure conformity:[12]

> Most children are habituated from their earliest years to the notion that the simplest way to get people to do what you want is to threaten them with violence if they do not. Why be surprised, therefore, if adult society is shot through and through with the same point of view?

Bill was later to recite, almost as though he had written it himself, the preamble to the constitution of UNESCO – 'Since wars begin in the minds of men, it is in the minds of men that the foundations of peace must be constructed.'[13]

After that the prescription for his Dartington almost made itself. The school would not be a copy of society as it was but as it should be, or as Sanderson of Oundle put it, a 'miniature copy of the world as we would love to have it'.[14] A place not for competition but for co-operation; with no more than a minimum of rules; without corporal punishment. Add co-education and an agnostic attitude to religion, and that was Dartington as he conceived it. His hope was that in such a setting children treated with 'reverence' would grow up more creative, more fulfilled and therefore more tolerant, above all people committed to settle differences by reason instead of force. Curry did not ask what would happen if such schools became the mode in England without any similar revolution in the Fascist countries.

The book from which I have been quoting was published in the year when German rearmament started in earnest. Curry pitched it all just right, both in some ways more utopian than anything conceived of before and more fully worked out in intellectual terms. Something new and exciting was clearly needed to replace the Elmhirsts' main idea up to then. The conjunction of estate and school, with children learning alongside adults who continued to do their ordinary work, had been called in question.

John Wales in his report of 1 March 1930 on 'The Present Position of the School' spoke of the unrest amongst the staff. 'Was there anywhere a clear plan for the school? Who really was in charge?' he demanded, as successive generations of people at Dartington have continued to do. He also noted that the estate was no longer the school's hinterland. The formation of the company – Dartington Hall Ltd – in 1929 had made commercial viability the first goal for all the departments. The company could not be lumbered with the education of funny-looking and funny-behaving children. How could the employees revere children at the same time as balance sheets? Slater, the Managing Director, had been saying, 'very fairly', that 'the Estate was on the way to being a flourishing place with a growing outside reputation, and that it would be disastrous for this to be imperilled by being mixed up with a questionable school'.

The Bonsers had recognised problems. Workmen were not necessarily good teachers. It was good luck if they were. Albert Fincham was an excellent one. With him a child could hardly go wrong. But others did not have the skill or patience to hold the interest of a child. Some of the teachers were not all that keen either. Making arrangements for children to join in the work of the departments could be a taxing business. With a big effort it might still have gone as well for others as it seemed to for me. Leonard was sorry his original scheme – Siksha-Satra translated to Devon – was to be abandoned. But he half recognised that he and Dorothy, by establishing commercial departments, had set in motion the forces which would reproduce in Dartington the specialised institutions which had proliferated generally. Once, he had not wanted to use the word 'school' at all. Those days were past.

Curry did not mind the title of Director of Education although he kept it right out of his new prospectus. He was willing to look after the budget (or try to) of Margaret Barr in the School of Dance-Mime and of the other adult educators on the estate. But he was not really interested in much that went on outside his school and he was glad to put an end, formally, to the use of the estate as its workshop. Some children, like me, had kept going with their poultry and gardening until he arrived and administered the final chop. Instead of making use of the farms on the estate he went the other way and actually started his own school farm, made up of twenty-five acres, a small herd of cows and a string of ponies.

The separation made Dartington more like other schools. So did the emergence of more orthodox teaching. The advocates of learning by doing had not admitted that learning itself, even of ancient history or biochemistry, *can* be a sort of doing, an affair of the mind as alive as anything people do with their muscles. Even Curry was not prepared to follow that line of thought very far. He would no doubt have agreed with his teacher, Russell, that the individual should 'mirror' the world:[15]

> The man who holds concentrated and sparkling within his own mind, as within a *camera obscura*, the depths of space, the evolution of the sun and planets, the geological ages of the earth, and the brief history of humanity, appears to me to be doing what is distinctively human and what adds most to the diversified spectacle of nature.

To become that kind of mirror the individual needs a great deal of painfully acquired knowledge. But to have put much emphasis on that would have changed the school too drastically. Curry was not ready for it. He had, however, been a teacher of science at Bedales and Oak Lane and henceforth it was to figure along with other conventional school subjects. He carried further the change already set out in the 1929 prospectus when he said in 1932 that 'Normally each boy or girl would take English throughout the school, take Mathematics at least through the elementary stages, take at least one foreign language, some History, some Geography, and some Science', all leading up to the School Certificate examination of the Oxford and Cambridge Joint Board.[16]

Curry also extended self-rule. He did not do this at once. Mistrusting the extent of children's tolerance of each other, he feared self-government would mean too much government:[17]

> I was convinced that a school community could run satisfactorily with far fewer rules than are commonly thought necessary and with practically no punishment, and to begin with, therefore, the system was a sort of philosophic anarchy tempered by benevolent despotism.

When he was persuaded that the children themselves no longer believed in punishment he began to introduce a measure of democracy. While numbers were still small he called general meetings of the whole school. As numbers increased he instituted in the Senior School a School Council consisting of elected representatives chosen from the houses and the teaching groups, the teaching staff and the domestic staff, with the children in a voting majority. The chairman and secretary were always children. In order to spread the experience of Council membership as widely as possible there was a rule that no one might be a member for more than two consecutive terms. The Council met weekly, heard complaints, made practically all the rules and dealt with offenders. The character of the institutions changed after that. In 1944, for instance, a School Cabinet was set up in conjunction with the Council, and in 1952 the Moot and an Agenda Committee which was later renamed the Senate. In one form or another self-government has survived. But in Curry's time, although he had no vote, only a voice, that was usually quite enough. He was so persuasive in argument that the 'Dartington contradiction' between self-government in theory and paternal government in practice was hardly apparent.

All in all, Dorothy and Leonard were convinced enough by Curry's ideas and practices to be quite happy to hand the school over to him. They had plenty to do without having to run it as well as everything else. The next few years justified their trust. There was a general air of optimism.

This was partly due to sheer physical expansion. New building is usually a tonic, and one that both Leonard and Dorothy were always ready to prescribe for themselves. At the time they appointed Curry they decided to have a new school halfway down the hill to the village, at Foxhole. Curry was still in Philadelphia and Leonard chose the architect, an Englishman this time. The same Mr Delano who was the architect for the Willard Straight house also designed the first completely new school buildings at Aller Park. They were a failure. He hardly left his New York office while the building was going up and chose, from that distance, a local stone whose properties had not been tested. The walls leaked. It took years to deal with them. Despite many efforts they are still not quite damp-proof in the 1980s. The Englishman was Oswald Milne, appointed by Leonard on Fred Gwatkin's recommendation. His standard neo-Georgian Foxhole was not at all to Curry's taste. For the moment Curry was in such high esteem with the founders that he was able to bring in William Lescaze as his own chosen architect from Philadelphia to build his own headmaster's house, at High Cross, just above the senior school at Foxhole, shown in Plate 24, and then other buildings for the junior school at Aller Park.

The neo-Georgian touch made it look more like an ordinary school and the numbers of children rose steadily. When Curry arrived the school had 51 pupils – 17 in the nursery, 11 in the Kindergarten, 11 in the Junior School and 12 in the Senior School. In the following two years the roll more than doubled, to 124; and went on rising all through the 1930s.

Curry himself did a lot to publicise the school by his writing and speaking. Dartington became quite famous, for its school. It was not yet known for anything else. The school was an attack on an important English institution. People who favoured public schools or their counter-parts in the state sector were affronted by almost all Dartington stood for. But a minority of the intellectuals already mentioned, predominantly left-wing in the 1930s, who were also critical of the Reptons and Manchester Grammar Schools, were as much *for* Dartington.

The new fame attracted new teachers. Curry sacked all but two of the old staff upon being appointed himself. His writings, his speeches and the general reputation of the school, as it began to get one, enabled him to replace them with ease, and to add to their number as the size of the school increased.

W. H. Auden came to look over the school and did not stay to teach. But Curry was more successful with Raymond O'Malley, teacher of English in the Senior School and later at Cambridge, who was certainly the best teacher I ever had. I can remember still the delight of spending a whole hour with him trying to find the most apt word for the noise a latch makes as it falls into place when the door is shut. Click? Clank? Rattle? Clatter? Tickle? Scratch? Rankle? Runkle? He later on became known through his books to a much wider audience.[18] Boris Uvarov taught science and later compiled the *Penguin Dictionary of Science*.[19] Our maths teacher was Oscar Oeser (one of the former students of Professor F. C. Bartlett of the Psychological Laboratory at Cambridge) who went on to become Professor of Psychology at Melbourne University. Bridget Edwards in the Junior School was, in Curry's words, a teacher of 'great skill, experience and resource'.[20] Bill Hunter was not just a good geography master; he interested a whole group of pupils in the making of movies and set up the Dartington Film Unit. Staffed entirely by children and other amateurs, it made a series of films not just on geographical subjects but on bird trapping (for the British Ornithological Society), timber and trees (for the Timber Development Association and the Forestry Commission) and on the school and estate. The films were widely used in other schools for teaching purposes. The Unit was carried on by John Wales after Hunter's death in the war.

David Lack taught biology and also carried out at Dartington, with the aid of his pupils, the research on the life of the robin which brought him world fame amongst ornithologists. The territories of robins as he marked them out in the 'woodland, orchards, quarries and fields at Dartington' are mapped for eight different periods in his Penguin book.[21] The main fieldwork was done between 1934 and 1938 before he left to become Director of the Sir Edward Grey Institute of Ornithology at Oxford. Leonard was particularly interested in Lack's work. Birds remained one of his passions. He therefore got to know Lack better than many of the new staff. After Lack died, Leonard wrote to his widow:[22]

> David was a great teacher, devoted to his pupils and to his birds. What a delight it was to go with him and a bunch of kids to the Exmouth estuary. We actually witnessed a swoop by a peregrine at a redshank. . . . I loved my time with him always. The last occasion was when he lectured at Foxhole on the swifts and asked me whether I still ever saw the peregrine flying over. My answer was, 'No, not often, but the best place for watching is from the station platform at Totnes where you may see him come over between Dawlish and Dartmoor.' Two days later I got a postcard back. 'Saw the peregrine from Totnes Station.'

For the rest of his life Leonard carried on the Lack and the Storrs Fox tradition by gathering around him a few children from the school who were or could be interested in birds. One of these, David Cabot, wrote after he left the school that:[23]

> I still retain a very vivid impression of the times you used to bundle us all into your car, shower binoculars upon us, and then take us over to Powderham and Turf for bird watching. Strangely, it had a most powerful influence on me.

Leonard paid David £5 a year for some years after he left for looking after the nesting boxes for the swifts at the Hall, rather as he himself had been paid at St Anselm's. Leonard took another pupil, Nicky Beeson, on a caving expedition and made a great impression. When a lot of Junior School children in their pyjamas were watching Francis Chichester on TV, the age of the hero was mentioned in his favour by one of the commentators. Nicky said:[24]

> Well, I know someone who I think is a good deal older and of course sailing is not in his line, but if it were I bet he could have done it too, and even more – and that's Leonard.

Birds and the many other interests encouraged in the school were all reflected in the summer camps which were one of the high points of the year. Curry told the Trustees what children did in the summer of 1937:[25]

> Mr Lack took a group of biologists, Mr Hunter took a geography group in the Quantocks, and made a detailed map of the area near the camp, Mr Uvarov took a survey group in South Cornwall, Mr Neylan took a group to Stratford to see several performances, Mr Wales and Mr Seyd took a group mountain climbing in Wales, another group went to Ireland, and those who wanted something less strenuous just camped with Bridget and Magda in North Cornwall. Two boys went off walking on their own.

The fame of the school also attracted parents, including some well-known ones who helped to draw in yet others. Bertrand Russell I have already mentioned. He sent his two children by his marriage to his second wife, Dora. Kate and John had been pupils at Beacon Hill, the school on the South Downs which their parents had started partly for them in 1927, in the same way as the Elmhirsts had started Dartington partly for Dorothy's children. In 1934 the marriage had broken down and, although Dora kept the school going, Russell wanted his children to move and in choosing Dartington began the relationship which mattered so much to Curry. Curry wrote 'As I think I told you when you were down, I always think of you as my spiritual father and there is no one whose children I should think it a greater privilege to have.'[26] He got drawn into the wrangling between Dora and Bertie. Dora wanted sole custody, which would have meant the children not coming to Dartington, Bertie a continuation of joint custody which meant they would. Curry was taken aback to be asked to support his hero. 'My feelings about you over a long period of years make it a somewhat embarrassing service: after all curates do not write testimonials for the Archbishop of Canterbury!'[27] He wrote one anyway. Russell spoke several times at Sunday Evening Meetings: some of his subjects were 'The Revolt against Reason' and 'The Case for Complete Pacifism'.

Bertie seems to have made the right decision. Kate Russell has written about her period under Curry:[28]

> Dartington was a very good school. The headmaster believed in reasonableness, moderation and sound learning, and his belief set the tone for all of us. We had a high degree of self-government and individual freedom, which rarely degenerated into aimlessness or licence, either in class or out. There were fixed rules, based on age, about bedtime and pocket money and a few other matters, but beyond that most things were managed by the enlightened commonsense of the school council. . . .
>
> We were indeed happier than at Beacon Hill. The teaching was good, the atmosphere pleasant, and Dartington had one great advantage over Beacon Hill: enough money. . . .
>
> The cultural advantages of the school, however, were not the cause of my contentment; other aspects of school life meant much more to me. I could live detached there, with nobody making emotional demands on me, retiring to my own room with a book whenever I liked and following my own routine, which could include or exclude others as I chose. Classes were interesting, living was comfortable, the environment was lovely and it was a blessed relief to be able to live for a while away from the unspoken demands of home and the frightening tensions of Beacon Hill.

Bertie and his third wife, Peter Russell, also sent their son, Conrad, to Dartington after the war, but he did not like it and was taken away.

Matthew Huxley, who arrived at about the same time as the first Russell children, did not get on quite so well. His father, Aldous, thought it would be right for his son, since the school was 'an experiment which may, I think, turn out to be something very remarkable'.[29] But Aldous was distressed at the outcome, for Matthew. Curry within limits allowed children to work when and at what they chose. Matthew chose to concentrate on carpentry. To Aldous this was not in line with family tradition and he said as much to Matthew who thought he had been getting on very well with his woodwork. At the Elmhirsts' request their mutual friend, Gerald Heard, persuaded him (despite the woodwork) to speak at a Sunday Evening Meeting. He took as his subject 'Religion in the Modern World'. Dorothy was especially interested.[30]

> Men still desire [he said] to be ascetic, still feel the urge to give to something greater than themselves . . . they still hunger for certainty . . . the emotional substitutes for religion still persist but the

intellectual premise in which the emotions could express themselves
has been taken away. Those who in the past have worshipped
supernatural beings now find it impossible to believe in their existence
. . . and set up natural beings who are worshipped instead. . . . Our
problem therefore is to find a new religion that is better than the old in
that it accepts science, and better than the new substitute. We want to
live in a world that makes some sort of sense, we want to find some
intellectual basis for our efforts, we want to know where we stand in
relation to the universe at large.

Aldous and Maria, his wife, let Matthew stay at Dartington for just
over two years. They then decided all at once that he was not learning
enough and that Curry's assurance that he was overcoming the handicaps
of an unsettled childhood and the disadvantages of his trilingualism were
not convincing enough. Matthew was taken away at the end of the summer
term in 1936, without being told he was not to return. Curry pointed
out that the usual notice was required, subject to a penalty. Aldous would
not pay.

Russell and Huxley added, if briefly, to the appeal of Dartington. So
did Freud. Ernst Freud, the architect son of Sigmund, was one of the first
refugees from Hitler's Germany to make an appearance ar Dartington.
Indeed he entered his three sons before finally leaving Berlin. They all
started at the same time in the autumn of 1933. The eldest, Stefan, stayed
two years, Mrs Freud writing to Curry that 'He goes on asking to visit a
school with some competition in the work and with organised games.'[31]
The youngest son, Clement, and the middle son, Lucian, stayed somewhat
longer, into 1936.

Freuds left. Others came: Ben Nicholson and Barbara Hepworth,
Victor Gollancz, Jacob Epstein, Richard Church, Stephen King-Hall. The
new school had made it in a certain circle. Dartington became an interna-
tional school and so remained until later when British were mixed with
German, Austrian, French, Swiss, Polish, Spanish, Persian, Danish, Dutch,
Egyptian, Italian, Indian and, of course, American.[32]

Some of the parents were still decidedly odd, their children likewise.
As a precaution, Curry insisted as an article of policy that parents should
come and be interviewed before their children could be admitted. He could
tell more about suitability from the parents than from the children.

It is so important, however, [said the prospectus] that we should have
the full understanding and co-operation of parents, that we make it
our practice to admit no child to the school without having seen, if
possible at the school, both parent and child.

Curry had a long-lasting correspondence about problem children with another headmaster of a progressive school, A. S. Neill of Summerhill. Quite a number of pupils came to Dartington from there – Dick Jennings, the co-owner of my Triumph, was one – and a few moved in the opposite direction. Neill came to talk at a Sunday Evening Meeting in 1933. Curry put up good-naturedly with fairly constant sniping about all the money he had to waste. To Neill the only thing really wrong with Curry was Dorothy:[33]

> Why the hell should Dartington Hall have more than it needs and Summerhill have to go on living on wish-fulfilments? But in heaven I'll have a golden harp while you and Dorothy will be in hell playing mouth organs.

Curry later admitted that on one point at any rate 'my friend A. S. Neill' was quite right.[34] When Foxhole was opened Dorothy bought for each house a set of gaily-coloured Swedish crockery, with a different colour for each house. The crockery was all broken within a few weeks though the house names derived from the cups – Blue and Green, Red and Yellow – have lasted into the 1980s. Dorothy's sofas and chairs lasted only a little longer than the crockery. Curry said that Neill could have saved Dorothy the money if only he had been asked. He knew better than she how destructive children can be.

Neill envied everything about Dartington – Curry's luxurious house; his Auburn Straight 8 with which his own Hillman Straight 8 bought for £75 hardly compared; the marvellous washing-up machine in the school kitchen. He wrote to Russell about 'our millionaire friends at Dartington Hall':[35]

> I am always sending on the needy to them . . . hating them all the time for their affluence. When Elmhirst needs a new wing he writes out a cheque to Heals . . . Heals! And here I am absolutely gravelled to raise cash for a pottery shed. Pioneering is a washout, man. I am getting weary of cleaning up the mess that parents make. At present I have a lad of six who shits his pants six times daily. . . . His dear Mama 'cured' him by making him eat the shit. I get no gratitude at all . . . when after years of labour I cure this lad the mother will send him to a 'nice' school. It aint good enough – official indifference or potential enmity, parental jealousy.

Curry assured Neill that 'If I come across a sick millionaire you can count on me not to be God in the mangerish.'[36] The sort of criticism Neill made of 'the millionaires' was of course made by many other people as well, usually behind their backs.

The two heads passed on staff and parents to each other, Neill usually trying to say something soothing to people he had no jobs or room for:[37]

> Fact is that crowds of people come round asking for jobs and to get rid of em I say sweetly: Now there is Dartington Hall. What about applying there? Sometimes I send em to Beacon Hill. Most of em I send to hell but not audibly.

Sometimes Curry did offer help, even if it wasn't financial. Neill wrote:[38]

> I have begun a play analysis room for the smaller kids, but am handicapped by lack of proper or rather improper material. You should have seen the salesman in Abbatt's toyshop when I asked him where I could get a doll with an unscrewable penis. Finally he suggested Paris.

Curry replied 'Sorry about the doll. Shall I get you one made in the workshop here?'[39]

Leonard and Dorothy knew most of the staff, some closely, and invited them to have meals at the Hall, which remained the social centre of the estate and the meeting-place for people from all departments. They knew some of the parents well, and sometimes their children too, especially their own relatives. The children of brothers Vic, Richard and Pom, and sister Irene Rachel, all went to the school. They still had Bill and Ruth there. From them, when they saw them, they heard about the school. But they had little hand in the making of policy. Curry made the decisions and informed them and the other Trustees afterwards in the quarterly meetings which he tried to keep as formal as possible. He never forgot the lesson of Oak Lane.

Dorothy was sometimes driven to direct action. She could not persuade him to plant anything in the courtyard at Foxhole, so she planted a walnut herself in a holiday when he was away, and waited to see if he would remove it. He did not. The tree is still there. Curry could afford to make an exception now and then.

They were brought back into policy not by Curry but by a conflict between him and the commercial departments. Far from wanting school and estate to be one, some of the salesmen said that the separation could not be sharp enough for them. This was not a new view. We have seen that Slater was anxious about the effect of the school upon his customers as early as 1929. The anxiety got a new edge in the mid 1930s when people in the commercial departments were making more of an effort than ever to become viable and meeting more resistance than ever from their competitors. Mr Harrison was the Sales Manager. He considered his staff, shackled by the school's anti-establishment reputation, had an almost impossible job to do. He told Curry that the school could be closed down if it took action against someone who libelled the school in public, and lost. The school was already, he wrote to Slater, costing the company £1,000 a year, 'the fee we pay the Editorial Section of the London Press Exchange merely as a defensive measure, to prevent, as far as we can, the Yellow Pages from champing its jaws over sensational tit-bits scented within the Schools'.[40] He did not know for how long the defences would hold.

Slater wrote to Curry that:[41]

> Your staff and pupils could also help by avoiding as far as possible that exhibitionism which is always present in those who are being different intellectually without conviction and certainty. You for example do not find it necessary to dress in a slovenly fashion or to bathe naked in the Dart in order to convince the world that you are intellectually free.

There was something in the complaint. We children welcomed the notoriety that our naked adolescent bodies seemed to attract. We bathed nude in the river Dart as a matter of course, and to delight the outsiders would sometimes jump high out of the water when the train from Totnes to Ashburton passed by. It was said that local people crowded the train in the hope of seeing something they could wax indignant about. It was also said that Slater went to church in a bowler hat to make up for the children who stayed away from church with nothing on.

Feeling in 1936 was running high on the estate partly because Curry had in the previous year parted from Ena. Divorce was rare then, especially amongst headmasters. This did not prevent Curry from falling in love with one of his staff, Marsie Foss, a housemother. He left Ena in High Cross and went to live in the school with Marsie, his stated view being that the children should be able to see what a really happy marriage was all about. Practically everyone on the estate took sides for or against Curry, almost all against. Dorothy and Leonard wavered, being persuaded in the end by the argument advanced by one of Curry's influential friends from America, Mrs Sidonie Gruenberg, that the school could not afford to do without such an outstanding head. Gerald Heard and others took the opposite view and did not come to Dartington again.

I should also explain as background to the crisis that if Curry was in some respects less radical than his predecessors at Dartington, in two other respects, co-education and religion, he was more so. People did, of course, get more worked up about these two questions than about anything else to do with the school. The one sentence from Dewey often quoted was that 'the only way to prepare for social life is to engage in social life'.[42] If one believed that one could not at the same time believe in segregation. Social life amongst adults (said Curry) is not just for men or just for women; nor should it be just for boys or just for girls on their own. Boys and girls at school should be together as naturally as they are in the family.

Dorothy and Leonard were ready to accept such an approach even at the beginning when they wanted to set up a Girls' Department. But the school as it was then would have come under Curry's fire as not much more than one in which both boys and girls happened to be enrolled but one which kept them apart for much of the time. He was more sarcastic about such schools even than about segregated ones. One school he knew allowed girls and boys to talk to each other only for forty-five minutes after supper; in another they could go for walks together provided they were brother and sister or first cousins; in another they could walk together only in one particular field overlooked by the staff common room.[43] Such absurdities made the association of boys and girls artificial and self-conscious, defeating the purpose of having them together at all.

In Curry's view the only proper position to take was that the two sexes should live quite naturally together, with none of the sense of sin and adventure which will always be brought on by suspicious adults worrying about the mischief they would get up to if left to themselves. Their rooms should be next to each other and no one should be prevented by any school rule from going in to any of them, night or day. So one of his first and most controversial actions was to transfer all the girls from the Girls' Cottage into what had been the Boys' Building. Dartington became the first boarding-school in which boys and girls had the same living quarters. Labels, 'Boys' and 'Girls', were removed from anywhere in the school: everyone should share the same lavatories, bathrooms and showers for the positive benefits it would bring. It is 'desirable for boys and girls to see each other wholly or partially undressed as, so to speak, part of the day's work'.[44] This on the grounds that 'nudity, after the first few occasions, diminishes rather than increases sexual interest'.[45] I, among others, did not find it so.

This openness was made acceptable to Dorothy and Leonard and to some but by no means all of the other residents by the persuasiveness with which Curry could excel once he had convinced himself. One of the arguments which appealed to Leonard, remembering Repton, was about the homosexuality rife in ordinary boys' and girls' schools. Curry referred to it in the way conventional then as a 'danger', but one greatly diminished by co-education. In co-educational schools there is hardly any homosexuality or lesbianism. Curry admitted there was a risk that a girl could become pregnant but it would always be small as long as he and his staff managed with the aid of older pupils to build up a tradition which excluded sexual intercourse. He was not necessarily against instant traditions, taking the American rather than the English side when he told, and laughed at, the story about the American university which erected a notice – 'From tomorrow there will be a tradition in this university that nobody walks on the grass.'[46] On the question of sex he also comforted himself, and perhaps the Elmhirsts, with the belief that 'for the majority of boys and girls below the age of eighteen, certainly in a climate such as we have in England, conscious desire stops short of complete sexual experience'.[47] Curry was proud of the fact that at Dartington there were hardly any pregnancies amongst Dartington girls and seldom any pornographic drawings or writings on the walls of lavatories or anywhere else. He was fortunate in the paucity of pregnancies; it was not for want of trying.

Religion was hardly less combustible a subject. Since religious instruction was incompatible with the scientific temper – hardly a single proposition of a religious nature can, he would say, be regarded as 'true' – he did not want to have any of it, though he was always happy to discuss any sort of religious question with anyone. He considered children his natural allies: 'religion is not a natural appetite in children'.[48] His God was not God but reason, and he hoped his children would worship at that altar as passionately as he tried to himself.

The controversy over these two issues was never hotter than in 1936. After the onslaught led by Slater and Harrison Curry agreed to defend his stand at a Sunday Evening Meeting on 1 March 1936. Curry said, a bit oddly, to Slater:[49]

> Owing to the quarantine restrictions the children are not at present attending the Sunday evening meetings, and I am taking special advantage of this opportunity, which may not recur for a long time, to talk with greater freedom on the school than I like to do when the children are present.

It was a very tense occasion and sad for those who still cherished the original notion of school and estate as one. Dorothy and Leonard were in the audience, appealed to by both sides, by people from the commercial departments who hoped to convince the founders that they were right, and by Curry who was sure he could convince them they were not. He was not so sanguine about his outright critics. As it turned out, even Harrison admitted in a Memo entitled 'Recipe for "Curry" – All Hot!' that:[50]

> For almost three hours, I suppose it was, I sat, in a very uncomfortable chair, without once recharging my pipe, in enjoyable surrender to the charm of his spell-binding eloquence and brilliant display of mental agility.

Curry charmed: he did not convince Harrison and his friends. But he again convinced Dorothy and Leonard. They made it clear to Slater and Harrison they would have to put up with the school, nudity, co-education his attitude to religion, Curry all hot – the lot.

The following years justified their confidence. By the autumn of 1938 the enrolment was 194 (131 boarders and 63 day). The school was nearing economic viability, the staff eager and devoted, the children by and large full of zest. Bertie's prophet was in his prime.

The school was prospering, under a head who kept Leonard and Dorothy out. They had plenty of other things to do. Dorothy had the arts to engage her and Leonard, amongst other things, education outside Mr Curry's self-governing empire. Education elsewhere, in Devon generally and the Totnes area in particular, was not a new interest. Even while Leonard was shaping the early school at Dartington he also had a hand in organising courses in 1928–9 for rural teachers, the subject being handicrafts not as they were but as they could be taught in ordinary Devon schools. These were the first of literally thousands of courses for teachers and others held at Dartington, most of them after the Devon Centre for Further Education was set up in 1963, many others before as well. Outside Devon, Cambridgeshire was the county that appealed most to him and to Dorothy. Henry Morris was at that time setting up the Village Colleges. The Elmhirsts made several grants to Morris to help the Colleges get started. It was about the Cambridgeshire vision as much as anything else that Leonard was writing when he said:[51]

> Further, or adult education, as it is being framed today, can help each
> one of us to sharpen our sensibilities, to deepen our powers of
> compassion, to enlarge our capacity to comprehend and to broaden
> the horizons of our consciousness. In the struggle to find a new
> meaning to life, a new sense of inner peace, of calm and strength, we
> may, as invited guests upon this lovely earth, learn how to leave it
> before we depart a trifle more beautiful, more humane, more full of
> joy, serenity and love than on the day we arrived.

Education should, therefore, feature the arts above all else. The chance came to conduct a welcome experiment in Devon when F. G. Thomas was appointed the County's Tutor Organiser for the Workers' Educational Association. He believed in music and drama as much as the Elmhirsts and, against much opposition but with financial and moral support from Dartington, did a great deal in the 1930s to foster the arts in villages and small towns throughout the county.

In 1937, a year after Curry defended himself with such flair, Leonard was elected an independent member of the Devon County Council for the Harberton District and became a member of the Education Committee. He was also a member of the Council of the University College of the South West. It showed how much local opinion had changed in little more than a decade. He remained a member of the Education Committee for nearly thirty-five years and eventually became the Chairman both of the Managers of the Dartington Primary School and of the Governors of the Comprehensive School in Totnes.

There is very little, either in the County records or in Leonard's own, which show what he actually did apart from attending these interminable meetings. There is no sign of the man from Siksha-Satra, no voice appealing for fundamental reform. The impression is rather of a squire who has settled down amongst his fellow-squires to do his duty by the county as they were doing theirs, and as others had done for many centuries past on and, in Leonard's case, off the field of war.

Most of the members of the Education Committee were Conservatives, many of them diehards. Leonard on the left, if the Council could be said to have one at all, was always ready to work with the more open-minded of the other members, especially on the issue which came to dominate educational politics in the post-war years, comprehensive schools. Leonard was fully for the new schools, large as they were to be. 'I see no solution', he said, 'to some of our social ills except by comprehensive educational provision so that all children feel they are members of one society even though their capacities and gifts vary enormously.'[52]

Much of his time as Governor of schools in Totnes, and eventually Chairman of the new Comprehensive School Governors, was spent on this same issue. Many of the Foundation Governors of the old Grammar School in Totnes, Kind Edward VI, were opposed. As in other parts of Britain, they did not want their school to lose its identity by being merged into the new comprehensive. Leonard had to face them down and at the same time get as much as he could out of the county in the way of resources for the new school. On one occasion he used a trick he had learnt in India: he invited Viscount Amory, who had been Chancellor of the Exchequer and formerly a fellow member of the Devon Education Committee, to open the new school and then urged upon everyone the necessity to exert themselves to impress the big man. He wrote in April 1971 to the Chairman of the County Council:[53]

> During my years in India I learned what a difference it could make to
> road repair if you were blest with a visit from the Collector, the
> District Commissioner, the Provincial Governor, and if you were
> lucky enough, the Viceroy, from whose visit you could expect a
> completely new surface to the road! In inviting Viscount Amory to

come and open the new set-up for Edward VI Comprehensive we had hoped to have everything decent and in good order.

Two and a half weeks later Leonard was able to write again to the Chairman, 'There is now such an army at work on the surrounds of Edward VI Totnes, and a promise of everything being in shape for the opening, so that I can only think some Vice-regal pressure has been in operation and I am most grateful to you.'[54]

Peter Snape, the headmaster of Totnes comprehensive as it came into being from 1964 on, describes Leonard as a supportive chairman.[55] When visiting, he would always talk to children, cleaners and other domestic staff. But he was curiously uninterested in the internal working of the school except for corporal punishment which he was, of course, very much against.

The war was an almost crippling blow to Curry's school, at any rate after May 1940:[56]

> During June I doubt whether there was a single day on which I did not receive a telegram or telephone message announcing some child's imminent departure, usually to Canada or the United States, but sometimes to South Africa and in a few cases simply to Scotland or the north of England. In a little more than a month we lost nearly seventy children.

Under pressure from parents Curry contemplated moving the whole school to the USA; this was stopped by exchange control. The drain of pupils, and staff, continued. Everyone had to take salary cuts. Curry himself acted as headmaster, school bursar and maths teacher. The situation was saved only by the evacuation of schoolchildren from London. Emil Davies, the Chairman of the Education Committee of the London County Council, was at Dartington attending one of the Fabian Summer Schools, which had become an annual event, at the very moment when the Army was threatening to requisition the Junior School. Davies arranged over the telephone that the LCC should forestall the Army by taking over the Junior School immediately; the Army had the Dance School instead. Curry got a substantial rent from the LCC for the rest of the war. The main school just survived.

One of the main problems was Curry himself. He had put so much store by peace, and the role that education could play in preserving it. Now here was another war. But he was not completely put down – there was one last hope: that some kind of world government would emerge from it. He diverted his energies from the school to politics, and specifically into

Federal Union. This organisation had quite a following while there was just a possibility, however faint, that national governments might be prepared when the war was over to surrender some of their sovereignty to a supra-national federal world government, which would put an end, in Wells's words, to 'this drilling, trampling foolery in the heart of Europe.'[57] and the world. Curry wanted advocacy of a world government to play the same kind of part that propaganda for the idea of a League of Nations had between 1914 and 1918. 'It must play indeed not the same part, but a better part, for the League we got was only half a League.'[58]

Curry was away a great deal from Dartington:[59]

> Indeed I was so active that the School became jealous and resentful, and once when I returned from a long weekend speaking tour I found the School covered with placards saying 'Down with Federal Union. We want our headmaster.'

There was sufficient discontent for the Trustees, this time mainly Dorothy, to make their presence felt once again. She wrote about it to Leonard who was in America:[60]

> Precious One,
> Tex McCreary brought your letter of Jan. 21st, and then a week later came the earlier letter of Jan. 16th, and now I have Beatrix's cable from Pasadena, so I feel I can follow you all around the world. Anyway, it's a comfort to feel you will be turning eastward again once you leave California. . . .
> Well, Dartington — what news have we from here? First of all Trustee meetings which were long and arduous, and on one occasion rather painful. Pom and I felt impelled to challenge W.B. because the evidence had been coming in from different sides that the school was in a most unsatisfactory state. Pom started off boldly by saying that he felt W.B. had lost interest in the school and that Federal Union claimed his main attention. Bill was struck dumb and couldn't answer for a moment, then he defended himself somewhat heatedly by saying the future of Europe for many generations depended on the settlement after the war, and that education was too slow a process to effect this particular settlement. Then I went on to say that we felt disheartened at our inability to draw out from Bill at Trustee meetings anything save the old factual reports. Why could he not give us some idea of the experiments being tried — of what new insight had been gained, of the modifications of policy taking place in his mind — and so forth? The school, I said, at the start had seemed to contain the germ of something vital, but within a short time it appeared to settle down into the comfortable ruts of its own making and has never seriously

questioned its premises since – nor its processes, nor its products. I don't believe Bill has done any real talking about the school for years, and I told him so.

Well, the result was electrifying. Bill went as white as a sheet and became angry in the way that a child becomes angry and almost cries. We carried on the discussion a little longer and then he left, agreeing to bring the kind of report we wanted at the next Trustees' meeting. But of course it was a vote of lack of confidence in him and he felt it, and I don't know what the result will be. I wish he could give his full time and attention to Federal Union, but unfortunately the organisation is broke and quite heavily in debt, and I'm afraid financial arrangements do, of necessity, determine one's actions. Well, there it is, and I haven't had any talk with Bill since because I myself have been in bed for ten days.

After that Curry did spend a little less time on Federal Union, though he did not give up the one or two lectures a week he gave to servicemen in Southern Command.

One question much discussed generally as well as in the debates leading up to Butler's 1944 Education Act and in the 1944 Fleming Report, *The Public Schools and the General Educational System*, was about the relationship of independent schools like Dartington to the State sector. I was a Trustee by then as well as a keen supporter of the Labour Party. I was much in favour of closer links. I could not get anywhere with Bill. If not suspicious of world government he was very much so of national government. His reason was always the same – the State would discourage experiment. Quite apart from anything else, mixed houses and mixed bathrooms would never be allowed in a State-supported school:[61]

> I naturally wonder a good deal about the place of this school in the post-war educational system. . . . Much as I regret present class divisions in English education, I cannot convince myself that we have yet reached the stage when an all-embracing State system will permit, let alone encourage, as much experiment and diversity as are needed. Many of the most important advances in education have been done in schools for which no Board of Education, or Director of Education, could have taken the responsibility at the time they were initiated. . . . I hope very much therefore that schools like Dartington will still be able to enjoy an independent existence, making their own independent contribution to educational progress through the freedom to practise ideas and methods not yet widely or generally approved.

His hope was borne out. The school slowly recovered after the war, reaching a peak of 218 pupils in 1951. Two years before that the Trustees finally persuaded him to put up with an official inspection by a team of His Majesty's Inspectors under an agnostic, Mr Christian Schiller. I remember arguing to a stony-faced Bill that surely it would be valuable to have ideas from outside, from people who had great experience of State schools. Their report, when it came, may have been more disappointing to Curry than he was ready to admit: the Inspectors did not seem shocked or even surprised. They thought it on the whole a good school with a good head. 'Carefully unobtrusive, his influence is the more widely felt. He knows every boy and girl, and they know him. With humbleness of mind, singleness of purpose, and complete integrity, during eighteen years he has created this school; his powers are still at their height.'[62]

Their really wounding criticism was about the standard of teaching. Work not good enough, they said. 'There is only little of distinction and much that is mediocre.'[63] Raymond O'Malley in English and Margarita Camps in biology were outstanding. Not so many of the others, which they attributed to the low salaries and to the lack of anywhere for teachers to go if they left Dartington. The school was not part of a more general system; which was how Curry wanted it.

Curry wrote the formal minute of the special meeting of the Trustees called to discuss the HMI's report in July 1951:[64]

> Mr Young felt that the whole issue of the place of experiment in the State system, in a world in which it would become increasingly difficult to find private endowment, had not been faced, and he felt that we, at Dartington, should make our contribution to the study and solution of these problems. The Headmaster replied that at the moment his nose was much too near the grind-stone for him to be able to give adequate thought to these large questions, and that, in any case, he felt too much out of sympathy with the planned egalitarianism towards which we appeared to be moving. He felt that the problems created by this new trend were the business of those who believed in it.

In arguing for his independence he was again thinking just as much of the Trustees (joined now by a tiresome ex-pupil) as of the State. He became more querulous with them, almost always about the problem which like a toothache kept him awake at night – money. The Trustees' endowment of £15,000 p.a. was the same as before the war but only in money terms. Inflation had eaten it away:[65]

> We have equipment and a general set-up all designed and developed on the assumption of an endowment with a *real* value of £15,000

pre-war. Our present endowment has a pre-war value, I suppose, of around £6,000.

He repeated this whenever he met the Trustees.

Gradually, the zest went out of him. The school was right in the mid-1930s; to restore it to that state, and then to maintain it, was the proper task of the post-war years. Writing in 1956 he said, 'The views which I set out in *The School* in 1934 are still substantially my views in 1956.'[66] If he was constant about that, his health deteriorated – he had diabetes – and he complained more and more of tiredness. His morale fell lower and lower. He wrote:[67]

> The grim realities of the Cold War and of inflation, coupled with the apparent inability of governments to deal effectively with either; the reaffirmation by the Great Powers, through their insistence upon the veto of the Security Council of the United Nations, that they still regarded themselves as Greater Breeds Without the Law, and the consequent failure of the United Nations to become even a faint shadow of that approach to effective World Government upon which so many of us had pinned our hopes; the failure to secure agreement upon armaments together with the appalling competition in ever more frightful nuclear weapons; all these, I think, subtly infected our morale. A world which appears to be so obstinately uninterested in its own survival is one in which long-term hopes for our sort of education are hard to sustain.

He had by this time wholly lost the confidence of the Trustees, and his staff were at sixes and sevens. His resignation, which was virtually enforced, came in 1956 and he left Dartington in 1957. He died in 1962, as a result of a traffic accident.

His departure from the school was at Easter. Raymond O'Malley stood in as temporary head for one term until the new heads, Hubert and Lois Child, arrived in September. The Trustees were won over by them as individuals and responded too to their belief that it was[68]

> psychologically right that both a man's and a woman's point of view should be represented at the head of affairs, not only where matters of general policy are concerned but also when, in considering the personal problems of individual children, the insight and influence of one or the other sex may be of paramount importance.

Hubert (Hu, as he was known to everyone) had been a Superintendent of Education in Northern Nigeria and a teacher at Bedales before joining the staff of the National Institute of Industrial Psychology. From there he moved to the London County Council as its Senior Educational Psychologist. Lois also taught at Bedales and, at the time of the appointment, was a lecturer at a teacher training college.

For Dorothy and Leonard the biggest change was that they were welcomed back into the school. They again felt they could walk around anywhere, at any time, without anyone frowning at them and that if they met either of the heads they would be invited in, smilingly. Curry wanted to keep them out to preserve his own independence; the Childs wanted them in to learn from them and also, perhaps, to gain their moral support for the changes *they* wanted to make. Many of the staff appointed by Curry stayed on. There was no general sacking on this occasion. In returning to the school the Elmhirsts did so with some confidence because at long last the fortunes of the Trustees had changed for the better. We did not receive any new endowment but we were given freedom to use our existing capital and income as we liked, and to invest the capital as we thought fit. Up to then the entire capital had been invested in 5 per cent debentures which could not themselves be touched, all under the control of Dorothy's American Trustees rather than those at Dartington. At last there was money for expansion. Capital could be drawn on if it promised to yield a good return.

The result was a wave of new building. The Childs chose a brilliant young architect, Michael Smith, who had been on the staff of a local authority which at the time had a great international reputation for school building, the Hertfordshire County Council. He designed for Foxhole a new assembly hall, a new library, a new boarding-house for thirty-nine additional boarders, a new dining-room, new laboratories and a new art and craft block which were all opened in September 1961. Aller Park got a range of new buildings as well. The plans and then the buildings helped to raise morale. So did the decision to raise salaries to the Burnham scales in force for teachers in State schools.

There was certainly a need for a new impetus. In Curry's last years the numbers of senior boarders had been dropping fairly steadily. One boarding-house at Aller Park had been closed for want of demand. There were no sure bookings for September 1958 for either the Senior or Junior Schools. Too many difficult children had been admitted because of the financial need to fill as many places as possible.

The new heads quickly showed their spirit by confining mixed nude bathing to before breakfast. There was uproar amongst existing and former pupils alike. Nude bathing was for the opposition a symbol of all that was good in the school. The Childs persisted and brought in other changes as well. Their underlying view was different from Curry's:[69]

Paradoxically, perhaps, the adult has to learn to reaffirm his authoritarian role. His efforts to divest himself of this led to the rediscovery of the young child's primary need for security and consistency, for protection against being overwhelmed by his inner feelings, his inadequacy and his lack of experience. The adolescent, left to find his own way, was seen to find it all too easily back to childhood rather than along the steep path to adulthood.

It was decided that classes should not be missed, that academic standards should be raised and that bedtime rules should be strict – all without abandoning the central Dartington belief in the value of freedom, co-education and self-government. The Elmhirsts were now consulted before each of these changes happened, not told afterwards.

The mixture restored the fortunes and the morale of the school. The number of pupils rose again and again. More than ever went on to university. The feeling of dissolution gradually disappeared. Everyone realised that the school could continue, and grow, without a Curry to fan it. The school was in far better shape when, owing to Hu Child's illness, he and Lois resigned in 1968 than it had been when they came.

The Childs' successor was Royston Lambert who took up his post in January 1969 after I had introduced Dorothy and Leonard to him in Cambridge. Aged 35, he came straight from a Fellowship at King's College. He had been in charge of the Research Unit established there to enquire into Boarding Education. He had lived for six weeks in the Senior and Junior Schools at Dartington as part of his research; he had won the confidence of some teachers and many children. Leonard was for him almost from the moment they met. Leonard wrote to Mr Schiller, who became a friend after his inspection of the school was over:[70]

> We know he has not had any experience as a Headmaster before and that in the realm of matrimony he so far has only 'prospects', but we need to relate much more closely to the State and its operations if we can without losing any of our essential freedoms.

Dorothy was equally taken by him. The new head had charm, fluency and, above all, ideas which flowed as freely as from Bill Curry in his prime.

Not the least of his attractions was that, when he went through the papers in the Records Room I have been using, he proclaimed that in his view the first phase in the history of the school, up to 1930, was the really exciting one. He therefore set as one of his aims the need 'to reintegrate the school with the community, which in the years 1926–30 it had been created to serve'.[71] This was not just flattery, though Leonard *was* flattered:[72]

Royston Lambert is trying to refound our School as it was once
conceived of – 1st Prospectus of all – typed by Dorothy under the
Luccombe Oak. 'This School is for Adventure!' was the first
sentence – in 1926. How people laughed at us. It will be a reality one
day.

Lambert proceeded, with bravura, to take a number of steps to reduce
the school's 'isolation from the community which Dartington shared along
with nearly all the other boarding schools we visited on our research'.[73] He
saw an extraordinary opportunity:[74]

Here, under the direction of one body of trustees, and close to each
other, were on the one hand a collection of educational
units – school, college, adult education centre, youth club and so
on – and on the other a set of industries, among them farms, forests,
building contractors, furniture factory, textile mills, sawmills, plant
hiring works, all containing young people on apprenticeships and
training.

The two should be brought together again. Children who did not know
what they wanted to do when they left school should come to Dartington
for a year and in that time have the chance to sample work in one or other
of the industries at Dartington until they found the job they liked, while
also continuing with their broader education.

The first move was to link the school with the Gardens Department
where there was already a horticultural training scheme and with the
Woodlands Department which had a similar one for woodmen. Both kinds
of trainee came to the school for their basic teaching and some pupils from
the school went to live in the garden hostel. Dartington pupils were also
encouraged to use the local youth club and joint teaching in some subjects
was arranged with the comprehensive school in Totnes. For a period,
unfortunately only brief, it looked as though Lambert was going to bring
together not just school and community but several different departments
and stages of Leonard's life. It was not to be, not yet anyway.[75] Too much
opposition built up in the Gardens and Woodlands Departments. 'The
failure occurred partly because I was too precipitate.'[76] The plan had to
wait until after Leonard was dead and Lambert resigned before it was put
into practice in Roy Robinson's Work Experience Scheme, which later still
became incorporated into the school under John Wightwick's head-
mastership. It was fitting that eventually the new trainees were housed in
the 'sixth-form college' which had been built at the Postern, as the Old
Parsonage was now called. This had enabled the sixth form to 'live in
conditions of greater freedom than in any other school in the country and
greater than most students in residential universities'.[77]

Almost as appealing to Leonard was Lambert's other chief initiative –
the link with the State system well beyond Totnes:[78]

> Frankly I was not prepared to become head of a school solely for the
> education of the rich. Apart from my own delicate moral scruples on
> the matter, the conventional English boarding school which operates
> as a sort of closed ghetto for children of one social, economic and
> cultural group seemed to me to be profoundly non-educative,
> confining instead of enlarging the experience of young people and
> their awareness of their society and its diverse cultures.

The school eventually chosen for the link was emphatically not for the
education of the rich. It was Northcliffe, a mixed comprehensive without a
sixth form in a grim mining town at Conisbrough in Yorkshire not far
from the other Elmhirst estate. Pom and Gwen Elmhirst played a leading
part in the experiment from the beginning. So did Sir Alec Clegg, then
Chief Education Officer for the West Riding and later a Dartington
Trustee himself. The West Riding put in some money, Dartington a good
deal more. In the first two years of the scheme about sixty pupils, all
eleven-plus failures, came to Dartington as full-time boarders and 400
others from Northcliffe for shorter spells. Dartington children moved in
the other direction, for short courses, and stayed at 'The Terrace' (a large
house bought by the Dartington Trustees very close to Northcliffe) which
was also a base for local children to live in and come to. Lambert and many
other people at Dartington agreed that the Yorkshire children brought a
new variety and stimulus into the school, which benefited the ordinary
middle-class children, and that the newcomers also gained in self-
confidence and adaptability.

'One can say already and with confidence that the progressive educational approach applies as much to the working class adolescent and to the
less able child as to those presocialised and highly able.'[79] Unfortunately
the main scheme did not survive the destruction of the West Riding
Education Authority by the wild reformers who did more damage to local
government in the early 1970s than anyone could have thought possible.

Lambert also opened another outpost in a much less probable place,
in the tiny peasant village of Scopello in the north-west corner of Sicily.
Students were prepared to go there by intensive study of Italian and Sicilian
and of the history and culture of the island, and by learning a craft designed
to be of use in the village. When all was at its best[80]

> The craft centre run by the students in the village, serviced by a
> brick-built kiln in the open air powered by an old vacuum-cleaner,
> now recruits numbers of young people from the region. The group
> also not only tends its own fields but works in those of all the other

peasants for nothing. Out of this practical gesture, out of the presence of the group in the village with no material gain of its own in view, out of the reconciling and negotiating work of the group leader, the peasants in the village, who have never until now been able to combine for any positive purpose, have formed an agricultural co-operative, acquired government grants, bought a tractor in common, and are working together in amity – a state which five years ago seemed impossible.

That centre too had, for financial reasons, to close in the end.

The Elmhirsts were not original in their utopianism about education. It has been the affliction or benediction of educators and their popular followers that they have hoped for too much. Only identify a fault in behaviour and out comes (or used to come) the secular faith so characteristic of the century. Are people too acquisitive? Too loosely attached to their marriages? Too self-interested? Too destructive – especially the teenagers who have become the butt for so much adult wrath? Too bored in front of their TV sets? Too whatever it is – the stock reaction is that it is all the fault of education, implying that if only education were 'better' people would be less acquisitive, selfish, destructive. Admittedly, the true believers in this particular faith do not usually go on and say just what they recommend should be done in the name of education to correct the multiple abuses which totter our tottering world. They are believers all the same. Or used to be.

The faith has diminished since the 1920s and 1930s. At that time education beyond a very bare minimum was reserved for a privileged minority. In 1924 Tawney wrote his then celebrated pamphlet for the Labour Party, *Secondary Education for All*. The 'for All' was so revolutionary because so far from all had it. Once they did, in some distant future, and when what they got was improved in quality, when the whole nation was educated, then what miraculous transformations would be possible! Then, the proposition had not been put to the test. Now it has, up to a point and without any obvious access of virtue.[81] Many would argue the opposite. The Elmhirsts, along with everybody else, would be less hopeful if they were starting again.

It is the same for many particular expressions of the faith. Russell said that 'Nationalism is the chief force impelling our civilisation to its doom'[82] – even more true today, when nationalism is nuclear nationalism, than it was when he wrote it. Curry not only saw the truth in that but also believed that a new, humane, rational, tolerant, co-operative school in its Anglo-American setting could take the fire out of nationalistic feeling and then, having shown the way, persuade other schools to do the same until in the end, but before the end, the world would be led into the green pastures of peace by a troop of high-minded headmasters. Happy head-master himself until another war took the edge off his idealism.

The school in the first phase which Lambert so much admired was different. In summarising the initial approach of Dorothy and Leonard the key sentence in the *Outline* was the one I have already quoted. 'For us it is vital that education be conceived of as life, and not merely as a preparation for life.' The emphasis there was not on what children would become, war-makers or peace-makers, hate-makers or love-makers, top masters or bottom hewers, but on what they *are*. This belief was less utopian than the secular faith I have just been talking about. The school was not seen as the gateway to the new Jerusalem. It could itself be the new Jerusalem. The central belief has under four heads, including the present one, John Wightwick, who was appointed shortly before Leonard died, remained the same. The focus has been on what children can be now, not on what they could be or will be when grown up.

CHAPTER 8

THE LARGER SPIRIT
THAT INFUSES
ALL LIFE

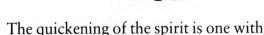

The quickening of the spirit is one with
the great mystery of life.

Outline, 1926

There was in Dorothy's mind and to a lesser extent in Leonard's no sharp break between their interest in the arts and in education. Education was to heighten awareness of the world, not just the world of fact but of the imagination. Education had to work through the arts, just as the arts had to work through education.

The balance between the two was tilted first one way and then the other. In 1926 the principal part was given to the school, and in the *Outline* arts were confined to the paragraph, though a long one, recalling the Tagore period:[1]

> To release the imagination, to give it wings, to open wide the doors of the mind, this is perhaps the most vital service that one being can render to another. So often we attempt to stifle the dreamer for fear that he may never grow up a practical man, and yet it is to the man of imagination that we owe all that is greatest in human enterprise and discovery. Here we enter a realm beyond the bounds of livelihood and the discipline which it imposes, a realm where the child is entitled to the utmost respect, the utmost freedom. We can neither chart his course nor attempt to guide his adventuring. There are few children to whom the realm of emotional expression, the world of the spirit, is not a very real thing indeed. We may stimulate by discussion, by the promise of regular opportunity for music, singing, and every creative activity, we may encourage, we may sympathise, we may attempt to provide the means and the opportunity, in fact a congenial atmosphere, but if we are honest in our desire to give the child freedom to grow, we shall be very careful not to superimpose our own

rules, creeds and theories. The quickening of the spirit is one with the great mystery of life.

This freedom was not to be manipulated by adults – a paint brush stuck into an unwilling hand, a flute pushed between unyielding lips. Children had more to give than need to take; they had in their state of innocence a gift of expression which society gradually robbed them of as they grew up:

> Shades of the prison house begin to close
> Upon the growing Boy.[2]

Children were born, if not good, at any rate with an aesthetic sensibility to the world around them which they would naturally express through boisterous dancing, singing, splashing about with water and colour. The belief that all children were artists, and few adults, was part of the idealisation which helped to justify child-centredness.

School it might look like; in aspiration it was an educational experiment in which everyone, without being cut off at any of the conventional ages – starting at 5 and finishing at 16, or 21, or 30 – was to remain throughout life a learner, especially in the arts. This being so, it was only logical to make the head of the school also head of the arts with a wide responsibility for adults as well as children. Wyatt Rawson doubled as the Adult Education Officer, and adult education was in large part to do with the arts. The Elmhirsts became grander with Bill Curry and, as I said, appointed him Director of Education. He was in that capacity supposed to embrace the arts. Much as Dorothy's heart was in it, his was not. He preferred to be headmaster, and the increasing number of artists no doubt preferred him that way too. As Director, he lapsed. This did not mean the arts lapsed. Far from it. Indeed, for Dorothy at any rate, once the school was held within the grasp of a head who disliked being bossed about by other adults just as much as he wanted his children to dislike it too, her centre of interest switched away from the school and into the arts. If the 1920s was the decade of innovation in education, the 1930s was the decade of the arts.

It was as if in the course of time the deeper interest was revealed. There were three strong reasons why it should be so – family history, personality and (most important of all for Dorothy) the alliance of art not with education but with religion.

Dorothy was bred a patron. In her eyes this was her father's favourite role. Distasteful as were some of the ways he earned (or amassed) his money, splendid were the ways he spent it, on a Van Dyck, or a Kreisler, in the tradition of the Medicis, the musical princelings and dukes of Germany, the rich merchants of Holland or even (closer to one of Dorothy's abiding interests) the Earl of Southampton.

Dorothy did not need to earn the money. Nor did she need to justify having it except by spending it wisely. I do not remember her ever defending her right to her wealth or her children's right to inherit as she had; she took it for granted.[3] I do remember, though, in Leonard's study, hearing the famous words of Southampton's protégé from *Troilus and Cressida* once spoken by some actor with great gusto over the wireless:

> The heavens themselves, the planets, and this centre
> Observe degree, priority and place,
> Insisture, course, proportion, season, form,
> Office, and custom, in all line of order. . . .
> Take but degree away, untune that string,
> And hark what discord follows. Each thing meets
> In mere oppugnancy.

Dorothy and Leonard nodded slightly, and smiled, and said nothing.

If she had been pressed to mount a defence I think one point would have been that without great concentrations of money much great art would never have been created at all. The human race would then have been the loser. If the twentieth century was a leveller she did not have to conform completely to its demands before being forced to.

> In the period that concerns us here [said Herbert Read], there is one broad economic development of the utmost significance – the gradual decline of private patronage due to the severe restrictions imposed on the accumulation of wealth. Private collectors still buy works of art in the open market – to that extent there are still patrons, if only through the medium of the art-dealer. But they no longer *command* the artist like the monastery or the guild, the court or the castle.[4]

The Elmhirsts were patrons wealthy enough to defy the trend. From 1925 until the war they bought one work of art after another. Their approach was described in the catalogue of a public exhibition of their purchases arranged at Dartington for the 1951 Festival of Britain:[5]

> Mr and Mrs Elmhirst do not consider themselves as art collectors. They have bought works of art to furnish and decorate their house, collecting many of their most interesting objects either in the course of their travels or in their desire to help and stimulate living artists and craftsmen. They have not specialised in any one branch of art, nor have they set out to acquire 'museum' pieces. Almost everything they have has been bought for its intrinsic interest or appeal to the eye.

They had very few of the kind of pictures Dorothy's father delighted in. The old things they purchased were pots; some medieval French and Byzantine sculpture; some drawings by Turner and a painting by Constable; several West African masks; a good deal of walnut furniture made between 1680 and 1730; and a very large Persian rug decorated with the 'Tree of Life' design.

As a collector, however much she disliked the word, Dorothy was in a relatively small way following her father. But she, and Leonard, were also different from him. William C. Whitney, like the other robber barons who were at the same time collectors if not connoisseurs, bought Old Masters painted for his counterparts in the past. The Elmhirsts were more like them: first-time patrons. They bought from living artists, generally trusting their own taste rather than relying on experts to buy for them, though sometimes taking advice from friends, as over their large collection of Christopher Woods. Jane Fox-Strangways advised them to buy paintings by him when he was still young and his pictures still cheap. The most they paid for one of the Woods was £150 to Mrs Wertheim in London. In 1931 Dorothy was taken in hand by Mark Tobey. She wrote to Leonard:[6]

> Today we have been to three galleries with Mark and he has discovered for himself and for us a young English painter who is the real thing. His name is Ben Nicholson and his pictures are on view at Arthur Tooth. In a moment of weakness I bought two, but I think you will like them and they are very cheap.

They also bought a Picasso, a Rouault, a Sutherland, several paintings by Winifred Nicholson and Frances Hodgkins and Cecil Collins and sculpture by Gaudier-Brzeska and Henry Moore. They also invited living artists to their court. William C. Whitney had introduced famous musicians into his palace. Dorothy was far to outdo him, by bringing people – and not only in the theatre – to stay in 'The ancient manor of Dartington Hall' to fight back (with her money) against 'The capture of the professional theatre by moneyed interests', as she put it in the prospectus she wrote for the Chekhov Theatre School.

Leonard was very much the prime mover in one department – pots. Bernard Leach, the potter who was not famous when they first met him in 1925, started him off. He and Dorothy wanted advice about starting a pottery for the school. Leach said, 'For your students you should have a small collection of pots by living British potters and some from China and Korea and Japan.'[7] To begin with, Leonard relied on Leach telling him which ancient Chinese pots of the Han, Wei, Tang and Sung dynasties to buy. Leach took him to a dealer in the City. 'I must have gone with Bernard

2 or 3 times, but only once on my own, and I dared purchase nothing without his guidance.'[8]

Gradually he began venturing out on his own. At the end of 1926 he bought a Korean jar in a secondhand shop in Torquay – a bargain at five pounds, he was later told by an expert – and from then onwards he built up a collection of old Chinese items and pots by the best Japanese and modern English potters such as Bernard Leach himself and Michael Cardew. Jane Fox-Strangways, who was the resident potter, produced her pots in the Dartington Hall Pottery Department, a converted stable below the present Barn Theatre. The demands of her kiln for electricity plunged the rest of the courtyard into darkness when it was being fired.

Leonard would lead visitor after visitor to his tall glass-fronted cupboards and talk at length on the history, techniques and aesthetic qualities of the pots in them. In 1967 he gave a special guided tour to David Leach, potter son of Bernard, his wife and a Japanese visitor. Afterwards he began a record of the collection in a specially bound large notebook, from which this information comes. David Leach wrote:[9]

> It was a great treat to go over all those pots together, and although you first showed some of them to me some thirty three years ago, I have never seen half of them before or so thoroughly. . . . Once you got the bit between your teeth you were difficult to restrain in your enthusiasm! . . . You begged for little bottle vases to hold single fritillaries, or other single flowers for the small space that is left for such things on your desk, and these I am making in porcelain.

Dorothy's interest in the pots was more as larger receptacles for Emily Thomas's elaborate and brilliant flower arrangements.

The second factor in Dorothy's concern with the arts was her personality. The account I have given of her so far may not have made her shyness sufficiently plain; it became more pronounced after Willard's death and, even more, after her marriage to Leonard and her move to England at the age of 38. Even in the country regarded as the citadel of reserve, people commented on it. She was said to be 'inhibited'. If the onset of shyness was gradual so was a coincidental growth of interest in the arts. They had the power to release in her feelings that would otherwise have been buried. She became most aware that this could happen in one of the happiest periods of her life, when she was a student at the Chekhov Theatre Studio, as she explained to Leonard in a letter she wrote to him on 5 November 1937. Michael Chekhov, its Director, was called Misha:

> Misha has been making so clear to me this business of going out. The other day he asked us to imagine the moment in Hamlet when

Claudius falls down before the crucifix and cries – 'My offence is rank ...it smells to Heaven', and then, one after another, to show him that moment. I felt that my performance was so weak that I asked him afterwards where the weakness lay – was it in my will or my feelings or my imagination. He answered – in none of these regions. But he told me a certain weakness lay in outward expression – that some fear seems to get hold of me, and that a long habit of suppression and the willingness to remain passive prevents my getting everything out. After he said this to me such a strange thing happened, I began crying, and I cried on and off for the whole day. But I believe that some deep inhibition has begun to break, and Misha with his clairvoyance has done more than any psychologist. Why is it necessary to learn the origin of one's bad emotional habits provided one can learn how to deal with them! And that's what Misha is doing for me – and oh Jerry, I owe it all to you for urging me to go on and to Biddie for drawing me in at the start. How can I say thank you, my Sweetheart, for understanding so deeply what I needed.

The third reason for her devotion, though linked with the second, was the most powerful of all – the common ground between religious and artistic experience. This is of such importance, to Dorothy in particular, and through her to some others at Dartington, that it requires some explanation.

There was no kind of organised religion in the new community, early and late, and the Elmhirsts were much criticised for it. Why would they not come to church? Why did they not insist on it for their pupils? Questions asked not once but a thousand times. 'Irreligion' became a prominent feature of Dartington's (and hence of Dorothy's) public image.

The practice, in the school at any rate, was spelt out in the revised school prospectus of 1929. The criticism made it necessary to be more specific than in the first *Prospectus* or the *Outline*:

No specific religious instruction of any sort is given; there are no school prayers, nor is Sunday treated in the school as more than a day of rest. If a child wishes to go to church, every opportunity is given, and a church car is run each week for those members of the community who care to use it. We take this attitude because we feel that growth in this, as in all else, can come only through the desire for growth: for the quickening of that desire we can be indebted in many ways – to Drama, Literature, Music: to life in the community, which inevitably, as time goes on, makes us realise the existence of other values – values which are neither personal nor material.

In the 1920s 'free-thinkers', so called, were still as much abused in Devon as elsewhere. If the parsons had been less hostile, or more willing to listen, there might have been more of a dialogue. This had to wait until much later. Ironically, in 1948 Dorothy was told (without being invited) that she had been unanimously co-opted as a member of the Dartington Parochial Church Council. She declined:[10]

> I am not an orthodox church member, in other words I am not a communicant nor a regular church attendant nor can I subscribe to some of the dogmas of the church.

She was indeed the most prominent non-attender in the place; yet she was certainly 'religious', in a century where a once-straightforward word has come to need the dress of inverted commas. In this she had in the course of time reversed the conjunction in which she started her life, if we leave aside the possible early influence of Ma Bonne and her tiers of candles in the darkness of St Patrick's Cathedral. She started as a church-goer without being obviously much more. Diary after diary dutifully records the fact, usually without comment. Her parents were the same, Flora having adopted her husband's Episcopalianism on marriage.[11] It was automatic for Dorothy to be confirmed at 15 in 1902, by the Bishop of New York himself. She would certainly never have let that fact slip out to the rector of Dartington.

The change in her, away from orthodox churchgoing and towards the spiritual side of religion, as she might have put it, did not come with her marriage to Willard, nor was it obviously much influenced by the more general changes in society, though she was of course affected by them. Willard was more interested in the painting in which he had such skill. What made the difference was his death, and the misery and ill-health it caused. This was the greatest shock of her adult life, recapitulating and intensifying her earlier grief over her mother's, her stepmother's and then her father's deaths. I have already mentioned the séances that followed.

After the séances, she attended not church but a course of lectures given by Dr Fosdick, a popular Presbyterian preacher of the day, given at the Union Theological Seminary! The exclamation mark is not mine but Dorothy's in a letter to Leonard and itself suggests she may have been on the way to recovery.[12]

In one of her commonplace books she prescribed the sovereign remedy for the anxiety from which she suffered so much: laughter. She goes on about Fosdick, 'I hope it will incidentally arm me for my contests with you!' Another exclamation mark! Leonard had been brought up on the Bible; that was what the lectures were about. Her sheaf of typewritten notes still exists to prove it. But they end with the Old Testament, suggesting that either she or Fosdick did not stay the course.

Her friends were her main comfort. She had two very religious ones whom she saw a lot of in the early 1920s, Ethel Derby and Ruth Morgan.[13] Ethel Derby gave her some prayers which she kept all her life, copying them into *My Special Anthology* which she put together during the Second World War:[14]

> O Lord Jesus Christ, who didst reveal Thyself more fully to Thy disciples after Thou wast taken from them; Grant us faith to believe that no separation of time or place can sever Thy servants from their eternal union with Thee who art with the Father and the Holy Ghost one God, world without end.

Ruth Morgan (after whom her second daughter was named) did not approve of her dabbling in spiritualism but she always hoped Dorothy would accept Christianity.

Throughout most of her life she could recognise a few other religious believers like herself. She made no attempt to impose her views, or even let her views be known to people who might not be sympathetic. She maintained, except with other initiates, a sort of layman's vow of silence appropriate enough in a country where most people do not anyway like talking about their deepest beliefs or even pretend not to have any. Such hints as I have about her religious ideas come from the letters she exchanged with some of her intimates and from her conversations as reported by Margaret Isherwood.

In what sense was she religious? It is difficult enough for anyone to say for himself, let alone for another. The meaning given to the word is so personal. It certainly was with Dorothy. I can only describe some of the forms taken by her religious interests. The first thing to say is she was clearly a humanist – that is someone who accords respect – but preferably more than that, reverence – to man. Beyond that she was also a 'nature worshipper', that is had reverence for all life, not only human, and even for things which are no longer alive or never were, and in this was like many descendants in England of the Fellowship of the New Life.

That is only a bare beginning. To justify the use of the word a person needs to recognise that behind the surface of things, outside and inside human beings, is some all-pervasive spirit. That spirit can take the form of a personal God, a superhuman being worshipped as having power over nature and the fortunes of mankind. To Dorothy it did not: that was clear. She was sufficiently of the twentieth century to have put that idea aside. God was much more the Holy Ghost present in everything than he was God the Father, or God the Son.

Yet she was prepared to say she believed in God. She wrote to the Rev. R. A. Edwards, one of the most sympathetic of the rectors of Dartington, who arrived after the initial hostility in the neighbourhood had largely evaporated:[15]

> Religion plays a central part in my own life – in fact it is the basis from which many other beliefs spring. I believe in God; I believe in a universe that has purpose and meaning, and I believe that the spirit of man is connected with a larger spirit that infuses all life. Prayer and meditation are means by which my own spirit finds its way to this larger life, and I cannot imagine any wholeness of living without this contact with a spiritual world that is all around us. But the church fails to hold for me these deepest experiences of the human spirit. I find its forms dead, and I believe the insistence on the historic Christ is a real stumbling block. . . . From the point of view of gaining spiritual help or insight I admit I find this elsewhere – I find it in talking with you and with other friends who are attempting to live the life of the spirit, I find it in books, in poetry, in nature, in art, in the goodness of human beings, and in any experience that opens my heart to reverence and to the wonder of life.

A vital question is how people convince themselves if they do that 'the spirit of man is connected with a larger spirit that infuses all life'. Many people would recognise they have their occasional moments of hyper-perception or enlightenment, or as some would go so far as to say, extrasensory perception, when they love deeply,[16] or when they look out of the window and for a moment everything has the clarity of crystal; or when they are moved by a work of art or the play of nature.[17] Most would not create any general attitude to life out of such chancy experiences, marvellously welcome though they are. But Dorothy regarded them as having a common form, of feeling alike in so far as on each occasion her spirit seemed to be coming from the deeps of herself and achieving a temporary union between the spirit inside and the one outside.

She sometimes wrote about the more or less common-or-garden experiences she had of this kind, for instance one night at 'The Chalet' in Cornwall in 1967:[18]

> Impatience nearly deprived me of great beauty last night. Opened my window – could only see lights at Looe and Eddistone – but after *waiting* a few minutes I began to see patterns of light and shade in sky – clouds – stars – clear patches in night sky. Marvellous revelation of pattern.

About a similar experience in the Bahamas in 1959 she wrote a poem:[19]

> I rose this morning with the dawn
> And watched the slow suffusion of the light

Restore to earth the pattern of the whole,
And, in the sky, though clouds obscured the sun,
I knew that he was there. Far, far, above
A great cloud caught the flame
And carried high the flow from far beneath –
This is the way, I thought, God shows Himself to us,
Never directly, since the fire would be too great,
But through reflection of this light in human souls,
And in the whole creation of his world.

She also attempted many times in her life to bring on such experiences deliberately by meditation. On 16 September 1967 she began her morning by gazing long and intently at a flower arrangement by the window:[20]

Lime coloured tobacco plant with wine red small dahlias. How incredible tobacco plant is. Long-long neck – with flower at end – simple open form 5 petals and 4 spots in centre – sticky substance. Marvellous invention of the Inventor. I felt at peace after this contemplation – and no urgency to read papers.

In the same direction, but further, is the experience to which the word 'mystical' more properly relates, a state of rapture in which the spirit is liberated from the body. Also further on is the belief, or knowledge as some people would express it, that the spirit from inside is liberated upon death and either rejoins the general spirit or remains as a form of consciousness separate from the body in which it has been incarnate. Dorothy had the kind of experiences – I do not know when – which made both beliefs plausible. She wrote to Michael Straight on 25 November 1958:

It is a revelation of that kind that really changes one's whole outlook on life. Three times, in my own life, it has occurred – a kind of sudden lifting of one's whole being to another level of vision where everything falls into place – where every object, every person, every detail of the pattern assumes an undreamed-of perfection that makes one want to cry. I suppose it is really a state of ecstasy – so intense that one can hardly bear to move or speak lest the spell should break. But, once having had such an experience, one can never doubt again that life and consciousness can be stretched beyond anything we have ever imagined and that death is only a transition to another plane.

Her intense experience of art, especially poetry, took her a little way along the same road. One of its embodiments was the Anthology already mentioned in which she put pages typed or hand-written which she wanted to cherish, poems she would go to sleep on. It seemed to have been kept private even from Leonard for he wrote on the title page after she had died

'Around the years of war I suspect, Dorothy put these together – 1939–1945'. The war may be the reason why she felt the need to keep the poems by her. Her first husband had died in the American Army. Whitney was in the RAF, Michael in the American Air Force. Nearly nine years of her life had been years of war, and another ten a period of recovery from the first or preparation for the second.

Out of some eighty poems and verses, with a piece of prose here and there, all but a handful are 'religious'. There are verses from the New Testament and Psalms:

> Thou shalt tread upon the lion and adder;
> The young lion and dragon shalt thou trample under feet.
> Because he hath set his love upon me, therefore will I deliver him;
> I will set him on high, because he hath known my name.[21]

> God is love, and he that dwelleth in love
> dwelleth in God, and God in him.[22]

Apart from Ethel Derby, other friends are quoted in the collection. Louise Croly, after Herbert's death, became a special friend. She figures in the Anthology with a letter she wrote to Dorothy:[23]

> I have every faith in your wisdom, my darling, and I hope above everything you can continue to keep your sense of something back of all which maintains the system of the universe – the rivers flow in the sea – the seasons come and go, there is birth and death, and you must forget yourself to touch it – and relaxation is one of the answers.

Gerald Heard calls for a training for the Life of the Spirit:[24]

> We can evolve further; evolution is essential if we are to be adequate to face our present crisis; evolution is spiritual – it is a growth in consciousness, in awareness, in power and control through understanding our connection with all life and with the Eternal Life which sustains all life. That evolution is now achieved and achieved only by the skilled, conscious training of some spirits.

The Anthology also contains religious poems by Robert Herrick, Henry Vaughan, William Blake, Francis Thompson, Edward Campion, Helen Waddell, Emily Brontë and Elizabeth Barrett Browning. The only ones without an overtly religious tone are from Shakespeare – Sonnets XVIII, XIX, LXXIII, CXLVI, CXVI.[25] She also quotes Shelley in *Defence of Poetry*:

> Poetry enlarges the circumference of the Imagination . . . (and) strengthens the faculty which is the organ of the moral nature of man, in the same manner as exercise strengthens a limb.

Poetry was Dorothy's bible if the theatre her church: both for her more potent means of communication with the world of the spirit than the music which is the more common pass-key.

She must have kept the book by her, for she copied out many of the entries from it into another book she gave to Leonard soon after her recovery from a severe heart attack in 1955 when she was 68. She enclosed a card:

> This is a personal gift – my Precious One – that I give in all humility – But you know, that in addition to the Lord, it was your love that carried me through. Your Dorothy.

Was she a Christian even if not practising? She certainly regarded Christ as an 'avatar', but only one. She refers in another notebook to the

> manifestations of central power of God – the creator, both wonderful and terrible; avatars such as Christ or Buddha and others – and the Paraclete of the Holy Ghost in all of us. We can give greater life to the Paraclete within us until it takes full possession.

What she was seeking was present in Christianity and in other religions as well. It was not for nothing that she paid for the publication of Arthur Waley's *The Way and its Power*, a book about Taoism.[26]

Since she was so eclectic it is perhaps surprising that at any rate at one time she regarded herself as a Protestant:[27]

> When I hear [she said] that someone like Malley speaks of the possibility of becoming a Roman Catholic I realize more than ever the vital necessity for Protestants to offer an alternative Way that includes all the available knowledge of ourselves with the necessary training and techniques – and with creative outlets as well, in art – in beauty – in harmonious relationship to our whole environment.

She elaborated that last view, without the Protestantism, in a statement she wrote for a Trustees meeting in 1950. Leonard had it printed:[28]

> What after all is the meaning and function of art? Like many other problems, art is subject to a very personal interpretation. I see it as a process of discovery: discovery about ourselves and discovery about life. What an exciting experience it is when, for the first time, we discover the effect of a shadow: how it changes everything around it; or when we realise the gesture of a tree, its inner movement and form; or when we ourselves are swept away by the rhythm that catches us: the rhythm of rising smoke or trees swaying in the wind or flocks of birds or the movement of clouds or whatever it happens to be. We may have looked at these things a hundred times without being really

caught into some fundamental rhythm in nature; and then suddenly a moment comes of intense realisation; one becomes aware of a profound unity and harmony underlying everything else; and it is perhaps this moment of vision that one longs to express in some form of art. Perhaps you will want to express it through dancing: through a form of movement that unites you with this larger movement in nature; perhaps music will be your form of expression – or painting, or poetry. In drama, too, we are able to go out of ourselves: to extend the limits of our own small personalities: to put ourselves imaginatively into another human being, another human situation; to touch the springs of feeling that lie beneath the surface.

As for Leonard, once he had finally made up his mind not to go into the Church, he turned his back on it. He had been through the valley of darkness and had no wish to return. Henceforth, he would use the word 'empty' when referring to the dogmas of the Church, or to some of its most cherished beliefs. He continued, it is true, to think of himself as 'religious' but what mattered was the way people lived, not what they professed. He expressed his mature view in a letter written forty years later to his sister-in-law, Gwen:[29]

> Remember, I still think religion is the most important thing in the world and that it isn't preaching or church attendance, or music, whether organ or strings, or praying, but it's concerned with the way we live, the way we draw guidance from inside ourselves and the way we behave to everyone else, and how to make a unity of these two so that we are happy inside and happy with people and nature in the outer world.

But to say that he had disposed of the problem to his own satisfaction would be to ignore the relationship with Tagore and with India. He was not impressed by Hinduism – Buddhism was more attractive – but he did not get anywhere near to substituting an Eastern for a Western faith. Nor was he taken aback by India as Goldie had been. Forster said of him, 'It was a revelation that man could take such constant and passionate interest in the unseen, and less of a revelation that neither their conduct nor their art seemed to benefit thereby.'[30] All the same Leonard had many vivid moments when with Tagore or at Santiniketan, as he wrote to Dorothy, on 13 March 1922, describing a performance by a vina player:

> Imagine to yourself a cottage with a thatched roof and wide verandah, around it a gravel walk with a carpet spread upon it, and then a parapet, with the open country stretching for miles under the stars on three sides. Through the Ashram trees to the East the full moon of

spring is just rising. Close to the verandah sits the poet in a low chair, and then in absolute silence men come down the road, up the path into the garden, make their bow of salutation and take their seats on the low parapet. A few of us sit cross-legged on the carpet. A group of women in saris flits in through the gate and is going to seat itself shyly out of the way but is beckoned to the verandah behind the poet. Still in the pleasant silence, broken only by the screech of a bat from the distant trees, the vina player arrives with his accompanist . . . this man is an artist and the melody is merely the body into which he breathes his own soul. First he converses with us and keeps up a kind of accompaniment of chords with the tune. Just as when two friends approach, their first medium of approach is conversation, so at the beginning the instrument seems to chatter and then, as the sense of intimacy and understanding increases, all conversation is dropped and the gentle wavering of the tune and the rising and falling of the poet's interpretation achieve such an intimacy that the conversation seems out of place, there is only a holy communion between the soul of the hearer and that of the instrument.

After his Indian period, whatever Leonard believed about religion, he had reached a state of mind with which he was content. He did not speculate about the hereafter. He referred to his own death as 'when I pop off' as if it were no more than catching a plane to an unspecified destination. But he did not exclude prayer. His sister Rachel said he would always stop at Durham Cathedral on his way to Scotland as if he had been a horseman travelling north in the Middle Ages. Once she came on him kneeling by the tomb of the Venerable Bede in that tremendous Cathedral, his favourite in all Europe as it was Dorothy's and is mine.[31]

But he was not a searcher like Dorothy. Their temperaments were different. If they had without questioning remained of the Church, as they might have if they had been born fifty years earlier before that cake of custom began to crumble, he would have been somewhat hearty low church and she introspective high church. He was not inclined to melancholy and she was, which was one of his attractions for her.

If he was not a fellow traveller of the spirit she had, at all periods of her life from 1919 on, other people who were, four in particular: Gerald Heard, Margaret Isherwood, Arthur Waley and Irene Champernowne.

Gerald Heard was not the first of her familiars, by any means, but he may have been the first from England, in England. From Cambridge too, he came through Leonard. He first arrived at Dartington on 20 June 1929; then and even more when he returned in 1932, it was not so much to Leonard as Dorothy that he responded. He was well known at the time as one of the first radio gurus discovered by the newly founded BBC and especially as a populariser of science; but this did not exhaust his range – he was also a historian and student of government and in addition he believed with passionate conviction that man is above all else a religious animal. In 1932 according to the Visitors' Book he stayed at the Hall eleven times, in 1933 thirteen times and in 1934 three times. Usually he came with his close friend, another Christopher Wood, a pianist. They brought with them from London two splendid dark green Sunbeam bicycles with oil-bath chains. Aldous Huxley spoke of him as 'Gerald very Grand-Inquisitorial in sharp profile'.[32] He and Wood were two handsome and elegant young men in light-coloured tweeds. They would glide on their bikes slowly and silently up and down the drive through the garden, crosses between fashion-plates and ghosts. Gerald held regular seminars on 'current affairs' at the school. Even then he was making predictions about the cataclysmic war that was on the way. He told Huxley that the entire might of the British Home Fleet assembled in the Channel would be rendered helpless within one hour by aerial bombardment. Quite often, when he was not teaching, Gerald talked to Dorothy about the subject they both found so compelling. On one matter they were completely in agreement. Gerald thought it pointless to proselytise. 'Those who know don't tell; and those who tell don't know.' The only people one can help or be helped by are the few 'travelling the same road'.[33]

'Mysticism', he said, 'is the only form of religion which can do without a creed or a theology, but must have a method.'[34] Under his tuition she tried to gain experience of the method. She agreed with him that 'One of the weaknesses of organised religion lies in the promise of the Church to do it all for you – prayers, confession, communion, absolution. No great effort required of the individual.'[35] Dorothy did exert herself. She sat cross-legged on the floor for half an hour in the morning and half an hour in the evening. What happened was

> Serenity – then meditation – this world a construction, man's faulty construction – might be the perfect world we dream of save for our inability to grow out of evil and negative passions – greed, fear, malice, pretentions. Coming back from meditation one has sense of returning to darkness. . . . A medium told Gerald the other day he would not live long.

On 30 November 1934 she wrote about a particular day:[36]

> This morning I attempted 10 minutes meditation along these lines and to my surprise found my mind far more composed than on previous occasions – perhaps due to the posture. I was not fully aware of the effects of this quiet period until later in the morning when I realized

that I felt unhurried – most unusual for me – my temper was quiet and my mood more patient – no tensions in my body. Food seemed quite unimportant – and I began to realize why Gerald speaks of requiring so little.

Not long after Bill Curry parted from his first wife Gerald went off to California where he established a religious community. Ena Curry settled near him. Gerald continued up to the end of his life to write to Dorothy, always on the same fundamental subject, and, often, also on the related one of Time. He usually used the capital letter, as he did also for God; like God's opposite, the Devil, Time also deserved its capital:[37]

> I feel increasingly that Time and its symptom – haste – is at the bottom of nearly all our mischiefs. You remember Plotinus thought so – urging that we can and must go neither slow nor fast but exactly on the beat of the great conductor of the orchestra – our eyes upon his wand. I am beginning to realize that if I can see each event as a unique opportunity for immediate understanding and each contact as an offer for creative compassion, then regret and anxiety, remorse and apprehension fall from us and we begin to live in the only place where Eternity is to be found, Now.

That last sentence was typical. He was always 'beginning' to do something, try something or realise something.

Margaret Isherwood, delicate, pretty, at once serious and humorous, was an intimate friend over a much longer span, half a lifetime. As Margaret describes it, she and Dorothy 'recognised each other as kindred spirits from the first'[38] in 1929 when Dorothy visited her, briefly, in America, and then when Margaret came to England that summer. She was offered and accepted the job of head of the school's 'Girl's Section'.

As it turned out, by the time Margaret returned from Philadelphia the job she had accepted had ceased to exist. There was no Girls' Section. Her brother-in-law, Bill Curry, had finally decided it would be a nonsense to have anything like that in a school he meant to be as thoroughly co-educational as his wit and writ could make it. No matter. A quite different job was invented for her, as head of a Teacher Training Department it was decided there and then to set up within the school. Margaret had herself been trained, after she left Cambridge and before she went to America, at the Froebel Institute and so knew about young children. The new depart-ment was to concentrate not on preparing teachers for Dartington's own school but for nursery schools, kindergartens and junior schools else-where. Margaret's students – over 60 between 1932 and 1946 when the department closed – were closely attached to Dartington's own school while they were taking the course. It closed because State schools would not recognise the department's Diploma.

After the closure Margaret returned once more to America to be near her sister, Ena, and also near Gerald. Dorothy was sad:[39]

> Dartington is strange and empty without you. I have the unconscious sense each day that something is wrong and then I remember consciously that you are not here. I miss you even more than I had imagined possible.

They corresponded regularly, amongst other things about Margaret's first book on religion, education and psychology which was later published as *The Root of the Matter*.[40] Soon after she finished Dorothy pressed her harder than ever to come back to England:[41]

> I had been in the USA seven years when I received from Dorothy a letter asking if I would not return to England. She indicated she would see I had somewhere to live. . . . Dorothy meanwhile, unknown to me, was building two bungalows in the large garden at Quarrenden, near Totnes. In one of these I have been able to write quietly and keep in close touch with Dorothy until she left us. At least once a week I went up to the Hall to lunch and to discuss with her what I had been writing.

Margaret said that she, Dorothy and Gerald were completely at one in their attitude. They were all disillusioned with the Church though not with churchmen. Dorothy had high hopes of one of the rectors, Mr Edwards, who had the great advantage of looking like a medieval saint. They all recognised that man needed something in place of church. He had not, and has not, ceased to have religious cravings just because the age is said to be a secular one. They all wanted to keep what was of value in religion, indeed all religions, and to prize as myth that which was of value, but which they could not accept as fact. They were searching for something that was more universally accepted than orthodox Christianity, not in conflict with but congruent with science.

Arthur Waley first came to Dartington in 1933, introduced by Gerald Heard, and then again on many occasions. In 1941 he visited ten times in the year and not all for short periods. He always came with Beryl de Zoete, a dancer who was the author of works on Balinese, Indian and Ceylonese dancing as well as of a book which includes a lecture she gave at Dartington in 1941.[42] They were a striking couple. Arthur was called Waley-Waley-Up-the-Bank by Hiram Winterbotham, manager of the Dartington textile mill, in an effort to make fun of a man who usually looked so serious. Slim and slow-moving (except on skis), withdrawn and ironic, with a high voice, his gentle mask-like face with skin stretched over it like ivory made him look a little like the Chinese poets whose works he translated. He refused to visit the Far East lest his visions of China and Japan should be destroyed. Beryl was in almost complete contrast. She was small, dark, with wizened skin even in the 1930s, full of vitality and snapping humour. In 1940, when London was being bombed, she introduced Frederick Ashton and Robert Helpmann and others from the Sadler's Wells Ballet to the refuge of Dartington and for a period Sadler's Wells had its existence in Devon.

Waley is important here because he brought into Dorothy's, and in this case also Leonard's, stream of thought the influence of China. Religion and humour had been in separate realms for them in a way they were not in China. Both Dorothy and Leonard read a string of his books, starting with *The Way and Its Power – A Study of the Taote Ching and its Place in Chinese Thought*, dedicated to both of them. Something of the flavour of the book and of Waley himself is given by this passage:[43]

> But, says the Taoist, by admitting the conception of 'goodness' you are simultaneously creating a conception of 'badness'. Nothing can be good except in relation to something that is bad, just as nothing can be 'in front' except in relation to something that is 'behind'. Therefore the Sage avoids all positive action, working only through the 'power' of Tao, which alone 'cuts without wounding', transcending all antimonies. The type of the Sage who in true Taoist manner 'disappeared' after his victory is Fan Li (5th century BC) who, although offered half the kingdom if he would return in triumph with the victorious armies of Yueh, 'stepped into a light boat and was heard of no more'.

His widow, Alison Waley, has summed him up by recalling how, shortly before he died in 1966, he was almost overcome with delight at a children's jingle:[44]

> The wind, the wind, the wind blows high.
> The snow is falling from the sky.
> Maisie Drummond says she'll die
> For want of the Golden City.

The fourth familiar was Irene Champernowne. Irene's husband, Gilbert, was the brother of the man who sold the property to Leonard. He would have inherited Dartington eventually if it had not been sold. Born in 1884, he was the ninth child of Arthur Champernowne, 'Squire of Dartington Hall'.[45] He remembered what the Hall was like in the 1880s and his father pretending to be a roaring lion when he chased his children down the back corridor of the Hall's Elizabethan Wing.[46] This background made for a special bond between him and Leonard. But the dominant one of the two, for Dorothy in particular, was not Gilbert but Irene. He was tall, thin and frail. She was as large in personality as in person, with tremendous energy and presence, a psychotherapist who had been analysed by Jung himself, in Zurich, and for twenty years from 1942 practised in Exeter.

On the personal level there was the same early recognition of Dorothy and her being kindred spirits. Their eyes lit up when they looked at each other. As an ardent follower of Jung, Irene was as much concerned with religion as psychology, and with the arts also as a member of the same great trinity. They corresponded regularly. This letter on Good Friday 1952 from Dorothy is typical of many:[47]

> Dearest Irene, as Easter approaches I realize with great joy that new life has come to me and it has come from you. I tried this morning to think of all the ways in which you have helped me, but I saw that behind all the particular things you have done, and the enlightenment you have brought, lies the tremendous quality of what you are yourself. I think I have never known in anyone such love and such power combined. It is, of course, your knowledge that gives strength and direction to the driving power of your love; it is the greatest force for life that I have come across. And Easter will be for me a day of infinite gratitude for knowing you, and for being able, here and there through my contact with you, to glimpse something of the Holy Spirit.

There was a formal break between Dartington and Irene's establishment in Exeter in 1960, but the two women continued to keep in touch. In 1966 Irene left Exeter for Stanton in Gloucestershire. Two years later she wrote[48] that one night

> [I] heard a noise in my study. I went to see what it was – there standing by the fireplace looking down into the fire was Dorothy. When I expressed surprise that she had not told me she was coming from Dartington to see me, I found she was no longer there. She disappeared. I was told the next day over the telephone of Dorothy's death the night before.

Irene wrote to Leonard, 'We shared some realm of the spirit, she and I.'[49]

For many years there was also a link between them on the institutional level. The Champernownes set up their therapeutic centre at Withymead when they first came to Exeter. It was intended as a retreat where people who had had a breakdown or for any reason could not make their way in the ordinary world could get support without being regarded as patients or treated with the drugs and shocks which were the staples of most mental hospitals. Irene and a staff of psychiatrists attended to treatments; another lot of people, trained as artists, did their best to show people how to find themselves through self-expression in the arts, in painting, pottery, music and movement. Gilbert was the administrator. Since he and Irene never wanted to be part of the National Health Service, for fear of being overladen by bureaucracy, they were always short of money – by 1950 so much so that the two of them decided they would have to close Withymead down.

Before doing that they spent a weekend at Dartington. Irene did not dare tell Dorothy about the impending disaster until on the Monday morning, early, Dorothy came in to her bedroom to say goodbye. Dorothy was off to Southampton to catch the boat on yet another voyage to New York. She asked, 'Irene, dear, what *is* the matter with you?'[50] Irene came out with it. Dorothy was immediately sympathetic and asked Irene to speak to Maurice Ash, her son-in-law and fellow trustee of Withymead, later in the morning. This she did. He reported to Dorothy and Leonard and they immediately pledged their support. Leonard told Dr Stevens, a doctor who was himself nurtured at Withymead:[51]

> Dorothy and I were entirely in sympathy with their work; like them, we were convinced of the fundamental importance of creativeness and intuition. When we settled in the wilds of Devon we gave priority to providing facilities for the creative use of leisure: we saw the escape from routine on the one hand and intellectuality on the other as the essential need. We must never allow ourselves to be led down the drain by the academics: we have to use and understand intuition.

Over the next ten years they gave £70,000 to Withymead. The centre was not only saved; it expanded. In the following decade hundreds of people stayed there and many benefited. In its heyday it was a remarkable place, without the rigidities which beset mental hospitals, without divisions between 'patients' and 'staff', but with almost continuous around-the-clock care for all who needed it. The intent was to surround people with an environment which was consistently curative. During this period Dorothy wrote to Juliette Huxley:[52]

> Irene herself is one of the two or three most remarkable women I've ever known – with extraordinary intuitive powers combined with profound knowledge of human beings . . . she was determined to establish . . . a centre where the arts could be used as a means of psychological revelation and healing. And now such a centre exists at Withymead where painting, modelling, music, movement are all used as an expression for the unconscious to make itself known and understood – thereby enabling our inner conflicts to be more quickly reached than through other techniques and balance restored in a

remarkably short time – I only wish I could tell you of some of the people we know who have gone to Withymead and been almost miraculously restored.

To Margaret Isherwood she wrote:[53]

I can't help feeling it holds the key to a whole new development in the art of healing. It becomes so clear to me there, in the art studios, that not only the illness but the cure as well lies in the unconscious and that the arts provide a language whereby the individual spontaneously portrays the unrealized or repressed aspect of himself.

Withymead came to grief, literally and figuratively, after Gilbert died in 1959. His had been the unobtrusive hand which had kept the finances and Irene within bounds. When he was gone the place fell apart. Irene became suspicious and temperamental. She could generate a terrifically charged atmosphere. As the Chairman of the Withymead Trust Leonard bore the brunt of it. Irene was so overpowering that Leonard developed a peptic ulcer serious enough to keep him away from the International Conference of Agricultural Economists, an occasion he hated to miss since he had founded it. Irene also tried to divide Dorothy and Leonard as many others tried to do, before and after; she failed too.

Despite his ulcer and all that had happened Leonard had no regrets. Dr Stevens asked him shortly before his death what he thought about it all. He replied, 'Dorothy and I never regretted a penny of it. It was money well spent.'[54] As late as 1970 he wrote to Irene:[55]

I know of no member of the original Board of Trustees or Committee of Management who would hesitate to make the same sort of investment for the same purposes and for the support of Gilbert and yourself. The vital thing is, I suppose, to recognise and face both positive and negative results for what they were and to learn from both.

The interest in psychology did not start with Withymead. In 1919 Leonard attended a Summer School at the Psychological Laboratory in Cambridge, just as Dorothy took courses on psychology from Dr Dewey and Dr Coates at Columbia University a year or so later. They both knew that a place such as Dartington would attract largish numbers of adults and children who would be unstable as well as unorthodox and would therefore need psychological help – 'brilliant people whose minds have run only slightly off the rails':[56]

From the first Dorothy and I were concerned with how best, or at all, to season our educational enterprises from 1926 on with the findings and wisdom of Freud. Down the years we used psychoanalysts at arm's length, Pailthorpe, Winnicott, especially for children, later Sue of course, and Hoffa, Schmideburg too.[57]

The Sue he mentioned was Dr Susanna Isaacs who became his second wife.

Leonard hoped to use £10,000 which had been loaned, not granted, to Withymead in order to set up a psychiatric clinic for the students at Exeter University on whose Council he sat for very many years. The sum repaid was in the event only £200. So nothing of that kind could be done until eventually Leonard succeeded in getting Dartington House built in Oxford for the Institute of Agricultural Economics and included a walk-in psychiatric clinic (established by Littlemore Hospital) on the ground floor. Leonard wrote to Alan Bullock, Master of St Catherine's College, Oxford, and Vice-Chancellor of the University:[58]

> I believe Oxford city is the first in the country to have a day and night service available for people in mental trouble, including the University students. It is sad for me that the Professors of the University working in the fields so closely allied to this subject exhibit such a mild interest in a first-class piece of pioneering work.

Dorothy had little time for the contemporary Church. It was positively painful to her to be with people who went through the outer observances without any feeling. The worst hypocrisy. But the Church of the past, that was a different matter, when it was the foremost patron who 'commanded' artists in Herbert Read's sense. The arts were then a part of the sacrament woven into people's everyday lives as they were in primitive societies. Eliot said that 'without sentimentalising the life of the savage, we might practise the humility to observe, in some of the societies upon which we look down as primitive or backward, the operation of a social-religious-artistic complex which we should emulate upon a higher plane'.[59] They would have agreed. If in our civilisation the Church could no longer perform that unifying function, the arts (with patronage coming from different sources) might still have in a community something of the same kind of force. Dorothy expressed her hope in the same prospectus she wrote for the Chekhov Studio. Her beloved Theatre has the same capital Heard used for Time:

> The Theatre goes back for its origin to religious mysteries. On the stage, as well as in religious services and ritual, men have attempted to lift themselves out of the humdrum world and to see themselves, their neighbours, and the world around them from some new and more spiritual point of view. The development of civilisation has progressively imposed restraint and privation upon human feeling as

well as upon the ideals and aspirations of human nature; and it has been the special function of the Theatre to attempt to meet these emotional and idealistic needs so often left unsatisfied in the round of everyday life. For this purpose each pattern of culture has in the past developed its appropriate entertainment, that is, the presentation before people of some spectacle that fulfils a need often deeply felt, sometimes frustrated and seldom consciously recognized. Such entertainment tends to be as varied as man's experience, and ranges in the different ages from the Cretan bull-ring to the Greek theatre, from the pageantry of mediaeval jousting to the mystery play, from bull-baiting to Shakespearian drama, and from the dirt-track, the boxing ring, the football arena and the music hall to the performing drama and concert hall of today.

Dorothy and Leonard were not nearly as sniffy as many of their contemporaries who complained continuously and bitterly about the 'vulgarisation' brought about by the new influence of a mass market.[60] Dorothy was entranced by the 'ballet' of soccer. Jackie Charlton, when England won the World Cup, was one of her heroes.

She thought that the arts might permeate the new Dartington as the Church had presumably once done. This became an article of faith on which the two of them could wholeheartedly agree. Rather before Dorothy's prospectus Leonard wrote two articles for the *Countryman* which, reprinted as a pamphlet in 1937, were used as the first publicity brochure for Dartington as a whole. Its title recalled his period at Cambridge, and in particular the Student Christian Movement – *Faith and Works at Dartington*:

> Besides the need for a sense of adequacy in economic, social and sex life, man has always shown a hunger for some sense of direction in the scheme of things around him and for a sense of balance and satisfaction and peace within his soul. When inner feelings, intuitions and sensitivities are alive and active, and are balanced by reason and a sense of social purpose, a civilization begins to produce something we call personality in the individual and in society something we recognise as culture. As village churches and chapels lose their individual resident ministers, as shooting syndicates and hunting stables replace the squire, as the nearest cinemas and dance hall take the place of home or village-made recreation, what is to be the alternative? The town as yet, with all its wealth of material resources and services, seems to offer little of cultural value to the individual or to the community as a whole. If once its economic base were sound, might not a rural community become the source of an original contribution to English culture and civilization in the future? The

question we had to face was how and where to begin, how to grow and develop standards, intellectual, cultural and aesthetic, while we were busy establishing a sound economic base? What emphasis were we to place, and of what kind, upon music, drama and dance, the function of the artist, the poet, the writer? Till the Reformation the Church attempted such an aesthetic synthesis by means of the Mass and of its ritual, its mystery play and holy day festivities. It aimed to guide the feelings as well as to steer the reason of its varied flock.

I have discussed religion not because it had an effect on Dartington – except in a negative sense – for there was no outward show of religion at the place – but because of its intense interest to Dorothy. The arts found a place at Dartington, partly because Dorothy, and Leonard to a lesser extent, had something like a religious attitude to them. The arts were not to fill people's leisure time. They had an importance far beyond that. They were the means by which the Elmhirsts themselves, every one at Dartington, everyone everywhere, could transcend the boundaries of self and enter into a communion with what lies behind the surface of life. Hence their significance. They were not just veneer plastered on top of industry and agriculture. They were themselves the very substance of the real life.

Here once again the utopian tendency shows. 'Art is always a bringing together; a synthesis'; and Dorothy thought it might offset the divisiveness, the fragmentation which specialisation has brought to the modern world. She probably would have remained hopeful even were she alive today when that same divisiveness has become sharper still.

CHAPTER 9

A NEW DAY
FOR THE ARTS

⟨⊃∘⊙∘⊂⟩

If once its economic base were sound,
might not a rural community become the
source of an original contribution to
English culture and civilization in the
future?

Faith and Works, 1937

The attitudes described in the last chapter predisposed both of them, especially Dorothy, to favour the arts, but without telling them what to do about them at Dartington. For some years they waited for something to happen, receptive but too unsure to *make* things happen, except on a small scale in and around the school. Since they knew they wanted everyone at Dartington, all the amateurs in the place, to have access to the arts, the only immediately obvious thing was to make use of whatever talent or enthusiasm anyone might have. Erica Inman, the Secretary of the school, had some experience of amateur theatricals and started the Drama Club which later became the Dartington Players and then the Playgoers. The only professional in the early years was a member of the school staff, Nevison Robson, who taught music to me and other children and ran the Estate Singing Club.

Before long came the first happening, as a result of a chain of introductions. Ruth Morgan introduced her niece, Evelyn Preston, who introduced Ellen Wilkinson, the Labour MP who became well known later when she led the Hunger Marchers from her constituency of Jarrow. After that she was Minister of Education in the Attlee Government. Ellen in her turn introduced Maurice Browne. Maurice, an Englishman, brought in another Ellen, Ellen Van Volkenburg, soon known to everyone at Dartington as Nellie. It was their good fortune that she was an American, with a fine name even though it was not Vanderbilt. Between the two of them

217

Maurice and Nellie had started the Repertory Company at the Cornish School in Seattle[1] and the little theatre in Chicago. Though divorced, they remained great friends.

Maurice was a small dynamic man, an excellent actor and play-reader. In 1927 he achieved a success in London playing *The Unknown Warrior* and agreed, on Ellen Wilkinson's suggestion, to give three performances of it in the Solar, the by now restored meeting room by the Great Hall. A temporary stage was built at one end. Leonard and Dorothy were as impressed by him as he by them, and by their money. He dedicated Book Four of his Autobiography, 'Somebody', to them.

> This was the first household which I had known where, when a course of action had to be decided, the governing consideration was always, not *What is convenient?* nor *What is expedient?* but *What is Right?*

Leonard 'was better informed historically than anyone whom I had known.'[2]

They for their part 'believed' in him sufficiently to lend him £2,000 and offer another £2,000 later on a fifty-fifty basis to put on a play not yet found, while advising him to wait until he found a play which he *had* to do. He waited a whole ten days. He then heard about one by an unknown writer called R. C. Sherriff. It had been given two private performances by the Stage Society. As soon as he got the text of *Journey's End* (as it was called) he took it straight down to Dartington in the train, as though the manuscript would lose its charisma unless it were brought to life immediately:[3]

> Five decorous Englishwomen and two decorous Englishmen contemplated with shocked amazement the spectacle of a middle-aged fellow-countryman alternately laughing and crying in a third-class smoker. That evening I read the play aloud to the Elmhirsts. Afterwards Leonard walked round the grounds alone for two hours; it was a cold December night.

They agreed this was it. Browne returned the next morning to London to arrange for the production. Dorothy and Leonard were at the first night at the Savoy. It was an instant, smashing success, and remained so. Within a year *Journey's End* had been performed by seventy-six companies in twenty-five languages, including every European language and Japanese. In Germany alone forty companies were performing it simultaneously.[4] 'It was', said Bernard Shaw, 'worth having a war to get such a play as this.' It was perfectly timed for the moment when people were at last (after ten years in which it had been too painful) prepared to talk openly against the war.

Leonard and Dorothy did not know at first what to do with the profits which started coming in immediately after the opening at a rate of £1,500 a week and went up from there. It was the only large sum of money they ever made out of the arts. Browne (according to his autobiography) wanted to put the money into the talkies which had just appeared in the cinemas.[5] His chief adviser thought they would be forgotten in six months. Leonard unfortunately believed the adviser, as did Leonard's own man of affairs, Fred Gwatkin. Instead of the talkies the profits went into the purchase of two London theatres, the Globe and the Queens.

Dorothy and Leonard were now 'in' the theatre with Browne and Van Volkenburg as partners. Browne's next production was *Othello* with Paul Robeson in the lead. He brought the company down to rehearse at Dartington. 'Night after night, unaccompanied, by the light of a great log-fire in the music-room Robeson sang "spirituals".'[6] The performance in London was a hit with the critics but not the public.

Another performance which figured more prominently in local history was at Dartington itself. F. G. Thomas suggested a village drama festival in the Hall gardens and Wyatt Rawson made it more precise by proposing the festival should in fact consist of a performance of *Comus*. Dorothy asked Nellie to produce it. It was the first grand occasion for the estate: something of a medieval atmosphere was created in the new community, with art uniting everyone. The cost was covered from a fund for drama at Dartington set up out of some of the profits made on *Journey's End*.

The performance was on a late evening in July 1929, at ten o'clock. Dusk was falling over the gardens. From the ruined stone arcade came a man's voice:

> Before the starry threshold of Jove's Court
> My mansion is, where those immortal shapes
> Of bright aereal spirits live insphear'd
> In Regions milde of calm and serene Ayr,
> Above the smoak and stir of this dim spot,
> Which men call Earth.

One of the performers still remembered, fifty years later, how those lines 'sounded unearthly and thrilling'.[7] The arcade had black curtains hung behind its arches, blocking out the view of the Great Hall. The Bowling Green became a stage and the arcade the set. Braving the midges and the advancing chill, the audience sat below the Bowling Green, near the top of the terraces but at a higher level than the ground lies today. The advance publicity for '*The Masque of Comus* by John Milton' had warned 'that it will probably be unwise to bring children of under 10 years of age owing to the possible eeriness of some of the effects'.[8]

The actors expressed themselves with gesture and movement as well as words. The leading characters wore masks designed by Jane Fox-Strangways. The Lady had a dead-white expressionless face. The Attendant Spirit had a priestly head-dress built on top of his mask. The monsters of Comus's Crew wore stylised animal heads with horns. The Villagers wore seventeenth-century costumes and their own faces but, masked or unmasked, everyone moved and stood in choreographed groups and sequences. Comus's Crew crept up, strung out in a line, masks in profile, arms raised in menace. Three youthful and pretty shepherdesses, in full-skirted short dresses, with bare feet and arms, danced together, or stood one above the other on a short flight of steps, holding masks on sticks in front of their faces. To back up the rhythms of Milton's blank verse seventeenth-century music was performed by a small orchestra, a choir of twenty and a chorus.

Leonard and Dorothy were the Attendant Spirit and the Lady. According to some of her friends Dorothy proved herself a 'natural actress'. As for Leonard, he made an impression with the opening speech which he delivered from the top of a ladder above the arcade. Vic Elmhirst was cast as the Elder Brother, his bride, Helen, as the Younger Brother, Richard Elmhirst as a Shepherd and Beatrice Straight as a Shepherdess. Whitney Straight played in the orchestra.

Comus was the first entertainment (out of tens of thousands to come later) at which outsiders were welcome. Now they come by car; then a long file of people walked each night up the main drive from Totnes and paid to see a spectacle which belonged with all the other strange goings on 'up at Dartington'. Such estate employees as came to watch or were in the cast, making music or behind the scenes, were already in the new transport age. Buses and cars brought them up from The Plains at Totnes for 6d. the round trip.

The Elmhirsts had wanted things to happen in the arts and they had. They had also begun to realise the need for professionals. *Comus* was a triumph for the amateurs in the school and on the estate. Amateurs could do work of reasonable standard if – and this was the most important new lesson they learned in the four years – they had professionals to help them. Nellie was a professional producer. Without her they knew that they and everyone else would all have floundered through the Milton.

But having the odd visiting professional to produce a play or work up a choral performance, valuable as it could obviously be, was just as obviously not all that was required, particularly in arts like dancing or painting or pottery where technique was needed as well as effort and enthusiasm. A man from the sawmills or a boy from the school might be able to put on a passable and spirited show in a sort of pageant in the garden. The boy, untutored, might be able to paint with naïf freshness. It would be too much to expect him to make decent pots without guidance or the man from the sawmills to paint without the inspiration and support of a teacher. This led them to the conclusion that they needed professionals as teachers, for the estate as well as the school.

Nellie pushed them towards this conclusion by telling Dorothy and Leonard about the Cornish School. The school's founder was yet another Nellie, Nellie Cornish.[9] The more one Nellie told her about the other, the more interested Dorothy became. The Cornish School required every student to study the arts – not just the single art which might be his chief interest:[10]

> The School believes that an actor, for example, will be a better actor if his background includes Music, the Dance and the Graphic Arts in addition to the technical knowledge involved in writing, producing, or acting plays. . . . Its origin dates back to the Golden Age of Greece, when every educated citizen was, as a matter of course, expected to possess an understanding of all the arts.

A model for Dartington? 'We regard the Cornish School', Dorothy said, 'as an example and an inspiration to all other Schools attempting to give a co-ordinated training in the Arts.'[11]

The Cornish was not quite to Dartington arts what Cornell was to Dartington agriculture. But Cornish did suggest the need for professional teaching. It posed the question whether Dartington should not do the same and have students of the arts who would train as professionals; and more immediately to the point it was a recruiting ground for artists who came to teach at Dartington.

Richard Odlin was the first from Seattle in 1929. He was a small, wry, homosexual puppeteer who made a famous almost naked puppet of the black dancer, Josephine Baker. The figure was almost as big as he. Next to arrive was Louise Soelberg, a beautiful young dancer who before long was married to Richard Elmhirst. The one from Seattle who had the biggest effect was Mark Tobey. Beatrice accompanied Nellie Van Volkenburg to Seattle in the summer of 1931 and was as much struck by the handsome young painter as by anyone else she saw there. She wanted Mark to teach *her* painting. At her request Dorothy sent Mark an invitation without any specificity about what he was expected to do, and perhaps because it was so vague Mark accepted. He taught amateurs of all ages on the estate, including me. I remember sitting in his studio with other children from the school and adults from many different departments of the estate, looking very awkward, as though they had never held a brush in their hands before, but all intent on their drawing. Mark moved around continuously, making jokes and encouraging more by words than by demonstration. Everyone an artist – he at any rate believed it.

He gave a little speech to his class at the opening of the autumn term in 1931. He wrote it down and the piece of paper has survived. His theme was the need to overcome the fears which prevent people finding voices of their own:

> Now, why should a class like this, a so-called Drawing Class, enable us in any way to do this; or set us on the road? First, because we are taking the creative point of view, however puny or weak the results, and to me the immediate results should not be dwelt upon too long. They are like steps on a ladder, experiences through which we grow and move onwards to the next stage. . . . Again, I want you to feel in this class you are, through making an effort to express your ideas on paper, freeing yourself, opening up great powers for living the life of the artist within us all.

His manner of teaching has been best described by Bernard Leach:[12]

> Those who came never forgot. Mark did not teach by any ordinary standards, yet he taught everything, even by silence. In particular I recall a summer evening when he did not appear during the first hour. Everyone set to work at a long table with a board, ink, pens or chalk, silently seeking some private expression. The fine weather had kept a few away. Suddenly Mark entered quietly and stood in the open doorway. We glanced up. He paused, then said: 'I too have been out for a stroll, watching some of you move freely in the sun on the tennis-courts, not stuck with your noses on drawing-boards. Is there a piano? Play, for God's sake! Now leave your boards – dance! Let go! That's better – dance, you emotionally tied-up English! Now stand up and dance with your chalk on your drawing-boards!'

Tobey discovered at Dartington the mode of painting – the 'white writing' – for which he later became world famous. It came upon him in the middle of one night in his studio above the entrance to the courtyard, with its skylight which opened on to the stars like an immensely wide-lens telescope. He was so excited he sent for his friends to come over, even at that hour. He began a long series of paintings made up of lines whitish in tone made up of brush strokes against a dark background.

Leonard and Dorothy had known Bernard Leach since 1925. During the years when he was helping Leonard to build up his collection, there was a standing invitation to him to come to settle in Dartington whenever he wished. He was impressed enough with it – he called it 'the most remarkable decentralisation of culture in England'[13] – to accept in 1932 and move there from St Ives. At first he taught pottery in the school and also began producing pots for sale, with the assistance of his son, David. In the summer of 1934 he and Tobey left together, at the Elmhirsts' expense,[14] to spend a year in Japan with Japanese craftsmen. Tobey went to China as well. When he returned Leach concentrated on building up the pottery which had been established for him at Shinners Bridge – a pottery which is still in production, now under Marianne de Trey. Until 1940 he produced slipware there and experimented with stoneware:[15]

> I employed the English slip-ware technique, using the chocolate-coloured Fremington clay from North Devon, which is the same as that used at Lake's Pottery, Truro – the last of the traditional Cornish Kilns. But I vitrified the body by taking the temperature to over 1,050C and used an excellent black englobe or slip – often trailing white over black and dipping into transparent iron glaze so that the effect was yellow on shot black.

The experience of Japan influenced both Leach and Tobey as artists and created a bond between them that lasted.

The Elmhirsts took another step when they decided to build on what they had already done with the dance and establish a small professional troupe – the first professional group at Dartington – under Margaret Barr. To foster dance seemed to them particularly appropriate. In primitive societies, and to a lesser extent in medieval England, village dance had marked every important stage and event in the life of the individual and of the society. It had been a unifying force. So might it become in the new Dartington. The performance of *Comus* had shown that in dance-mime – the combination of ballet and acting to tell a story without words – amateurs could acquit themselves creditably.

Dance, in general, had obvious attractions and so did Margaret Barr. She was recommended by Nellie and Maurice together, having worked with them in theatre in Carmel in California after her training with Martha Graham in New York. She had an impeccable family background – English mother, American father, and to cap even that she was born in Bombay before being brought up in California. She looked like a tigress with wild black hair and had very large breasts which bounced about as she danced. She seemed always ready to spring, and often did. She combined training in contemporary dance and a deep interest in community participation.

She brought with her a nucleus of women for her own troupe and added others to it, including, soon, Bridget D'Oyley Carte. It was harder to get going with the amateurs. Putting oneself out for *Comus* in a grand performance was one thing; to turn up regularly for rehearsals as part of 'The Labour Movement' in Miss Barr's ballet *The People* was another. She needed men most of all as partners to her women professionals. She gradually made headway but even the glamour of her dancers was not enough for the boys in the school. Her report for her second term was almost despairing. 'Even working in the Adult classes has not helped with the two I especially wanted – Michael Young and Michael Straight.'[16] But by dint of copious bribes she eventually corralled us, as I described earlier. We duly appeared in *The People* for the opening of the mammoth dance school. I thought Michael was rather good, all the more because of the oddness of casting a millionaire's son as the leader of the workers. (Dorothy herself was soon after giving money to the Left Theatre in London.) As for me, I was terrible. Pom said my dancing was as farcical as Dorothy playing cricket for the Yorkshire Gentlemen. We 'dancers' could hear him laughing up on the balcony through the most moving passages, that is when the thunderous Sibelius music quietened enough to allow anything else to be heard.[17] I only had a small part in her next production, *The Bread Line*, and none at all in the following one, *Virgins*.

With Edmund Rubbra and Alan Rawsthorne as her resident musicians and Peter Goffin as stage director she put on other remarkable performances, one of *A Midsummer Night's Dream* in the parish hall at Liverton, in which many of the villagers took part. She also wanted to do another and better *Comus*, a Spring Festival this time, also in the garden. The plan for it went to the Education Committee:[18]

> The Ancients are discovered seated around the ashes of a fire – on the terrace above, prone on the earth, are the Adolescents asleep in a long line. Dawn music awakes them followed by a Hymn to the Sun. At this moment the Adolescents see the Ancients. They spring down on them and the Mock Ritual Battle of old Pagan ceremonies occurs between the old life force and the new.

Margaret wanted an orchestra of 60 as well as mountains of forest-green costumes for the 25 Tribal Men and spring-green ones for 35 Tribal Women, and 4 horses, 5 cows, 1 bull (if possible, she said – Frank Crook had a rude but pertinent comment on that), 15 sheep and 1 goat (if possible). The Education Committee, when it came to the point, for once said the money was not there: there had to be some limits. Margaret was not helped very much by the stage-struck Beatrice who had been appointed Secretary of her School of Dance-Mime. She wrote letters like this to the Director of Education:[19]

> Mr. Curry Mr. Curry,
>   Shame on you trying to get out of paying for cleanleness! I am disappointed in you sir! . . . So you are doomed sire to be royal in your generosity, and present the noble Dance School with a Hoover. And me Lord if not asking too much could this perchise be made before the change of the moon? Faith we grow sick with waiting, and most

unseemly growths spring before our eyes in the chinks and crannies of our shelter.

In all good faith, I remain one of your past

Beatrix Rex

In June 1934 Margaret brought in another dancer, Uday Shan-Kar. He performed in the Open Air Theatre and followed it up with a short school. Beatrice was his most enthusiastic pupil. She fell in love with him and he with her. They went off together to India. Out of this came the Uday Shan-Kar School in Almora in what was then, under British rule, the United Provinces. An older friend of Leonard's, Dr Boshi Sen, suggested Almora. He was a plant physiologist who bred improved seeds for fodder crops. For twenty years Leonard and Dorothy gave financial support to his Vivekananda Agricultural Research Laboratory at Almora until he eventually got Indian government money behind him.

The next troupe to arrive was much larger, more fully fledged and complete with an international reputation. The Jooss Ballet, named after its founder, Kurt Jooss, had jumped to fame on the strength of his single masterpiece, *The Green Table*. It was a savage comment on the injustices done by the Versailles Peace Conference which weighed almost as heavily on the victors as on the vanquished. Would one Peace lead to another War? The question was hanging over Europe long before Hitler. The white-gloved, black-suited and masked dancers portraying the statesmen around the conference table seemed to say yes; they were more sinister than ridiculous. As a choreographic achievement, this was far and away Jooss's most successful blend of Diaghilev and German expressionism. Jooss himself gave a powerful performance in the role of Death. With his height and sharply etched face the part was made for him, and he for it.

Jooss drilled his dancers quite as exactingly as any classical ballet master until every little movement was just as he wanted. They seemed like marionettes. This added to the effect of *The Green Table*. The statesmen – Lloyd George, Clemenceau, whoever they were – were meant to be puppets on strings pulled by Death. But the method handicapped his other ballets, with the partial exception of *Big City*.

Beryl de Zoete took Dorothy and Leonard to see *The Green Table* in July 1933 when Jooss had his first London season in the same theatre where *Journey's End* had opened. Perhaps it was a good omen. Beryl pushed them into the dressing-room afterwards. According to Jooss's account in the English he never mastered,[20] Dorothy said mainly 'M-m-'. She also invited him to tea at her London flat or if not that, to Dartington. 'We have a very nice place in the south; maybe you would like to come?' He said yes he would and then didn't, until his troubles with the Nazis began. These hit him a month later, in Essen, where his ballet had its headquarters, alongside the companion ballet school under Sigurd Leeder. The Nazis wanted Jooss to sack his principal composer and musician, Fritz Cohen, to play his music without his name, and do the same to his stage designer, the painter, Hein Heckroth. Fritz was Jewish. So were several other members of the company, thereafter likewise under threat. Jooss refused. He escaped across the border eighteen hours before the police came to arrest him.

Where to? During the crisis Beryl was in Essen at a Summer School of his. She said, 'To England, to Devon, to the Elmhirsts.' Jooss had no idea what Dartington was. The name had not been mentioned in his dressing-room, only 'the south'. He had ahead of him a tour in Holland and a six weeks' season on Broadway. He sent Sigurd Leeder to Devon. Sigurd reported back that it was a magnificent place, something unheard of. Then on the way back from America the *Île de France*, with the troupe aboard, stopped outside the breakwater in Plymouth. A small motorboat threaded out with passengers for Le Havre. Leonard and Dorothy were on board too. Leonard had a little notebook which he took out to make notes in as they stood on the deck. 'Well, now, how many people do you reckon would come over when you move the School to Dartington?' 'I see, yes. And the company, that would be so many? And there would be musicians and so on?' Leonard put it all down in the little book, and said, 'We'll see to it.' Jooss remarked that neither then nor at any other time did he get from his patrons a sense of patronage:

> Never. Not a single time. Dorothy, who was so passionately interested, would never open her mouth to give any kind of advice. Never. Just 'M-m-m. Oh I see. Give them a chance.'

Soon there were twenty trained dancers at Dartington, with a general manager, a stage manager and two pianists, and also, in the school, twenty-three students and three teachers. A large house was bought for them at Redworth, on the outskirts of Totnes.

Having made up their minds on the Ballet they did not lose interest in it; but they left it pretty much to itself, doing their duty, of course, by attending first nights of new ballets and student performances or by talking to Kurt and his colleagues whenever they returned to Dartington from one tour of Europe or America to rehearse for another. They were not involved partly because they did not have to be. The company prospered, even if none of the other ballets was up to the standard of *The Green Table*. Audiences were waiting both in the part of Europe which had not yet fallen to the Nazis and in America. Students were also waiting to enter the Jooss-Leeder School which supplied the touring company with its new recruits. The School had thirty-six students by the summer of 1939 and forty had registered for the following term. By the time the war began there was a good prospect of eventually building up to fifty students – the break-even figure.

With the arrival of Jooss artists were sardined into Dartington. Preventing them from quarrelling was almost a full-time job. Whose job? Dorothy and Leonard were as much away as they had ever been and when in residence had much else to do besides dealing with one complaining artist after another. Fred Gwatkin, observing the Jooss Ballet jostling Barr's School of Dance-Mime and Louise Soelberg's other dance group, watching drama and puppets, Mark Tobey, Bernard Leach, Jane Fox-Strangways, and noting how much money was being spent on them, proposed that a department should be created and an administrator appointed. He knew just the man for it. Christopher Martin was related to Theodore McKenna who was still the senior partner in Gwatkin's firm. His wife, Cicely, was a McKenna on her mother's side. He had business experience as well as interest in the arts. The fact that he was nephew to the Rev. J. S. Martin of Dartington who was such a staunch opponent of theirs was a twist which also appealed to them both. He got the job; the Arts Department was set up.

Martin did not take long to size up what was going on. His first report dated 14 July 1934 was incisive. 'Is the Arts Department to be primarily a professional undertaking', he asked Dorothy and Leonard in the report, 'having amateur work with the Estate as an offshoot of its professional activities, or is the Department to be primarily amateur and dilettante with professionalism only as a chance consideration?' It was to be out with the amateur, in with the professional, and the Elmhirsts agreed. Jooss was in, or just about to come in; Barr was about to be out. She and Jooss were not friendly to each other, and she had apparently offended Dorothy and Leonard that same spring with a dance burlesque with words and music called *Subject to Alteration*. This was about the conversion of an old building for heaven knows what purpose. Scene One may have been intended as a kind of satire on the satire of *The Green Table*. It was set in a 'Board Room in which a Committee has been sitting long and unprofitably'. Then comes on the architect who leads the draughtsmen in their work:

> We'll cube the root of the Bunkum tree
> and multiply it all by three.
> Measure twenty chimney stacks,
> observe the laws of parallax,
> model the moon in sealing-wax
> and circumvent our Income Tax.

An Expert kept appearing but each time only to say

> As an Expert, I agree
> As an Expert, I agree.

It all ended with a chorus about the converted building:

> What can it be, what can it be.
> A club, a school, or a menagerie.
> A place for observations
> of planets like Mars
> or a prison designed
> without iron bars.
> A gallery for abstract art
> or ancient farm with place apart
> for a new hygienic dairy.

It did not appeal to Martin either. The decision to get rid of Margaret Barr and her troupe was finally taken after Leonard and Dorothy had left for their summer holiday in the Adirondacks. Margaret wrote to a friend at Dartington that she was specially resentful that the message, 'out', came from America and was not communicated to her personally. She was given a handshake, large enough to keep her group together, in London, for another year. Margaret left and Paula Morel, a pillar of the arts at Dartington from that day to this, went with her for a time.

Margaret had no friendship with Dorothy and Leonard she could draw on to prevent herself from being sacked. For them her combination of the professional with the amateur did not sufficiently offset her combination of artiness with politics. Her amateur students did not agree at all: they wanted her to stay. These were not only at Dartington itself. Some of her greatest successes were with villagers. When German refugees took her place, all thoroughly professional to the tips of their white-gloved fingers, many people at Dartington felt neglected. It would have been unimaginable even at Dartington for Jooss to give dancing lessons to villagers. A peak period for the professional was a trough for the amateur. If Margaret had stayed she might have inaugurated much sooner the developments which occurred only after the war, although by then the emphasis was on music rather than dance. As it was, the Arts Department became more isolated from the estate, and from Devon, than it had ever been before or has been since. It was brilliant, but it was not transforming life through the release of the imagination of many local people.

Professional ballet was in; so, said Martin, should be other professionals. While the Ballet was riding high with him and with the Elmhirsts, Jooss was able to introduce some more of them. One was his old teacher,

Rudolph Von Laban, whom Kurt called 'the originator of the New Dance in Europe'.[21] He had worked with Mary Wigman as well as Kurt. By using the system of movement notation he had invented (the Laban Kinetographie) he was able to bring together 10,000 dancers without rehearsal and put on a gigantic spectacle both in Vienna and then, before he fell foul of the Nazis, at the 1936 Olympic Games in Berlin.

He came to Dartington in 1938 and stayed until he and Lisa Ullmann, from the staff of the Leeder School, took refuge in 1940, when they had as Germans to leave Devon, in the Elmhirsts' flat in Upper Brook Street. Showing great ingenuity, he adapted his methods to ease the efforts of manual workers in wartime factories. After that he and Lisa set up the Art of Movement Studio in Manchester to train teachers and others in the dance. It moved to Weybridge and then to Goldsmiths' College at the University of London. One result of this English phase of Laban's work is that the dance has become a regular feature of the programme of many ordinary primary schools, starting in the West Riding and spreading from there. Laban has been the most enduring legacy of Jooss in England.

Christopher Martin's most important recommendation in 1934 was that, whatever else Dartington did, it should seek a counterpart to Jooss in the theatre. With Beatrice in mind Dorothy readily agreed. They prepared for the coming by making more room. The first step was to finish the conversion of the Barn Theatre in the courtyard. To do the design yet another professional was invited in who could perhaps have had a larger impact on Dartington than any of the others if he had been given his head. He was Walter Gropius, founder of the Bauhaus. It was a curious relationship. In 1932 Nancy Wilson Ross, a great friend of Dorothy's in America, asked her if she could give money to help the Bauhaus.[22] She did, but only $500. In the following year Dr Slater wrote from the Managing Director's office at Dartington to 'Herr Professor Dr Gropius' in Berlin, inviting him to visit Dartington. The enticement was that 'We at Dartington are doing a considerable amount of building, in particular in the development of land and the building of houses.'[23] It was apparently in Slater's mind that some part of the Bauhaus might be recreated at Dartington. He must have discussed the possibility with Dorothy and Leonard. The visit in the summer of 1933 was presumably to put Gropius on trial. If so he did not pass.

Although Gropius did not get what he wanted – to create a design studio at Dartington – he was commissioned as the architect for the last stages of conversion of the theatre. He did it by respecting completely the old barn and altering, without any embellishment, the arrangement of the space within. Once he had come to live in England Dorothy and Leonard also gave Henry Morris in Cambridgeshire the money needed to employ

Gropius to design a much more famous building, the Village College at Impington,[24] built in conjunction with Maxwell Fry and completed in 1937.

For a professional man of the theatre the initiative came from Beatrice. One of her drama teachers in New York, Madam Daykharnova, told her about a Russian actor and director called Michael Chekhov, who was also in New York. She went to see him act, in Russian, with an all-Russian group. One of the plays was Gogol's *The Government Inspector*, in which he was Khylestakov; the others were based on stories by his uncle, *An Evening with Anton Chekhov*. She was captivated. There and then, although she did not understand a word of the plays and Chekhov knew no English, she decided that he was the man she had been hoping for. She 'called' her mother and step-father, one of the first appearances in Dartington life of the telephone, and said so.

On their next visit Dorothy and Leonard saw him play in Philadelphia; they were as impressed as Beatrice. Stimulated, perhaps, by competition from the Group Theatre in New York which Dorothy also gave money to – the Group wanted him as well – they at once invited him to Dartington. He agreed, sight unseen, and arrived just over a year after Jooss, in October 1935, to prepare for the opening of what it was decided should be called his 'Studio' a year later.

Dorothy had a big part in drawing up the plans for it. Once it came into being it was not long before she was fully involved:[25]

> One day I went over as a visitor to his class. Several people were sitting with me on the little balcony and I watched an exercise. Mr Chekhov was showing the different qualities of emotion in the way we approach someone. He walked across to Esme Hubbard in one tempo, and then in another, taking her hand and saying 'How are you?'. It was a simple exercise, but what he gave to it was such a revelation to me that I knew I had met the man who was for me, the Master. Then Beatrice urged me to join the group for an hour a day. I did this with certain misgivings, but soon it was two, three, four, five, six hours a day and even more. I hardly dared ask myself where I was going. I only knew the work opened up new vistas of life for me.

She had found in Misha (as she called him – Leonard always wrote it Mischa) the most important man in her life after Willard and Leonard.

His first virtue was that he was indisputably a genuine man of the theatre. None more so. Born four years after Dorothy, in 1891, he had it in his blood. He was the nephew of the playwright who was second only to Shakespeare in Dorothy's regard. He was trained exhaustively. His uncle got him into the Moscow Art Theatre whose first big success was *The*

Seagull after it had been a flop in its first production. There he was taught by Stanislavsky that what mattered most was the 'feeling of truth' in everything that happened on the stage; by Nemirovich-Danchenko that every work of art must cleave to its guiding theme; by Meyerhold about the power of fantasy and by Vachtangov that the audience must never forget they are in a theatre. Taking something from all of them, he elaborated his own special approach – the need for all the elements in a play to be fused into one rhythmic whole. Director of the Second Moscow Art Theatre in 1923, he remained with it until he (like Jooss with the Nazis) fell out with the Soviet authorities, in his case because they disapproved of his interpretation of *Don Quixote*. For a time producer for the Hebrew Habima Players, he had never settled anywhere after his escape from Russia. He was longing to have once more his own school and his own theatre.

A further advantage was that despite his credentials he was not like other men of the theatre Dorothy had met in London and New York. He was not the least bit pretentious. A slight, light man, he was in ordinary social relationships almost retiring, somewhat like Dorothy herself, and always ready to make fun of himself, also like Dorothy. He had, for instance, a comic nose turned up in such an absurd way it showed, as he said, that he was not meant to take himself too seriously.[26] Dorothy loved that, especially when humility was combined on stage with an imagination of enormous power. He could become so fully the character he was acting as to be uncanny. Day after day there would be this metamorphosis into a person so different yet so true to life it was more than life.

Another asset was being a foreigner, like Dorothy and sixteen others out of the first twenty students. Paul Rogers and Iris Tree were two of the few English ones. Twelve were from the USA or Canada. It was very obvious, too, that he was. His English was bad even after he had spent a year concentrating on learning it. But this only made him the more lovable. Dorothy laughed along with the others when he said to his students, 'Now we will play with our balls.'[27] Not at him.

A still more appealing quality was his religious attitude, in many ways similar to Dorothy's though she did not share his faith in Rudolf Steiner who was Misha's mentor. Shortly before Beatrice burst in on his dressing-room he had asked Steiner whether he should give up the theatre and become a monk. The reply was, 'No, go on with your art.'[28] He felt Steiner had blessed the Dartington enterprise and he wanted to bring some part of his message into the new venture. He described it as follows:[29]

> In the last four to five decades, within the big stream of the development of science, art, philosophy and religion, one can clearly distinguish a new movement arising, the tendency of which is directed towards the *unification of science, art and spiritual knowledge*. The

231

initiator of this movement, Dr Rudolf Steiner, through his encyclopaedic knowledge, his sharp, clear thinking and his outstanding spiritual faculty, was able to give concrete practical advice to scientists, philosophers, artists and other specialists who wanted to develop, to refresh, to widen their professional knowledge.

Though not a follower of Steiner Dorothy certainly hoped for some 'unification' of science, art and spiritual knowledge. Even more, she was attracted by the attempt Misha said must be made to get out of and beyond one's ordinary body. To him imagination was the greatest of man's gifts: we must all, especially if we are actors, learn to let it run free. He was elaborating what Gerald Heard had already told her.

One of the many things that attracted her about the exercises the students had to repeat was the similarity between Gerald's meditative techniques, as a method of passing over the threshold of self-consciousness, and these dramatic ones which Misha taught her. They were both means of passing over that same threshold and into the essence of a character at once oneself and not oneself. It could only be done by letting the imagination run free:[30]

> When in the evening we are alone in our room, with the light out, what comes out of the darkness? The faces of people we have met, but also (at any rate for the person with an imagination trained as Misha would have it trained) the faces of people we have not met, perhaps in unusual situations strange to us, developing an independent life of their own. These others belong to the world of the imagination, yes, but they are just as much objective as the people we *have* met. When people let their minds run free in this way they are opening themselves to the possibility of creative experience, as Dickens was when he said he had been sitting in his study all morning 'waiting for Oliver Twist who has not arrived', Raphael when he at length saw the image in his room which became the Sistine Madonna, Michael Angelo when he saw not just the muscles and sinews, the folds of cloth, the waves of hair and beard of his *Moses* but also the inner might which he found behind that first membrance of his imagination, following the path towards Goethe's 'exact fantasy'.

The only setback for her and the group generally was that they could not persuade any playwright to join them. Dorothy had written in the Prospectus that the new theatre must 'evolve' its own playwright to work with the group. She tried to evolve some unlikely people who all turned her down – R. C. Sherriff, T. S. Eliot, Denis Johnstone, James Bridie and, most persistently, Sean O'Casey. He was completely opposed to Chekhov's ideas, as he wrote to Dorothy:[31]

The expression that 'the theatre of today suffers from too much literature and too many words and too little action' is the very opposite to what I believe. . . . Instead of 'the theatre losing itself in literature', it has lost itself in inanity and ignorance, and must find itself again in literature.

On Bernard Shaw's advice, Sean and his wife Eileen moved to Totnes in 1938 so that their children could attend Curry's school as day pupils. They stayed for seventeen years. Eileen felt Dorothy was 'ignoring something splendidly worthwhile upon her own doorstep' in not accepting her husband in the way he wanted to be accepted. She wrote rather bitterly:[32]

> Sean, thoroughly honest and down to earth, had nothing arty-crafty in his make-up; he had no admiration for the Chekhov Theatre at Dartington. While appreciating that Michael Chekhov was a clever man, he could not endure a set-up in which the actors wore long blue robes and went round capering and bowing to each other.

Dorothy could not see it that way at all. The Studio was just as it should be, all except for the lack of an O'Casey who would be as humble as Misha seemed to be.

The idea was that the Studio would eventually have a touring company based on Dartington, as Jooss had. For want of a playwright they had to fall back for their first main production on an adaptation for the stage by George Schdanoff, the Studio's assistant director, of Dostoyevsky's novel, *The Possessed*. Dorothy was given the part of Mrs Stavrogin, a rich elderly lady. It became her everyday struggle to be more like Misha whose every word (even in English) she thought was spoken with his whole person. He appears on almost every page of the daily notes she kept:

> 15 March 1938. Scene: Church – Mrs Stavrogin and beggar woman. Misha gave me bag to carry and while I am speaking I must be fumbling in my bag to find pennies. While beggar woman is speaking I merely hold penny, listening, then give it to her and pass on. But whole action must be done with same quality of intensity and significance.
>
> 17 March 1938. Scene: Nicholas' return.
> Misha kept telling me to be more commanding.
>
> 21 March 1938. Scene: Mrs Stavrogin and Nicholas in his room.
> Criticism – my voice was like a weak mouse.
>
> 13 June 1938. Scene: Mrs Stavrogin and Nicholas.
> Found difficulty with 'Now I know you love me'. Misha asked me to say it to him, quite simply and directly – and then it seemed to come more easily.

She loved him, without any of the eroticism which Misha was not keen on.[33] Her closeness to him, strangely enough, is most evident from the letters she wrote to Leonard. Perhaps she was especially affectionate because she realised he was jealous and wanted to comfort him: perhaps, too, some of the fondness she felt for Misha flowed quite naturally over to him, with no restraint imposed by fear of impropriety. The two men are conjoined:

> When I realise how patient you've been with me during this strange new experience of concentrating all my energies on one thing, on one idea – I see, with a kind of overwhelming gratitude, that perhaps only you would have been capable of supporting and helping me in this way – asking nothing in return, and only eager to see new vistas of life opening for me. As time goes on I hope I shall learn to take it all more easily in my stride, and thereby have more vital experience and more sympathetic attention to give to others. But I know that, there again, you will help me, by believing that I can do it. (25 March 1937)

In 1938 Hitler was already stretching himself towards England. Munich was only a respite. Most of Misha's students remained American. English students stayed away. Some of the Americans felt insecure anywhere in Europe, including England. It was uncertain how many more would be prepared to come into what might soon become a theatre of war. Beatrice, who had brought them from West to East, now took them back again. Within a few weeks of Munich she found a large house at Ridgefield in Connecticut and started interviewing prospective new students for the reopening in January 1939. The existing ones, only some of whom would be able to follow, gave their first and also their farewell performance in the Barn Theatre in December 1938. One of the sketches was the death scene from *Peer Gynt*, with Dorothy taking the part of Aase, as shown in Plate 23. This was the bit the Dartington people who had crowded in were waiting to see. They almost held their collective 'breath stream' (to use a Chekhov phrase) when she appeared. She was intensely concentrated on her part and full of feeling which was, however, more fully directed inwards than outwards. The wonder, to the audience, was that the shy Dorothy they knew (or rather did not know because she was so shy) could get up there with a white wig, a radiant face, a hank of wool and perform at all.

She decided at first not to accompany Chekhov and his students. But the pressure on her began to mount. Misha was to present *The Possessed* on Broadway in the autumn of 1939. He said he could find no one else to play Mrs Stavrogin; he needed her. She went on with the exercises he had taught her – they were a bond.

In March she decided to give in and get ready for her Broadway première, at the age of 52, before all her old friends like Eleanor Roosevelt, Ethel Derby, Susie Hammond, Bruce Bliven. They would be waiting with even keener anticipation, some with more dread, than the audience at Dartington. It would be front page news for the *New York Times*. She explained her departure by saying that given six more months with Mr Chekhov she would have much more to contribute to Dartington when she returned. When she left Leonard behind physically, she made up for it as much as she could by a flood of letters.

Eventually Dorothy became too afraid that war might cut her off from England. Before its outbreak she was back. In an emergency her commitment was to Leonard and to Dartington. *The Possessed* opened in New York in October without her and with Ellen Van Volkenburg as a stand-in Mrs Stavrogin. It was a failure; only the performance of Beatrice and a few of the other actors earned any praise from the critics.

Dorothy left Beatrice and Michael behind her in America. Beatrice's appearance on Broadway that October proved to be the first of many there, as well as in the other major cities of America and, many times, in Hollywood. With talent and energy she did what Dorothy would have liked to have done herself. Dorothy always attended one of Beatrice's first nights if she could, even if it meant putting off a trip to America until the opening of the new play. In 1947 one particular performance was postponed for four weeks. She wrote to Margaret Isherwood:[34]

> You know – we were planning to go over to the U.S. in September for four weeks – but since Biddy's play has been postponed – and of course we were intent on being there for her first night – it seems better to wait a bit. She is putting on a most moving and lovely play about Emily Dickinson – the poetess – Biddy taking the part of Emily. An Englishman, called Jack Hawkins, is going over to play with her, and I feel very happy about it, because I like Hawkins so much and because the play is about something real and deep. Do you remember the lines of a 16th century poem –
>> But true love is a durable fire
>> In the mind ever burning,
>> Never sick, never dead, never cold,
>> From itself never turning.
> That is really the theme of Biddy's play – and you can see why I care so much about it – and about seeing her make her debut, as it were, in such a part. So we will try to arrange our American visit to coincide with Biddy's plans – and that will probably mean either November or January.

The next year Dorothy saw her in another success:[35]

Biddy's new play is lovely and she is so happy in the part. The story is based on Henry James' short novel – *Washington Square* – but the play is called *The Heiress*. Wendy Hiller has been playing in it all winter and now Biddy takes over the part. . . . I think she has really established herself as the rising star – and I must confess she has the power – so rarely found in an actor – to reach the deep emotions of an audience. It is extraordinary to look around and find nearly everyone weeping in the theatre.

When Michael left Cambridge in 1937 with a First Class Degree in Economics, gained when Keynes was his star teacher, he too had decided to make his future in America. He was deeply interested in politics. In Britain nothing was happening to excite him; in the USA there was Franklin Roosevelt, and he was the man Michael wanted to serve. In his last Easter vacation, before the exams, Leonard took him to Washington and to the White House to see Franklin and Eleanor. Leonard was fearful about it in advance. Arriving in New York with Michael, after a voyage with Herbert Morrison as an argumentative companion, he wrote to Dorothy:[36]

I had terribly cold feet as the boat reached Quarantine – knew I couldn't measure up, felt no one would want me, that I was just a four flusher, putting one over, barging in on the White House just as an exercise for my sudden self conceit.

But Michael was offered the job he wanted. He came back from England for it later that year instead of staying on at Cambridge for a fourth year to become President of the Union. He was for nearly four years close to Roosevelt as speech-writer for the Cabinet.

Dorothy was full of pride in him as well. Shortly before Michael left the Administration to join the staff of *The New Republic* (of which he later became Editor) she wrote from New York to Miss Hull-Brown, her secretary at Dartington:[37]

Michael continues to forge ahead through his articles and speeches, and last week he presided at a big public meeting in Washington at which Congressmen and Senators and journalists spoke, and the Attorney General himself. There's a wonderful story around Washington to the effect that if you want to get something done 'you'd better take it to President Roosevelt because he has more influence with Michael Straight than anyone else!'

These two children by Dorothy's first marriage were joined in America by the two children of her second marriage. When she herself returned from Ridgefield to Dartington Ruth and Bill, who were in America on holiday in the summer of 1939, stayed on after the outbreak of war to live in New York. Miss Jefferies was in charge, of them and of the two children they were brought up with, Dorcas Edwards and Eloise Elmhirst. They went to school in the city and spent many of their weekends and holidays at Westbury for the next four years. Leonard saw more of them in that period than Dorothy. He was more often in America. When Dorothy managed to get across the Atlantic in 1941 she too was full of the delight of seeing the children again. She wrote to Leonard's mother:[38]

> We drove down to Westbury for the night; and what a gay evening we had. I felt as if I were walking in a dream all the time, as if I had slipped over some border and entered Heaven. The next day we all set out for Chappaquiddick – such a lovely island off the Massachusetts' coast. And Jeff had discovered a house that is absolutely ideal with its own beach and sailboat, and a tennis court and an old barn for the goats and the pony. I watched Bill do the milking early next morning, then he washed the car most thoroughly while I helped weed the tennis court, and finally, at the end of the morning we all had a swim. The next morning Michael and Bill were up at 6 fishing, and later we played tennis – such a good four – Michael and I played against Bill and Leonard. And then in the afternoon we sailed. And so the days passed: four heavenly days which brought home to me, with terrible intensity, the fact that there is nothing in the world which so fills one's emotional life as a family. . . . Thank God for Russian resistance. I keep saying this every day.

The war brought an abrupt close to a brilliant period for Dartington. It was not only part of Devon and England; it had become part of the world, an international centre. The man and woman walking in the garden were talking in Russian about Vachtangov's influence upon the theatre. The two girls were talking in German about the difference between the reaction of audiences in Chicago and Paris. The figures in their blue robes running and dancing in pairs were talking American to each other or Australian.

For a few years the courtyard, itself a cross between a theatre and a Court, was teeming with young Germans, young Hollanders, young Americans. When the Ballet was back from the acclaim of London, Paris and New York and at home alongside the Leeder School there were sixty dancers to add to the score or more of actors and actresses in the Chekhov Studio, the singers and other musicians working for Hans Oppenheim (a distinguished musician, also a refugee from Germany) and the painters or sculptors like Hein Heckroth, Willi Soukop and Cecil Collins. A fine day could produce a rare spectacle. Leonard swore there were more beautiful women per square yard at Dartington than anywhere else in the world. It was certainly more magnificent than in John Holand's day. While Bill Curry in the White Hart Club was standing drinks to Hiram Winterbotham, the young manager of the textile mill, and debating the theory of natural selection, Hein Heckroth, the designer, and Frank Crook, the farmer, could be arguing furiously in the same place. Frank reckoned that photography would in the end make painters redundant, Hein of course hotly denied it. Prize cows and beautiful women were used as evidence by both sides.

Robin Johnson, the Dartington archivist, remembers the whole courtyard abuzz with talk, people standing on the grass arguing or flirting, others hanging out of the windows of the students' rooms. There were endless parties. Almost every day was someone's birthday; and people moving around in the large dining-room where the different groups of students and artists ate together would set up a party for that night. Johnson or another pianist would play – no canned music any more than there would have been in medieval times – and others would dance or talk or look at the moon. Leonard and Dorothy were quite often invited. They came early and left after half an hour or so; there was always a slight feeling that they were visitors from a different realm, Duke and Duchess, the deeply appreciated but rather distant patrons from whom many mercies flowed. People relaxed more easily after the ducal visit was over.

It was not all one long delight, of course, day or night. Many of the refugees were doubly difficult, being both artists and displaced people. It was hardly any help that they all had the English to contend with. Why were they so prone to laughter, and especially that wounding mocking laughter? One of the main questions put by Germans devoted to expressionism in the arts was this: could the English possibly be good dancers, good artists of any kind, with the proper intensity, and *laugh* so much?

There were also problems of rivalry. They were all drawing on a common pool of money. Some of the Jooss dancers criticised Chekhov as a charlatan. Chris Martin said he was a supreme actor who knew exactly how to act as head of a drama school.[39] Jooss had the international reputation Chekhov did not yet have outside his own country, the large professional troupe who hero-worshipped him, and a large school from which the troupe could draw a constant supply of new talent – all things Chekhov hoped he too would have one day. For the time being, he had to be content with a school and build up slowly from there. But Chekhov had a trump card – he was Dorothy's master. For her nothing he could do was wrong, and Jooss knew Chekhov knew that full well. When he saw them together, strolling around the courtyard or, worse, going up to her room, he was bound to feel jealous. Amid all the joy even his face was sometimes anxious and if his so much the more others.

When the courtyard was the centre of an artistic world, it was not of the Dartington estate. Never has there been such a distance between the two. Some of the heroes strutting around the Hall knew their way around Berlin or New York better than they did Dartington village. Almost the only link many of the amateurs had with the Ballet was through attendance at its Annual Ball. There was much bitterness amongst the employees. They were told there was no money left. They were at various points in danger of dismissal. Yet vast sums were apparently being spent 'up at the Hall' upon foreign artists who made almost no contribution to the estate. In the 1920s the Elmhirsts aroused hostility *outside* the estate; in the 1930s they did so *inside* it. By the outbreak of the general war there was much damage to repair.

For all that, Leonard and Dorothy, looking back on the decade, did not have that much cause for regret. They had had no policy for the arts since the beginning of Dartington, unless the welcome given to refugee artists constituted a policy. The reason for the welcome was as much humanitarian as anything else. But it had made the arts so prominent in the Dartington scheme that they could never again be really eclipsed unless England was to lose the war.

For the moment the curtain was down. After the conquest of France in May 1940 many of the refugees were interned, some sent off to camps in Australia or Canada. By mid-1940 there was little left to show for the previous decade. Dorothy was as disheartened as anyone.

Leonard was away more than ever, in London working for the Ministry of War Transport, in the Middle East building up the Middle East Supply Centre, in India and in the USA. For the most part Dorothy stayed at Dartington while Leonard was not there and played more of an executive role than at any other time, before or since. She found her solace in the garden. Her artistic energies went into it. She could not compose music or a play; she composed the garden. This was her work of art.

There was a link with Chekhov. She tried to use her imagination and to concentrate in the way he had taught her. He encouraged her to consider the garden as preparation for her return to the theatre. In October 1940 during the blitz on London he was still urging her to rejoin him:[40]

> I understand you so well when you write to Biddy about your gardening. If I dare say something it would be the following. I think all your experience with flowers is the bridge which links you with us, with your future acting with us, and with your flowers you are undoubtedly rehearsing your future parts in our group.

Dorothy saw the Chekhov and the garden phase rather as successive ones. She wrote to Leonard:[41]

And how can I ever thank you, my darling, for your endless patience with me – watching me go through such queer phases, immersing myself in drama, and then in gardens. But you never desert me, in fact you go along with me in the deepest kind of sharing and understanding – like Orpheus bringing his Eurydice back.

In this new phase Leonard, not Chekhov, was her chief partner, with the head gardener and the other gardeners in supporting roles:[42]

Another thing I must tell you about myself – I have no saviour, no father-figure at the moment, and I don't seem to need one! Do you think it's possible that I'm really growing up? I wonder!

Whenever apart, they wrote to each other constantly about the garden, *their* garden as Dorothy called it, Dorothy's garden as he called it, as it revealed itself anew each year, each season, each day:[43]

It has been wonderful to watch the way in which different flowers force their way up through the crust of the earth. The snowdrop bud is pressed tight between two leaves that are just like swords, and they carry it up to where it can fend for itself; the aconite with bent head presses up by the back of the neck, then once through, it lifts its head and shakes itself free; and finally the cyclamen in that coiled spiral unfolds its magic.

They had private names between each other for the trees that with the old buildings were the special feature of the garden. Frinswith was the name they gave to the slender upright Deodar on the terraces and Ghond to the stouter, spreading Monterey Pine. It was a great grief when Frinswith was blown down in the late 1950s – 'frightful gale last night from south but twisting and whirling like a cyclone'.[44] Fortunately the gale could not topple the Henry Moore woman who in all weathers gazes calmly down from the top terrace – a sculpture commissioned as a memorial to Christopher Martin – which can like other Moore statues be seen and appreciated equally well from any viewpoint, while itself being a view-point.

Not that the work on the garden originated only in the war, merely Dorothy's devotion to it. Though the other arts, like Dartington itself, had no detailed plan behind them, the garden was the great exception, perhaps partly because it was more malleable and also, right outside their own house in the Hall, more nearly personal than anything else at Dartington. Being so wealthy, they had almost no really private property. The garden, as much as anything, belonged to them, though always thrown open to the public, and they moulded it over a long period. In this one respect Dorothy was both planner and executor.

As patrons, and more than patrons, they were like the makers of the great eighteenth-century landscape gardens for which England is famous. Dorothy was herself conscious, as shown by her talk to one of the weekend gardening courses, in 1953, of the link with the romantic gardens which were influenced by Pope and Addison as writers and Claude and Poussin as painters. She needed no persuading to agree with William Kent and Capability Brown in their always fresh appeal to put formality on one side and plan gardens as landscapes. She was also much influenced by two late-nineteenth-century gardeners, William Robinson and Gertrude Jekyll, who were in sympathy with the movement of the century before. Dorothy quoted Jekyll with approval:[45]

> I am strongly of the opinion that a quantity of plants, however good the plants may be themselves and however ample their number, does not make a garden; it only makes a collection. Having got your plants the great thing is to use them with careful selection and definite intention . . . the duty we owe to our gardens is so to use our plants that they shall form beautiful pictures.

They were in a long tradition of garden-creation, playing something of the same role at Dartington as Lord Cobham had done at Stowe. They were particularly unusual in the twentieth century which has had so few patrons to build on a really large scale. The garden at Dartington covers thirty-eight acres, not quite the size of Blenheim or Stourhead, but not very much smaller either. Dorothy and Leonard had the means to be horticultural patrons in an age when for the most part only municipalities and other public authorities have been able to operate so handsomely; and they had more to contribute than just money.

In his book, *The English Garden*, Edward Hyams picks out Dartington as the most modern of the great gardens 'made in the light of all the traditions, all the knowlege which had been accumulated during the long slow growth of the art of horticulture':[46]

> This is the kind of garden with which it is possible that today's and tomorrow's institutions, industrial, administrative, educational, even residential, could well surround themselves. It provides recreation not for one man or one family, like the great English gardens of yesterday, but for a working community of people who, despite jeers which one sometimes hears at Dartington's 'monasticism', are very much *dans le siècle*. It is, in short, in gardens like those of Dartington Hall that the traditions of the great English garden will, if at all, find their continuance.[47]

Right from the beginning it had been obvious to them that something had to be done, although not necessarily so grandly. Brambles and creepers had to be cleared off the courtyard walls to enable Mr Fincham to inspect the stonework to see where it needed replacing. The walls and chicken-wire that divided the courtyard had to be removed, as did the large box-tree growing inside the roofless Great Hall. John Holand's tiltyard was so packed with a formal Dutch garden as well as shrubs and a giant monkey-puzzle that its form could hardly be picked out at all.

Having begun to reveal what lay under the clutter their next step was to seek advice, in the first place from Avery Tipping, previously editor of *Country Life*. He proposed planting new yew hedges and retaining walls. He also introduced Mr Stuart Lynch as the first Gardens Superintendent, whose immediate achievement was to clear the tiltyard which was found to be on two levels. The lower one Leonard was convinced had once been the site of a pit for bull- and bear-baiting. In *News of the Day* for 26 October 1955 he recalled that the old Miss Champernowne had told him, 'When I was a small girl in the nineties my very old great aunt told me that when she was a very small girl, she remembered being pulled away from the nursery window at the top of the house and being forbidden by her nanny to look at the bear and bull-baiting then going on in the "sunken garden".' The twelve apostles or Irish yews may have been planted to screen the bullring from the nursery windows. To Leonard, the historian, there was no doubt of it.

Mr Lynch did not have the vision they had hoped for and some years later, in 1934, Dorothy asked Mrs Beatrix Farrand to advise her. Already famous as a garden designer who had continued in America the English tradition of the grand garden, she was a niece of Edith Wharton, the chronicler of New York at the time Dorothy was a girl, and had worked for Dorothy and Willard at Westbury. She was known as Queen Elizabeth to the gardeners, Trix to Dorothy. She began by redesigning the courtyard and then made four new paths through the woodland, planted with camellias, magnolias and rhododendrons. She was a great planter of shrubs, and never singly. Dorothy learnt this lesson from her. 'She believed in using the native plants to full advantage, especially yew, bay and holly, for "backbone" planting (to give shelter and background), arranging against these a wide variety of magnolias and rhododendrons and other woodland shrubs.'[48]

Unfortunately Mrs Farrand could not return to England either during the war or after; she was succeeded by a leading English landscape architect, Mr Percy Cane, who had a special eye for vistas. He made the Glade which provided a new vista from the temple down to the bastion from where, according to Dorothy, the 'land in the distance seems to take the form of soft green waves, silently rolling in'.[49] He created another vista from High Meadow at the top of the garden. He built a steep flight of steps at the side of the terraces to connect the glade with the rockery as witness to his wish (and Dorothy's) both to have separate parts of the garden and to connect them up with each other to make a whole.

Up to the war Dorothy and Leonard had been unobtrusive patrons of the garden as well as all the other arts except the theatre. From 1940 for the rest of her life, when she did not have other duties, she was to be seen on almost any fine day in the garden in her blue woollen trousers, windcheater, old boots and large blue hat, carrying a trowel and a small fork which she used assiduously, often so absorbed she did not see other people at all, except for William, the old gardener she worked with; Mr Calthorpe, the Supertintendent; later on his successor, Mr Johnson, who, when Dorothy was away, would hold back a lot of planting until she returned, because 'she so enjoys helping with it',[50] and his successor, Terry Underhill.

In 1943 she started a day-by-day gardening diary which she kept up for a quarter of a century, recording her never-failing appreciation of all that was happening in it. If the garden was a picture it was certainly not a still:

2 January 1943: Great spread of winter aconite on top terrace walk – utterly entrancing.
18 January 1946: Strange light on everything today – with white earth and dark sky. The planes looked tawny and the beeches and oaks very dark grey. All the values are changed, as if under spell of an eclipse.

On 31 March 1968,

Corylopsis willmottiae – top glade one of heaven's gifts and Percy Cane's – it is rapidly becoming one of my favourite shrubs and the scent in the study and my bedroom is one of the joys of Emily's arrangements. Must increase the heavenly shrub in Eldorado and Glade and Dell.

She also increasingly took the lead, the artist-gardener, deciding everything on aesthetic grounds. She said in her guide to the gardens, as she often said emphatically in conversation, that 'this is not a garden of botanical specimens; it is a garden based on personal choice and dis-crimination, where only those plants will be found that seem to flourish and to fit into the total design'.[51] She had a feel for the general composition and for getting each of the colours right within it. Many of the day-to-day comments in the diary were critical of colours 'swearing with each other', as she put it, colours that to her eye did not quite match:[52]

I've had a bit of a shock – I've decided we have too much Rhodo Praecox! It looks dingy with the orange-brown effect of beech leaves on the ground. They kill each other completely. I'm afraid we must remove half the clump – perhaps all Praecox this side Davidia.

Half the clump was promptly taken away. On another occasion:[53]

> Horrors! All the Coccinea Azaleas are frightful when seen from steps with crimson Tricuspidaria in foreground and deep blue-purple iris siberica.

She had favourite colour combinations. Most of them are still there in the herbaceous border as she herself described it:[54]

> The border itself is restrained in colour to blend with the soft grey wall. Pale yellow predominates, provided in the main verbascum, rue, fennel, Hemerocallis citrina baroni, lupin Sunshine, Thalictrum glaucum and Potentilla fruticosa Vilmoriniana. Delphinium and salvias have been introduced here and there to give patches of blue and purple, and grey artemisia acts as a link throughout the length of the border. In July, when the season for flowering shrubs is largely over, the Sunny Border is at its best.

She had two especially favoured colours – blue – used as much in the garden as in her own hats and dresses, and white – white hyacinths, white ox-eye daisies, white chrysanthemums, especially the small American variety, white lilies of the valley, white lily-flowered tulips. She even liked pink. After waiting twenty-five years for Magnolia Campbellii to bloom, when it did so, on 7 May 1958, she wrote in her diary 'Glory, glory Halleluja!' Neither she nor Leonard agreed on this with Goldie who said, 'I don't like pink. I did speak to God about it; however some people do, and anyhow it can't be helped.'[55]

To the gardening staff all this could sometimes seem wayward. They could not understand why, on what seemed like a whim, she would rip out this and plant that instead. According to Miss Hull-Brown, Dorothy's long-time secretary, one of the gardeners used to say to plants as he put them in, 'I don't know how long you'll be there: you'd better start blooming quickly.'[56]

One of the comments of Terry Underhill, when he was Garden Superintendent, is to much the same effect:[57]

> Someone she highly respected – I believe it was Julian Huxley – said, looking at a double marsh marigold in the Dell, 'Why on earth have you got that there?' I said 'You've always liked it.' 'I don't now,' said Dorothy. So I took it up but moved it to another part of the garden. She saw it next year and said, 'How nice! Why haven't we got some more of it?'

But to Dorothy there was an enduring sense of the 'wonder of it all'. She wrote to Margaret Isherwood:[58]

> How I wish you could see the garden. It is the moment when daffodils and primroses cover the terraces and the grass slope down the drive — and the magnolias are in bloom — and forsythia a golden haze that I can see from the study window — and rhododendrons just coming out. Jerry and I rush out whenever we can to have a fresh look at the wonder of it all.

Soon after Dorothy found her second vocation after the theatre Chris Martin produced a report in 1941 on the Arts Department which proved to be of great significance for its future. He was by then assisted by Peter Cox who had come in 1940. Martin's health had never been good. He suffered from TB. In the first years of the war he was in bed a great deal; he had much time for reflection which he put to good use. What should Dartington aim to do in the future, he kept asking himself, his wife, Cicely, and Peter.

To answer he had to look back at what had been done so far, particularly since his 1934 report, written when Jooss had already come over from Essen. He had been all for professional standards then, decrying the dilettantism of the amateur. He did not say, expressly, that he had been wrong. Rather that the opportunity Dartington had had then was very unlikely to recur. It had been able to draw in professionals with the highest standards where they would not have been able to (and could not now) attract comparable English people. Their English counterparts, if there were any, would have been deterred by the geographical distance from London as the centre of the arts (and of much else) for the whole country, whereas the refugees were attracted by the distance put between them and Essen or Moscow. For this reason they could not build a future on a new English Jooss or a new English Chekhov. They had to look in other directions.

The amateur could again emerge from the shadows. The arts were important not just for the good life they could afford professionals, and the pleasure (and more) they gave to their audiences, but also the fulfilment they could give to amateurs when they stopped being audiences and became practitioners themselves even though not professional ones. The more this happened the more would the amateur and the professional nourish each other in a mutual dependence. For music this had happened in England in the second half of the sixteenth and at the beginning of the seventeenth centuries at the time of Byrd, Morley, Dowland and Gibbons. It happened in Germany where even a small city like Essen could support an opera house (and a ballet). It still happened in England north of the Trent, though not in the south:[59]

> The reason for the musical race north of the Trent is that every second man either belongs to a brass band or, more important, to some choir, chorus or choral society. While in his band or society his standard of performance may not be very high (though it is often very high indeed), he has a knowledge of music and an appreciation of it which draws him in large numbers to support opera, orchestral performances and concerts. In other words, musical appreciation is founded upon musical experience. It is my firm conviction that the same is true, to a lesser degree, of the theatre.

This line of argument led, quite naturally, to a reversal of Martin's position in 1934 when, fresh to the job, he was sensible enough to tread the same path as his employers. It would be for the best if professionals could be found, with high standards themselves, who would devote themselves to fostering experience amongst amateurs of all the arts. The future department should be built around them.

He wanted for each of the arts one such person to form a small school with no more than twenty students, one in dance, one in drama, one in music, one in painting. The professional head of each school would be kept engaged and stimulated by other professionals amongst his staff and by students. The amateurs would be served (and being served, serve) by being cultivated by the professionals. They were waiting to be picked up where Margaret Barr had left them at Dartington (though he did not say that) and in the rural area around it. Amateurs would also be served by the students being trained not so much as performers as teachers.

Not for nothing did Martin call his plan what very few people at Dartington had ever dared to call theirs, a blueprint. Obviously it has not been followed in every particular. But it still has, over a longer period than for the school or any other local plan I can think of except the garden, partly because, with Peter Cox at his side, Martin carried his successor with him. If Martin could be reincarnated at Dartington today, he would perhaps be most surprised by the scale of the College of Arts, surely not by its design. From 1941 onwards there was for the first time a policy for the arts that deserved the name.

The policy included short in-service and refresher courses for teachers, often isolated in their work as they were. Up to 1963 the Arts Department organised a variety of them, for teachers, for people in other jobs and also for societies or individual members of the public who wanted to pursue an interest like folk dancing or gardening. In 1963 all such courses were taken over by the Devon Centre for Further Education, opened in the East Wing of the courtyard as the joint responsibility of the

20 Leonard and Dorothy on holiday at Klosters, Switzerland, 1927 or 1930

21 Dorothy's five children, c. 1931. From left to right: Bill and Ruth Elmhirst, Beatrice, Whitney and Michael Straight

22 Dorothy (centre) with Michael Chekhov and Anna de Goguel, a student, in the Chekhov Theatre Studio, Dartington, *c.* 1937

23 Dorothy as Aase in a scene from *Peer Gynt,* a Chekhov Theatre Studio production in the Barn Theatre, Dartington, 1938

College of Arts and Devon County Council. Many of the classes at the Adult Education Centre, launched at Shinners Bridge in 1947, gave people living locally the opportunity to learn about and to practise the arts. So from 1964 onwards did the annual Summer School of Art. The Playgoers Society from 1946 on has been responsible for one performance after another, often combining amateurs with professionals. The Dartington Summer School of Music which moved from Bryanston in 1953 brought amateurs and professionals together for a month at a time and gave local people a chance to attend concerts by musicians of international standing. Concerts, plays and exhibitions were also one of the responsibilities of the new Arts Department until the function was taken over in 1966 by the newly formed Dartington Arts Society.

Martin had, of course, to carry Dorothy and Leonard with him. As to the content this was not too difficult. They did not want to go back to the 1930s. Jooss had too many imperfections and Chekhov too few: for Dorothy it was in the highest degree unlikely that there would ever be another like him. Another effort of that kind could easily be an anticlimax. They were ready to start again as they always were when anything was over, without too many regrets. But it was another matter when it came to accepting the consequences of adopting a policy. Would they continue to choose whoever took their fancy and sack whoever did not? Would they accept in practice that they should not choose a dancer on the strength of a visit to a dressing-room at the Savoy, an actor because Beatrice said his performance was fantastic? If they could not, any policy would be so much chaff blown about in the Devon air.

Peter Cox needed to know. After Martin died in 1944 he stayed on as acting head until a new appointment could be made. Fred Gwatkin, for one, was impressed by him, particularly by the work he had done along with Martin on the Dartington-financed Enquiry into the present state and future prospects of the arts in Britain. The reports were published by PEP (Political and Economic Planning). They covered music, drama, visual arts and the factual film. The relationships the two of them established with a very wide range of artists in the course of making their investigations helped them to fill out the 1941 plan.

While Cox was still only acting and Leonard in India, a painter turned up at Dartington. Dorothy was intrigued by him and wanted to appoint him a resident artist. Peter hesitated and, when Dorothy pressed him, he threw his notables at her. He said that the people who had helped him with the enquiry on the visual arts – Sir Kenneth Clark was a member of the group along with John Rothenstein, Henry Moore, Eric Newton, Barnett Freedman, Philip Hendy and others – should be consulted before such appointments were made. They might know of someone better. Peter knew by her look that 'you did not tell the daughter of a millionaire that she ought to take advice'.[60] Despite that, he asked to see Dorothy again, which he did at tea on the loggia, with Thomas there to hand around the same famous cucumber sandwiches. He told her she would have to think very hard about the future head of the department. She would have to decide whether she was going to run things herself, with someone else to do the administration for her, or appoint a director and leave the choice of people to him. She could not go on as she had with Chris Martin, appointing people herself and leaving him to cope with them or get rid of them if they did not come up to snuff. He won. Peter was appointed, the painter not. It looked as though she, and if she then Leonard when he got back, would after all be prepared to back a man and a policy and accept the implications of doing so as they had done before with Bill Curry. In general, this was how it turned out from that time on.

Martin and Cox might not have succeeded with their plan had it not been for a remarkable woman, a virtuoso who could balance between professional and amateur. She showed the Elmhirsts there were such people as Martin dreamt of. Imogen Holst first visited Dartington in 1938 at the instance of Marjorie Wise to lead the carol-singing before Christmas.[61] The members of the Elmhirst family sang rounds at the breakfast table. This won her heart. Her head was put off when, returning into the private house after the singing, she found Thomas bending down at the house-side of the door to look through the keyhole at what was going on in the Hall. On the one side carols with (it seemed) 'everyone' on the estate joining in, on the other someone, obviously a servant, *not* joining in. Imogen's father, Gustav Holst, was one of William Morris's followers who conducted the first Hammersmith Socialist Choir in Morris's house. She knew artists such as her father needed patrons, and the Elmhirsts were obviously that. It was still difficult to stomach the riches surrounding them and, still more, the fact that some people like Thomas were excluded, or excluded themselves, from the fruits thereof. It was a tiny illustration of the Dartington contradiction in practice.

The next encounter was in the early years of the war. Imogen was appointed a travelling music organiser in the south-western counties to encourage people to make music as well as war. She visited Dartington before and after she came under the wing of the newly created Council for the Encouragement of Music and the Arts (later the Arts Council); and there talked to Martin before he wrote his plan. The travel was eventually too exhausting for her and when he asked her to help with his report on music she accepted. From that came her proposal that Dartington should train teachers for the Rural Music Schools which Mary Ibberson had founded in 1929, their job being to supply rural people of all ages and occupations with a good musical education. What could be more

appropriate for Dartington and, after its international phase, more English, than that? Chris dressed up the notion into a 'Rural Morley
College' – Gustav had made that college in London famous for music
when he taught there – and persuaded Imogen (Imo as she was later called
by everyone in the locality) to take on the job of running the music bit of it.
From Chris, who was a friend of Benjamin Britten and Peter Pears, came
her introduction to them. Chris wrote about the start she made in 1943:[62]

> This term Dartington has begun to make music for itself in a way in
> which during the nine and a half years I have known it, it has never
> been able to do before. This is entirely due to Miss Holst. There is
> something in music open to everyone on almost every evening of the
> week. On Sunday there is choral, on Monday gramophone recital, on
> Tuesday composition, on Wednesday orchestra, on Thursday a music
> lecture, and on Friday part-singing. Saturday is a free day. My only
> anxiety over this very exciting development is lest Miss Holst should
> overtax her not very robust strength. There is, however, no holding
> her, and she regards her present schedule as only a beginning. . . . But
> the Estate music is only one half of Miss Holst's activity. She now has
> a group of four students who are taking pre-service training in music
> under Miss Holst, with the idea of building up a supply of competent
> leaders in the country at large for rural and adult classes. This is
> unquestionably our most important development and is, I know,
> attracting some attention outside Dartington.

Dartington had been strong in the past in the other arts: now with Imo
in the lead it was going from strength to strength in music. Four students
did not stand comparison with those sixty dancers and the marvellous
people in blue. But they were a pointer.

The movement into the new phase was made all the smoother because
Imo had in abundance the asset Margaret Barr did not possess – the
affection and admiration of the founders.[63] She even helped them to get
pleasure out of music, without being in the least sloppy in the way she
treated them. Leonard was in her amateur choir, a leading tenor, with
perhaps the best voice she had, but poor at sight reading. She was
conducting a final rehearsal for Verdi's Requiem. There was about to be an
entry for the tenors. She saw by Leonard's expression, the way his eyes lit
up and the way he lifted his copy of the vocal score, that he was going to
come in a bar too soon. Her only hope was to dash in one slide across the
room, smash her hand down on his copy and slam it to the floor; she knew
that otherwise he'd bring the others in as well. Poor Leonard. He looked
up, blinking. The music went on without him while he picked up his paper;
the other tenors came in at the right place, this time with vigorous direction
from Imo. He showed no resentment; he liked her all the more for her

punctiliousness. She encouraged him to learn the cello, then the recorder. She wrote out two or three books of Bach Chorale tunes for the recorder and for over twenty years he would practise, usually before breakfast in his bedroom. For visitors to the house it was their well-known alarm – the recorder mingled with the birds in the morning air. Dorothy spoke about the comfort of it when he was in bed nursing his ulcer after the Withymead crisis and had time to practise much more than usual.

Dorothy could not sing. She hardly made a squeak even in the breakfast rounds, at least when Imo had her ear cocked, although she would open a soundless mouth to show willing. But she joined the orchestra, sixty strong, with many players who could not read a note, some quite small children, others quite old but who had never played an instrument before. Imo wrote special parts for open strings on the violins and lots of percussion. Dorothy attempted the guitar, to Imo's special satisfaction:

> One of the things I shall never forget was looking out of the Ship Studio window just before an orchestra practice . . . and Dorothy came out of her house and went down one side of the courtyard towards the Hall for our rehearsal swinging her guitar in one hand with an absolutely marvellous happy expression on her face. Completely relaxed, going to an orchestral rehearsal.

Imo was as pleased by that as by her achievement in persuading the four who blossomed forth as the Amadeus Quartet to come and play for the first time at Dartington. Among the many musicians who visited Dartington during Imo's time one was specially dear to them. Ben Britten performed often at Dartington and they went often to Aldeburgh and sent money there as well. One year Dorothy was not able to go and Leonard wrote to her about the Festival:[64]

> Ben was worried that he was neither seeing me nor doing anything to entertain – I absolutely refused I said to be a burden during his very busy time . . . I think we might consider stretching out a little more help to them in the coming year.

For the sake of Imo's students as well as her own pleasure, Dorothy held weekly classes on Shakespeare for sixteen years from 1945 until 1961, well after Imo finally left in 1951 to join Britten and Pears at Aldeburgh. Music and other students joined the few regulars like Helen Glatz, a music teacher, and Mrs Powell, housekeeper for the courtyard. After supper in the private house there were quite often too many for the chairs. Some had to sit on the floor, including always Dorothy who insisted on the floor whenever there was a chance. The main business was the reading of one of the plays, introduced, always, by Dorothy and interspersed with comments from her and with discussion. Dorothy cast the parts and sometimes read herself. The students noticed how this usually quiet person, who talked so slowly and with such reserve, lost all her shyness when she was reading Shakespeare's lines or talking about them, and managed to communicate her excitement to others. She prepared for each evening by consulting her copious notebooks, added to whenever she saw a new production at Stratford, London or Dartington. She would travel 1,000 miles for a new performance of almost any of the plays, many of which she knew almost by heart. She could be shaken even by another reading of one of them:[65]

> My Shakespeare class has just disbanded. There must have been 25 here tonight, all eagerly reading Hamlet, and we had – what I've long been waiting for – a really animated discussion. I threw out a new idea, derived from the book Irene suggested – the most exhilarating study of Shakespeare I've come upon in many a year, by Prof. Goddard of Swarthmore. He spent 15 years writing the book, and being a man of imagination and a psychologist himself, he is able to penetrate more deeply into the poetic imagination of a genius than the more purely intellectual critics of the present day. At all events his treatment of the father–son relationship opens a new vista, as it were – a relief after all the mother–son business of the past. And what a play it is! I found myself shaken to the core as we were reading it tonight.

The character of the Arts Department was largely set in the war and early post-war years by Martin, Cox and Holst. Music became the queen, not drama or the dance, although joined later by both of those and by the visual arts on a much larger scale than in the days of Mark Tobey. There were many crises and transformations to go through after 1951 when Imogen left thirty music students behind her. The college was brought gradually closer to the Ministry of Education and to the Devon County Council. In 1961 the Ministry, after long-sustained efforts by Cox, agreed to support the training of specialist music teachers. They had their musical and dramatic education at Dartington and their training in how to teach at St Luke's College at Exeter (for men) or Rolle College, Exmouth (for women). The Arts Centre became what is now the Dartington College of Arts. A constitution was adopted the following year which gave the County and other bodies the right to nominate members of the Governors along with Dartington Trustees. A new building programme was started. Degrees and diplomas under the auspices of the Council for National Academic Awards were introduced in 1974, starting with a BA in Music and following with one in the Theatre (including Dance) in 1976 and a

Diploma in Higher Education in Art and Design in 1978. The Dartington String Quartet was associated with the music department and also toured the country.

The Elmhirsts' interest was for many years reinforced once again by their family, as it had been before the war when Beatrice was working with Dorothy. Bill followed Beatrice. He was a student of movement at Laban's Centre at Weybridge and in one respect as unusual a student as Beatrice had been: he paid for the building occupied by the centre and gave them continued financial support. After that he studied drama under Michael MacOwan at the London Academy of Music and Dramatic Art, and from there got a job in the Theatre in the Round at Scarborough and in the Shakespeare company at Stratford. Dorothy visited him there in 1957:[66]

> I've just had three heavenly days with Bill. On Sunday he drove me out into the country up to a lovely hillside, where we parked the car and lay in the sun, and he read aloud bits of AS YOU. I had never really penetrated to the startling beauty of certain lines and speeches until Bill brought them to life for me. He himself so completely absorbs Shakespeare's thought and meaning that it is like seeing something for the first time to hear him read and expound. It was a wonderful experience for me, full of revelation.

For a time Bill taught drama at Dartington in the college.

Though wanting to bring education and art together Dorothy and Leonard did not have any plan for achieving a synthesis. They always believed with Coleridge that 'deep thinking is attainable only by a man of deep feeling' – their criticism of Bill Curry, and of me, was that we were too much men of the head – and that the arts could bring about creative action only by marrying feeling and thought. They would have agreed that if man is the work of art that education seeks to form, art could be the chief means of fashioning it. To that end, the Elmhirsts let things happen. Their hopes were enigmatic and often confused. But perhaps that is more the way of the artist – to begin with confusion and trust that, through the struggle of making and discarding, some sort of order will be created. Crystallisation, especially if imposed by any founders, can be death. The work of the last substantial private patrons of the arts in Britain (along with the Christies of Glyndebourne) has at least stood the test of time, so far.

CHAPTER 10

TOWN – COUNTRY

Could the relics of an old English manor
such as Dartington Hall, that is 900 acres
out of an ancient total of 9,000, be used
as the basis of a modern business
enterprise?

Faith and Works, 1937

The two aspirations for education and for the arts that guided Dorothy
and Leonard have dominated the last four chapters. I have hardly touched
so far on their hopes for the local economy. The school would produce
men of peace not war; the arts channel emotions otherwise choked – yes.
But where was the money to come from, that is after the subsidies to the
Devon village from New York City's subway system had been exhausted?
The founders did not have to earn their living. Almost everyone else did,
and had to go on doing so.

The outcome was unusual because Leonard in particular combined
two strands of thinking ordinarily kept apart. It was common enough for
people like him to be very conscious of belonging not just to a country in
the more embracing sense of the word but also with a special intensity of
feeling to the country in the other sense of the word. Leonard was made
into a country boy by watching his father mount his horse at Laxton to
visit his parishioners, by being trained to observe the good crops raised by
some farmers and the poor by others, by the practice he was given on the
cricket field. He acquired a hundred country skills, from cutting stakes to
large-scale rat-catching.

After that prosaic training had been further sharpened by the Indian
poet, Leonard could take for granted where he stood in the long-drawn-
out and never-yet-resolved tug of war between country and city. Before he
proposed the 'English experiment' he was already saying to Dorothy that[1]

> I don't know why it is but somehow I have begun to suspect that city
> life has a devastating effect upon human nature. In the city man
> becomes the sole manifestation of life. He misses certain aspects of
> it – that throbbing, pulsing, creative, fruitful force which surrounds
> man on every side in the country.

His mind was already made up. If there was ever to be a 'Dartington' it
would not be in Detroit or Derby.

In making his choice Leonard was in one respect working against the
grain. The balance had been swinging against rural areas ever since the
Industrial Revolution. Already by the middle of the nineteenth century the
urban population for the first time exceeded the rural. By the end of the
century the urban population was three-quarters of the whole, and when
he bought Dartington it was four-fifths. The country's wealth and power
were securely concentrated in the towns and cities, above all in London. In
another respect he was working with the grain, although he did not know
then just how much – it gave Dartington part of its dynamic. The paradox
of Britain has been that as it has become more industrialised and commer-
cialised so have the supposed or actual values of rural life been more highly
prized – one of the reasons, it is alleged, for the failure of people to put a
more vigorous effort into the performance of British industry in the
twentieth century. If your heart is in the country house or cottage you go to
for weekends or look forward to moving into when you retire, industry
languishes from lack of commitment. Raymond Williams has expressed it
in this way:[2]

> Rural Britain was subsidiary, and knew that it was subsidiary, from
> the late nineteenth century. But so much of the past of the country, its
> feelings and its literature, was involved with rural experience and so
> many of its ideas of how to live well, from the style of the
> country-house to the simplicity of the cottage, persisted and even were
> strengthened, that there is almost an inverse proportion, in the
> twentieth century, between the relative importance of the working
> rural economy and the cultural importance of rural ideas.

To the partisans the country excelled on one criterion after another.
Beauty – were the bowler-hatted commuters pouring out of the station
any match for the birds flying through the air, fish jumping from the rivers,
the foxes stealing from their lairs in the moonlight? Space – would you
rather be edging your way through the crowds on a city pavement, where
Rousseau would have it 'Man's breath is fatal to his fellows',[3] or walking
on your own through a lane or down a footpath between the hawthorns in
blossom? Silence – is the traffic's roar by day and hum by night preferable
to the quietness of the country which allows nature to speak through wind
and rain? Monotony – should each day be enclosed in the routine of a

factory or an office or enlivened by the variety of weather and season? Size – who could fail to feel dwarfed by a city, and not feel country life more to the scale of a man? Dehumanisation of work – can there be any doubt that a worker on the land, with his wide range of skills and with his jobs changing constantly, has more satisfaction than most townsmen? Acquisitiveness – is not the anonymous city-dweller puffed up by his anxiety to surround himself with material goods? Busyness – is not the city-dweller always being driven into frenzies of futile activity which waste his spirit instead of allowing time for contemplation?

Leonard would certainly have agreed with all that. But he also remembered from his childhood the misery of many country people with their long hours of work stretching into the night, their poor wages, their cottages no less damp, cold and overcrowded for having roses over the door. Devon in the 1920s was not all that different from Yorkshire at the beginning of the century. Country life, in both counties, was not country-house life. Many of its mainstays had gone. He said that 'The trouble with the "deeply rooted old world of the English village" is that it is no longer deeply rooted – squire and craftsmen have gone, and half the country parsons are either pensioners or have already disappeared – population declines and it is the villages not affected by D.H. [Dartington Hall] that have declined most rapidly.'[4] Such big people as had stayed put in their big houses often made themselves comfortable by exploiting the poor. Sidney's *Arcadia* was written not in the Peloponnese but in a six-teenth-century park from which the tenants had been evicted by an early and ruthless enclosure.

Leonard's Arcadia could not be brought to life unless all manner of these small and large miseries could be allayed. 'I have, as you know, insisted from the start that the bread and butter end of this experiment must come first, and that we are not an ordinary country house for entertainment and leisure.'[5] In other words, Leonard combined love for the country with respect for the city and hankered after the advantages of both: the good life of a kind which only the countryside can sustain and the material assets which the city enjoyed. Dorothy could not see the signi-ficance of what he was saying until she arrived in Devon. In America the 'countryside', being vigorous and thriving, was not the cue for nostalgia it was for many people in England. There the cities were regarded as suffering from neglect, not the country. But when she saw what material conditions were like in Devon she could understand.

Moving as Leonard did with such ease and frequency between the best of four worlds, between Westbury in what was then the country of Long Island and the flat at 1172 Park Avenue, or between Dartington in what was then the deep countryside of Devon and their other flat at 42 Upper

Brook Street within a stone's throw of Hyde Park, the contrast between country and town was part of his everyday experience. The theme was taken up by many visitors to Dartington. One was Captain Ellis, Secretary of the National Council of Social Service. In 1931 Leonard asked him to make a detailed assessment of the place,[6] what Ellis in reply called a 'Social Audit'.[7] Although offered a fee, the Captain was too busy or the fee not large enough; at any rate no audit was produced. Three years later came Professor Bartlett from Cambridge, one of the foremost social psychologists of the century.

After his visit he wrote Leonard a long letter which set out the views about the good community he had been developing over many years. It would look like Dartington. 'I can only feel very humble about the whole thing, that while I have merely been chucking words together you have been putting it all into deeds.'[8] Leonard was delighted by the tribute from his old university. 'I think perhaps for the first time it gave me a feeling that there could be a meaning to all our struggles during the last seven years, and our hopes for the future – a meaning that I have felt rather than known was there.'[9]

Bartlett put a new slant on the town–country debate. What appealed to him about Dartington was that it was a community differentiated into several distinct functional groups. No rural area would be properly balanced if it depended on agriculture alone. People working in it, while often solid, determined and reliable, were, if they met no one but each other, also prone to an inert sort of contentment not much removed from stupidity. An alive rural community would be made up of people working in industries and in education as well as agriculture. They would stimulate each other, keeping their intelligence 'bright and burnished', rather as Frank Crook and Hein Heckroth were doing when Frank was declaring that photography would put paid to painting. People from diverse occupations would also, being all within the bounds of one community, generate sympathy for each other instead of calling farmworkers dolts, as townspeople were liable to do from a distance, or making farmworkers jealous of industrial workers because they enjoyed much more in the way of possessions and amusements. At Dartington they were all individuals, people not type-clusters, the difference in their standard of life being to some extent justified by the obvious difference in their functions and responsibilities.

Leonard took up Bartlett's argument in a speech he delivered a few months later to the Agricultural Economics Society at Oxford.[10] His attack there on rural areas which could boast only an agricultural occupation was almost identical with Bartlett's. More down-to-earth than the professor but along the same lines, he also came back to the better services that such areas needed:

water, power, sewage, gas, electricity, baths, milk supplies, playgrounds, shops, decently equipped schools, clinics, hospitals and clubs: most of these are still beyond the reach of many of our rural areas. In addition to these material services there are libraries, picture galleries, museums, the pursuit of games, and of the arts, all of which are out of reach of any but the larger and better-off communities and the few wealthy individuals.

His argument was for making the rural more urban. It had always to be complemented by the case for making the urban more rural. Leonard did not like either the large cities or many of the attempts then being made to replace them:

> On the other side of the picture when the urban centre grows too large, certain other desirable things of life are denied to the individuals that dwell in or near to the great city. Miles of asphalt and houses cut them off from green grass and health-giving open-air recreations. . . . Already there is an outcry for the geographical re-planning of the industrial and urban centres to meet this need for work, living and green area to be much more closely associated. A recent example of the need for this can be seen at Becontree, where, with other good building land available, wide areas of the best market garden land in Essex were acquired by the L.C.C. for the building of a town of not less than 120,000 inhabitants. Preference was given to those who worked in London, no open spaces were allowed for between this and adjoining shopping areas, and no central shopping area was provided for the weekly or monthly shopping. Lacking its own industrial and shopping development, morning and evening traffic is all in one direction and though, when compared with isolated rural areas, more services are available, there was here no proper attempt at social planning at all.

When he was talking almost in one breath about the arts and sewage Leonard was at one with the supporters of the garden cities who have had such a large influence on the physical landscape of Britain. All the New Towns (and more recently the authorities for reconstruction of Liverpool and the London Docks) stem from the original garden cities of Letchworth and Welwyn just as the modern Town and Country Planning Association stems from the work of the progenitors of those cities, Patrick Geddes, Ebenezer Howard and Frederic Osborn. They were just as averse as Leonard to old-fashioned cities. Osborn thought they exemplified all the most dreadful errors of 'town canning'[11] when there was an alternative to hand. The Town–Country idea had been worked out by William Morris in *News from Nowhere*, Robert Blatchford in *Merrie England*, Peter Kropotkin in *Fields, Factories and Workshops*, and H. G. Wells in *Anticipations*. Wells prophesied in 1901[12] that 'the London citizen of the year AD 2000 may have a choice of nearly all England and Wales south of Nottingham and east of Exeter as his suburb'. He went on:

> It will certainly be a curious and varied region, far less monotonous than our present English world, still in its thinner regions at any rate, wooded, perhaps rather more abundantly wooded, breaking continually into park and garden, and with everywhere a scattering of houses. . . . Then presently a gathering of houses closer together, and a promenade and a whiff of band and dresses, and then, perhaps a little island of agriculture, hops, or strawberry gardens, field of grey-plumed artichokes, white painted orchard, or brightly neat poultry farm. Through the varied country the new wide roads will run, here cutting through a crest and there running like some colossal aqueduct across a valley, swarming always a multitudinous traffic of bright, swift (and not necessarily ugly) mechanisms; and everywhere amidst the fields and trees linking wires will stretch from pole to pole. . . . The same reasoning that leads to the expectation that the city will diffuse itself until it has taken up considerable areas and many of the characteristics, the greenness, the fresh air, of what is now the country [leads to the expectation that the country] will take to itself many of the qualities of the city.

In the year before Leonard first went to St Anselm's, Wells might almost have been anticipating Dartington.

Leonard was thinking how in specific places town and country could be combined before he met Dorothy, for instance in 1918 when his fantasies in his Indian diary were still about what he might do with his father's estate if only he could get it into his hands:[13]

> Whole of that valley must be colonised. Near town must be suburban houses each with enough garden to grow vegetables the year round and playground for inhabitants. Then small holdings economic enough to support family co-operatively completely. There must be a large hall and a domestic science institute combined with a rural elementary school, secondary and college, and training school for adult small holders, complete hostel accommodation and playing field. . . . Co-op. Soc. must finance scheme.

In 1929 he wrote to A. R. Pelly, a friend who had been at Trinity and who was then working for Welwyn Garden City, saying 'Some time I want you to come down and see our embryo Welwyn in Devonshire.'[14] Leonard was introduced by Pelly to A. E. Malbon, General Manager of Welwyn Builders Ltd, which did all the building for the Garden City. Leonard appointed him Managing Director of Staverton Builders Ltd, Dartington's own building firm which was to do the same job for Dartington's 'garden city'.

One difference between Dartington and the garden cities is that Dartington as a rural version of them has been more like a village than a town, although an exceptionally well-endowed one. Letchworth, Welwyn and all the New Towns have been for migrants from old-fashioned cities. Dartington was meant for country people, even though in practice many also migrated to it from London and other cities. But despite the differences the basic similarity was that both garden city and Dartington were to be town–country. Dartington was to be country but with local employment so that people would not have to travel far to work and have many other amenities of the town as well; and so it has remained.

Visitors can see for themselves that the mixture, as things have turned out, is an unusual one. Dartington is recognisably a village. There are houses, farms and woods, a river lined with trees and a brook that runs into it. The boarding-school and the college are not particularly out of place: many schools and colleges are in the country, in old buildings and in new. But the place also has some features that would ordinarily be thought of as belonging to the town.

The most obvious is that there are simply so many buildings of all sorts, including houses of many different sizes. Most of these have been put up since the Elmhirsts came. The Census for 1921 showed the number of houses in the parish of Dartington was 123; it grew four times by the Census of 1971, to nearly 500. During the same period the population rose from 492 to 1,560.

The growth of Dartington's population has been sharper than any other parish in Devon which is not contiguous to a large town: so much so that the density judged by the number of people per acre has more than doubled, not by any means to the level of cities or towns proper – the earlier new towns had a density of some eighteen persons per acre[15] – but to a point a good deal higher than most other rural parishes. Its density is something of a town–country one, even if nearer the country than the town.

Town is suggested (too much so for some local residents) by the kind of buildings as well as by their number. The shops could exist in a thriving village. Not so easily the tweed mill or the furniture factory, nor the large office cluster – what could all that be for in an ordinary village? – nor, above all, the amenities. I don't know any other remote parish which has a Hall for concerts and meetings, two theatres, one doubling as a cinema, a studio for dance performances and several others for small concerts, four club bars, three restaurants, a residential adult education centre as well as a non-residential one for local people, a state primary school, an independent day and boarding school, a nursery school, a playgroup and a special school for handicapped children, a large variety of sports clubs, the big garden open at all times free of charge, and sheltered housing for elderly people.

Dartington was, and is, like garden cities in another respect as well. The ownership of all the land has been vested in one body, the Dartington Hall Trust. There are no private shareholders, no private interests – and in principle it has immortality since the Trust does not cease to exist when any of its Trustees do. This constitutional feature has had two lasting consequences for Dartington as well as for the garden cities. The land can be planned as a whole. When there are many different landowners such planning becomes very difficult, which accounts for the common use of compulsory acquisition when land is needed for any large common scheme such as city-centre reconstruction, a motorway or even a small housing estate. This is not to say, of course, that the use of the land is planned in practice; but at least it *can* be.

The second effect is that increases in the value of the land brought about in part by the development undertaken by the Trust belong to it. The Trust automatically gets the 'betterment' resulting from its own activities instead of the benefits going to other landlords who have done nothing themselves to raise the value of their land. Thus the Trustees have been much more ready than they otherwise would have been to invest in the land and what stands on it. The land, raised so much in value by their own efforts as well as by the general inflation, is a much larger asset than it was in 1925, and still growing.

These advantages, plus the tax relief open to a charity, were indeed so great that Leonard, and with him Fred Gwatkin, believed in the 1930s that a Land Trust might be a general remedy for the plight of agriculture in Britain. They were looking for an alternative to the land nationalisation being vigorously campaigned for at the time, and one which could perhaps solve the same problems – how to stop large estates being sold up and fragmented into too many small units, how to get more money invested in land improvement, how to get skilled management into land ownership. The proponents of nationalisation like Leonard's friend, C. S. Orwin,[16] and also Viscount Astor and Seebohm Rowntree,[17] argued that the need for more capital to go into the land was only too obvious and that the State was the only possible source with sufficient resources. The State could not be expected to put money into private land in order to benefit private landowners. If it was to be capitalist the State had also to be owner.

Leonard did not want to go as far as that. The Land Trust he envisaged and recommended in that same Oxford speech would not own all the land any more than President Roosevelt's Tennessee Valley Authority (which Leonard greatly admired) owned the whole of the Tennessee Valley. But the land was 'a national asset in which the community had a predominant overriding interest and before which private interest had to give way'.[18] Leonard's Trust was to act as an intermediary between the State and the landlords, channelling grants, loans and tax reliefs from the former but only to the latter if they conformed to high standards of management. The duty of the Land Trust would be to work out the treaty with each landlord and then to supervise him.

Leonard did not succeed in persuading others to take on the idea. But, tenacious as ever, he stuck to it and achieved some success (see p. 287) when he adapted his original proposal to forestry land. 'All owners of timber or forest lands', he said in 1935, 'shall be required to register with their land trust registry office a working plan for such areas, to be approved by the Land Trustees.'[19] He also went on propagating the general notion of Land Trusts after the war to audiences that were as lethargic as he was still enthusiastic. He would have been pleased by the formation in the late 1970s of a Land Trusts Association which stands by the belief that for land a charitable trust has important advantages over both public and private ownership.[20]

Leonard also had the chance to apply the same sort of idea not so much to ordinary agricultural land as to land which, whether agricultural or not, was primarily of recreational value. In 1945 he was appointed by the Minister of Town and Country Planning to the Hobhouse Committee on National Parks. The interest for him lay partly in a new kind of public body, more in the link between town and country and, still more specifically, in the enlargement of opportunities for townsmen to get into and enjoy a countryside not too much contaminated by the influence of the town. Speaking of Britain the report said:[21]

> Here are no vast expanses of virgin land, rugged mountain ranges, primaeval forests, or great stretches of savannah, teeming with big game, which can be set apart for popular enjoyment and recreation or for the conservation of wild life. . . . Four-fifths of the population dwell in urban areas, many of them in the smoke-laden atmosphere and amid the ceaseless traffic and bustle of our industrial towns and larger cities. They need the refreshment which is obtainable from the beauty and quietness of unspoilt country.

Leonard greatly enjoyed the tours he made with other members of the Committee, his old friend, Julian Huxley, and his new friends, Clough Williams-Ellis and John Dower, who had written the previous report[22] which established the framework which the new Committee was being asked to fill out. Leonard visited several of the areas that might be designated as National Parks: Dartmoor, Exmoor, the Lake District, the Norfolk Broads, the Pembroke Coast, the North York Moors, North Wales, the South Downs and also the Peak District with whose delights he had so many times regaled the Mesopotamian troops. The nights in inns and hotels were almost as pleasurable as the days. Julian and Clough were famous storytellers. Leonard recorded[23] how on one day, for instance, when they were visiting the Marlborough and Berkshire Downs they stayed at the Three Swans at Hungerford. The day's highlight was the house at Compton Beauchamp; originally a Benedictine monastery, it was deliberately built there to counteract the strong magic radiating down from the White Horse, Dragon Hill and the Druidic (so Leonard said) Uffington Castle on the ridges above it. 'The springs came out of the chalk into a moat around the house, full of young carp.' One of Julian's evening stories became a standard part of Leonard's repertoire:

> A lady who had trouble with her dog was advised to take it to consult a vet but by mistake she turned up at a GP of the same name. 'I'm in trouble,' she said, 'I'm losing all the hair from my Seluki, what am I to do?' 'Oh', said the doctor, 'I expect some ointment will fix that. Just lie down on the couch so I can have a look. And don't ride your bicycle for a while.'

Dorothy nearly always managed a wan smile when it came out again.

Dartington was not at all like a garden city or new town in either of the founders' countries. Many of the New Townes built by the American colonists were the same as the modern new towns in Britain: planned:[24]

> Maryland and Virginia selected sites for settlement under their New Towne acts, and like New York and New England, gave them distinction through a unified architectural style. William Penn laid out the central city of Philadelphia and surrounded it with open spaces.

In Britain most new towns including Welwyn and Letchworth as well as the Harlows and the Cumbernaulds have a 'consistent overall character and in each case the chief designers remained with the development corporation over a long period'.[25] Dartington is very different. There could have been a plan. As it is, there is no unified architectural style, nor a consistent overall character.

Partly because neither Leonard nor Dorothy was nearly as sensitive to architecture (let alone planning) as to the other arts, they never saw the need for the appointment of an overall designer for the estate as they did for the gardens.

Bob Hening was the most important architect. He had a hand in the work for forty years, first as estate architect and then on commission for many buildings. But he was never on his own, and he never had a brief from the founders that allowed him to determine an overall design. Leonard now and then wondered whether the lack of it was something that mattered. Bob Hening wrote to him in 1963, 'I continue to feel some anxiety about possible incoherence in the appearance of various new buildings on which I gather you are likely to embark.'[26] It was hardly any wonder. In the previous year, 1962, seven architects were employed by the Trustees simultaneously. Almost every design by these or by very many other architects was a one-off or at best a two-, three-, or four-off. Leonard may have been tempted to tolerate this, even not to notice what was happening, by his passionate interest in the small detail of buildings.

In later years it became standard practice for the lord of the manor and his wife to attend a site meeting before any new building was put up and decide where on the site it should be placed. They were usually attended by several other members of the 'household' – the estate architect, the estate steward, the estate forester if trees were to be felled or planted, occasionally a new professional whom John Holand would not have recognised, a town planning consultant; and with them the user, often frightened that all these important people were just about to take a wayward snap decision he could not possibly live with. Dorothy's overriding concern was for the landscape: the building must not be allowed to mar it. She almost always got her way. At the site inspection in 1960 for the new college hostel at Higher Close, a large, ugly building near the courtyard, she said nothing about the effect on the view until right at the end came the very quiet words – 'Couldn't it all be two feet lower?' It could, and it was, although it meant two feet more of very expensive excavation into the stone.[27] Leonard's concern at the same meeting was with the view from a particular bedroom window.

Dorothy recognised, of course, that buildings (like the Hall itself) could also enhance landscape. On one occasion she knew what she did not want much more clearly than what she did. She opened the subject by telling Hening she had a little problem and could they walk together in the courtyard to discuss it. She wanted a special shelter at the top of the glade in her garden as a point on which her eye and others could focus, but not (it transpired later) a stone one of the kind Percy Cane proposed, which Dorothy described as 'like a bus shelter in the Cotswolds'. Hening tried to visualise what she wanted, suggesting various sorts of oak and other summer houses, all of which Dorothy brushed aside. At last he thought he understood. A classical temple as in eighteenth-century gardens. She beamed and said in her low, long-drawn-out way, 'Of course. Good for you, Bob.' She immediately thought it might be circular. Hening agreed and then realised a circular roof might defeat him. 'Semi-circular then,' said Leonard when he was told about it,[28] and that is what is there now.

They both disapproved of haphazard planting in their own or anyone else's garden. Leonard was at his most caustic about municipal parks where a garden with no sense of overall design was made up of trees and shrubs 'pepper-potted' almost at random. The 'pop-it-in-there' principle ruled most of Britain; even such a treasured spot as the Westonbirt Arboretum was becoming a ' "pop-it-in-there" garden'.[29] Leonard only narrowly saved the campus at the new Exeter University, on whose Council he sat, from being ruined in the same way. The Vice-Chancellor was told that 'The botanic garden which you are getting, and which has ruined the great 18th century plan for Kew, not to mention Stourhead, is slowly creeping up on you.'[30] Avoiding action was taken in time. But as for buildings at Dartington *they* were popped in all over the place. Why so sensitive to one and not the other?

The restoration of the old buildings around the courtyard was a magnificent success, from the giant hammer-beam roof in the Hall down to the stone mullions which replaced the wooden windows in the private house. They were also a handicap, and not just for the Elmhirsts. For they posed a dilemma. New buildings could match the old only if they were in the same medieval style. But if they were, the new would in the eyes of many people be phoney. At first the Elmhirsts, finding it difficult to decide, ditheringly leant towards the medieval. The first staff cottages built in Park Lane, near the courtyard, have a picturesque traditional look to them, being faced with the same porous limestone as the old buildings, roofed with the same Delabole slates and with such an inconvenient internal non-plan that this too could have been medieval. The nursery school at Aller Park was in the same vein, mock-medieval as seen from New York City, with the same stone and the same slates.

But this picturesque style obviously would not continue to serve, let alone the dingy grey roughcast which was the nearest the Barton farms could get to medieval. Quite apart from the objection of phoniness, the stone buildings were too costly even for the Elmhirsts. Also, even at that time there were not enough stonemasons. They had therefore to jump forward from the fourteenth century and if they had at that stage appointed one or a team of like-minded architects to be responsible for the rest of the buildings the new ones might at least have been coherent and consistent. Few would have blamed them for not continuing in the John Holand manner. Yet the chance was lost. When the decision was taken to build a new school Leonard was satisfied with a 'country-house architect'. This was an odd idea. They already had their country house. They now needed houses and schools *in* the country, which was rather different.

Anyway in Oswald Milne they got a fashionable architect. That meant he belonged at that period of the century to the third-time re-run of architectural styles – Georgian had copied classical, and now neo-Georgian was copying Georgian.

So the Elmhirsts got a neo-Georgian school. Milne also designed the dance school and a number of large houses in Orchard Park for executives like those he and other architects with an eye to the main chance were building in many wealthy suburbs. As Hening said of them: 'Dancers depart, weavers wend their way; Orchard Park houses remain forever Esher on the skyline.'[31]

Bill Curry prised them away from this attachment into the arms of Lescaze and the 'modern movement' where they remained until the criticism of his flat roofs and over-boxy stuccoed buildings became too insistent. By then it was too late for an overall plan. After that they let things happen. Architects came and went, leaving only a mark, never an imprint.

Louis de Soissons, architect for many of the houses in Welwyn Garden City, was introduced by Malbon. His job was to design the first housing for Dartington workers. In 1932 twenty-four were built in a cluster at Broom Park for an average of £508 each and twenty-one for £537 each at Huxhams Cross. The latter are shown in Plate 25. In order to demonstrate to other landowners that they, too, could build good houses for their estate workers cheaply and without subsidy the price was kept down – too much, according to some critics. The houses were not only cheap; they looked it, and on the inside it was a penny-pinching mistake to leave washbasins out of the bathrooms, all the more so when the Trustees were willing to spend £3,827 on a new house in Warren Lane for Kurt Jooss. There was also much criticism about the meanness of other houses for 'workers', for example in the terrace by the Parsonage farm. The labourers and their families living there had to share a muddy approach road with sixty cows. The houses were small-scale Milnes, a near replica of others he was building simultaneously for a factory owner in the suburbs of London, at Perivale.

If one major charge against Dartington has been that too many styles have been picked from the architectural supermarket in a century when there has been a plethora of styles, rather than a dominant one, the other has been the absence of any unifying idea in the layout of the buildings. They *are* pepper-potted. In good part this is the responsibility not of the Elmhirsts but of topography. There are two or two and a half chief centres to Dartington – the Hall at the top of the hill; Shinners Bridge at the bottom where the main road from Totnes divides into two, one way to Plymouth, the other to Buckfastleigh – where the primary school, shops and the Dartington central office all are; and a subsidiary centre at the parish church on the Buckfastleigh road. There have been some new buildings, or conversion of old ones, around each of these centres, and a good deal in between as well. Foxhole is a massive affair, itself the size of a small Oxbridge college, half-way between Shinners Bridge and the Hall. But again it has just happened, and looks like it. The new building was not related in any coherent way to the old village centre. Nor for many years were there footpaths between the new hamlets and the old or between the main centres. It would be quite wrong to criticise the Elmhirsts for not creating a village as many English landowners of the last two centuries did, especially when they could lay their hands on industrial wealth. They were not seeking to do that. It would have meant imposing too much on what was already there. The criticism is that they did not place or connect their new buildings in ways that could have made more sense of them, both in aesthetic terms and in day-to-day use.

Up till the war and for a short time after, the Elmhirsts and their agents could do as they liked: it was 'their' land. After 1947 and the Town and Country Planning Act it was no longer theirs in the same kind of way. Thenceforth they had 'nothing more than the bare right to go on using it for its existing purposes',[32] except that they could apply to the new planning authority (the Devon County Council until responsibility was, ridiculously, divided between the County and the South Hams District Council) for permission to do what they would before have done without restraint.

The planners did not impose a plan on what had previously been unplanned, though just conceivably they might have done if they had existed twenty years before. Building went on apace and was accepted as being, by and large, in conformity with one of the dominant concerns of the planners, that new building should be concentrated where building already is and not allowed to sprawl between existing settlements. The major institutional buildings of the post-war years were extensions or near-extensions of the buildings the college occupied in and near the courtyard, the school at Foxhole, Aller Park and the Postern, and the conversion of the old Cider Press at Shinners Bridge into a large shopping complex. The main new residential building has not been in new hamlets, as it was before the war, but inside the existing settlement at Cott. The Trust has built a new estate there at Hunter's Moon.

That there was no clash with the new planners was partly due to the recognition by the Elmhirsts that they were needed. To show how far they conformed, and also to influence the authorities, they appointed their own Dartington planner in Miss Elizabeth Chesterton. She had worked with Professor Sir William Holford, the planner who at Leonard's instance was given the main commission for Exeter University. Leonard fell in very readily with her frame of mind. She had to ensure any ideas the Trustees had should, as he put it, always be 'related to an overall strategy'.[33] More specifically, her job was to advise about planning at Dartington and to prepare an actual plan not just for Dartington but for Totnes and District. This she completed in 1957,[34] with two others on Dartington Hall alone in 1965 and 1971.[35] Both were submitted to the County Council and influenced what they put into their own published plans which described what should, and should not, be tolerated on Trust land. They went a long way towards meeting Dartington's needs. 'The plan recognises the special significance of the Dartington Hall campus by allocating land for educational and ancillary residential uses.'[36]

There was no great conflict with the new planning authorities until after Leonard had died. Maurice Ash succeeded Leonard as Chairman of the Trust. He took the leading part, with Tom Hancock as architect and planner, in preparing the first scheme conceived of for the parish as a whole. The hamlets which were there before 1925 and those which the Elmhirsts had created since were to be joined to the centre of the whole village at Shinners Bridge. The linking was to be done by a series of clusters of houses which would, however, not be like ordinary ones. Each would have a piece of farmland attached so that the householder could work on it part-time while also having another job, or jobs, as well. The farming would be labour-intensive rather than energy-intensive at a time when energy was a great deal more expensive than when Dartington was founded, and threatening to get more so in the future year by year. This fundamental attempt to introduce an 'overall design' was foiled. A plan to build 70 council houses which could have been the first step towards achieving such a design was turned down in 1977 (though having the support of the District Council) by the County Council and then, on appeal, by the Secretary of State.

Dorothy and Leonard were private patrons of architecture on a grand scale, responsible for the largest collection of privately-funded buildings in England in this century. With some exceptions they are not inspiring. But their intention was not to create a twentieth-century estate with a unified plan to it, though they can be criticised for not doing so. Their intention was to create an estate which would combine some of the advantages of town and country.

Dartington is less country than it was; it is also more town. One measure is the extent to which leisure opportunities have been provided. Dartington was unusual almost from the beginning in what it had to offer people in their spare time. In June 1933, to take a month and year at random, there were nine events open to the public of sufficient interest to be worth advertising separately in the Dartington newssheet – two concerts, a dance performance by Margaret Barr, a travel film and five talks, Leonard with lantern slides on 'Russia and its Schools', H. N. Brailsford on 'Can the World Reconstruct Itself?', Andrew MacLaren on 'Political Pantaloons on Economist Donkeys' and Dr Henry Dagger on 'Care of the Teeth'.

By June 1979, to take another month at random, despite television, the number of events had quadrupled, to forty. Twenty-eight of these were concerts, plays, films and dance performances put on under the auspices of the Dartington Arts Society. Many people came to them by car from a wide area embracing the nearest cities of Plymouth, Exeter and Torquay. There were more societies, including an Astronomical Society which put on a lecture by Jack Hamshere for the Einstein Centenary, and an active Natural History Society. There were far more student performances at the college in music, drama and dance, and more exhibitions. Politics were right out. If the quality of life is measured by the opportunity to see and hear performances and take part in non-political discussion then in relation to the number of people served it is not lower than in many cities and certainly higher than in many towns.

I quoted Raymond Williams at the beginning of this chapter. At one period it was certainly the case that the wellbeing of the rural economy was inversely related to the attraction of rural ideas. It is less true now. Today it is the cities, and especially the inner cities, which can claim to be neglected, not in a very general way the rural areas, though of course some parts are deprived. The old question is now raised in yet another context – what should the proper balance be between town and country if the town itself is not to disappear as it once seemed the village might? Leonard was aware of the new problem. He wrote to Miss Chesterton on 10 August 1971:

> We have been warned by M. Dower not to favour indefinite growth and expansion of our artificially planted and developed rural community. But the sudden demand for sites and (Cott) houses compels us to realise and recognise that the combination of choices of schooling for kids, choices of live entertainment, and choices of practice in the arts, Hall, Shinners Bridge and Totnes, are exerting an ever increasing pull on London and escapees from aeroplane noises, expensive commuting etc. etc. Of late we find we can draw on increasingly expert brains and capacities just because the will to flee industrialism is increasing. . . . Chris Zealley and Michael Dower are other moths caught by our sticky paper! If only other old Ducal estates could be converted to similar ends! But we don't want to become a Welwyn in our turn.

The Michael Dower mentioned by Leonard is a planner and Director of the Dartington Amenity Research Trust. He is the son of the man Leonard worked with on the National Parks Committee. Christopher Zealley is a Trustee who had previously worked in Imperial Chemical Industries and the Industrial Reorganisation Corporation.

CHAPTER 11

CULTIVATION OF
THE LAND

━━━━◁•◉•▷━━━━

The life of the community must then be
rooted in the soil.

Outline, 1926

The appeal of the town was its material standard of living. This was not to
be obtained at Dartington by packing more people into the space or even
by widening their opportunities for leisure. It would only come in full
measure if people could earn more money, first in agriculture and silviculture and then in industry.

'Efficient economic organisation', said Leonard, 'is essential to that
high standard of social existence within which all individuals may grow
and flourish.'[1] The point is worth re-emphasising, because at every period
in its history some observers have insisted that Dartington was intended to
be self-sufficient, feeding, clothing, educating and amusing its people from
its own resources. Leonard played with the idea when he was writing the
Prospectus for the school – never again; after that he was always ready to
round with as much fierceness as he ever showed on anyone who said that
was Dartington's purpose. He must have read what Graham Wallas said in
the book so strongly recommended by Goldie, even if he did not remember
it:[2]

> It is true that [William] Morris, for all his greatness, never faced the
> fact that we cannot both eat our cake and have it, cannot use slow
> methods of production and also turn out without overwork large
> quantities of consumable wealth. Once while I listened to him
> lecturing, I made a rough calculation that the citizens of his
> commonwealth, in order to produce by the methods he advocated the
> quantity of beautiful and delicious things which they were to enjoy,
> would have to work about two hundred hours a week. It was only the
> same fact looked at from another point of view which made it

270

impossible for any of Morris's workmen, or indeed for anyone at all whose income was near the present English average, to buy the products either of Morris's workshop at Merton or his Kelmscott Press. There is no more pitiful tragedy than that of the many followers of Tolstoy, who, without Tolstoy's genius or inherited wealth, were slowly worn down by sheer want in the struggle to live the peasant-life which he preached.

Leonard's mind harboured another idea he thought intrinsic to efficiency – the need for scientific experiment. It was not until later that a conflict between the two became gradually more and more apparent. The educational experiment had been shown to be to some extent in conflict with the economic experiment. The same dilemma emerged within the one sector of agriculture.

This emphasis on experiment came from Cornell. Leonard learnt there most of what he knew about husbandry, animals and farm management and along with all the detail absorbed a whole attitude to farming. The School of Agriculture had its own farm on which experimental work could be done to guide local farmers. Leonard could not equip himself with a university demonstration farm like that of Cornell; he could not set up a host of field trials of new seeds and fully controlled experiments for testing new machines and methods. But within its limits of size and staff Dartington was to embody something of the same scientific attitude. Every venture was to be in a looser sense an experiment and therefore assessed by an appropriate 'yardstick of measurement'. Leonard got the term from Cornell and used it constantly throughout his lifetime. In principle everything done at Dartington should be subject to an economic yardstick: retained, if successful, discontinued if not.

This phrase was like another he used even more frequently – positive and negative results. If the attitude came from Cornell, in this case the words did not, but from Sir John Russell, Director of another 'Cornell', an English one, the Rothamsted Experimental Station. Thanking him for what he had done when he visited Dartington in the 1920s Leonard wrote much later:[3]

> I do not know whether you remember your fully justified criticism of me when we first went to see those replicated plots in the early days of Dartington. I have told the story over and over again to different people and it is now embodied in the Proceedings of the International Conference. I apologised for what I called failures, and you said, 'Never let me hear the word "failure" about a scientific experiment. There are either positive or negative results. If you call them failures you will forget about them and not learn from them. For me they are the most exciting part of this experiment. I hope to learn something

from them.' Ever since then I have tried to apply that wise injunction and have found that it not only covers scientific experiments but experiments in human relations as well.

The sceptical spirit of science was not welcome to many people at Dartington; but Leonard drew such comfort from it that I have considered it as the essence of one of the utopian hopes underlying Dartington. He could not help feeling depressed by the failures that occurred. He succeeded in moderating his depression by repeating Sir John Russell's words to himself and others almost as though they were an incantation. There are no failures, only negative results; no failures, only negative results; no failures, only. . . .

This scientific approach meant, if a new venture with one regime could be compared with another following a different, something of special value might always be learnt. As it happened, the configuration of Dartington suggested some such experiment. It was made up of two farms, one of 202 acres with the original farmhouse at Shinners Bridge and the other of 390 acres, the Barton Farm under Frank Crook, at the Hall. At the former the Codd family, three unmarried brothers and an aunt, were scraping along at a near-starvation level when the Elmhirsts bought the estate. Despite their poverty they refused to quit even though tempted by compensation. If they had agreed, Leonard wanted to put in at once a new manager for the farm and establish a collecting centre at Shinners Bridge for milk, eggs and fruit from the estate; they would be sold there in a small shopping centre probably run as a co-operative and the residue transported to other markets. The Codds did not finally leave until Lady Day 1928. By that time the Old Parsonage had been purchased from the Rector to be the centre of the second farm which eventually took in the Codds' territory.

There was little doubt on one point – Dartington, like Devon generally, should concentrate on dairying. The high rainfall produced good grass for cows to feed on; the hills and in some areas the poor soils discouraged arable farming. All the advisers whom Leonard summoned from Cornell, Professor Myers, Dean Ladd and Professor Roehl, agreed that Dartington should float towards the future on milk. But there were different means to this end: traditional Devonshire represented by Crook producing milk indeed but combined with beef; and the modern, represented in Europe by the Danes who were admired even from the heights of Cornell. Follow science and there was only one conclusion – let us compare a Devon and a Danish farm, each learning from the other.

Danish farm needed Danish manager. A few weeks after moving in to 'Elmsleigh', their first house in Totnes, Leonard was off to Denmark with his brother, Richard, and another new man, Roger Morel. He was the son of E. D. Morel who had before the war exposed the exploitation of Congo tribesmen by the Belgians; he was introduced by Kenneth Lindsay. Their first stop was the Elsinore People's College. Dorothy had given some financial support to it from New York. Its Principal, Peter Manniche, told them about a C. F. Nielsen whom he thought might be just their man. When he saw him, Leonard thought so too. Neilsen had been trained as a farmer in Denmark and in Britain. He spoke good English. In the following autumn he became the manager of the Old Parsonage Farm. He had plenty to do to get buildings ready and a foundation stock of good cattle purchased. Strange, in view of what happened later, that Nielsen, good stockman though he was, advised against bringing in from his own country the Friesians which later carried almost all before them in England and devoted himself instead to the improvement of the South Devon breed. Leonard and he hoped by getting good stock and then by selective breeding to put South Devons amongst the world's leading milk cows, adding quantity to the already good quality of their butter fat and colour. He took advice from Henry Wallace, a geneticist who was later Secretary for Agriculture and Vice-President of the USA. Wallace thought it could be done and told him how.

Investment was not spared at the Old Parsonage. Nielsen destroyed two miles of high Devon banks – it was all done in those days by pick and shovel – as he thought them too expensive to repair, a refuge for rabbits, rats and sparrows and a hindrance to machines.[4] Banks removed and Dartington had the largest field in the district, over seventy acres in one piece. It was and is still known as Sneezle's Prairie. Nielsen, a burly man with blonde hair, was known as Sneezle by all but his employees, that is to his face. With advice from others he also designed the new buildings. These were for a time well ahead of current practice, being flatteringly reproduced in the Agricultural Research Council's farm at Stafford. Milking machines and mechanical equipment for cooling and bottling were introduced to make them labour-saving. They gave all-weather protection to men and animals. They ensured the comfort of stock and the cleanliness of milk by having adequate space for each cow, glazed mangers for the cows to lick clean and a wide gutter to take liquid manure into an underground tank. It was curious, though, that among all the experts, including most prominently the agricultural economists, no one foresaw the coming of the tractor. Five horses were to be the only power on Sneezle's farm.

Meanwhile, Frank Crook was continuing in rather the same way he had always done up the hill at the Hall, not specialising nearly so fully on dairy as Nielsen, keeping his pigs, hens, sheep and some beef cattle. Crook had to move out of the main courtyard to make way for the school and into new buildings just outside. Improvements were made on what he had before but not on the full scale of the Old Parsonage. He agreed to convert the mixed farm he had run under the Champernownes, where beef had been as important as milk, into more of a dairy farm supported by the same dual-purpose South Devons on which Nielsen was going to depend.

If these were the two main pieces in the new design, there were several others as well. Roger Morel, thought by many to be the most handsome man on the estate as his wife, Paula, was the most beautiful woman, eventually became Manager of the Orchards Department. It too had an experimental bent to it. As well as cider apples at Dartington he grew kinds of eating apple not grown before in Devon on a farm purchased at Marley. Inspired by the daffodils grown in the Scillies and in Cornwall, he raised early ones further north than before in an 11-acre field near to Foxhole. At the peak of the season, between March and May, his department was sending 200 boxes a day to Covent Garden. He made cider in the Shinners Bridge Farmhouse (which then became known as the Cider Press) under the names of Dartington Hall Mark and Devon Valley, and later on coupled a quite new product, apple juice, with cider. When juice manufacture started in 1935 it was the first time it had been done in Britain.

Before that Morel had helped create a Poultry Department. Leonard was particularly keen to experiment in Britain with an American-style poultry farm. He had studied poultry at Cornell, and he hoped that by following their methods a new way forward might be found for Britain. Thousands of British ex-servicemen and others had set up intensive poultry farms after the war; thousands had failed. There must be a better way. At Leonard's invitation Gustave Heuser, Professor of Poultry at Cornell, came to Dartington in 1926 expressly to get the new venture started. Brother Richard was also sent off to Cornell for a short poultry course before becoming Manager at Dartington. The Poultry Department eventually had 6,000 laying birds in batteries and was selling 200,000 eggs a year as well as many day-old chicks and table birds. This kind of large-scale poultry farm has since become commoner. At that time it seemed to be doomed, mainly by disease. Richard had some success with egg marketing co-operatives, Poultry Farmers of Devon Ltd and then Devon Egg Producers Ltd, but not with poultry. The Department was a negative result.

Clifford Bridge Farm near Moretonhampstead was an experiment in moorland farming which produced the same instructive outcome. But Harry Tope, its manager, if the farm as a whole did not prosper, showed himself a highly skilled pigman and he moved to another Dartington-owned farm at Yelland where he bred pigs with success. His example was followed after the war by Harry Jonas with similar success – a very positive result.

Leonard took the main decisions, to have two farms for comparative purposes, to let Morel go into fruit and flowers and to set his brother up as a poultryman. But much of the detailed planning he left to J. R. Currie, the man who was to become Leonard's closest collaborator at Dartington, head of the Agricultural Economics Research Department and an endless source of confusion at Dartington because of his similarity in name to the Director of Education when he too arrived from America. On the surface he was a bluff Scotsman, every inch an extrovert.

Professor Myers had taught Leonard that farming must always be understood as a business. He was also an agricultural economist and convinced Leonard of the value of this new science. If (he said) farms were to yield better incomes to people working on them the inputs and outputs had to be more carefully costed. Ordinary economists were beginning to be recognised by governments and business. Agricultural economists should have like recognition from farmers.

The idea came from Cornell. So did the man. Jock Currie took a higher degree at the School of Agriculture there after studying agriculture at Glasgow and after managing his mother's farm on the Isle of Arran. He had no job to return to at home. His amalgam of experience was on the face of it as ideal as the other Curry's. He could almost have been appointed unseen. He wasn't. But Leonard liked him when he saw him and said that the Dartington farms would be his laboratory. He was to advise on what should be done to them and collect from them information which would be useful to others outside, 'inspiring them until their farms became, not experimental, but demonstration farms in the true sense of the word: i.e. demonstrating results of applied thought by figures measuring failure and success'.[5] They would thus create around Dartington a miniature version of the agricultural extension service which radiated information from Cornell to farmers in New York State. In addition, he was asked to advise on new business enterprises of any kind at Dartington; it was taken for granted that all new businesses or industries would grow out of the land.

Jock did not accept at once. To a Scotsman Dartington seemed too rum and too English. But he liked his fellow ex-student and eventually he said yes. Starting in December 1927, he was soon at work on the design of Frank Crook's new buildings. His new stables were one of the first to have windows for the horses to look out of. The view improved their tempers.

Currie's first large job was to make a survey of 205 farmers within fifteen miles of Dartington. He did it jointly with W. H. Long of Seale-Hayne Agricultural College.[6] This was at Newton Abbot, well within the 15-mile radius, and Leonard and Jock wanted to improve their relations with the college. The conclusion of the survey was comforting: the basic strategy for the Dartington farms was right. It would be more profitable to produce fluid milk, fresh eggs and poultry than the traditional beef, mutton and butter. The higher the percentage of receipts from dairy products on a particular farm and the higher the percentage of dairy products sold as fluid milk, the higher the income. With that assurance Jock and everyone else who put any faith in surveys could throw themselves with confidence into the work at the Barton and the Old Parsonage.

As economist, Currie was the arbiter between the two farms; but since they were being compared they were also in competition, which meant both the farmers were very wary of him, and naturally ready to blame him for his ignorance or misinterpretation if he blamed them. He was always liable to be caught in the middle between the Dane and the Devonian. He was hindered, anyway, by the unwillingness of farm workers to provide figures whose purpose was obscure to them and by farm managers who were not all that anxious he should get any figures at all. But despite his discomfort with his role of judge he always insisted that Dartington was, first and foremost, a Project or Experiment, and only secondly a business enterprise. He did not use the term, negative results, so freely as Leonard. His attitude was the same. A venture that lost money might be even more valuable for the lessons it could supply than something that was profitable.

Currie's fellow researcher from 1929 on, J. B. E. Patterson, was in charge of the Laboratory. This was also modelled on Cornell. He had an easier time. He was not called on to adjudicate. He made a soil analysis of the estate and kept rainfall and temperature records which helped both farmers, and conducted investigations at their request, for instance into different methods of making grass sileage and of fertilising grassland. Patterson drew nothing but cheers when he proved (and reported in the journal, *Nature*) that pining in sheep, an established Dartmoor disease, was due to cobalt deficiency.[7] There were only regrets when he left in 1946 to join the National Agricultural Advisory Service which took over the work of such private ventures as the Dartington laboratory.

Another Dartington figure was Dr Slater. He was at first appointed Estate Scientist on the recommendation of A. V. Hill whom Leonard knew as a Fellow of his old college at Cambridge. He was soon promoted to be Managing Director of the new company, Dartington Hall Ltd, when it was founded in 1929.

As a scientist he could sympathise with Currie's stance; as Managing Director emphatically not. He found it insufferable that a Company which had to pay its way could be regarded as an Experiment. Why could Currie not come down from his perch? Tell him in what ways each of the two farms was being successful? Advise him on what to do to make them pay? There was one tussle after another between him and Slater, and Leonard was always being called in to arbitrate between the arbitrator and his detractor. Leonard nearly always came down on Currie's side.

Slater did not get on with Nielsen either. He thought Nielsen far too resentful of any interference from the management of the company, that is himself. Nielsen expressed disdain for what he called 'amateurs' in management without having the right to, because he was not making a profit at the Old Parsonage, despite all the heavy investment, whereas Crook was, even though in education and as a stockman he was no match for Nielsen. Slater determined to get rid of him if he could, and seized his opportunity when Nielsen admitted to disposing of a small quantity of milk as Tuberculin Tested when it was not. Nielsen was sacked and Crook appointed joint manager of both farms. So the experiment was brought to an abrupt end, and with it, to Currie's chagrin, the effort to build up the South Devon herd. Crook decided almost at once to sell off and disperse some of the best heifers, the product of ten years of skilled and selective breeding by Nielsen. To Crook they did not have the appearance of a proper South Devon.

Dr Slater as Managing Director certainly had the nominal right to do what he had done. The Company had been set up so that power should be devolved. But devolution in the commercial departments did not work quite in the way it had done in the school. The Dartington contradiction was in evidence. Leonard was still the final arbiter; to him came running everyone who considered Nielsen had been hard done by.

Morel was the first on the scene, writing to Leonard that 'one wonders if a very big issue is not at stake – the whole structure and future of Dartington seems involved'.[8] Leonard sent Morel's letter to Slater, who summoned the offender to his office at once. Slater reported to Leonard, 'I pointed out to him that I cannot have members of my Staff writing letters of this kind to you.'[9] *My* Staff – Leonard was meant to pay attention:

> Morel's defence was that he wrote it in a moment of agitation, and that he was really referring to something which he calls 'the tradition of Dartington', and which, so far as I can see, is simply a general reaction against the attempt on the part of the Company to be a normal, enlightened business concern. He has at the back of his mind an idea that Dartington has certain peculiar principles which should override all conditions of finance and trading.

But the issue was not settled just by decrying the 'peculiar principles'. Leonard havered. He asked his brother, Vic, to prepare a report on the whole affair. Vic interviewed Slater and Nielsen and others and concluded that Slater had been far too severe. Still uncertain, Leonard called for yet another report, this time from Bill Curry, of all people. It must have been galling indeed to Slater to have to give evidence to the headmaster whom he had himself so strongly criticised. Curry says in the report he delivered on 21 March 1939, as though he were a visiting French magistrate, doing everything by the book, that he had examined the documents bearing on the dispute between Nielsen and the Managing Director and had interviewed the principal witnesses. His conclusion, however, was not quite like a French magistrate's. Nielsen, he said, is 'neither a bad man nor a hopeless man, nor one proved to be unfit to follow his profession . . . and some responsibility rests upon the authorities at Dartington to assist him to resume it'. The authorities – namely Leonard – did not reinstate Nielsen but gave him money and lent him more later on so that he could get started on his own farm. Nielsen succeeded; well before he died in 1965 he repaid the whole of the loan to Leonard, unlike most of the people Leonard lent money to.

That was not the end of the story, by any means. Frank Crook ran the Dartington farms in a mainly traditional manner, and in the war he made large profits by doing so. Yet Leonard was never too happy with him and when a new and very promising young farmer arrived in the district Leonard thought he might help to introduce a new era in which there would once again be some pioneering. Peter Sutcliffe, the new man, had been told about Dartington by his sister, Jennifer, who was teaching in the Nursery School. Crook did not take to him. Dr Slater had in 1942 been given leave of absence to take a government post and in 1945 he resigned, and when Peter was appointed a Director and General Manager of the Company in Slater's place Crook too resigned.

When Frank moved out of the Barton Farm House in 1945 he gave up farming and retired. But he stood for election to the Devon County Council in 1946; he opposed Leonard. This was a brave move in a still deferential rural society, even if Dartington did not fit decorously into it and even if Frank was the local man. Leonard's campaign was organised by Peter Sutcliffe, a further aggravation to Crook. Leonard wrote to Basil Liddell Hart about the election on 21 March 1946:

> Frank Crook fought me for the County Council with every weapon the Tories had (and some dirty ones) but lost by over 200 votes. It meant a voyage of discovery around 61 sq. miles of fascinating Devon, and meeting some very sterling people. It was really in one sense a vote of confidence in Dartington.

Frank called Leonard a socialist, still a word to send shivers down some Devon spines.

Amity was restored in the end. Shortly before his death in September 1970 Frank Crook wrote to Leonard in March, 'Although living in Paignton our roots are at Dartington. We would like our ashes strewn up there somewhere.' He chose the spot just inside the Hall garden at the top

24 High Cross House, Dartington, designed by William Lescaze, 1932

25 Houses at Huxhams Cross, Dartington, designed by Louis de Soissons, 1932

26 W.B. Curry, headmaster, Dartington Hall School, *c.* 1946

27 Outside 7 Warren Lane, Dartington, home of Maurice and Ruth Ash, 1948. From left to right: Dorothy, Maurice Ash, Fred Gwatkin, Ruth Ash, Leonard, Michael Young, Pom Elmhirst, Adam Curle (social psychologist), Peter Sutcliffe, Robert Appleby (a Director of Dartington Hall Ltd), Barbara Jewell (secretary to Peter Sutcliffe and Secretary to the Trust). The little girl is Adam Curle's daughter

of High Cross Hill, looking out over the fields. Leonard went to investigate and wrote to Frank, 'I was up among those pine trees this morning cleaning off the old seat where people used to sit when walking up from Cott to church in the old days.'[10] He suggested to Frank that his ashes should be scattered near the seat. He was being matter-of-fact, not macabre. Frank agreed. The stone seat was set into the wall of the Hall garden. Frank and his wife with the fine voice used to like to sit on it and admire the view over the sweep of his farmland. In September 1970 the Crook family gathered there after Frank Crook's cremation. Leonard met them at the gate into the gardens, talked about Frank and served sherry and biscuits. He then left them on their own but went back afterwards to fetch the tray and the glasses.

The next farm manager was Ronald Hawtin. He had worked at the Old Parsonage Farm under Nielsen from 1931 before he was sent on a course at a Farm Institute and became manager of a farm in Cornwall. He could hardly have had a worse start. Frank was so angry he refused to show around either Ronald or Peter Sutcliffe or tell them anything, and he withdrew from the dairy his three daughters who had been looking after the records. No one else knew who the registered customers were for the retail round. Ronald also found nearly all the equipment obsolete. The milking machine buckets were so worn that pieces of rag had to be stuffed into holes in their sides. Here was no experimental or even demonstration farm. The Dartington farms, at any rate at the Old Parsonage, had once been a model. They were no longer.

The re-equipment of the farms began immediately and the decision taken which Frank had always avoided, to become more fully a specialised dairy farm, with meat very much secondary. This forced a further decision about the kind of cows to have. South Devons were not immediately discarded. Leonard, Jock and Peter Sutcliffe went to Scotland in 1946 to look over some herds of Friesians and Ayrshires. Ronald wanted Friesians and that was (according to Peter) clearly right. But Jock out of pride in all things Scottish succeeded in persuading Leonard to favour Ayrshires to accompany the best of the South Devons. It was not until 1961 that the farms went all-Friesian. Long before that the size of the herds at Dartington had been much increased.

The farms did not have again the glamour they had at the time of the experiment. They were also more soundly run. Hawtin proved himself an effective manager, usually making good profits which contributed to the income of the Trust. In 1963, for example, the return on tenant's capital was 17 per cent and the profit per acre over £10.[11] Ronald said Leonard always knew what was happening in any part of the farm, walking over it frequently and attending every possible Farm Committee meeting.

Leonard was 'a first-class practical farmer with sufficient theoretical knowledge to keep his end up with any professor of agriculture'.[12] He did not have a hand in the appointment in 1974 of Ronald's successor, Francis Huntington, but he would certainly have taken as much interest if he had been alive and perhaps especially approved of the return to experiment, when the decision was taken to develop one of the Dartington farms at Rattery for 'low-input' farming under the management of Harry Jonas. The idea was to use a good deal less of the inorganic fertiliser which the chemical industry requires so much energy to produce and generally to cut down on the use of energy by adjusting cultivation, seeds, stocking mix – the whole metabolism of the farm. Following that, in 1980, all the farms cut down on cow numbers and so became more self-sufficient on the strength of home-grown forage.

It cannot be said that Leonard's scientific attitude, his interest in experiment, study and research, bore fruit on the farms. Far from prompting efficiency, the experiment impeded it. The outcome was indeed a negative result, so negative that experimentation on any scale was stopped, too much so many people thought. The pressure for further pioneering at home may have been lifted because he had other interests outside Dartington, in other ventures in which Jock was his full partner.

This was notably so in the International Conference of Agricultural Economists. It had its first meeting at Dartington in 1929, and its first fully-fledged conference at Cornell in 1930. Two Cornell-trained Britons held key offices. Leonard was elected President and remained so until he resigned in 1958. He was then elected Founder-President, a post he held for the rest of his life. Jock Currie was Secretary-Treasurer until 1955, and Secretary until his death in 1958. They were joined by John Maxton as Editor of the Proceedings and also as the Director of the Institute of Agrarian Affairs at Oxford, this being financed from Dartington. The Conference turned into the International Association of Agricultural Economists in 1964. By 1980 it had some 1,600 members spread throughout the world. Leonard played a part in the growth on a world scale of a new profession.[13] A book in his honour was published in 1964. Economists from twenty-four countries contributed to it. The book opened with a formal tribute:[14]

> For nearly thirty years you, L. K. Elmhirst, have been the President of IAAE, and, since 1958, our Founder-President. Not only have you been the leading personality of the international gathering of agricultural economists in a formal sense, but also you have been an inspiring and encouraging spirit in it.

Dartington gave rise to the Conference and the Association. But there was hardly any influence the other way: the Conference did not influence Dartington. There was one notable exception. Leonard, usually with Jock and John, travelled a great deal to create support for the Conference. One of the countries he went to in 1932 was the Soviet Union. He was miserably depressed by almost everything he saw there except for one thing. Russian agriculture, generally so backward, was ahead of the world in one respect: artificial insemination was quite widely used for cows. It had two great advantages. Contagious abortion could not be spread by bulls who ordinarily caught it from infected cows. The only cow seen by the bulls in the AI centres was a teaser cow they were not allowed to get too near to. The semen of the best bulls could also fertilise many hundreds more cows than if they mated in the normal way. Leonard came back excited by what he had seen. There was an obvious link with what he and Jock were hoping to do with the South Devon breed. He was soon in touch with Dr John Hammond at the School of Agriculture at Cambridge, who was experimenting with AI himself. Trials were made at Dartington in 1933 and on a large scale in 1937 and a pilot service scheme begun in 1938. There was a pause till 1943, when Leonard and George Hayter Hames, Chairman of the War Agricultural Executive Committee, agreed to start a Cattle Breeding Centre together. Leonard and Hayter Hames put up £1,500 each to get it going. It was not part of the Dartington Trust. Jock did not want it to be and the two founders thought it would have a better chance of County Council backing as a private venture. As it happened, such backing was never needed. The new service was successful almost right away and, under the chairmanship of Peter Sutcliffe, has remained so ever since. Over 5,000 farmers in Devon and Cornwall are now members. They can call for an almost instant insemination from one of the bulls which live out a peaceful existence at the Centre at Dartington or from bulls at other similar Centres throughout the country.

Another enduring outside interest was in PEP (Political and Economic Planning), a research and policy-making body which achieved a national reputation almost from the moment it was founded. Its vital first meeting was at Dartington in April 1931, two years after Leonard first rang a cow-bell to open his first agricultural conference.

It was partly his interest in agriculture which made him back the new organisation. Agriculture was clearly in need of a 'plan'; but when planning was generally a popular notion amongst people dissatisfied with society as it was, a plan was obviously needed as well for the country as a whole. Dorothy's fortune may have escaped almost unscathed from the Wall Street Crash and the worldwide depression that followed it. This was partly because she had a large shareholding in British American Tobacco which her father helped to start, and consumption of tobacco was not hit by the depression as much as other sorts. Few other fortunes survived without suffering, and few other people of any kind. The worse the straits of the economy the more strenuous the search for a way out. This particular group of planners stemmed from the *Weekend Review*. Max Nicholson, its Assistant Editor, wrote a supplement to it, called *A National Plan for Great Britain*.[15] The ideas were bold. They also needed amplification, and for that a permanent research body was needed to gather the facts about major national issues, to form working groups of knowledgeable people to consider them and to publish the results in easily understood language. Apart from Max, the leading protagonist was the same Kenneth Lindsay who had prepared the way for Leonard's courtship of the New York Princess. Kenneth asked him and Dorothy to take an interest, which they did, handsomely.

The initial group which met the Elmhirsts at Dartington was, apart from Max and Kenneth, Sir Basil Blackett, Gerald Barry, Noel Hall, Julian Huxley, Lawrence Neal and J. C. Pritchard. Dorothy and Leonard were immediately won over by their earnestness and practicality; they were rather like Lippmann and the others who had met ten years before at *The New Republic* meetings. These people were open-minded, they were not taken together attached to any particular party, they were determined that something should be done to relieve the miseries of the world and they believed that reason could point the way. Dorothy and Leonard were glad to advance the first money for it, enough at least to pay the salary of the first Secretary after the new organisation was officially launched two months later. They were joined as the other long-term financier by Israel Sieff, then Vice-Chairman of Marks & Spencer. He and Leonard became close friends and remained so for the next forty years. They swapped around their roles with each other. Israel was PEP's Chairman from 1933 to 1939, and Leonard from 1939 to 1953 and they both served on many working groups, Leonard on those to do with the land and agriculture, Israel more on those to do with industry. Apart from them Max Nicholson was the main driving force in the 1930s and beyond. I followed Max as PEP's Secretary.

Like the International Conference, PEP continued to thrive throughout Leonard's life. It celebrated its 50th anniversary in 1981 with the publication of a history which has only two photographs in it, Leonard's and Israel's.[16] This was in fact shortly after it had merged to form the new Policy Studies Institute which is one of the largest bodies of its kind in Europe. With some 600 'broadsheets' or pamphlets published and 150 books there is hardly a subject of public policy PEP has not touched during the fifty years. If the quality of policy-making by the government has not markedly improved in that time it has not been for want of trying by PEP.

Dorothy did not after the beginning have much to do with PEP except when it had meetings at Dartington, and did not go with Leonard on any of his conference tours, if only because she was not fond enough of Jock or John for that, and Leonard could not normally go without them. The only agricultural tours she made with him were in the war. While Britain was on its own fighting Germany but heavily dependent upon supplies from America Britain's friends in Washington needed all the help they could get from Britain in return. Leonard and Dorothy, as Anglo-Americans, were just the kind of propagandists they were after, for they did not seem propagandists at all. Leonard had many friends in the US Department of Agriculture, the closest of whom was M. L. Wilson, one of its senior officials. They met through President Roosevelt. Wilson saw his chance and cast first Leonard, and then Dorothy, as Britain's propagandists-without-appearing-to-be-so to America's farmers and farmers' wives. The means of delivering the message was to hand, his hand: the land grant colleges like Cornell and the extension services cobwebbing out from them.

Leonard made his first American tour alone in 1941. He wrote to Dorothy in February:[17]

> Really the tour is going well. Each new place is like a deep plunge, and
> one comes up spluttering, but the discussions go on and on, and the
> questions are good and the newsmen keep control of themselves so
> I've never been accused yet of being a 'propagandist', and anyhow the
> general feeling is that unless Uncle Sam and John Bull can pull
> together from now on, we're sunk in war and peace.

In July he was back, this time with Dorothy. They travelled almost continuously for six solid months, moving from one college to another and to many meetings outside them in all but four states of the Union. It was one-night stands and packed houses all the way, talking to tens of thousands of people. Every Dean of every College of Agriculture was told in advance from Washington that Dorothy was the daughter of President Cleveland's Secretary of the Navy, and that Leonard had been a student at Cornell and was the founder of the International Conference of Agricultural Economists.

Dorothy used the same basic speech. She wrote it out in a notebook. Leonard had it typed after her death. She starts with an account of the city in the west of England from where they began their journey to Butte, Montana; Boise, Idaho; Albuquerque, New Mexico and all the other places they visited. The city was Bristol:

> After supper we walked through the streets looking at the
> devastation, here and there a wall left standing, sometimes the front of

a house gone showing the whole interior, like an open doll's house, the staircases often still in place and the fireplaces, and a cupboard or two and clothes hanging on a peg – and sometimes a clock and ornaments still on the mantelpiece. One turned away with a sense almost of indecency as if one were prying into the private life of individuals. Then there were churches open to the sky with the tracery still left in the windows; and sometimes just the façade of a house with only a charred mass of blackness behind it.

But for many blocks there would be nothing at all – just rubble piled high – occasionally a pile of long frayed strips of wood looking like jack straws – the remains of what had once been a floor. It looked as if an earthquake had shaken down all the buildings – levelled them to the earth. But not all the historic monuments had gone – one church, to my mind the second most beautiful church in England [St Mary Redcliffe, the first favourite being Durham], still remained, and we found many an old and precious building still intact. As we walked about we asked ourselves, how much of the old England will still remain – will there be anything left in our cities – any of the old beauty that we cherish so dearly – or must we let it all go and build the whole thing anew. Who knows! . . .

You will remember that on the night of September 7th, 1940 the Germans began their concentrated night attacks on London and for four months London was bombed relentlessly every night save for an occasional lapse. We had imagined that such attacks would last an hour or two. Never had we dreamed that from 8 o'clock in the evening till 6 in the morning these attacks would continue – with relays of bombers coming over, sometimes every fifteen minutes. On the evening of Sunday 8th September we returned to London by train from the North. Half an hour before we were due the lights suddenly went out in the train and we slowed down to a crawl. No one spoke in the carriage – only the familiar exclamation – 'Air raid'. Slowly, slowly the train crept along until finally one hour late we drew up in the station. Still no lights. The porters had small torches and with the help of these we collected our baggage and walked to the entrance. What a scene as we stepped out into the night. The sky a great sheet of crimson to the east – and a stillness like death in the streets – not a sound – no taxis – no buses – no human beings. Deserted and yet glowing with sinister crimson light. . . .

Then for the first time I remember becoming aware of the planes direcly overhead – buzzing over us like angry mosquitoes. Suddenly there was a swish and a whine and a sound like crunching pebbles on a beach – falling through the air – and then the thud of the bomb as it landed. Another almost immediately and a third – so often in three's

– and then the sound of a building falling – glass breaking – bricks crashing – I had been trying to learn a Shakespeare sonnet by heart so I concentrated all the harder on the words. It seemed the best thing to do. An RAF officer and a girl were carrying on an animated conversation opposite – entirely unconcerned. Whizz – whine – I counted the seconds until it fell with another thud. They went on talking – not even listening apparently – I felt better. . . .

The former Chekhov student went on to speak about food rationing and diet in wartime England to show the need for food from American farms. After her the wives of Butte had to listen to an hour of Leonard on wartime farming in Britain. Dorothy enjoyed the tour immensely, pleased, it seems, that she had become garrulous enough to steal time from Leonard on the platform.

This chapter has dealt mainly with agriculture. The subject left to the last is forestry. It was for Dartington itself more of a success story than agriculture. This is mainly because Leonard picked the right man and put him in undisputed charge. Wilfred Hiley first visited Dartington in 1926, introduced by C. S. Orwin. He went on teaching at the Imperial Forestry Institute at Oxford University up to 1930. At the age of 45 his job disappeared when expenditure was cut and he was happy to accept Leonard's invitation to become Dartington's first research officer on forestry. But when the Woodlands Department was created in April 1932 Hiley, without giving up his responsibilities for research, became its Manager. It was as if Jock Currie had been made wholly responsible for the farms.

Not many men could have done both jobs as well as Hiley. A forestry business had to be established. That meant, on Hiley's recommendation, buying further land on the edges of Dartmoor that was particularly suitable for tree-growing and adding it to the woodlands on Dartington estate to make in all about 2,000 acres under woods, nearly all of them to be freshly planted. He calculated that with costs as they were then, the techniques of woodland management as they were then, and the interest rate what it was, Dartington would need these 2,000 acres to produce, eventually, a profitable forestry undertaking which would more than cover the costs that had been incurred during the long years of waiting for the newly planted trees to reach maturity. His forester's utopian dream did not seem too utopian even if it was to take fifty years to achieve. By then the 2,000 acres should contain a 'normal forest':[18]

A forester's ideal is a forest, or group of woodlands, in which an approximately equal volume, or value, of timber can be cut every year. This is the principle of *sustained yield* which is one of the

fundamental conceptions of continuous forest management. . . . A
normal forest is one in which all the age classes are appropriately
represented.

Like a stable human population, he might have said. Hiley explained
further:[19]

> The easiest way to make money in forestry is by selling trees, felled or
> standing. . . . But our object was the converse of this. It was to build
> up a new capital value in the woods by planting, cultivation and
> growth, in sufficiently economic a manner for the investment to prove
> *continuously* profitable.

Such a long view Leonard found very appealing.

It was in sharp contrast to the common attitude. In his Introduction to
Hiley's *A Forestry Venture* Leonard recalled the state of affairs in 1925. He
was talking about landowners like his father:[20]

> Woods, as part of a landed estate, tended to be considered good or
> bad in so far as they offered, or failed to offer, good sport: a
> comfortable home, in fact, for game, foxes or pheasants. Country
> houses were useful to the new rich only if you could reach them easily,
> with your friends, from some industrial centre or from the city of
> London, for weekends, and for sport. Serious forestry was liable to be
> criticized because it was said to interfere too much with sport. In the
> gloom of unthinned conifers there could be little ground-cover and no
> food for pheasants. For the Master of Foxhounds, wire netting was a
> '_____ insult', and his Whip must carry wire-cutting pliers in his
> pocket to teach the forest owner and the tree-planters a lesson.
> 'Whatever would foxes do for food if rabbits were persecuted? . . .'

A further merit in Hiley was that he saw what he was doing not just as
a business but as an experiment which had seldom if ever been tried before.
To find out if the results were negative or positive, the most careful costings
had to be kept. These would show in the end whether the woods were
continuously profitable and meanwhile would tell Hiley and his staff
which growing regime produced the most timber most quickly. Hiley was
keen on much more drastic thinning than had been customary and was
able to pick the right degree of it by relating different densities of trees to
the annual growth in their girth and their height. The research department
remained a long-lasting part of the whole venture.

Hiley wanted to show how the damage done to Britain's remaining
woodlands by the war — when vast numbers of trees were felled — could be
made up. He was not thinking of what the State could do — the Forestry
Commission was already planting new woods on a large scale — but of

private woodland owners. It was to them that the Dartington experiment was addressed.

To this end Wilfred and Leonard kept up an almost continuous attack on the Forestry Commission for not giving more help to private owners. They worked through the Royal Forestry Society of England and Wales; each was its President, Leonard from 1946 to 1948 and Hiley from 1950 to 1952. For the most part they achieved very little, but with one shining exception. Leonard's idea of a scheme of dedication for forestry was polished up for the Society's submission to the government in 1944 in *Post-war Forestry: a Report on Forest Policy*. The details were worked out by Fred Gwatkin in conjunction with the Treasury Solicitors and the whole plan had a strong influence on the Forestry Acts of 1947 and 1951. The outcome was that an owner who agreed to dedicate his woodlands in perpetuity to productive forestry, in accordance with a plan agreed with the Forestry Commission, became eligible for grants from public funds. Leonard claimed that he took the word, dedication, and the idea, from one of his heroes, the Venerable Bede:[21]

> It was the Venerable Bede who pointed out to his King, whose brother was Bede's Bishop, that by handing out land without clearly stated obligations attached, he was taking undue risk with the safety of the realm. The land owes two duties, said Bede, and must be dedicated either to God and to the service of the Holy Church, or to the King for the protection of our shores against invasion.[22]

The Hiley plan for Dartington did not work out as he had hoped. By 1980 some of the woods planted in the early 1930s should have been reaching the ideal of normality and no doubt they were. But the number of acres Hiley recommended under normal forest did not after all turn out to be sufficient for a profitable business. The economic size had, unfortunately, increased. Leonard explained it:[23]

> The economic unit for forest management tends to be more than ten times as big as our original 2,000-acre unit at Dartington and big capital sums are involved. Our 2,000 acres of woods could not any longer today support the costly overhead of good management as well as the demand for capital with which to operate a whole battery of large and expensive machines essential now for the extracting, hauling, processing and transporting to the factory, that a modern forestry industry requires.

For these reasons the commercial operation of the bulk of the woodlands was handed over in 1966 to Fountain Forestry Ltd, who worked in consultation with the Dartington Woodlands Department. After Leonard's death quite large acreages of wood were sold. Inflation made them a good investment, but not in the way Hiley had expected. Under Hiley's successor, Michael Harley, the rest of the woodlands were still one of the Trust's most sizeable assets.

Leonard was fond of trees. He liked other people who liked trees and if the kind of people who did so numbered amongst themselves members of the aristocracy that was no disadvantage either.[24] Leonard enjoyed acting host to many visitors to Dartington woods, from the Royal Forestry Societies, the Country Landowners Association or the Land Agents Society. He could sit for hours on a shooting-stick in a clearing, talking seriously to other men in plus-fours, all of them craning their necks to look up at the 'canopy', to use one of the favourite words of both Leonard and Hiley.

He also worked in the woods himself in a way he could not easily do on the farms. Hiley said in his book, *A Forestry Venture*, that Leonard's 'personal enthusiasm for cultivating trees has been the main influence in building up a successful forestry business. . . . His active participation in forestry has included manual work as well as administrative perspicacity, and we have always left some plantation for him to thin or prune in his spare time.'[25] The other enterprises at Dartington demanded either special-ised skills, as in the various industries, or continuous application, like farming or horticulture. In forestry, however, Leonard could indulge a hobby spasmodically, when it suited him in the midst of a busy life. Gladys Burr, Leonard's secretary from 1958 until his death, said:[26]

> Leonard's favourite occupation was going off to the woods. He had a little rest after lunch and then he would say, 'I am off to the woods.' I could see him through my window with three large axes over his shoulder and his yellow helmet.

His collection of ferocious-looking forestry implements still stands in the porch of the private house, in startlingly incongruous proximity to the pots, paintings and antique furniture just within. The tools were kept there so that they were handy for Leonard to pick up on his way out. Dorothy wrote to Pom and Gwen about them in 1943, just before Leonard was due to go to see them on one of his many visits to Houndhill:[27]

> I think you should tell him, Pom, to bring all his new woodsman outfit! You've never seen such implements! They keep arriving every week – each more murderous than the last – and Jerry is just like a small boy collecting his first tools. The moment he arrives for the weekend we rush out with a new and faster snipper, pruner, weeder, hoe, axe or saw – and we experiment in the garden before setting off to the woods. On Monday morning every path and road around the Hall is blocked with Jerry's fellings and poor Calthorpe [head

gardener] spends the rest of the week tidying up and getting ready for the next onslaught.

These occasions must have been among the very few in his busy life when he was alone. He kept it up until the time he left Dartington in 1973, when he was 80, still stripping to the waist as he wielded one of his axes. In his late 70s he fell into a badger's sett which collapsed as he walked over it and recounted afterwards how he had been unable to get out for some time. After this Stuart Bunce who was Leonard's frequent companion in the woods gave him a whistle to hang around his neck while he was out to summon help if he needed it when he was on his own. Later on they found the whistle rusted and hanging from the branch of a tree, where Leonard had put it while he was working and then forgotten it.[28] In *Who's Who* Leonard gave his recreation as 'care of trees'. Israel Sieff in his own autobiography said that if this was Leonard's recreation his vocation had been the 'care of his fellow men'. Sieff spoke of Dorothy and Leonard together as 'liberal pioneers in a dark age'.[29]

The two aims – efficiency and experiment – proved to be incompatible on the Dartington farms. Experimentation had to be dropped in order to make them as commercially viable as possible. Leonard's interest in science had to find other outlets, which it did in the International Conference. Starting at Dartington in 1929 this was one of his main outside concerns for forty-five years. In silviculture there was more harmony between what went on in and outside Dartington. Commercial operation and experiment were not in conflict, and they were both related to national policy in forestry. In forestry Leonard came close to the classic model of the improving landowner.

CHAPTER 12

REVIVAL OF RURAL INDUSTRY

<hr>

The striking of a happy balance between
rigorous efficiency in the pursuit of
material ends and the growth of a
co-operative and vital corporate life is
never a simple task, and personnel
problems occupied a considerable portion
of our energies in the first six years.

Faith and Works, 1937

Improvements to agriculture and forestry could not by themselves do all that much to raise the standard of life generally. Too few were employed on the farms and in the woods. Dartington, like any other village, needed the wider choice of jobs that only industry in conjunction with agriculture could offer.

This was not in the minds of the Elmhirsts at the beginning. In the departments of the school listed in its *Prospectus* only three out of twelve sounded much like industry – the Building Department was to 'control' all existing resources for construction but the students were to do the building work; the Workshop Department was to employ students on repairs in the Carpentry and Machine Shops; the Crafts Department was to enable students to develop their natural capacities in dyeing and wood carving. It was not a plan for an industrial conglomerate, which was hardly surprising since Leonard was as distant from industry as any other English gentleman. Dorothy was even more so. Her father knew how to make money out of industry; she did not need to. She and Leonard could do what thousands of other couples in England had done for several centuries: transfer the money made in industry to the land; like them also, they were turning their backs if not back to front then half way around on cities and the industry which made life in them so prosperous and so stultifying. If they had not been so much more ignorant of industry than of education, art or forestry they would not have made so many mistakes with it.

It was once again the place which determined what should be done. They were led into agriculture on a larger and more professional scale than they had intended when contemplating the 'English experiment' by finding a working farm all around their school. They acquired Mr Crook and his men with the land. They were led into construction by the cry for help from the crumbling buildings. From there by another step that seemed perfectly natural they were drawn into the sawmilling industry. The sawmill set up at the Hall in 1926 was to cut up the timber needed in the renovation of the buildings, and in the turnery shop within it Bob Cawsey, brought over from Barnstaple, taught his first two apprentices, George Clake and Stanley Tucker, how to fashion surplus wood into broom stocks. The sawmill was doubly justified: a supplier for the local consumer in the reviving courtyard, a user of local raw material drawn from the countryside.

If a sawmill was justified by using a rural raw material, so on that line of reasoning could other industries. A few years later Leonard gave some examples:[1]

> Tanning, saw-milling, and wood-working, specialised woollen fabric weaving, furniture making, the canning and preserving of fruits, vegetables and meats, all belong by right to rural areas. Many of these do survive in country districts, but too often they have failed to move with the times.

The reason they belonged by right was the source of their materials. This alone should give them an important advantage in transport costs and, more important, in the feel that country people would have for the materials they lived amongst and for their local uses.[2] There was therefore only welcome for Roger Morel when, as mentioned in the last chapter, he established, or re-established, the cider press at Shinners Bridge to make high-quality Dartington cider. It was not fully realised at the start that the necessary materials, although they should have been available locally, were not; some thought it rather reprehensible to go to Brittany for cider apples in a short year, or to New Zealand for wool or to north-east America and Scandinavia for timber. Never mind – they were still rural products though not originating in Devon.

There was another strand too in the industrial estate – the special suitability of the crafts for such a place. Leonard had had a success with Leach the potter when he persuaded him to launch out at Dartington. Other crafts too had none of the disadvantages of mass-production – the Elmhirsts would use the cliché, soul-destroying, to describe factories in the Midlands or Clydeside that they had never been inside. Crafts could provide real jobs, humanly satisfying jobs, which combined artistic and manual skills in one. The crafts could unify work and leisure, the professional and the amateur.

To this kind of thinking Dorothy was very receptive. She showed it in a letter she wrote to Leonard in July 1925. She had been driving through Cullompton when she found what she wanted:[3]

> Half-way between Taunton and Exeter there is a sign: 'Hand weaving here'. Do you remember? I resolved today to investigate – which I did. I discovered a tiny two-room house and an Irish gentleman named FitzPatrick hard at work on a loom, which he had himself constructed. He makes delightful tweeds of his own design and wonderful soft woollen materials. I asked him whether he would construct a loom for us and start our work going at Dartington. To my surprise he jumped at the idea. Then I went a step further and enquired whether he would take a boy as apprentice. 'Yes', said he, 'I'll take anyone who is intelligent. I won't take women.'

The ban on her being taken was no deterrent. Herémon FitzPatrick, Toby as he was eventually called by Seniors and Juniors alike, was the kind of man she wanted at Dartington. Leonard took the precaution of checking up on him. He sent some of the cloth Toby had woven to his tailor in Savile Row. He pronounced it to be good quality. The tailor did not know, nor did anyone else, how much the cloth cost to make. It was enough to know that Toby, as well as being a short, bustling, enthusiastic Irishman, had experience of hand-weaving in the West of Ireland and then in Cullompton, and that he was willing to teach the Juniors.

His plan, which became their plan, was for him to build a small textile factory, water-powered and with hand looms, like the mills which still survived in the mountains of Wales. The carding and spinning machinery and the looms were bought second-hand from there and had to be heaved up cliffs with a block and tackle to get them to a road. Such old machinery obviously needed a new building to go into. Made of stone and powered by water, this was built on the Bidwell Brook as a place 'where five or six people will get permanent employment and, we hope, a good return for their labour'.[4] The water wheel unfortunately proved itself a liability. It determined the site; but there was no room for expansion so that later a second mill had to be acquired at Fordingbridge in Hampshire. Toby had in full measure the interest in research so dear to Leonard's heart. He researched into dyeing and into spinning and above all, into machinery. He also built looms in his workshop for use in other rural areas in Britain and in the poor countries of Africa and Asia. These were early examples of the intermediate technology which E. F. Schumacher did so much to promote in the 1950s and 1960s. Toby's machinery was an adjunct to rather than a replacement for manual work in the crafts.

Toby's water-powered mill was not unrepresentative of Dartington's workshops. It was eventually meant to be a commercial one, like the pottery. If the pots which Leach made there had sold at anything like the prices they now command from collectors the world over it would have been a resounding success. But of course they did not.

Another venture was known as Dartington Craftsmen or the Craftsmen's Studio. The building itself was for once made out of second-hand materials, the remains of temporary pavilions at the Bath and West Show. Rex Gardner put the building together and was the organiser of the craftsmen when he was sacked as the first Estate Architect. The Studio sold garden and other furniture designed by Rex and made by craftsmen on the spot. Customers could see their furniture being made before they decided to buy. As Rex added other craft goods to his stock it gradually became the retail shop that is still at Shinners Bridge.

So Leonard and Dorothy had by 1929 rather haphazardly collected two farms, an Orchard Department linked to a cider press, a poultry farm and also a sizeable Building Department (with several hundred men employed), a sawmill, a textile mill and a carpentry shop. They all had to be managed. How was it to be done? The question has haunted Dartington for fifty years.

It was not to be done by any single-minded concentration on management. The heads of departments were to be rather like Leonard, men of many parts with time for other interests than their ordinary jobs. Leonard wrote to John Wales on 8 June 1928:

> You will be interested to hear that in three departments at any rate, forestry, poultry and orchards, plans are in hand to relieve the head man of a great deal of the drudgery, and thus enable them to do much more thinking in relation to outer contacts with school and world than they have been able to do in the past. That is to some extent true of myself also, though the final touches have yet to be added.

Dartington in the 1980s is still waiting for those final touches, fortunately.

Even if the managers were not to be too single-minded it was clear that in the time they could give they had to be efficient. Both of them, and especially Leonard, wanted the efficiency without which the new rural industry would not be able to compete with the urban. All the new ventures had to be 'economic', to be 'put on an economic base', that is become self-supporting, not immediately but after a period of experiment. Leonard was not consistent about how long should be allowed for the experimental phase. A fairly standard statement of his went like this: 'Then we drew up a ten-year programme for each section which ran like this: two to three trial years in which to discover the economic unit of production, one to two to plan and build the unit, two to three to bring it into full operation, and one to two to find the best market for that resulting production.'⁵ After that each section had to cease 'digging into Dorothy's pocket', as Leonard would put it – never his own pocket – and become self-supporting. Education and research in agricultural economics and forestry could not be expected to pay for themselves, nor the arts. But commerce – that was different, it could not go on being subsidised, not beyond ten years at the most.

Cornell left its mark again. Until it became an economic unit (the word 'profit' was hardly ever used) each manager was meant to be an experimenter, taking decisions, yes, but checking their correctness or incorrectness by careful measurement and modifying them accordingly until he got them right. Indeed, to start with it was not thought there was really any difference between agriculture and industry. Jock Currie could help in each case to set up the experiment and to assess it.

The Cornell doctrine made several managers feel dizzy, not knowing whether they were supposed to be experimenting or to have got beyond that into the boring state of being economic. About another guiding belief the founders were perhaps not so much more explicit as more emphatic. They were for efficiency; they were also for humanity. Dorothy was its more forceful exponent: if Leonard was Mr Efficiency she was Mrs Humanity, always ready to say that whatever they did it must not be at the expense of the individual:⁶

> Another value that is more and more important: here at Dartington the individual still counts. You read everywhere, in every paper you turn to, that the individual is being killed by our mechanistic and technological society. That is not true at Dartington – the individual here is still very very important, thank Heaven!

Leonard also spoke for, and interpreted, Dorothy, in the same vein:⁷

> Immediate educational and arts problems take the place for Dorothy of these various cow, hill, field and tree activities for me, and still more – and most vital of all, that intimate giving up of herself over the intimate problems and difficulties in personal relationships that no one measures, that few notice, and that, when the story of Dartington is written, will go largely unrecorded, and yet this is the lubricant that has made it possible so far for so many diverse souls to be busy in one isolated insulated community with comparatively so little of the kind of disturbance and backbiting that one has experienced in similar communities elsewhere, army, missionary and YMCA and

government in India, University communities in the USA or in Cambridge.

To begin with, Leonard was the squire and with Dorothy ran everything, either through one of their stewards like brother Vic or directly by themselves. On 9 January 1926 Leonard arrived 'home' (as it could now be called) to Totnes from the visit to America after the Willard Straight Hall had been opened. Early next morning after a quick look through the letters which had been piling up for him he went out and found Mr Fincham, the Clerk of Works. According to Leonard's notebook, Mr F. had discovered a 'single Tudor hand of clock with Champernowne arms on'. They inspected the private house and decided to try to put a new lift and stairs into the flue that led from the kitchen up to the dining room, and to tuck away their miraculous new toy, a telephone, behind the Hall steps. Having settled that, Leonard was off to the garden to have a long talk with Mr Woods; he gave an American machinery catalogue to Mr Tucker, the woodman, and met Mr Martin in the churchyard where Leonard suggested they should move 'the top' by three feet 'to give more room to living than dead'. Unfortunately, it is not clear what he meant by 'the top'. Tree? Bank? Wall? He broached his wish to buy the Old Parsonage for use as a hostel. Martin was agreeable. The man who leased the shooting rights on the estate called to offer Leonard an old picture of Dartington. He met Mr Crook and they decided against growing maize in the 1926 farming year (pest too much of a danger – unlikely to be enough sun) and to go for roots instead. Leonard wrote to Mr Weir asking him to become architect for the new roof of the Great Hall.

Next day, a Sunday, was almost a holiday. He cleaned the car until 12 noon, when he and Dorothy took a sandwich lunch up to Ugborough golf links, on the edge of Dartmoor, drove back by South Brent, and went to church at Dartington. Come Monday he worked on the prospectus for the school until 10.45 a.m. before looking over the Parsonage. He liked it more than ever, and particularly 'the myriad jackdaws and rooks that circle it morn and afternoon'. After lunch he saw Mr Fincham again about building at the Hall, especially about Dorothy's worries over 'the Bath Stone's yellow hue, rougher and lighter in quality than at Buckfast Abbey'. Both the men went to the music room 'where we eliminated the wall brackets and agreed upon plugs and ceiling lights'. He then invited himself to a cup of tea with the Crooks as he passed the Barton farmhouse. He walked around the sawyard. In the garden he found Mr Woods and his assistants digging out a border. He decided the gardener's cottage needed a proper water supply and more windows. In the evening Mr Tucker came in to the house for a long talk.

During the rest of January and February the notebook shows he interviewed Marjorie Wise for a post in the school, ordered a timber carriage, found a granite cider mill and arranged to have it dragged into the garden, discussed the scheme for hydro-electricity from the Dart at Starverton, saw to the re-stocking of the cider orchards at the Hall, approved the newly cut oak beam to be put in the Library, explored the woods with Vic and saw a greater spotted woodpecker, redwings and four goldfinches, greeted Nielsen on his arrival, discussed farming plans with him and Roger Morel, went to Exeter with Dorothy to arrange for the printing of the school prospectus, delighted in the crocuses, snowdrops, violets and primroses in the garden, settled a demarcation dispute in the orchard between Crook (farmer) and Woods (gardener) – 'first little rumpus . . . just like Surul days' – conducted negotiations for the purchase of the rectory and its land, went to the village school where he talked on woods and birds and gave leave for children to visit two of the estate's woods and 'asked children's assistance in keeping people from pinching ferns', decided on the site for the new Barton Farmhouse, and one evening visited the village hall at Dartington. 'My first session with working men's clubs. Great fun discussing farming the world over,' which Leonard knew a lot more about than the rest of them.

At that time Leonard and Dorothy were not just the fount of authority from which other managers drank. They *were* the authority and they acted for the most part personally as heads of a growing household to which almost everyone belonged. In so far as any balancing had to be done between efficiency and humanity they did it themselves. There was hardly ever any dispute. People were not being sacked. They were being taken on at a great rate, mainly to do the building. Leonard said that in the following years, 1927, 200 of them were employed on the courtyard, the rectory and the Barton.

It could not go on for long so informally and personally. They were away from Dartington so much; someone had to be left in charge. The number of enterprises, as Leonard called them, was expanding, and those in charge had to be vested with some of the founders' authority. Money was being spent; someone had to keep an account of it. Leonard could not play for too long at being a modern John Holand with power not from the King but from America. He had to make it possible for farmer Crook to decide for himself not to plant maize and for someone else to decide which printer to go to for a prospectus.

The first device was the good old one the English never tire of – a committee. Let us have a committee, several committees. Dorothy was delighted with them: they could provide the minimum of structure which was all Dartington needed. She wrote to Ruth Morgan in 1928:[8]

I believe that the place can be run without resorting to a great deal of organisation. There are five committees operating now with power and though we haven't yet arrived at a satisfactory co-ordination of interests and ideas and experience yet I think we are beginning slowly to move in that direction.

I am not sure which the five committees were with power – Dorothy took the minutes at some of them but not all. One was certainly the Education Committee I mentioned in chapter 6. It showed its mettle by appointing from its own members another Committee, an Executive Committee consisting of Leonard, Dorothy and Wyatt Rawson. Another, the Finance Committee, was Leonard, Wyatt and 'Doc' Watson who had known Wyatt in north London and became the first official with a title, Secretary/Accountant. He had an office first at the Old Parsonage and then, more splendidly, in the Staff Dining Room at the Hall. Leonard was very happy with him:[9]

> I originally met Mr Watson through his interest in boy scout work in Barnet, and since I was anxious that in all our enterprises here education should have its place, I enquired as to his experience in the City and found that he was fully qualified for the post of Secretary to the estate here. He has, during the two years he has been with us, had full responsibility for the expenditure of a sum not much less than £100,000. . . . He has also had to take the responsibility of fathering new departments which were being opened by specialists in their respective fields, who, though fully qualified in their own science, had never worked a business enterprise or been attached to one.

With the admirable Watson at the centre and the admirable committees around him all was decidedly well. The only thing still needed was a Management Committee to add on to the Finance Committee, the new committee consisting of the same trusty three together with the addition of Roger Morel. When this step forward was announced the first public signal was given that Leonard, even with Dorothy to help him, could no longer do everything. Everyone on the estate got a letter from him:[10]

> The experiment on the Estate has grown to such proportions that it is no longer possible for me, individually, to formulate policies for the Estate as a whole, or to supervise their execution. I have therefore decided to form a Committee which shall be known as 'The Dartington Hall Estate Management Committee'.

This must have been welcome news. The only fear was that it might mean he and his wife were going to 'withdraw'. They were always being asked by endless people at Dartington as well as by Miss Bogue, Mrs James and others in New York, whatever else they did, never to 'withdraw'. Some people must have found ominous Leonard's statement in the same letter that in future he 'would not be available to discuss business after 6.30 p.m.', the time that has remained ever since right up till the 1980s as the very latest hour for anyone at Dartington to continue working in their offices, that is except for the Trustees and top executives whose office windows are still lit up later. The work must go on.

The next step in the institutionalisation of the squire was the forma-tion of the first company. The ground had been prepared by their new solicitors at McKenna & Co. The solicitors said to the by now willing audience of the two Elmhirsts that they both had to be relieved of the executive management of the estate and that a company with limited liability was the way to do it. I suppose Leonard must have heard of limited liability; he may even have been dazzled by it. Dartington Hall Ltd was formed in July 1929, with a nicely balanced shareholding: Leonard having 64,999 shares, Fred Gwatkin one; neither Dorothy nor Doc Watson, the other Directors, had any.

The relief hoped for did not materialise. On paper the company controlled the new industries – textile, sawmills, ciderhouse, as well as the farms, forestry, poultry, quarries and works departments. In practice it changed nothing. Leonard showed that whatever he wanted to be relieved of it was not power, by appointing himself both its Chairman and its Managing Director. The only real change happened a year later when Dr Slater took over one of his jobs, Managing Director, even if he only obtained limited powers to start with. 'Mr Elmhirst, as Chairman of the Board of Directors, remains primarily responsible for directing the general policy; Dr Slater now becomes responsible for the detailed administration of company affairs with the advice and assistance of the Management Committee.'[11] Dr Slater was the same as Doc Watson in one important respect: he had no experience of business. Slater made himself felt all the same. He wanted to be a proper Managing Director, as the last chapter showed. He wanted to get out from under Leonard.

The Trusts when they came in 1931 made the formal still more so. At first there were three of them, the Land Trust which took over the ownership of all the land and buildings from the Elmhirsts, the School Trust which became the owner and manager of the school and the Dartington Trust to promote research and hold all the shares in the company. A year later the three were merged into one, the Dartington Hall Trust. Leonard was of course Chairman and so remained until 1972. The other Trustees were Dorothy and their two legal advisers, Fred Gwatkin and Pom Elmhirst.

Leonard explained in the Dartington news-sheet[12] that 'without depriving the experiment of the leadership and personal interest of Mr and

Mrs L. K. Elmhirst so long as they are alive' it was necessary to recognise that at any time they might not be:

> Without these Trusts the whole of the Estate would remain in the hands of one single person and it is not difficult to imagine the disastrous effect which his sudden death would have upon the whole of the Dartington Scheme. The death of a Trustee does not affect the continuity of a Scheme since new Trustees must be appointed by the remaining Trustees.

The other prime advantage was to do with tax. The new Trust was a charitable one and after long negotiations with the Charity Commissioners and Inland Revenue it was accepted as exempt from income tax. Any dividends the Trust received were not after that subject to tax.

They were thinking about taxes when the Trust was established, and they continued to do so. The Trust was tax-exempt, but not Dorothy's other money. In 1925 her fortune was worth $35 million. In the following eleven years she spent about $8 million on maintaining her two households in America and on charitable gifts there, the same sum that she spent in England on the household and capital for all the departments and everything else to do with the English experiment at Dartington. Despite having spent this $16 million her fortune was valued at $45 million in 1936 (allowing for price increases since then, the equivalent of some $200 million in 1980). The vulnerability of this $45 million to tax was pointed up by Leonard's failure in the first stage of a legal case he brought against the Inland Revenue. He claimed he was not liable to tax for the years 1925–6 on the grounds that neither he nor Dorothy had intended to stay permanently in the United Kingdom – their intention being the decisive point of law. They lost the first round and also the second in the High Court.[13] Even without this setback it was obvious that if either of them died death duties would have been very heavy, with more than one government squabbling over who should get how much. Leonard calculated that American and British death duties would at one time have taken one-fifth more than the whole value of the fortune.[14]

The device of the Trust had shown its worth. They had given away a small part of their money to it, and although they still controlled it, the money was tax-exempt. Why not do the same with their other money? The lawyers on both sides of the Atlantic advised them to. If they gave away most of their money nothing would be left to tax. The detailed preparation of the scheme was left mainly to Milton Rose, the New York attorney who with his wife, Emily, became their very close friends. He worked night and day on it for nearly a year. Under the settlement £1 million, about one-tenth of the fortune, was settled on the Dartington Trust, that is on top of the land and the other property it already owned. This £1 million investment has been the basis of the Trust's endowment ever since. Nearly all the rest of her money Dorothy also gave away, mainly to her five children but also to the group which ran her American publications and to two new Trusts, the William C. Whitney Foundation which acted as the more formal successor to the Committee of Friends and under the direction of her American children made charitable gifts from New York; and the Elmgrant Trust which did the same from Dartington under the direction of her English children.

After that their financial affairs were in order and a limit set to the amount of money that could be spent on Dartington; the legal structure with its companies and its Trust was as sound as lawyers could make it. The question was whether it could all be made to work in practice. This depended not just on them but on the man they had appointed Managing Director and on their relations with him. They picked him as someone who stood up well to the three cardinal tests which Leonard applied when selecting anyone. He told me what they had been in a talk I had with him shortly before his last visit to America:[15]

> A person must be technically competent at his job. Able to assess his effectiveness at his job with the aid of figures. Able to handle people. We put technical competence first. This meant we often got No. 1 but not No. 2 or No. 3.

Slater was obviously technically competent, but what at? Watson had been a scoutmaster, Slater a scientist, a sort of competence that was more or less irrelevant to the job he had to do. Leonard never mentioned competence as a manager, a quality which is something more than the ability 'to handle people' as Leonard understood it.

Slater's first grave fault was that he was no better at selecting people than Leonard. He sacked Watson, which may have been right, and appointed in his place as secretary, Mr Porter, who certainly had all the proper 'technical competence' – he was a chartered accountant recommended by Price Waterhouse, the Dartington auditors.[16] As with his boss, if he had been a manager as well all might have been well. As it was, he proceeded to build up a Central Office with the function not just of looking after the accounts but of 'monitoring' the whole experiment according to proper yardsticks of measurement. This notion, which was also Leonard's except that he did not intend any central office to become as dominant as Porter wanted it to be, greatly appealed to Slater the scientist. He wished to have the most up-to-date data on each experiment delivered regularly to the centre so that he could take corrective action if necessary. The Central Office in its new Lescaze building grew and grew on the base of very small production departments. It was disliked accordingly by all those being monitored.

The Central Office added more to its grandeur when a central Sales Department was set up as part of it. All the departments were having trouble selling. To Slater and Porter it seemed obvious that the design of the product or the price was not at fault; the only thing wrong was the lack of a sales force. In 1934 they appointed James Harrison to head it. He had been a marketing man for Lever's soap and proceeded to do what he would have done in the sort of large company he knew about – appoint a large London advertising agent, the London Press Exchange, and rent posh London offices and salesrooms at 106 Regent Street and 99 Mount Street. Early in 1936 Leonard's old friend from Trinity and Welwyn, A. R. Pelly, was appointed the London Representative, with a staff of seven under him. All sales except sawn timber, farm products and eggs had to be made through the Sales Department which added 10 per cent to the price for its services.

To make matters worse, there was fairly constant tension between Managing Director and Chairman. When Leonard had been the sole, undisputed boss he had built up many personal relationships with all manner of people on the estate. These could not be changed – the man or woman on the other side of the relationship with the squire made the greatest of efforts to stop them changing – merely because a new Managing Director had appeared. 'Slater's Central Office' some people called it, to draw a sharp line between it and Leonard's HQ up at 'the Hall'. The people with whom Leonard had a special relationship were called 'old-timers' even then, the words being used in a derogatory tone by many of the new-timers and with nostalgic approval by those who would so describe themselves, or, better, by others who would describe them in that way. Jock Currie was an old-timer and so were Leonard's brothers. Many manual workers were in the magic circle as well, bound to Leonard (and to a lesser extent, Dorothy) and he to them by fond memories of events in which they had shared and enjoyable times they had experienced together. In the first years Leonard symbolised the sort of relationship he had with them by behaving like his father in Yorkshire and on a local scale like the King or Queen with Maundy Money. His father gave Christmas boxes of a five-shilling piece to his coachman, groom, keeper and gardeners, and a new penny and an orange to each choirboy. At Dartington, on the pay day before Christmas, Leonard paid the wages himself to every employee, shaking their hands before he passed over the packet. To everyone also he gave cigarettes and toffees, to married couples towels and blankets, to single women silk stockings and to single men ties.

This practice in its full sweep did not outlast the appointment of Dr

Slater. Leonard would instead pay a Christmas visit to each department to shake hands with all their employees and give them his best wishes. Another Christmas institution which lasted for nearly fifty years was the Christmas party for all the children on the estate. This was more Dorothy's occasion than Leonard's. He was banished behind the disguise of Father Christmas. Dorothy was known to be rather indifferent to some of the fruits of her wealth. She once poured chicken gravy over ice-cream and pronounced it delicious. She was constantly giving away her own clothes when new or hardly worn, and did the same with her children's, even the possessions of her personal staff. She gave her long-time secretary, Miss Hull-Brown, a bicycle and then without consultation gave away the same bicycle to a lady visitor to the garden who said she did not know how to get home that night. In contrast, she could hardly have been more aware of all the objects she gathered together for the children at Christmas. By early November of each year her sitting room was stacked high with piles of presents waiting to be carefully chosen and ticketed for each child. Lists were preserved so that on no account would anyone get the same present several years running from the woman who on this occasion was not so much the Chairman's as the squire's wife. Sybil Newman, daughter of Frank Crook, remembers there was always a Christmas tree and tea and a bag of sweets and a balloon for everyone at the end of the party. It was slightly frightening to have to go up to receive a present from Dorothy when one's name was called; she was such a great person at Dartington.[17] Ann Collingbourne said: 'This is what made people so fond of the Elmhirsts, the fact that they met everybody and always wished them a Happy Christmas.'[18] Foundation Day was another time to meet.

Ann Collingbourne, later Welfare Officer and Secretary of the Sickness and Benevolent Committee, is an example of an old-timer. Her husband, Jack, is another. He was an electrician and (as I said before) came with four others from a London contractor for a six-week visit to wire up the buildings in the Hall and install a generator. When the first job was done Leonard asked Jack and all the others to stay. They did so gladly.

Jack called Leonard 'special' partly because of his knack of giving his whole attention to whoever he was talking to. He remembered the impact this made on him in 1926, when he and Leonard discussed the General Strike. Leonard sat on a box and said he sympathised with the miners:[19]

> And I thought, what an extraordinary man, I can't believe it. I mean, ordinary people working in ordinary jobs to come across a man in his position with this attitude was truly remarkable. . . . He had this habit of getting to know people by their Christian names, which everybody enjoyed, because it was unusual for somebody in the position he had – owning a big estate – to actually talk to people.

Leonard drew Jack into adult education and photography. From 1928 to 1934 he was organiser for some of the WEA classes in the Totnes area, including those on the estate. He worked closely with Margaret Barr and gradually became responsible for the stage lighting for almost all the amateur and professional stage productions until Horace Davis was employed by the Arts Department after the war. He also did the lighting for exhibitions of paintings, pottery and sculpture and for concerts, all on top of his full-time job as electrician. He was not paid for them, 'but time off was offered to balance out; except that we were so busy I couldn't get round to taking time off'.[20]

Jack also had a behind-the-scenes unofficial role, along with Wilfred Hiley and Jock Currie, as a member of the Praetorian Guard whom Leonard would consult:[21]

> He was always coming to me about extraordinary things but I never went to him. He in fact came to me at one time and asked what my feeling would be about the reaction on the estate if they had another Trustee known as Michael Young. He also came to me and asked me to come and see him in the study at one time and he wanted my advice on Peter Sutcliffe. Now Peter Sutcliffe doesn't know that and you didn't know it.

Leonard also relied on him in more workaday matters:[22]

> LK had a habit with people he knew of saying, 'I saw this blocked, or that not working, or that window broken – tell somebody about it'. . . . He couldn't resist doing it, he was so anxious if something was wrong that it should be known and he would just give you a direct order to do it and leave you to face the music.

People in positions of authority did not like receiving Leonard's orders through Jack.

For Dr Slater it was not so easy to manage with a boss who, without consulting a departmental manager or, of course, Slater, was himself liable to give direct orders to anyone and then to protect the people who carried them out. Those whom Slater had appointed he had control over; those whom Leonard had appointed or built up a special relationship with, like Jack, could always appeal to him when they were in trouble, especially if they were subject to dismissal – an even more serious threat as the industries floundered. The prospect of Leonard's intervention was a threat to Slater, even though he had a good deal of backing from Gwatkin. Fred wrote to Leonard in 1934, typing with one finger at his flat in Piccadilly:[23]

> I know also that you and Dorothy hate to be ruthless, but it must be borne in mind that inefficient, or indolent people do not help the cause, and to tolerate them is an injustice to them and to others. . . . If people are treated fairly but at the same time discipline is preserved, they will always give their best.

Knowing Gwatkin's mind, Slater would often consult him about how to get rid of people who were in his view 'indolent'. If Leonard was agreed that someone should go then it was straightforward. George Turner[24] and Toby FitzPatrick were eventually sacked without fuss. With others it might be as well to bring the chopper down while the Elmhirsts were in America. One year almost the entire staff of the Drawing Office turned up on the morning after Leonard and Dorothy had been seen off on the New York boat, having received letters at home that morning telling them they were dismissed, with a day's notice. But whatever the time of year people who were close to the Elmhirsts could not be treated in this manner. Roger Morel was one. He had championed Nielsen in the dispute. Slater wrote to Gwatkin:[25]

> The cases of Lynch and Morel are different in character. As far as Lynch is concerned, in my opinion the major difficulty is that his salary is too high. . . . Morel presents an entirely different problem. I have been asked repeatedly by Mr Elmhirst to try and find an outlet for him. It is therefore, I think, extremely unwise in his case to start any discussion or to give him notice before Mr Elmhirst returns. It would be immediately assumed that I have taken this action now because I was afraid to take it in Mr Elmhirst's presence, and Morel would merely accept the fact until Mr Elmhirst's return and then approach him. To take the step without having first obtained the full agreement of Mr Elmhirst would, I think, be extremely unwise.

Morel did not leave the cider factory until 1941 and the orchards until 1944.

There were many pressures on Slater to recognise that, in Dorothy's words, 'here at Dartington the individual still counts'. If he forgot that doctrine, there were plenty of people to remind him – Jack Collingbourne, Currie, Curry, Morel and brother Vic. It was partly their hesitations that protracted the dismissal of Nielsen and procured the same sort of golden handshake for him as for Wyatt and many others. Even if Leonard had had sympathy for Gwatkin's plea for 'discipline' – and he would never have put it before humanity – he would have been held back by all the other people who did not think that way at all and had come to Dartington because it did not wholly belong to the world where commerce ruled over men.

The tension between Slater and his supporters on the one hand, and the Elmhirsts and theirs on the other, became greater after the 1936 reorganisation. The Trust had been set up with its £1 million endowment with the intention that from then on it would stand on its own feet, and, moreover, that the income on the £1 million should be for charitable activities like school, arts, research, not as a source of more capital for ailing industries. In 1936 a further £60,000 of share capital was, it is true, provided for the company and the cumulative losses of £325,920 incurred since 1930 were forgiven. Some loss-making departments – Jock's, the Lab, the moorland farms and pottery – were transferred to the Trust. The Poultry Department had been another heavy loser. Brother Richard resigned in 1936. He said later:[26]

> I think the real trouble was that Dartington was, for me, so exciting emotionally that departmental work became a chore of no special interest compared to the delights of dance and drama and marriage and mistresses! Further, I was nearer to being LK when lecturing at Harper Adams, sitting on directorate or buzzing up to London for PEP or what have you.

With losses forgiven, with additional capital, with notice served on everyone that if an Elmhirst could be dispensed with, so much the more could anyone else, the company with its 300 or so employees was from that time on itself under strict instruction to pay its way.

Having told Slater there would be no more handouts, Leonard could not nearly so easily turn round and tell him not to sack inefficient executives. He could not even raise much of an objection if Slater claimed, as he was bold enough to do, that the very presence of Leonard and Dorothy on the board of the company was a handicap. He did not tell them they knew nothing of business or were far too tolerant of feather-bedding; he said that as long as the names of two millionaires were there on the notepaper customers would not think they really needed to pay their bills and the company would suffer. The Elmhirsts did not like it but they had no answer. While they had been directors every department had made steady annual losses even after they had passed through Leonard's experimental period, or should have done. Drastic action had to be taken, especially as the economy of Britain and the world was still in the depression. But for the moment they did not come off the board. They merely stayed away from meetings. In their place two new experts were appointed: F. C. Lawrence, an industrial consultant, appointed as Technical Adviser, and M. C. Spencer of Price Waterhouse as Financial Adviser.

Even with all this shifting about there was no improvement. All departments continued to lose money in 1938. Slater threatened to close not only what was left of poultry but also the gardens department, textiles, ciderhouse and sales. Although he did not go as far as that, nevertheless his own man, Harrison, was dismissed and, with him, Pelly from the London office. Pelly made a strong protest about the inequity of saving money by sacking people like him while some people were living in such luxury. 'The number and the size of cars at Dartington and the money wasted in similar ways MUST go – or be explained – BEFORE economies are made on the defenceless young and efficient.'[27] Porter went from the Central Office and Hiram Winterbotham from his post as manager of the textile mill. Since even then there was still not enough improvement and the Trustees would advance no more funds, crisis point was reached at the beginning of 1939. Leonard and Dorothy at last resigned as directors although it was afterwards found that they had no right to: they were life-directors. Still, for the moment everyone thought they were out. The Trust's hard man, Mr Gwatkin, was made Chairman.

Another Elmhirst was also sacked. Leonard's old steward, Vic, was the personnel officer and Secretary-Treasurer of the Sickness and Benevolent Fund. The Fund had money to help out any employee or ex-employee suffering hardship. Vic was as greatly liked by employees as he was disliked by managers. He could always be trusted to back any employee in dispute with any manager, including Slater. He also had direct access to Leonard. Slater was much relieved when during the crisis period of February 1939 he was able to dismiss Vic. He gave no reasons. The only explanation Vic himself could offer, when three months later he wrote a report for the Trustees,[28] was that Slater had greatly resented the criticism from Vic that he had been too severe on Nielsen. Looking back on what had happened to him and to many others he could name, one of his main proposals about future policy was that anyone who was going to be sacked should first have a warning that he was likely to be, and be given the reasons why. Vic was too late to save himself. But he did not have to leave Dartington. He moved back to the school of which he had once been joint head and became manager of the school farm. In 1944 Dorothy bought a farm at Aish where Vic and his wife, Helen, could live and where Vic could have some land of his own to work. The main farm was run by Nielsen as Vic's sub-tenant.

As a further blow, the company's pension scheme was abandoned and salaries reduced. All staff were also put on short-term engagements. When early in 1939 a general meeting of all company employees was called in the sawmills at Shinners Bridge, there was not a light heart among the hundreds of men who looked up at the makeshift platform rigged up by the gantry. On it sat not Leonard, nor Gwatkin, but Dr Slater, Mr Wadhams, the chief accountant who had succeeded Mr Porter, and Mr Spencer, the man from Price Waterhouse. Surprisingly, the speaking was left entirely to the outsider, Mr Spencer, whom hardly anyone knew. He never once looked at his glowering audience. Keeping his eyes firmly on the planks in front of him he trudged wearily through his speech. It was remembered by many who were there:[29]

> For too long you've been doing nothing in this place. . . . It can't go on. You've all got to pull your socks up. Everyone, or it's the end. . . . Departments that fail to meet their targets will be closed and their staff sacked. . . . There's no other way.

No questions were invited, let alone comment, in public.

After the meeting employees began talking, angrily, in small groups. Who was this saying that they had been doing nothing? Frank Walters walked back to the Central Office with Mr Wadhams who said the stricture did not apply to Frank of course. He wasn't lazy. Frank was very angry. 'Don't talk silly. He was talking about everyone and he shouldn't have done it.'[30]

Leonard's absence suggested he was not fully behind what Spencer had said. Many people said it could not have been his doing. The boss was not that kind of person. He wouldn't let people be sacked. Others thought it could not have happened at all without Leonard knowing about it and that there might be a march up the hill to the Hall. Some said Leonard would be afraid for Dorothy's safety that night. She would have just come in from a long day in the Chekhov Studio.

As it turned out there was a small improvement in the year ending September 1939: the company's losses were reduced to £23,000 from £35,000 in 1938. But without the war the company still might not have survived. The departments had always had trouble selling as much as they produced. Suddenly it was easy. Imports of food were cut. There was demand for anything the farms could produce. Timber likewise, which meant the sawmills could sell any home-grown timber it could lay hands on, and at very considerable profit to the company. Cider sold at last. Textiles made a profit. After all the years of struggle in the 1930s the company was no longer making losses. Every department was more than making ends meet.

The war also brought the Trustees back into the centre again. Neither Dorothy nor Leonard had liked the symbolism or the fact of being pushed off the board of directors; very few of the other people on the estate, led by the old-timers, liked it either. Since that event there had been a sort of vacuum at the top. The need for personal leadership was made all the greater by the upheavals of the war. The economy of Dartington was stabilised. The hard-nosed managers lost some of their power. But it was not only the German refugees who were frightened by the threat of internment; everyone was anxious about something.

The founders were very much needed. As it turned out, for much of the time only one of them was there. War was the cue for Leonard to be off and away, as it had been for Willard two decades before. Always restless, he could not possibly have passed the time as a country squire even if one now happily restored to power. Dorothy's role at Dartington was for the first time solo rather than duet.

The American trip apart, she was much more continuously at Dartington than ever before or after and more nearly an Englishwoman than ever before. Almost the only place she could get to easily by train was London. She kept on her flat in Upper Brook Street. Sometimes she could see Whitney there, her one child still in England, now a Squadron Leader in the RAF and in the front line of the Battle of Britain. He had been shot down over France; after many months presumed missing he was smuggled back to England. Whitney gave her his news, and she passed it on to Leonard wherever he might happen to be:[31]

> He and the German spotted each other and both dived – Whitney after him. From 20,000 ft. to 1,000 ft. Whitney dropped at the rate of 450 miles an hour firing 1,200 rounds of ammunition. The Germans were firing at him, too, continuously, but thank heaven he escaped. Then at 1,000 feet Whitney brought his plane out of the dive – unscathed and whole – while the Heinkel plunged headlong into the sea and disappeared. It is wonderful and terrible isn't it?

She also met me – I was called Youngster – on many of her visits. In January 1941 she wrote that[32]

> Youngster had arranged a week's program of films in shelters to be run by Bill Hunter and Peter Cox, and it has proved a most unexpected success. . . . Walking through those streets at night, with a jagged skyline of broken buildings above you and only the sound of your own footsteps in the silent street was like making one's way through a city of the dead. But suddenly we slipped round a corner and through an alley, and there we were, in the warmth of the Brewery shelter – about two or three hundred people in all, sitting on their mattresses or rugs, or in some cases, in chairs.

She was intensely involved in the war. Her pacifism was fully abandoned. She could not fight; she could work.

Her mood was as it had been in the years after the previous war when she had been fighting the intolerance of the privileged in the USA. She wrote to Michael on 2 July 1940:

> We have been almost wilfully blind – enjoying life and leisure, refusing to see – everything so pleasant, so easy, so soft. The ruling

class have had every privilege – a life of comfort and ease, perhaps
unexampled – and the rottenness of the system which tolerates
poverty and unemployment and exploitation has been covered over
with a veneer of easy-going democracy that never looked very far
beneath the surface. . . . Soon, of course, the invasion will have begun,
then expectation will give way to something else. We shall
presumably be cut off from you, from one another, from the
world – but I can't believe we will be easily conquered. . . . But as I
look at these antique terraces and trees and buildings I know, if they
are spared, they will bring new life to birth, as they have done, for the
last five hundred years, and it matters little whether we are here or not.

At Dartington she made herself available even more fully than before
she had been gripped by the excitement of working with Chekhov. Anyone
could come and see her about anything at almost any time. She could be
relied on to consult Vic, back in favour on the Sickness and Benevolent
Committee as its acting Chairman when Leonard was away, and after that
as its permanent Chairman, and then to have a word with any manager
who seemed to her to be acting unjustly. Her word was almost as decisive
as in the 'early days'. She also got to know much more about what was
happening through mixing with people on the estate. The kitchen in the
private house was given up 'for the duration', as the phrase went. She, and
Leonard when he was at home, ate in the White Hart dining room with arts
students and the staff from the courtyard. She looked frail, especially when
she was tired, and young students would sometimes try to give up to her
their places in the queue. She always refused. She also took turns in the
White Hart kitchen helping to prepare the lunch. In the village nursery
school she looked after the children and, incidentally, talked to their
mothers about anything and everything, particularly everything at Dartington. 'It is a comfort – perhaps the greatest comfort in the world – to
feel that one can still be of some use to people,' she wrote to Marjorie Wise
on 1 July 1940.

When any new shift had to be made she was there helping to organise
it. She did this for the evacuee children from London who lived at Aller
Park. Links had to be created with Dartington people. Teachers and others
had to be persuaded to take an interest in the children; outings had to be
planned:[33]

> Dartington is undergoing a strange metamorphosis. But I find it rather
> wonderful to see how this place can adapt itself to any situation. We
> now have 150 soldiers quartered in the Dance School and the
> Chekhov Studio, and our own Junior School buildings are filled with
> evacuees. Last night a group of us met to discuss entertainment for the
> soldiers and the teachers; and I foresee a new kind of community life

opening up, based on singing and dancing, painting, acting and all the activities we love so much.

She was quickly on the spot when Plymouth was bombed, devastatingly, on 5 April 1941. Her old friend, Nancy Astor, was still MP for a Plymouth constituency:[34]

> Plymouth is a tragic sight. I went over there at once to have a long talk with Nancy. . . . In answer to my offer of hospitality Nancy decided to send us 20 Nursery School children, and they have been housed here in the Courtyard gym, and the Barn Studio above.

She welcomed successive batches of rescue workers on leave from the cities – ARP (Air Raid Precaution) men and women – and firemen. She got to know quite well men in their successive regiments, British troops first and then American, who were billeted in Margaret Barr's dance school. She called all the sixteen heads of departments together to hear two RAF officers appeal to them to offer work experience to badly burned airmen. When Dorothy added her voice none of the managers could possibly refuse even if they had wanted to. Called Guinea Pigs – Dr McIndoe at his hospital at East Grinstead was using on them his new methods of plastic surgery – the airmen worked in different departments until they returned to the hospital for further operations or were considered fit enough to return to active service. Dorothy did all the administrative work for the scheme.

After her practice in America she also took to speaking to servicemen and others, travelling all over the South West by bus and train or, when she could not get to the meetings by public transport, by official car or in her own car with petrol coupons supplied by the Ministry of Information. It was the reverse of the trip with Leonard. She explained America to English people who suddenly had stationed amongst them millions of American soldiers with plenty of money, plenty of food, plenty of soap[35] and plenty of extraordinary words – movies instead of cinema, automobiles instead of cars, light trucks instead of lorries, wrenches instead of spanners. She spoke so well on 'The Promise of American Life' (taking over the complete title from Croly's book) or 'Our American Allies', or 'Anglo-American Relations' that she was flooded with invitations from RAF, Army, Navy, ARP wardens, firemen, Women's Institutes, Townswomen's Guilds, the WEA, youth clubs. Leonard got the itinerary in his regular letters. Here are two extracts about the same week:

> Tomorrow I go off to Topsham and Dawlish, and the following day to Tiverton. Requests are coming in from Somerset now, and I'm being given the Town Hall in Torquay and heaven knows what else. You should see the cards advertising my meetings – 'Mrs Dorothy

28 Dorothy (centre) with
Imogen Holst and Peter Pears
at the Dartington Summer
School of Music, mid-1950s

29 Leonard in medieval dress at
Foundation Day, 1957

30 Leonard and Dorothy watching the
Plymouth Royal Marine Band,
Foundation Day, 1966

31 Leonard and Dorothy on holiday in
the Bahamas, with Michael Straight
(left) and Bill Elmhirst (right), c. 1960

32 Leonard (right) with Tom Brown,
Forester at Dartington, 1929–41, at
Foundation Day, 1952

33 Leonard and Dorothy
at Foundation Day, 1967

Elmhirst will lecture on Our American Allies' – oh dear – it's all so funny. I expect they will soon be tired of me, and I'll settle back to weeding the garden.[36]

I've had rather a broken week moving round Devon, speaking in Topsham, Dawlish, Tiverton and finally Princetown. The last was, of course, the most exciting – 340 prisoners in the chapel with guards seated in high rostrums down both sides of the hall.[37]

She was also busy at Dartington bringing to life a new institution – the Estate Committee. It was prompted, rather curiously, by something that happened in the Arts Department – a decision, taken it seemed to many people from on high and without consultation, like so many decisions at Dartington, to push out the Travelling Repertory Theatre. This company which Basil Langton and his wife Louise (formerly Richard Elmhirst's wife) had brought to Dartington in 1941 was extremely popular. It was not just that the productions in the Barn Theatre were highly professional and the actors, with Yvonne Mitchell and Margaret Leighton amongst them, highly talented. There was also a dearth of entertainment in the war and a great desire for it. The news that they were not to stay brought out more hostile letters in *News of the Day* than I can remember on any other occasion. A letter signed by Vic Elmhirst, Sean O'Casey and Terry Roper (head of the successful wartime Greencrops Department) started it off:[38]

> As we have a very high opinion of the artistic integrity of the Company, and as we believe that both Dartington and TRT stand to gain enormously from their continuing to work here, we should like to express publicly our urgent hope that every possible effort will be made to enable them to stay.

It sounds more like Vic's style than O'Casey's. The angry correspondence went on for weeks and broadened out. How was it possible for the top people to be so out of touch with ordinary opinion that they apparently did not know how much support TRT had?

On 8 July Dorothy responded:[39]

> Shall we resort to the principle of representation, and will all those at Dartington who are interested in creating a medium of exchange between Trustees and any member of estate, school and arts departments, elect a committee to meet with me, say once a fortnight, to discuss any problems, any criticisms, any points that they would like to bring up?

Dorothy was like a queen granting democratic rights to her subjects. The committee was to meet 'me' without any of the managers, except that they could choose one representative. Roger Morel, almost as prominent a humanity-man as Vic, was eventually selected.

News of the Day on 12 June 1942 reported her hopes as she had expressed them at a Sunday Evening Meeting:

> The reason she had put forward her proposal for the creation of an Estate Committee was to enable the Trustees to keep in closer touch with members of the Estate who, through the enlargement of the enterprise and the need for greater organisation, had tended to become increasingly out of reach of the Trustees. . . . In the early days of Dartington there had been a sense of close comradeship. Leonard and Vic used often to drive lorries themselves to bring the workers from distant villages to the job at the Hall. It was like a large family in which everyone played an active part. But as the place grew larger relationships, of necessity, became more tenuous.

The committee took some time to set up, for obviously nothing could happen while Dorothy was on the other side of the Atlantic from July 1941 to March 1942. When it did, Jack Collingbourne was the first Secretary. Dr Slater asked Jack to come to see him and show him the Agenda for the meeting. Jack at once reported this to Dorothy saying 'this is against your principle'. Dorothy agreed wholeheartedly. She said, 'I will see him.' Slater never asked for an Agenda again.[40] The committee was soon hard at work dealing with some of the issues that had caused so much distress in 1939 – To what extent should there be any subsidies for anything on the estate? Is the building programme complete? When is an experimental stage complete? Leonard should have been there for that last one. Slater was asked to explain the Trust and company finances, which he did. Dorothy was very pleased. The estate committee has lasted until today as a representative body at Dartington.

Dorothy even got directly involved in the companies. She reported to Leonard that there was a big wartime market for apple juice, the 'Saw Mill is making a profit – think of it',[41] the textile mill was producing 'some lovely new materials made of waste matter – wood pulp and so forth, and only a small percentage of wool'.[42] Almost the farmer's wife now, she even lectured the 500 farmers who came to a meeting at the AI Centre in 1945 on the work that Leonard had done in promoting Artificial Insemination and, although she had qualms about the 'unnaturalness' of it all, went down to the Centre with the farmers to watch the bull being encouraged to masturbate to the point where he 'did his stuff' as she put it. 'But it isn't going to be so easy to convert them all to milk recording, is it?'[43] The mood at Trustees' meetings was optimistic. 'Pom was very brotherly and sweet to me – and all went well.'[44]

Addressing farmers and speaking at the Torquay Town Hall, she was no longer an eccentric American millionairess. She was no longer the squire's wife. She was in her own right the leading figure in a community with an Anglo-American ancestry which had a special significance now that the two countries were allies. It was also a community no longer separate from the mainstream of society. Its people were as much engaged in the war effort as any others in Britain. The farms were sending food to the cities, the sawmills timber to the army. The Dartington Platoon of the Home Guard stood by to repel any invader. Corporal Cordy (Arts Department), Corporal Clake (Sawmills) and Corporal McTaggart (Woodlands) and many others were Dartington's Guardsmen.

Being caught up in the war meant being also caught up in post-war planning. It was one of the popular activities. Britain must not return to the unemployment, insecurity and disheartenment of the 1930s. There had to be a new start. PEP in London was concentrating on post-war reconstruction, and people at Dartington were thinking in the same way. Dorothy wrote to Leonard in Bengal on 14 August 1944:

> Dartington is going to have a great many decisions to make this autumn, and I can't help hoping that you won't be gone too long. . . . But what a chance we are being given, Jerry, to recreate Dartington. I don't believe many people have a second chance like this. It's why I feel I need you so much just now. You must finish the India job first, but then you must come back and give the best of your thought and vision to Dartington – at least for a time, until we get going in our Second Phase.

If Dartington was to be recreated, without Leonard more than part-time and without as much of Dorothy as there had been since 1939 – she would presumably start travelling again as soon as the U-Boats were penned back into Kiel – the most important question was about the managing directorship, from which Slater resigned in 1945.

Peter Sutcliffe was Slater's successor for the industry as well as the farms, though without his title to begin with. Leonard and Dorothy took to him from the start. Stocky, bright-eyed and humorous, he had an infectious sense of confidence. Leonard did not square him up to his standard criteria – technical competence, willingness to measure himself and ability to handle people – and then decide he had a respectable total score in points. It was enough for him to look as though he had the third ability in abundance, one, too, which had come to appear more and more important. In the event he also worked hard, going every day to his office early in the morning and staying there till late evening, so that almost anyone could see him at any time with or without an appointment. The different managers could get his concentrated attention. Joan Mitchell, his assistant, was equally reliable and equally good-natured and her husband, Fred Mitchell, was the ever-dependable accountant in the post-war Central Office. Sutcliffe was also more the all-round 'Dartington person' than Slater had ever been and with a delightful American wife. Leonard got the approval of Jack Collingbourne (and of Jock and Wilfred I am sure) and moved decisively though not quite openly, leaving the final pronouncement about Slater's departure and Sutcliffe's appointment to be made by Gwatkin. He always tried to avoid the final confrontation; Dorothy was tougher in such situations.

From the very beginning of the Sutcliffe era there was little friction compared to the 1930s. The division between the two headquarters – Central Office and Hall – was no longer nearly so sharp. Leonard had been somewhat detached in the war; he was never again quite so involved. He never again initiated a new industry or started a new venture with a commercial or semi-commercial character, like the Artificial Insemination Centre. He no longer talked, or talked so much, about the Dartington (let alone the English) experiment. Peter Sutcliffe made things simpler, too, by regarding him as the boss in a way that Slater had been loth to do, which was perhaps all the easier because Leonard did not look on himself as the boss in the way he had done until the war. Slater and Leonard were of an age. Peter was a good deal younger and looked up to Leonard not just for that reason but because he had such an attractive combination of the practical and the visionary. Jock first introduced Peter and Ann to him, taking him out to their beautiful farmhouse at Forder Green through Devon lanes so tortuous and past so many crossroads that although I have driven there hundreds of times I still lose the way as often as I find it. Peter remembers not the conversation but Leonard leaving. He looked at a door on one of Peter's barns and said it would rot if nothing were done. Peter said he knew that as well as Leonard but he did not have the benefit of an Estate Steward. Leonard, smiling, replied he did not think it would make much difference if he did. To Peter it was encouraging proof of Leonard's realism and his eye for detail.[45] Here was a man he could 'work for', which meant that he would (and did) consult him before taking any major step.

Peter did this not long before he was promoted Managing Director (but to do just the same job) in 1947. He wanted to get rid of Mr Wadhams who had continued as Secretary to the Company. He was a perfectionist who introduced an extraordinary regime of check and counter-check, counter-check and check, which was supposed to make the accounts proof against human error. All headings in the enormous account books were coded but had continually to be translated back into ordinary language before anyone could understand what the vast army of figures referred to. More and more staff had been taken on to make the system more and more proof against their error. Without the war Wadhams would not have lasted so long. As it was, Peter secured Leonard's assent and then fired him more or less in public at a meeting of Central Office staff. To many of the others it was like his decision finally to close the Poultry Department and the fruit farm at Marley, proof not of human error but the opposite, the wizardry of PS, as he was of course called. 'Where is PS? He's gone up to see LK.' He did not need the title of Managing Director once he was called PS.

Full employment conferred another advantage on the Sutcliffe era. How to preserve that in Britain had (for the moment, until the lesson was again forgotten) been learnt from the success in achieving it during the war. Full employment meant that purchasing power was maintained and with that markets for the products of industry, including Dartington's. But the conditions for Dartington departments became tougher all the same. The emphasis was no longer so much on the self-sufficiency of Britain. Goods began to be imported again, at the same time as home demand shifted away from austerity. The sawmill could no longer sell all the timber it could cut up. Apple juice was no longer in such demand when the juice of oranges and other fruits that had hardly been tasted for six years could again flow down English throats. The farms were desperately in need of re-equipment.

There were also some setbacks to the general economy, and even, temporarily, to full employment, which were also setbacks for Dartington. Dorothy wrote to Margaret Isherwood in California about one of them, the fuel crisis in the winter of 1947 after Wadhams was sacked:[46]

> I wonder if England has ever had such a winter! It isn't only the bitter wind from Siberia, freezing one to the marrow, but the heavy leaden sky that hangs like a dark pall over the earth and turns the day into a kind of perpetual twilight – that paralyses the mind as well as the body. I can't imagine how people in the north are enduring the hardship not to speak of those poor wretches in Germany and elsewhere who are short of food as well as fuel and clothing. There's a feeling of crisis in the air – not unlike certain periods in the war. . . . Mr Shinwell gambled on a mild winter – fatal – as the unwise virgins discovered when they gambled with oil![47]

The fuel crisis did not last long. These were smooth years for Dartington. She wrote again to Margaret Isherwood in December 1948:[48]

> Never have I known Dartington to be in such a state of harmony. I don't know how to account for all the good-will – perhaps there are

many causes. Peter Sutcliffe is a great success as managing director, and Alan Milton has created in one year an adult education centre that is just bursting with life and vitality – nearly 80 people a night fill his rooms – down at the Central Office – doing pottery, painting, machinery repair, playing in orchestras, singing in choirs, discussing local history, interior decorating, current affairs, philosophy and religion and heaven knows what!

Dorothy was particularly pleased as well that 'the Estate Committee is taking over executive responsibilities . . . all pointing in the direction of decentralizing controls'.[49] Three years later Margaret Isherwood was still receiving very similar glowing reports although beginning to be qualified a little:

We are wonderfully happy together – Jerry and I – and no longer anxious about our children, nor even about Dartington. I wonder if this is the resignation of old age![50]

Dartington is very peaceful these days. I sometimes wonder whether we do not need more prodding and questioning – more of an intellectual challenge to keep us more continuously alert. I remember Misha always said – 'it is so easy to fall asleep'. How different from the old days when conflicts of one sort or another seemed perpetual! The danger now comes from another quarter.[51]

The serenity was all the greater because Ruth returned from the USA to Dartington to live there in 1946. A year after that she married Maurice Ash, an economist and philosopher. Their first house was at Dartington. Ruth began the work which she took further in later years. Dorothy wrote of her:[52]

Ruth goes wandering in the fields gathering wool rubbed off by the sheep – and now she is dyeing and carding and spinning – and soon she will be weaving. She is finding her way towards setting up a complete little home industry.

As they were in England, Ruth and Maurice's children, Kate, Marian and Claire, were the grandchildren they saw most of. Again, Dorothy to Margaret, in 1952:[53]

I had a happy three weeks looking after my 3-year-old grandchild, Kathryn – I'm always urging Ruth to have a few more holidays and to leave Kathryn to me!

Although full employment was not abandoned there was a recession after 1951 and, as always, the Dartington industries suffered along with the rest. After some years of profitability the company made a loss in 1950, and large ones in 1952 and 1953. The Orchards Department, what was left of it, was closed down in 1951, and the Woodworking Department in 1952. The Textile Mill survived, just, despite a loss of some £14,000 in the bad year of 1952. A new manager helped. A Norwegian, his name was Gunnar Storvik. Storvik succeeded in getting a new mill built at Dartington in the former grass-drying station next to the sawmill. It was a big advance.

The sawmill was another worry. It had been far and away Dartington's main profit-earner during the war and for some years thereafter, producing railway scantlings, mining timber and furniture squares. As long as timber imports had to be restricted by the shortage of dollars it could prosper even though the quality of home-grown timber was falling all the time as less and less desirable parcels had to be bought from landowners and farmers. But when British Rail cut down on its orders for scantlings and imports began to increase the period of prosperity was over. Many expedients were tried – kilning on contract, staff reductions, an incentive bonus, sales of pallets from second-quality timber. Nothing was quite sufficient. In 1958 the Dartington sawmills (on the same site at Shinners Bridge) was merged with a mill owned by the large timber importers and builders' merchants, Reeves of Totnes. Dartington had a 50 per cent stake, Reeves the same, in a new company, Dartington Sawmills Ltd, which survived until 1981.

On the strength of the savings made and an upturn in the economy, the company returned to profitability in the mid 1950s. The farms made the biggest contribution (especially if the Yelland pig farm was included with the main farms). The retail shop under the management of Barbara Jewell, with very little capital put into it, was also providing increasing profits each year. The profits rose from £546 in 1951 to £5,849 in 1964 – this apart from those earned by the Tea Room which Miss Jewell also ran – and went on increasing from there.

Not a change was made, as I say, without consulting Leonard. After her wartime period of being in everything Dorothy left it to him, as in his turn he left most things to Peter. On a tour of this department or that Leonard would always stop for a few heads-down words with old-timers or new-timers whom he or Dorothy had got to know – Jim, Fred, Arthur, Dick, Charlie, Percy as he saw them – 'they there Elmhirses', in their eyes. He remained the gaffer for many, and Dorothy his kindly but slightly frightening wife. She was always liable to brake to a stop beside you if you were walking anywhere, and alarm you further (her erratic driving being well known) by offering you a lift.

But for the most part they were bystanders, warm and supportive ones, it is true, throughout the next stage of Dartington expansion which is associated with Maurice Ash and Christopher Zealley as well as with Peter. After a long period as a Trustee Maurice became Chairman of the Trust in 1972. Chris became Director of the Trust in 1971 and a Trustee in 1976. It was Maurice's idea some years before he became Chairman to expand into North Devon, as it was Peter who planned and executed one of the two main new projects, the Dartington Glassworks at Torrington. This was the first new industry that had no organic tie with the rural area in which it was placed. It turned out, along with Staverton Contractors, to be the most successful of all, by a long way, under the devoted management first of Eskil Vilhelmsson, a Swede who brought seventeen glass-blowers with him from his home country, and then of Jan Mollmark and Tony Easton. Frank Thrower was from the beginning the designer who created a style and a range of glassware to express it. The other main project, brought to life by John Lane, later to become a Trustee, was the Beaford Centre which began by being called the Beaford Arts Centre but could soon drop the Arts, it became so widely known for what it did in carrying the theatre, music and visual art into the small towns and villages of North Devon. Dorothy was delighted by the plan. She decided, as she usually did about buildings, that the Trustees should buy Greenwarren House at Beaford as the quarters for the new Centre. Neither of them lived to see the next steps after that – the building of the Cider Press Centre near the old retail shop at Shinners Bridge, as a cluster of many different kinds of shops, exhibition-spaces and restaurant, or the new partnership between Staverton Contractors and John Pontin's prospering design-and-build company, the J.T. Group of Bristol. Or the new merchant bank, Dartington & Co., which Christopher Zealley started with David Johnstone to offset, in however small a way, for the south-western counties the centralisation of financial power in the City of London. Or the Dartington North Devon Trust established as the first offshoot of the main Trust but in another region. Or John Pontin appointed a Trustee.

The Elmhirsts wanted to achieve efficiency for the sake of a higher standard of life, and also to incorporate the humanity which seemed so often to be forfeit in modern industry. Who would not? There is hardly an industrialist or manager anywhere who would not say the same in the same or different words, though many, I suppose, with rather less stress than the Elmhirsts on the humanity. Many too would be quick to point out that it is all very well to want both but that in practice this is not so much a choice as a dilemma – it is not so much a matter of going all out for both efficiency and humanity together as of deciding how much of one is going to be sacrified for the other. It is partly because there is a dilemma that skilled management is needed to do the reconciling and, particularly, to ensure that efficiency is high enough for an organisation to survive in the face of competition *without* losing humanity.

The rub comes only when there is a struggle for limited markets. Dorothy and Leonard did not have to face the issue squarely in the early years when everything that was done belonged to the one glorious experiment. Nothing was threatened with closure just because it was making a loss in the first five years, hardly anything even in the first ten. When the mouth of Dorothy's purse was still wide open the two of them could exercise direct, personal leadership – employees talked about Leonard as 'the chief', of both of them as 'the leaders' – in striving for what almost anyone would recognise as values more worthwhile than profit: the opening of people's hearts to each other, a sense of sharing in a high endeavour of consequence to mankind, the joy beyond any calculation that the arts can give, the pride of putting quality into sound work. When Leonard clambered up the ladders in the Great Hall with Mr Weir to praise the skill of the craftsmen he was not worrying about the cost of the hammer-beams. He wanted excellence. That would come only if the men had the pride in craftsmanship which the cathedral-builders enjoyed, before the advent of the money economy with its insistence that almost everything else should give way to the reign of pounds, shillings and pence. When the costumes were made for *Comus* no one asked about the cost of the cloth, as they were already doing by the time Margaret Barr wanted to clad her maidens in new finery. The purse was bound to close. It at last had to be accepted that high-mindedness alone does not make a business.

For my part I would pick out four failings which account for the setbacks in Dartington industries in the period up to the war. The first and most serious was their poor choice of executives. They did not select the right people as managers, not so much because they could not sum up a person when they saw him or her as well as most – they grew a lot sharper and more careful as their experience lengthened. It was more because they were looking for the wrong qualities. In the trio of qualifications Leonard sought, technical competence took pride of place. Managerial competence was nowhere. Leonard did not know, let alone Dorothy, that to add to all the many other arts, and as subtle in the skills it demanded as any of them, is the art of management.

In a money economy ruled by the cash nexus a general manager stands in the borderland between the organisation *for* which he is responsible and the rest of the world *to* which he is responsible. He has to ensure that the organisation responds to that world and meets its needs sufficiently well to be paid for doing so. This whether he is a headmaster who depends upon the State or upon parents for the sustenance of his school; the head of a research unit supported by foundations; or one of the heads of a commercial business which has to find and keep an ever-changing market for the goods and services that he can produce and sell to customers without loyalty except to 'good value'. That 'value' is judged by money explains the society of which Dartington is a part. The manager also, as the second main part of his job, has to make sure that everyone inside the organisation contributes as fully as possible to the common effort. This they will not do unless they all feel that what they are doing is worthwhile and have confidence that the management is competent to make it happen. Everyone needs to know what the goals are and as far as possible agree with them. Humanity enters into the whole affair but not so much undiluted, spontaneous, from the heart, as channelled – all the same 'humanity' which ensures that people receive real appreciation for the good work they do for the organisation. If sanctions are imposed upon individuals it must be done within a code of conduct recognised as equitable. To say all that is easy, but in the 1920s and 1930s, at any rate, it would have been foreign doctrine at Dartington, as would any attempt to go further than such bland propositions and enunciate the qualities a manager needs if he is to do such jobs or the ways to spot them, select for them and train for them. I am sure it would have been foreign because for all the well-known painters, philosophers, writers and men of the theatre, educators and politicians whose names are inscribed in Dorothy's Visitors' Book I can find no one who would have described himself 'manager'.

The Elmhirsts were persuaded, and rightly, that in one vital respect Dartington lacked management skills, that is in marketing. They, as well as Dr Slater, at one time had high hopes of Mr Harrison and his sales force. They got that wrong too. The best salesman in the world can do very little with the wrong product, of the wrong quality or design at the wrong price. Marketing men cannot be added on to a business without the right product but need to permeate the organisation, above all determining, or helping in large measure to determine, what is made, altering what is made in the light of customer reactions and all the time acting as a source of intelligence for their fellow-producers. The Elmhirsts hit on a crucial defect without going far enough, even with marketing management, let alone with the still more crucial general management that Dartington lacked until after the war.

If they learnt something from their mistakes in selecting people, and became tougher about getting rid of the wrong ones, if never as much so as a Gwatkin would have liked, their other three failings stayed with them. I have spoken already in this chapter of their notion of 'rural industries'. They did not recognise that these industries, the traditional ones that were in the countryside and especially on manorial estates in some form in Shakespeare's time, in Chaucer's time, even Bede's time, were also declining ones. In a free-trade Britain which was except in war open to the imports of the world the wool of New Zealand or the timber of Canada could be as well (probably better) made up in Bradford or Walthamstow as it could in Devon. With hindsight, it would have made more sense to leave aside the declining industries in which markets were contracting and competition therefore fierce, and plump instead for expanding industries nearer to relatively high technology. Leonard was a great admirer of science and (in common with so many of his countrymen in his class) knew little of technology. That was left to the Japanese and the Germans. The glass factory was not directly Leonard's doing. It was just luck (a few would say bad luck, most good luck) that a new industry expanded and expanded in the post-war years and lapped all round Dartington. There was nothing about tourism in the first *Prospectus*.

The third failing was, I think, that they did not stay with their early enthusiasm for the crafts or take to heart the reasons for it. The crafts were to be supported because the work they gave rise to was, or could be, so deeply satisfying. If they had followed up on that recognition they would perhaps not only have made a bigger effort even than they did to create more viable, small-scale craft manufactories. They might also have en-quired about other ways in which work could be made creative. They might have become more interested in experimental systems of manage-ment and in attempts being made to make every worker a partner in his enterprise instead of just an employee. If that kind of experiment had been a more prominent part of the general experiment Dartington could also have attracted into what was a remote district of rural Britain some young managers who were more than *technically* competent.

These three failings were bound up with the underlying failure to resolve the Dartington contradiction. Leonard never entirely stopped being the squire, Dorothy never entirely gave up being the grand lady even though they were surrounded with all the outward forms of modern commerce in limited liability companies, managing directors and accoun-tants. It was difficult for them to devolve power or for any devolution there was to be accepted as genuine by people at Dartington.

For all that, Dartington survived. It would not have done so unless there had been a lot of money to shore it up with. But it is still true that the main injections of capital were before 1936. Since then the Dartington venture as a whole has not just survived but, with comparatively little quite fresh money being put into it after 1936, has expanded, since the war fairly steadily. After write-offs the assets were valued at about £1½ million in 1936 – £1 million for the endowment, half a million for the land and buildings; they were worth nearer £20 million in 1980. Much of the increase was accounted for by inflation in the price of land and buildings. But it was not only that. The management, since the war at any rate, may not have been brilliant. But it has not been profligate.

CHAPTER 13

RETROSPECT

<hr/>

We shall avail ourselves of every
opportunity of linking our interests
with those of the neighbourhood, in
order to avoid the danger of becoming a
self-centred institution.

Outline, 1926

Without Hitler the Dartington company might well have collapsed in 1939 or 1940. If all the economic experiments had suffered such negative results as that, the school and arts departments might have been brought down too. The Elmhirsts could hardly have chosen a worse period for starting up new industry, let alone the favoured collection of rural enterprises which belied the name Leonard liked to give them. But they cannot be blamed for the state of the world economy up to the point when rearmament got rid of a lot of unemployment. Their attitude to management was another matter. Not appreciating the importance of the qualities a general manager needs, their mistake was to appoint further people in their own image, with the addition that they were to be technically expert.

This was in one way perfectly understandable. At Cambridge the magic of experts had not brushed off on Leonard; there weren't any. At Cornell there were – rafts of them, like Professor Heuser who knew as much about Rhode Island Reds as anyone else in the world and with his own hands built the first fourteen poultry buildings at the Old Parsonage. Dorothy had also generally favourable experience of one sort of expert, in artists, and another, in lawyers, supported as these were by excellent investment advisers who could prefer Dupont Common Stock to General Motors at one moment and the other way round at another with equally sage reasons. Her lawyers were between them so accomplished that at one period, although she was one of the richest women in the world, she was not paying much income tax at all. She thought this quite wrong and asked the experts to become a little less so and rearrange her investments so that she would pay more tax. Tax was not all; she and he were well advised about all manner of other legal matters as well, by Milton Rose in New York about their American estate, by Fred Gwatkin, Ian Wilson and Michael Bowers in London about trust and company law and about administration, and by Pom in Sherburn-in-Elmet about everything to do with the land.

They were not themselves amateurs through and through. Leonard was, for example, not far off from being a silviculturist. Balancing comfortably on his shooting-stick, he could expound on the relative vulnerability of *Thuya plicata* and *Chamaecyparis lawsoniana* to particular degrees of wind exposure with as much panache as any earl or forestry commissioner, and prune and brash so well his private wood at Chacegrove (where he fell into the badgers' sett) that foresters from all over England came to inspect it. He was also an agricultural economist and he knew backwards Roger Ascham's *The Schoolmaster* and the Venerable Bede's *History of the English Church and People*. True also, Dorothy, as well as knowing almost all her favourite Shakespeare plays by heart, and all the Sonnets, was a surprisingly skilful bridge player whenever she played, which was seldom. She had been well taught as a teenager, better than as a tennis player or a golfer. John Wales, who sometimes played bridge with her, said it brought out a steely, ruthless streak in her. She wanted to win and knew how to.

But they also had the special enthusiasms of amateurs. Leonard was a spotter of blocked drainpipes; an inexpert but very keen recorder player; a public speaker; a friend to children; an educator who would never use such a word of himself; a loving observer of birds as keen-eyed for new species in Tanzania as in the Yangtze Valley, above the Arctic Circle in Finland or on Hudson's Bay. Above all he was a conservationist. After he died Ian Mercer, Chief Officer of the Dartmoor National Park, called him a 'conservation hero' in the *Journal of the Devon Trust for Nature Conservation*:[1]

> In the last two decades society has developed a conservation ethic, a social component, still not all-powerful, but gaining strength. In its turn it has spawned new professions, new skills, and inevitably a new language. 'Nature reserve', 'heritage park', 'country park' – are all names for places. 'The quality of life' is not located, less precise, but more important, than the other designations. Leonard Elmhirst's Dartington was born before the conservation movement and its literary currency – it is nevertheless all these things, and quality remains the base of the wholeness. . . . Long may it go on – as an

inspiration to true conservators, and in memory of himself, your late vice-president.

Dorothy had many of the same interests, some of them caught from him. When Trustee meetings were on the lawn she would face him west so that he could see the swifts flying in and out of the nesting boxes he had built for them in the old church tower to remind him of the other swifts outside the silent dormitory at St Anselm's. She would follow the swoop of his binoculars, watching him as well as the birds. She was a keener observer than he of the way each actor on a stage said a line, so completely absorbed indeed that nothing escaped her unless the play was trumpery. She had keener discrimination between the different varieties of a plant species and a better sense of garden design. She was a better politician, not perhaps so much in Dartington's internal politics as in gauging the threats and, sometimes, opportunities of world and national politics in each of the turns through which they went in her lifetime. She was as much of a world citizen as he was, living in a country which before it began to shrink was the centre of an Empire. They were both interested not just in the Empire but in the rest of the world as well. As a listener she had a gift denied to him. She laughed more while making people laugh less: she never told the sort of funny stories of which he had such a large store. She longed to be able to. She was the same as Leonard in another vital respect – she had so many interests and had so many friends she had to spread herself thinly without ever appearing to. She was a mystic whose intense inner life she withheld from almost everyone else, including members of her family.

There was an asymmetry in their range. Leonard shared all Dorothy's interests. He tried harder to adapt to her than she to him, almost as though she had done enough in swapping countries with all the loneliness that induced, and did not intend to do much more, even in the early years of the marriage when Leonard, at his jubilant best in the period when the buildings were being restored, was much more the dominant partner than he was later. He felt acutely his inferiority in the arts, and did not get over it. In 1932 he was lamenting 'so with art and music and poetry – I'm the savage there and you must throw your weight in consciously please to prevent me tending potatoes and chickens all the time'.[2] Two decades later he was still saying:[3]

> In the most important fields your sensitivity is so acute that I marvel at it – sports, roofs, pantries, cow houses – yes, these are the fields where training has sharpened perception – but in how mundane a world these operate. In music and drama and decoration and the arts and above all in your perception in the field of human relations where did man ever find such a partner?

He always tried, attending every play he could with her, every Chelsea Show. She on her side was almost hostile to agricultural economics in all its manifestations, would not attend international conferences even to hear Leonard ringing the cow-bell, cared for the look of fields more than about their manner of cultivation, and was somewhat distant about Political and Economic Planning.

Travel was a powerful common bond. The Hall was always bursting forth into clumps of suitcases and trunks plastered over with yellow labels, CUNARD LINE – STATEROOM. The servants carried them to the cars for the journey to Southampton. Travel reflected and contributed to their many-sidedness, their Renaissance quality, and mattered a lot to Darting-ton. All the way from the period when ladies wore hats like inverted flowerpots to the period when most wore none at all they were away so much that they could not, for that reason alone, keep a tight control over what happened. They had to delegate even if they did not know how best to, in any formal way. Their departures were therefore welcome events to many who wanted to take action of which the founders might have disapproved – including, as I have shown, dismissing people who might have appealed to their overlords for clemency. To others more vulnerable, on good enough personal terms to count them as friends, their departure was a blow softened only by being so well advertised. It was almost as if the population of Dartington in general, who could not afford to travel and only had a week's holiday anyway, were being encouraged to find vicari-ous enjoyment in the sights and scenes that unfolded before the eyes of the founders in their staterooms above the Atlantic main, their Packards whirling down Fifth Avenue or on top of their elephants in the heat of India. *News of the Day*, the estate news-sheet which went to everyone, was a kind of court or manor circular. The doings of the ruling family came first in the list of events in the calendar. *Tuesday 16 July 1929, Mr and Mrs L. K. Elmhirst, Mrs Starr, Miss B. Straight, Miss E. Lindeman, and Whitney and Michael Straight leave on Thursday at 4.30 a.m. to catch their steamer to America.* Their times of return were as precisely recorded and often Leonard (or sometimes Dorothy) would write an account of where they had been and what they had done for publication in the circular. If it was a particularly notable trip, like the one to Russia, or India in 1944–5, Leonard talked about it at a Sunday Evening Meeting.

They never wearied of journeys. In England Leonard would never go on a direct route if he could, by leaving earlier, go roundabout to see something new or relish something already well known, especially if it was Saxon, with some supposed trace of King Alfred or Bede about it, or even Roman. He liked to trace a disused Roman road on an ordnance map and then follow it through farmgate after farmgate until his car could go no further. Like a one-man Automobile Association, he was always ready to suggest routes to anyone, especially to a close friend like Milton Rose:[4]

> From Wilton I would suggest keeping due west on the B.3089, through Chilmark and Tisbury, and so down to Shaftesbury with a look at the museum and the old Abbey site, and so through your Hardy country, the way you most like to go, but if through Sherborne, turn south there to the top of the hill at Lyons Gate, where you should turn due west to Evershot, Broadwindsor and Battiscombe to Axminster.

Then there was always the more serious, more distant travel which, even though aeroplanes now carried them much faster than the *Majestic*, kept them away as much after the war as before – almost half of almost every year. Even after Dorothy's severe heart attack in 1955 there was no abatement.

The travelling year started in February with a stay of some weeks at a chalet-hotel called Pink Sands on Harbor Island in the Bahamas. Every day, weather permitting, they went for a walk, to the village, to the harbour, along the beach, along the central island road to the red tree and the grey tree. Averse to alcohol and chit-chat, they found their own ways of dealing with their fellow-guests. On 27 February 1961 she wrote to Michael:

> We have found a new form of social entertainment: 'Come and Meet the Birds at 12.15'. We place chairs in full view of our two bird baths. Jerry offers Bourbon and Scotch and rocks, while we wait hopefully for the Painted Bunting. Then, as a parting gesture, he plays a few Bach tunes on his recorder! We managed in this way to entertain first the Twomblys, then the Hamiltons, then the Fraziers – really very successfully. I was even able to get by without noticeably failing to drink!

They did not keep to the routine in 1958. The Bahamas holiday was cut short by the news of Vic's last illness; they flew home immediately.

At Easter and in the summer it was 'The Chalet', at Portwrinkle, the house in Cornwall which Dorothy underplayed by calling it a 'cliff dwelling'. In the autumn, for several years, she returned to the Italy which she got to know so well with Beatrice Bend and particularly to the Venice where in 1907 she wrote her specification for an ideal husband, but to a different hotel, the Gritti Palace, with Leonard, Michael, Milt and Emily. On 24 October 1959, at the end of another of the by-now regular visits to Venice, she wrote in her diary, 'I had feared before we started that I might not be up to it all – but my body responded wonderfully – and only occasionally did my spirit flag when we seemed to be visiting too many churches, hunting for a single picture.' She was 72. Day after day in autumnal Venice Dorothy would get up to have breakfast with Leonard on the terrace of their room. She would wear one of her thicker woollen dresses if it was a colder day and always one of her blue hats. After breakfast they would take a trip in a motor launch to one of the islands, or walk nearer at hand to the first church of the day, to see a Pietà of a dead Christ upheld by several angels with sharp black wings outlined against the sky, or further away along the other side of the Canal to see the Tintorettos in the Scuola di San Rocco. After the sightseeing she and the others often 'made for', as she said, suggesting she could smell it from far off, a fish restaurant called the Poste Vecchie recommended by Ben Britten and Peter Pears. On 19 October Leonard 'of course' (the 'of course' gives an impression of the constant ritualistic leg-pulling which went on in the party, with Leonard being the butt of much of it) 'ordered all the most exotic fishy things available – fish soup containing everything scraped up from the bottom of the canals'.

A few years later in 1963, missing out on Venice for once, she was climbing over the rough stones at the top of the Acropolis with the aid of a good stick for her right hand and Leonard's arm for her left. A day or so later Leonard left her side as she was walking down to the stadium at Delphi from the spot where their driver had left them; Leonard rushed on, so that, when she and the others entered, he could be sitting on a stone playing to them on his recorder. All around were donkeys carrying chives, grapes and men while their wives trudged behind. The women wore black; in large families there was always someone who had died not long before. On such occasions, when they had a meal, Dorothy would sometimes harrass Leonard about the tip. One afternoon when they had eaten a very expensive tea in a Greek castle and were again sitting in the boat Dorothy said very sharply to Leonard, 'How much did you give the girl?' Annoyed, Leonard replied, 'Sixpence.' Dorothy nodded her head, saying, 'That's all right.' Despite those accounts on the walking tour in Wales she had no idea of the value of money.

Much of the travelling they did was to visit the children. In the immediate post-war years they still had the house at Westbury – the decision to sell it was not taken until there was a family conference about it at Dartington in 1951. Before that the family reunions were in the same old surroundings. Dorothy wrote to Margaret Isherwood in 1948:[5]

These flying visits are strangely and deeply satisfying. Just to be able to see Biddy and Michael and their children, once or twice a year – even for a fortnight only – gives a kind of continuity and binding tenderness to our relationship. Though their lives are full of problems we seem to reach together deep levels of peace. . . . Her [Binnie's] two little boys – and Biddy's Willard – are my great delight and we have the greatest fun together at Westbury. You can imagine how blest I feel in all these grandchildren.

In the 1950s and 1960s, with Westbury sold, they stayed with Beatrice or Michael. Beatrice was not always at home. Her busy life as an actress, not just on Broadway but in Hollywood – where she won an Oscar in 1976 – meant that on some visits Leonard and Dorothy could see her only fleetingly. Michael Straight lived for the most part in Washington with his wife, Binnie, and his five children. While living there he ran *The New Republic* for the many years he was its editor. From there too he did some of his writing, of the two novels that became well known, *Carrington* and *A Very Small Remnant*. Long after Roosevelt died, another President made him Deputy Chairman of the National Endowment for the Arts. Whatever else they did after one of their still regular trips over the Atlantic, they always stayed with Michael. In 1947 Dorothy wrote:[6]

> Michael always gives me a great lift of the heart – perhaps because he combines such strength with such idealism. The cause he so passionately believes in – true internationalism – is not very popular at the moment in the USA and he is bound to suffer much criticism and abuse. But he is unafraid of criticism and undeterred by abuse – and, since I am neither, I admire him all the more for these qualities.

She wrote about him in similar vein on many later occasions.

There were also the children in England to visit. Whitney was committed from the start to England rather than America. In the 1930s, after he left the school at Dartington, he became one of the champion racing drivers of the decade – in one year he came first in the South African Grand Prix and brother Michael, third. He also built the first airport at Exeter. In 1946 he was, as an Air Commodore, in command of the RAF Group in Europe which was later transformed into British European Airways, and from there he moved on to become Managing Director of the British Overseas Airways Corporation and Deputy-Chairman of Rolls-Royce. He lived for the greater part of his adult life at Southall in the western suburbs of London where Dorothy would often go out from her London flat to visit him, his wife and his two daughters.

Two years after Ruth married Maurice Ash they bought a house, Howe Green Moat, near Bishop's Stortford, which was another place to go to and another garden to care for and have ideas about. Dorothy wrote to Leonard about one of her visits in 1953 as she did about many of the others:[7]

> We have lunch out of doors and Kathryn runs around with nothing on
> . . . and the laughter rings in the air and makes the loveliest

accompaniment of sound. Maurice is busy with architects planning the reconstruction of the house and courtyard.

Both of them rejoiced when daughter and son-in-law moved back in 1962 to live at Sharpham House a few miles down the river Dart from Dartington. Grandparents and one set of parents and grandchildren were for the first time near to each other. The extended family was together in one place and the web of relationship became still closer when first Maurice and then Ruth became Trustees.

Dorothy only travelled to India once in 1930, with Leonard and Michael. In her notes she describes 'the poverty, the disease, the mutilations of human life, the leper asylum at Allahabad, the beggar ridden streets of Calcutta, the crowded, seething, struggling masses in the cities and the bazaars, and the seemingly hopeless tangle of the political situation'. She also goes into detail about particular days:

> Yesterday we saw Gandhi. He lives a few miles out of the city in an Ashram or small community, which has grown up around him, consisting of his friends and followers. He himself lives in what appears to be a one room house – his bed along one wall, a long low table opposite, and in between, himself and his spinning wheel. As we entered he ceased spinning and rose to greet us in the warmest, kindest way possible. Then he seated himself again on the floor by his wheel while Jerry and I squatted, cross-legged, on the rug in front of him. He was naked to the waist, and bare legged, with only a short white band or kilt to his knees. And, marvellous to relate, though the room was thick with flies and though Jerry and I were plastered with them, not a single one settled on Mr Gandhi. I watched, fascinated, to see if there might not be one vagrant fly brushing his shoulder with a playful wing – but no, not one broke the mysterious spell of non-interference with him.
>
> He talked at first with Jerry of mutual friends; of Jerry's work at Surul; with a sort of kindly, gentle simplicity that created at once a sense of friendliness and ease. . . . 'Some day', he said, 'your people and mine will sit down together as equals to govern India. That is what I want. But not till arbitrary power is broken will that be possible.'

She never went again – no China this – and became less and less happy about Leonard's fascination with the country, which was even more evident in the war and after 1945 than before. In 1944 Leonard was appointed Agricultural Adviser to Richard Casey, Governor of Bengal, at a time when the province was hit by a terrible famine. Out of that came a plan to prevent the flooding which caused the famine and after the war Leonard was appointed consultant to the great Damodar Valley Corporation. Its job was to prevent the Damodar river flooding, as it had done in the war and so often before, by building dams and preventing soil erosion as well as using the water for generating power and improving agriculture. In his capacity as consultant he went to India at roughly two-year intervals between 1949 and 1961. He always visited Santiniketan. He was almost as fond of independent India as he had been when it was under the Raj. He liked being asked 'and is this your first visit to India, Mr Elmhirst?'

Anxieties prompted by India or irritations by agricultural economists showed only occasionally. When they were together at 'The Chalet', for instance, they were at peace. Dorothy wrote to Susie Hammond on 7 September 1951:

> We have come for a few days to our beloved cliff dwelling by the sea where nothing intrudes save the sound of the waves and the call of seagulls and the fishermen from Looe who gather their little boats together at night close to our rocks and spread their nets all over the sea.

Nor was there any sign of irritation when they were sitting together of an evening in Leonard's study at Dartington itself or outside their Bahamian bungalow with the guava jelly on a saucer in front of them to attract the birds. Dorothy would often be reading, perhaps snorting now and then over a new book or the latest attempt to prove that Shakespeare was not written by Shakespeare, or indulging herself in the American's game she never tired of, 'Snip and Stick', cutting out pieces from magazines and pasting them in albums; Leonard reading, too, about William of Wykeham or John of Gaunt or catalogues from a historical bookseller until the Nine O'Clock News was turned on. They would read a line or two to each other or to whoever with them was constrained to the same slow rhythm as they adopted. It was as though they had moved, quite consciously, into a temporary retreat to prepare themselves the better for the hustle of a journey or of business to come.

In their bustling public life they were partners of another kind. Dorothy when on her knees in the study with scissors and paste or stroking Leonard's hair while standing behind his chair and saying 'I think it is time for bed, Jerry' was apparently a woman like other women. Dorothy at the following day's lunch for the Chairman of the County Council was different. She might lean forward rather awkwardly when she shook his hand and his wife's and her smile (at any rate for the Chairmen of County Councils) could be a trifle forced; but she was, despite her evident shyness, still the grand lady who could never disguise the fact. Leonard was the impeccably turned-out country gentleman who also knew the way (or some of the way) around Whitehall. Dorothy was something more than that. It was as if, without being told, people knew that she had once been at home with Kings and Presidents and Chinese Princesses, and could be again if necessary.

Her money also continued throughout her life to make her wary of anyone whom she sensed might be more interested in it than in her. Even for others who did not want anything for themselves it was still difficult to forget her wealth. Leonard could not forget, either, that the others could not forget, and might well be wondering what it was like for him to be a millionairess's consort – not the more usual Duke or Earl marrying American money but a poor man with no title. It did not worry him nearly as much as they might have expected. Once he had come to terms with it; once he had decided to live at her level, instead of asking what might have been the impossible of her, that she should live much more modestly, he did not ruminate over it endlessly any more than he did over religion once he had decided where he stood. It was not a subject which kept cropping up in his mind, although Dorothy's money continued (as it did at the beginning) to evoke, together with all the other feelings, some sense of awe.

She was a woman at a period when women were not supposed to be too forward. The 'position of women' was of course changing continuously throughout her life. Dorothy herself, having supported the suffragettes of America and the Women's Trade Union League, and by being an independent woman both before she married the first time and in the interval before she married the second, had done something to further the cause of feminism which has in the rich countries of the world been gathering strength throughout the century. But it was not in her circles considered a proper part of women's role to be pushy, at any rate in public. Rather than taking the lead, they were supposed to let their husbands do that and then give them support. Women's power was supposed to be exercised behind the scenes and Dorothy's was, in small meetings of Trustees. In these her word was final. A discussion might persist for several hours without her saying anything; then she would utter perhaps only two sentences and the decision was made. If the men could agree without her, fine; if they were havering she would decide for them – and we almost always accepted it. Outside the Trustees' private meetings it was rare for her to do what she once did when Jock and Leonard were throwing compliments at each other. She said, very sharply, 'Jerry, do stop exaggerating.' Jerry, and Jock, fell completely silent.[8]

It was implicit in the partnership – Dorothy was as much a Trustee as her husband, with a finger in most pies, like him too – that in public she should keep herself in the background. She was, as far as she could be, completely loyal to the compact. It was a rarity for her when she vented her spleen on Jock or when she stopped Frank Walters, the accountant closest to him, as he was going in to see Leonard in his study and told him that whatever he said he simply *must* not worry Leonard.

It was not possible to segregate the roles according to gender, as men do when they travel every day to their 'work' and leave their wives to theirs; and tensions in the public realm were bound to surface in the private. Just because night had fallen, the door could not always be shut on the little world they had created; troubles came whistling under the door, and may have sometimes blown aside the spontaneous tenderness which can come more easily to people whose lives are less cluttered. The demands of that world were also so persistent – in part because their failings as managers meant there were always troubles to face – that they got little time on their own together, or with the children who, when young, were largely pushed off to the nursery floor. When Leonard said in 1927 that he did not want to talk business after 6.30 p.m. he was expressing not so much a decision as a hope he was not able to fulfil. The feudal household in which private and public lives were inextricably mixed ceased quite early on to embrace the whole estate and all its officers; but for the two people at the top there was little relief from the continuous pressure. Imogen Holst tells a story which illustrates it:[9]

> I remember once running across the courtyard rather late for supper one Friday evening and as I arrived under the porch to go in to the White Hart dining room Leonard and Dorothy were coming through the Hall from their own house and there was nobody else there and Leonard, in one of those lovely asides to Dorothy that one so seldom heard, whispered to her anxiously, 'Have we got anyone staying?' – he'd just come down from London, you see – and she said, 'No', and he said, 'Good', and his face lit up and that taught me, you see, how he felt about it.

They would not, of course, have been able to manage the complexity of it, nor to maintain the multitude of their interests, had they not been rich. They always had someone else to do the shopping and the cooking and the laying of the table (I remember Dorothy once in America having a look almost of triumph when she actually succeeded in boiling an egg), someone else to answer the telephones and sort the letters, someone else to order the car and book their Cunard or White Star cabins before the war or their BOAC seats thereafter. The trivia of everyday living were managed for them, not by them. Being relieved of these they could more fully enjoy a partnership which embraced work as well as family and leisure. They were tied together by a far larger number of threads than is usual, far more than between Dorothy and Willard even after they had started *The New Republic* and revamped *Asia*.

Dorothy loved the theatre. She was therefore able to get *Comus* put on, and involve Leonard so fully, on and off the stage, that it became a common enterprise which led to all manner of things later. He was interested in agricultural economics and could organise the first conference at Dartington from which Dorothy could not stay aloof as long as it was happening on her doorstep. They did not just talk education to each other. They could make something of a school-like nature happen inside their household and at one stage guide it from day to day. They did not need to look at other people's gardens or cultivate a few flowers and vegetables on their own patch. They could create something grander in which Leonard could be almost as concerned as Dorothy. The windows of their house opened on to their great garden, the birds were there which Leonard had attracted, and over it hung before breakfast the notes from his recorder.

With so many common interests they could not easily be bored. They had hardly any hours when they were just following a routine that became tiresome or waiting for something to happen to relieve it. They were engaged in everything that was going on around them almost continuously. This was by no means all gain. So much activity could make them restless, causing them to weary perhaps a bit too easily of a face which had been around at Dartington for long and be a little too ready to turn to a new one for distraction, or be tempted by the pleasures of another journey and the excitement, once more, of boarding ship or plane and of seeing the dusk in a new setting.

The letters they wrote to each other do not capture their relationship. Dorothy, as I said before, was inclined to melancholy, occasionally perhaps to a state of mind not far from accidie. That rarely appears in the correspondence, nor Leonard's compensating quality of optimism and energy. He could get as depressed as anyone and as agitated. In meetings his foot would often shake incessantly. But depression and agitation seldom lasted. He would bounce back. The other way round, she with her will of steel could, when they were together, give Leonard, when he lacked confidence, a sense of support in any one of the 2,000 weeks of their marriage when he needed it. Underlying all was a pervasive sense of tenderness.

Their joint project cannot be comprehensively summed up. Most of what they helped to create is still there and therefore still changing. Dartington in the 1980s represents work in progress as much as it did fifty years ago.

They would not have wanted any judgment to be made as soon after their deaths as this, or at all. They tried to take a long view. Leonard would have agreed with Dorothy when she said:

> In regard to almost everything we do for Dartington we feel that we are not only doing it for ourselves nor for our generation only, but for

those who will succeed us twenty, fifty, and a hundred years hence. I know that the forestry department is working out a plan which has in view certain results which will be evident in 150 years. Well, Leonard and I regard this place in the same way. We can't regard ourselves as isolated and independent owners of this place. I think we are conscious every day, almost every hour of our debt to the past. . . . The man who conceived these two courtyards, his successors who planned the garden, and countless others who have added to the grandeur and dignity of the place – to all of them we are bound by a great tradition. We want to preserve tenderly what they have handed down to us, and we want to make our own additions to it in the same spirit. That means again a certain quality of work – a certain bigness of conception. We are only a link in a long chain, but I think it's worth forging that link as well as we know how, even though money is apparently wasted in the process.

But perhaps something can be said even this early about the effect outside Dartington. It was an experiment. While Dorothy did not use so often the well-known words which Leonard used, with inverted commas around them, they were always floating through the humid Devon air: the world or some part of it was to learn from the 'positive or negative results'. Has it happened?

It is clear enough that some of the innovations made at Dartington have ceased to be so, by becoming general practice. This is perhaps most evident in the world of what used to be called 'morals' where even the word, sex, had to be tiptoed around, cautiously – or as one is allowed to put it now, the attitude to and the practice of sex. It was because these were so unusual at the time that Dartington attracted such notoriety in the 1920s and 1930s. Mr Martin was thinking more of this even than of the outrageously high wages paid to agricultural labourers when he said that the Devil had moved his headquarters from Moscow to this new hotbed of sin. The Elmhirsts in their Kremlin at the top of the hill were as guilty as any of the parties more directly involved when they condoned nude bathing, girls wearing shirts so scanty that their breasts did not have to be imagined, and the awful things that obviously must happen in a co-educational school when boys and girls who had already reached puberty were let loose on each other. Against this half-imaginary background – the loud sound of kisses, the pants of delight from deep in the bushes – were the more particular horrors. Gerald Heard, Christopher Wood, W. H. Auden and others who came to visit the Elmhirsts were (to anyone not so innocent that the very notion of such strange behaviour was foreign to them) surely homosexuals.

Fifty years later co-education, far from being unconventional, has become so much accepted that it is not only state schools which have been won over. Even Repton is now competing not just for boys but for girl pupils and assuring them they will not be beaten on their bottoms by the boy prefects. In the holidays the girls as well as the boys amid the leafy suburbs of London or leaf-mould of Gloucestershire may even wear the expensively tattered jeans which were the scandal of Totnes when I raced proudly down the High Street on my red bicycle in 1933. Once upon a time a girl or boy like me was instantly identifiable and ridiculable. In the 1930s we were already more or less sexless, with our jeans and sweaters and old army jackets. The boys' hair was sometimes as long as the girls'. Dartington children still look like that; and now the Totnes children are almost indistinguishable from them, as in other towns or cities. In giving up uniform the Dartington children were the first to introduce a new and eventually much more widely worn uniform. The appearance stands for much else that has changed in the patterns of adolescent behaviour, with values and habits in a child-centred society being set by the children themselves rather than by adults. Children have become less influenced by adults, more alike, and more like Dartington.

More important than the acceptance of co-education and the new uniform, the novel belief proclaimed in the *Outline* that education is not just a preparation for life, it is life itself, has become something of a general creed. Here is another of the social revolutions of the century. The elevation in the status of the child has been as significant as the rise in the status of women. The change in actual practice has been most evident in State primary schools. Certain Local Education Authorities have been in the lead – the West Riding before it was wantonly destroyed, Oxfordshire, Devonshire itself. But every area has had some primary schools which drew praise and encouraged emulation from other countries in the western world for the way in which they created a school to fit the child instead of creating a child to fit the school. Primary schools have in short grown much more like Dartington than they were in the 1920s. Children have been demobbed from their regiments. They are not pinned into uniforms selected for them by adults. They are not lined up in rows of desks. They are not copying painstakingly from blackboards. The teacher may still have a ruler to hit children with, or even a large cane, but neither will normally be so ostentatiously displayed. Affection seems to be a more powerful motivating force than fear, co-operation rather more in evidence than competition, kindness than cruelty. On these and many other points the primary schools in the country generally as well as in Dartington village have moved a great deal nearer to Dartington than they used to be when Leonard criticised the old village school as it was in the 1920s:[10]

There were but forty children in it, and the Rector was able to say to me, 'Mr Elmhirst, I should like to remind you that this is a school for the children of the poor.'

The same change has not happened in secondary schools. Rather the opposite. I would say that Dartington in its senior school has since the 1920s moved in many respects nearer to the standard secondary school. Both are to an unhappily large extent governed not by their own teachers, heads or boards of governors but by external examiners who are in their turn subject to the universities. Competition to pass their imposed exams has brought all schools, including Dartington, into a common mould. Each bright new day is still divided up for millions of children into the same Geography 1, Geography 2, Eng. Lit. 1, Eng. Lit. 2 and so forth, with the most deadening effects on what goes on in and around the heads of young people who are being urged to put 'life itself' on one side for the sake of the jobs (that is, if there are any jobs) that exam-slogging will bring them.

In the arts it is not only the leisure of many people living at or near Dartington which has been transformed over the fifty years. No one can be sure what T. S. Eliot would say now if he were to produce an up-to-date edition of *Notes Towards a Definition of Culture*. Perhaps he would be as gloomy as ever about the kitsch and vulgarisation which the masses with their television sets have allegedly imposed upon culture. Surely he would also have had to recognise that at any rate within a minority which has been increasing steadily in size there has been a change of which he would approve. Not all of those who played in recorder consorts or sang in their school choirs or painted the pictures which hung on the walls of class-rooms at their primary schools have when they reached adult age put away childish things. More people make up passive, or not so passive, audiences for live concerts brought to the city or town or even village where they live, or in little theatres in places that never had them before, or for travelling theatres (like the Orchard Theatre based on Dartington's Beaford Centre) which visits them where they are. The range of artistic events at Dartington mentioned in chapter 10 may be rather large for such a small place; but similar lists could be reproduced elsewhere. More people, too, practise themselves, as Sunday painters or evening singers or players or attenders at ten thousand courses for all manner of ongoing and novel arts and crafts, while a majority of the houses of the country contain within them miniature craft centres going under the general name of DIY. The unusual of 1925 has, in other words, become the much less unusual of the 1980s. Dorothy would not have wanted to retract the statement she made in 1950 that 'We need the great artists; but we need also to be artists in our own way – taking time really to look at things around us: to listen, to feel, to relate one thing to another: to bring some order out of the chaos around us, and to express in some form the unity and harmony that we feel.'[11] She would probably also recognise that in certain respects there have been gains since then.

So much for the first two of the utopian hopes distinguished in chapter 4 to do with education and the arts. How about the third, the combination of town and country? That was no more completely novel in the 1920s than were the Elmhirsts' other aspirations. Ebenezer Howard was there before them and before that Rousseau, and St Augustine even further back. Their originality at the time was that, unlike the garden-city men who wanted to introduce wedges of nature into city living, they wanted to introduce wedges of urbanity into the countryside; but this too is original no longer. People have voted with their wheels for a new order. In the last century people piled into the cities where the industry was, and in this, as transport has improved, they have piled out again. They have moved first into suburbs which have expanded in ever-widening circles around the metropolitan centres and then, even further afield, into counties like Devon, as the 1981 Census showed so strikingly. In general, the danger now is almost the other way round – that the cities which are losing their youngest and brightest people will become progressively more and more neglected, deprived and uncongenial so that the migration outwards will accelerate into a general exodus. The cities may be saved by a still harsher energy shortage which could reverse the whole centrifugal movement and compel again the huddling together which industrialisation without easy transport of people and materials at one time made necessary. For the moment, however, the countryside has proved in the later parts of the century the magnet the city was before. What was not much more than a dream in the 1920s is now largely taken for granted. Lewis Mumford wrote to Patrick Geddes on 29 March 1922 about the new invention of the 'radio-telephone':[12]

> The countryside is now in direct communication with the city: even in the remotest districts it will soon be possible for the farmer to get storm warnings at much shorter notice than the present service. Will not this probably give a new turn to rural life?

It can, and it has, along with electricity, water, the car and television.

As for the fourth and fifth hopes, to combine efficiency and self-determination in industry and organisation as well as to imbue every enterprise with the scientific spirit, Dartington has not had much influence because it has not itself been notably to the fore. I have referred several times in previous chapters to the 'Dartington contradiction'. The Elmhirsts wanted the individual person to be respected in an atmosphere which

337

would, to recall Dorothy's words again, be 'relatively free from fear and competition'. They wanted self-determination for individuals. But there the two of them were, in a feudal setting, ensconced as the squire and his wife, and, although nearly always ready to laugh at themselves, not objecting to their status. Acceptance came all the more easily because this was what the people around them though was proper. When Leonard and Leonard alone stood at attention to take the salute on a Foundation Day as the band of the Royal Marines marched past in the courtyard, there would only be a few wry comments. The band, Dorothy and a seated Leonard are shown in Plate 30. Most of the observers took it for granted that this was how Leonard ought to behave. He *ought* to take the salute. He *ought* to take the vital decisions about the present and future of Dartington. He had all the more right to do so because he (and she) were benevolent. They were gentle grandees. Leonard did not like being called 'Sir', although he was, if not by the old-timers. Benevolent autocracy, however rare in human history, is a popular form of government. It is easier to believe in a person than in a system, and easy to over-believe too.

It would not of course have been like that if Dartington had been full of raging democrats. The two holders of power, and the Trustees who inherited at any rate some of it from them, would probably have bowed to the populace. But the Dartington they moved into belonged to a hierarchical county. However much they were at the beginning hostile to that county, and the county to them, they were bound to be influenced by it. Nor did the many newcomers from other counties make all that difference. Some of them came because they welcomed the sense of security that dependence upon a wealthy and benevolent squire gave them. Apart from the foreigners, nearly all came from other parts of a country which has over the whole century been beset by the same basic contradiction as Dartington. Britain has been a democracy at home and given way to the demands for self-determination in its Empire. Britain has, to protect the individual, built a welfare state which did not exist when Dartington had to provide most of its own social services in the 1920s and 1930s. But Britain has also remained a deeply class-divided society. Intelligence has continued to come from the top. It has not been interfused with the mass. Britain's industry and society have been plagued by consequential dissension. The upshot is that at Dartington there have been no great innovations in management, no experiments (scientific or other) in industrial participation which would show how individual employees as members of a partnership could not only fulfil themselves more completely but also contribute more to the collective life. Nor have there been many such innovations in Britain generally.

But it has to be remembered where the Elmhirsts' starting-point was and how far they came in a period of fifty years. They began their

experiment in a feudal style which John Holand would have recognised
and even envied. The White Hart mattered more as an influence than the
black Buick or the generating set which Jack Collingbourne installed. They
were the charismatic founders, the 'extraordinary people' whom it was an
honour to serve and an inspiration to be with, partly, it is true, because
their money allowed them to be not quite contemporary. From there they
moved within a short period not just from personal charisma to organisa-
tional bureaucracy (as happens generally) but also from a feudal household economy to a more or less modern industrial economy, from dependence upon a personal fortune to self-support in a world market, from the
structure of an all-purpose family to a division of labour, from a measure
of autocracy to at least a measure of shared responsibility, even if it has not
been enough. Looked at in one way they embraced within a lifetime the
changes which have taken the Great Society many centuries to encompass.

I come back to the question – what effect has Dartington had? Large
changes in mood and practice cannot be traced to any single people or any
single institution. They belong to the zeitgeist of the century. What can be
said is that the Elmhirsts were pioneers. They were ahead of their time.
Some of the main ideas they picked up from the progressive circles in which
they moved turned out to be winners.

The same point might be put another way. An alliance was formed
early on, without the Elmhirsts necessarily recognising what was afoot,
between them and the beard-and-sandals brigade which, despite Orwell's
derision, has had, and continues to have, some general influence upon the
movement of society. Dartington, not by issuing manifestos, not by any
ringing declarations about the new Jerusalem, but by itself being a
happening which is embodied in a place and in activities which people can
see and feel, has been just one of many pillars upon which the brigade has
been able to lean.

The bearded men have, as I said before, been part of, or on the fringes
of, socialism in the idiosyncratic form it has taken in Britain. William
Morris, the founder of the Socialist League, was a bearded man himself, as
was Bernard Shaw. Morris was also, as the founder of the Society for the
Protection of Ancient Buildings, a medievalist who would have approved
of what William Weir and Leonard did. He was also a man who insisted on
the life-enhancing quality that can emerge from blending art with craft.
His successors have together constituted what has sometimes been called
the libertarian element alongside the even more important egalitarian
element in the socialist movement.

Its other main element, the emphasis on nationalisation of the means
of production, distribution and exchange, has been introduced far more by
the producers of wealth than by its consumers. They have not been notably

successful, much less so than the brigadiers whom Orwell considered such a bane. The achievement of the beard-and-sandals men, along with many others who would not recognise themselves as fellows in any common cause, is there in the acceptance of the need for conservation which goes beyond ancient buildings. They have managed to force upon governments some continuing responsibility for sustaining the arts. They have succeeded for the moment in abolishing capital if not corporal punishment. They have liberalised the divorce laws. They have brought homosexuality within the pale, and as one item is crossed off the radicals' agenda another item has been added to the list.

The Dartington which gradually institutionalised the ideas of the Elmhirsts has never enjoyed (or suffered) independence from the general society. Its influence has merged with thousands of others to bring about some changes in the way people live, and as this has happened Dartington itself has become more and more a part of the general society. At the beginning it was a foreign body set down in a hostile environment. The boundaries between Dartington and its bit of Devon, or Devon as a whole, or England, were well marked. Morale on the other side of the brook over which Leonard's Talbot nosed its way was high indeed amongst the like-minded enthusiasts attracted by the Bostonian high-mindedness or/ and the New York high living. As usual, heresy-hunting tightened the bonds between the heretics.

Gradually the boundaries became more and more permeable. Many of the people from Totnes and the other surrounding towns and villages who came to work at Dartington were (and are) more strongly motivated by wages than ideals. They were a channel along which messages travelled in both directions. The children of the first and later waves of pioneers grew up as did the pupils from the school and went to work elsewhere; each carried into England some impress from the unique community of Dartington and so changed the whole. People were invited to cross over to attend a Jubilee Celebration or to take part, later on, in one of the Christmas Festivals organised by Bobbie and Peter Cox. Each one who did was another link. Students graduated from the College of Arts and taught in schools throughout the country or performed in repertories or in trios, quartets or orchestras, or just played in their sitting-rooms in Carlisle, Montreal or Auckland. Farmers used the Cattle Breeding Centre. Customers, like parents, came from far and wide. They had to be responded to. The island gradually joined up with the mainland.

The junction was made easier by a crucial feature of Dartington which was linked to the belief in the scientific spirit – its lack of a charter, its lack of what Leonard called pejoratively 'Benedictine Rules'. The 'English experiment' was notably vague in its outlines, and remained notably vague. There was hardly a declaration even of principle although it was inevitable that, as time went on and as the Elmhirsts had to meet more and more people who bothered them by asking what they were setting out to do, they should be driven into retrospective rationalisations. These were mostly not very crisp or very convincing to the insiders who remembered the vacuum which no one abhorred. In 1937 Leonard, after grouping his aims neatly into, first, the economic and, second, the cultural, proceeded to report in his *Faith and Works* on how nearly they had already been achieved in the short space of twelve years. Dorothy, much later, in the Foundation Day address of 1962 made another attempt, still using the word 'plan' at a period when it was well on its way out of favour. 'What appeared at the start to be the haphazard, fortuitous combination of activities was, in fact, the beginning of a broad-based plan.' Broad-based, yes. Plan, no.

But the rationalisations were also happily rather vague too and mercurial. At no time were the ideas underlying Dartington nailed to any door for zealots to draw inspiration from. No one could easily and convincingly claim to be more in tune with them than anyone else, though hundreds of people have claimed (as they will continue to do) that what they are proposing to do in the future is exactly in line with the Elmhirsts' original intentions. This usually fortifies them more than their audience. The lack of a set of precise objectives handed down from above meant that there did not have to be too much fierce argument about the extent to which the objectives had been achieved, or some treachery against them perpetrated. The absence of a plan meant there was on that account an inbuilt openness which allowed the walls to crumble.

One of the crucial dates is 1937, when Leonard was elected to the Devon County Council. He became one of the squires of the shires, ten years later serving on the Education Committee, Health Committee, the Planning Committee, the Care of Children Committee, and as Vice-Chairman of the Adult Education Joint Committee, Chairman of the Music Committee, Vice-Chairman of the Governors of three schools in Totnes, Chairman of the Crichel Hostel in Totnes, and member of the Council of the University College of the South West. Poor man! It all had many long-term consequences for Dartington. The support by the county for the expansion of the College of Arts in the post-war years is in lineal descent, and so is the Devon Centre for Further Education established by the county in the same rehabilitated stables where I once took bits of my motorcycle to bed. Leonard's joining the county was the precursor of Peter Cox doing so and Peter Sutcliffe and of such a two-way traffic along the A38 between Exeter and Dartington as must have contributed towards exhausting a small oilfield in the Middle East.

The erosion of boundaries has, naturally enough, brought about many changes on the inside. The scale of the affair has also changed. Everything is bigger, more departmentalised, more specialised, less amateur and with less of the enthusiasm of the amateur. The easy informal solidarity is no longer present. But 'Dartington' still means something special to many of the people who live and work there. The Trust is still landlord and, directly or through its companies, college or school, the employer, and with much more widely dispersed interests than most employers. The Trust is a formal front for the network of relationships between the people who make up or make use of the community. Dartington has not become an indistinguishable part of society in general. Dartington is still a lot more than a place-name, and it is changing more rapidly than at any period since the war.

Pioneers who are ahead of their time if only by a little often attract acclaim later in life. It helps of course, if what they have done is known. The Elmhirsts' range was too wide for all but a few to be conversant with it. It was not much of an asset in England (nor would she have wanted it to be) for Dorothy to have financed *The New Republic* and *Asia* and *Theatre Arts*, the New School of Social Research, the National League of Women Voters, the Child Studies Association, Margaret Mead in some of her studies, or Consumers Research and Consumers Union in the United States, although those led later to the Consumers' Association and its magazine, *Which?*, in Britain. Nor was it much of an asset for Leonard to have helped to start Sriniketan, PEP, the International Conference of Agricultural Economists, the Cambridgeshire Village Colleges, the Vivekananda Agricultural Research Laboratory, the Damodar Valley Corporation, or even the Cattle Breeding Centre at Dartington, although admittedly that last was to many eyes more of a glorious affair than most.

I am not saying there was no acclaim; there was some, especially when they were abroad. Dorothy's membership of a prominent American elite did not totally lapse when she moved across the water to the Hall, and her husband had access to it as well. He also had certain advantages not gained through marriage, connected at that time with his being an Englishman. England – although it was called the British Empire, England, not Britain, was its heart – was still the greatest power in the world, even if already on the decline. A quarter of the population of the world, and a quarter of the earth's surface, much more than the modern superpowers can muster in the present, or even Rome in the past, was ruled from London, Cambridge and Oxford. It was done not by the deployment of vast armies and secret services – the home base was too small for that – but by such men as Leonard although with thicker skins than his. As much as any of the rest, he carried around with him the awesome prestige of this Empire (coupled with a critical attitude to it, so that he had the best of both worlds) and at

34 Dorothy photographed by Juliette Huxley, late 1930s

35 Dorothy at Dartington, 1930s

36 Dorothy in Totnes, 1960s

37 Dorothy at Dartington, 1960s

38 Leonard in the Cotswolds, 1972

the same time was so much the gentleman – confident without being brassy, polite without ever being obsequious, well-dressed without being flashy, widely experienced without being boastful, superior if at all only because not flaunting it – that he fitted almost every man's stereotype of the world rulers who could rule without mailed fists. He hardly had to show his passport, until the Second World War completed the downfall which the First had started.

With such advantages Leonard was welcome in the White House while Franklin Roosevelt was President. Eleanor was Dorothy's old friend from Mr Roser's School in New York. There is an account in Joseph Lash's book, *Eleanor and Franklin*, of one such occasion in August 1933.[13] The Roosevelts were pushing a programme for the resettlement of the unemployed on the land in planned communities. At dinner Leonard, says Lash, explained how he was, like M. L. Wilson, who was in charge of the resettlement,

> trying out some of his ideas on how to halt the drift away from the countryside. In order to raise the standard of living they had introduced light industries and built housing, and they had encouraged the development of arts and crafts as a part of rural life and everyday amenity. Leonard Elmhirst, a student of medieval history, embellished his description of Dartington with references to the manorial system, where there had been security, a sense of belonging and rootedness, and, to a considerable degree, self-sufficiency. Everyone was fascinated. The Dartington concept was not too far from Wilson's 'community idea'.

Later that summer I was one of the party that stayed at the White House. At supper on the first night almost the entire Cabinet joined in the discussion about the plan to persuade farmers to grow less so as to keep prices up. Roosevelt turned to General Johnson, Director of the National Recovery Administration, and said that now he supposed they would have to give blue ribands to the sows that had the *smallest* litters – a reference to the reverse incentive which was operated in France and Germany for human mothers. After supper Leonard left the rest of us to join the President in a discussion with angry coal owners. In 1940 he was at dinner with him again and came home to England soon after Dunkirk to tell his brother, Thomas, then an Air Vice-Marshal, that Roosevelt had asked him to telephone if he heard of something vital England needed to withstand the then-expected invasion. Tommy asked right away for fifty American fighters to be flown off US aircraft carriers onto British airfields. Leonard thereupon rang the White House. Roosevelt did not understand Leonard's use of the term 'Fighter Aircraft'. Tommy remembered in time that the word from the First World War he would understand was 'Scoutship'. The

Scoutships did not come but fifty old US destroyers did that Roosevelt gave to the Royal Navy in September.[14]

In India Leonard was on sufficiently personal terms with Nehru to write to him about a whole string of administrative matters, about the Damodar Valley, about American architects in India, about Dr Sudhir Sen, the first Executive Secretary of the Damodar Valley Corporation. In England Max Nicholson, then head of Herbert Morrison's office when he was Lord President of the Council, rang me in 1946 and asked me, when I was in charge of the Labour Party Research Department, whether I thought Leonard would accept a peerage if it was offered. I said I thought not but he'd probably be pleased to be asked. The next step was a letter from Mr Attlee proposing that 'the dignity of a Barony of the United Kingdom be conferred upon you in recognition of your political and public services'.[15] Leonard sensibly refused by return of post, on 20 May:

> Your letter and proposal came as a complete surprise to my wife and myself. That you should think that our services were at all worthy of such public recognition moves us deeply and we should like you personally to realise how very appreciative we are of your willingness to recommend us for one of the highest privileges this country can bestow upon an individual. . . . My own work, however, as you know, has lain in the main among country people and with rural problems, in India, in the USA and in Devonshire. . . . Whether in Bengal or in agricultural circles in the USA, acceptance would neither be easy for me to explain nor easy for my friends to comprehend.

The 'as you know' to the Prime Minister was typical. A few years later, in 1949, the government appointed Leonard a member of the Development Commission whose role was to promote agriculture, fisheries and rural industry. He remained a member till 1965. In 1972 Leonard was offered a CBE[16] which he refused much more peremptorily.[17] Edward Heath wrote back to say he was sorry.[18]

The only honour Leonard would accept was an honorary degree – five of them. He was particularly pleased with the ones from Durham for Bede's sake and Oxford for the sake of agricultural economics. He wrote about the first one, at Durham in 1962:[19]

> That any University in Britain should have considered me and my wife and our doings seriously worthy of recognition was, I must admit, a considerable shock and a welcome surprise. I was told later that the mathematicians, the physicists and even the theologians voted for it!

Dorothy died in 1968, aged 81. Miriam Adams, theatre producer for the Playgoers Society for many years, met her two days before her death on a very cold morning in December at the retail shop, buying Christmas presents. Dorothy was frozen. She said, 'Oh Miriam, you do look cold.'[20]

A Trustees' meeting began on the next day. When I arrived for it she stood stock still looking down the stairs to me as if to a messenger. She was grey and grieved. The next day she took to her bed. A few hours before her death she was laughing gaily and loudly enough to fill the house. Leonard, Bill and I went for a Christmas dinner at the school. Leonard made a farewell speech to Hu and Lois Child. He apologised for Dorothy's absence, saying she was a little unwell. When we got back to the Hall she was dead.

Leonard married again in December 1972 in Worsbrough Parish Church in Yorkshire. How often he and Dorothy had discussed the possibility I do not know. I doubt whether she would have altered the view she expressed on 17 July 1931, shortly after she had heard she did not have to undergo what could have been a dangerous operation:

> Perhaps it will sound foolish to tell you now all the things that ran through my head today, but one thing I do want to tell you. I knew that I loved you so much that your happiness came before anything else and I knew that if I died I wanted you to marry again. I wanted you to have that complete and perfect relationship with another woman. The one thing I couldn't bear was the thought of you alone.

His second wife was herself linked with, and a link to, Dartington. Dr Susanna Isaacs was at the school at the same time as I was. Trained as a doctor and a psychoanalyst in Bristol and Chicago, she followed Dr Winnicott at St Mary's Hospital in London as Physician in Charge of the Department of Child Psychiatry at Paddington Green.

After the marriage the next months were spent with Leonard at Dartington and Sue in London whilst they each extricated themselves from their jobs. They then had a month at Dartington and two months in Italy, at her farmhouse. Leonard became known locally as Leonardo. He wrote to his secretary, Gladys Burr, again from Venice, on 6 August 1973:

> We took the local 'vaporetto' . . . to Murano and our favourite church and Dorothy's favourite Madonna. We found too a little local restaurant full of fishy foods, eels and soups and then visited the glass museum. You would hardly believe the pains to which the Murano workmen go to mutilate glass!

There were many new friends near them in Italy. One was Marion Iacopucci who had once been a pupil at Foxhole and now lived not far from Sue's farmhouse. She wrote to me about her memories of them:[21]

One could never really accept Leonard's age: everything about him physically and mentally belied it. Although his considerateness of others took the form of a certain old-world courtesy which is rare nowadays, everything else about him was young. His energy was amazing. He would clamber up terraced vineyards, over the fields and through the woods which cover this part of the world. He was very interested in the local problems of forestry and the abandoning of the land. He thought it would be a good idea to introduce sequoia and even pinched some cuttings from a local garden. Leonard was always interested in the tools local artisans used in their work, and he showed my husband how the walls of the Hall had been plastered in medieval fashion without a trowel so that this method could be used to plaster parts of Casa Figaro in Gombereto. He always wanted to know what people did and why they did it. And how things worked: for instance he didn't think much of the heat retaining qualities of our traditional fireplaces and drew up very detailed plans and sections of a system developed by an American University in the thirties for my husband.

He was a wonderful raconteur, and some of the most memorable times were when, to a chorus of 'tell us one of your stories', Leonard would retell stories from his life: being in India – before and after meeting Tagore; Cornell and the Foreign Students' Union; his and Dorothy's plans for Dartington; finding Dartington with his sister; the early life on the estate. He had a wonderful memory and was quite fascinating.

My lasting memory of Susanna and Leonardo (to their Italian friends) together is of a romantic tenderness and gaiety. They were good sounding boards to each other and one could feel their mutual understanding and concern. Their domestic life here was very loving and peaceful though they were often inundated by their friends and children, particularly during summer visits. Books, music, paintings, plants and gardens, people, food were some of the things we saw them enjoy together here in Italy.

That autumn Leonard and Sue left England to live in America. Sue had been appointed to a professional post at the University of Southern California in Los Angeles. In November Leonard made his last journey across the Atlantic, again by ship, not the *Majestic* this time, but the *Q.E. II*. They bought a house in Beverly Hills with a swimming pool in the garden. Leonard told Juliette and Julian Huxley about their arrival:[22]

A group of great long-eared owls sat on our Telly mast through much of our first night – discussing our arrival and hopping from the Telly to our tall and handsome Canary pines. In our lower hill side woodland what should appear one morning but three long-eared grey deer.

While Sue was at work during the day he wrote the book, *The Straight and its Origin*, which I have quoted from. He re-learnt typing. He was happy. He died in April 1974, aged 80; Susanna brought his ashes back to England. They were not taken to the family grave but strewn in the same place as Dorothy's, in their garden.

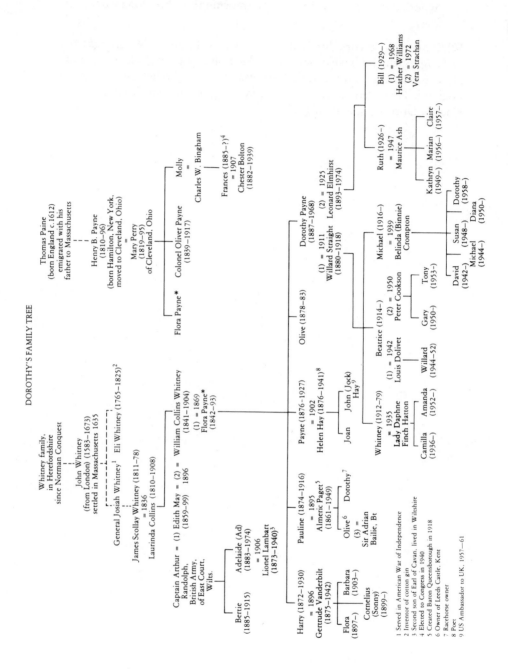

DOROTHY'S FAMILY TREE

1 Served in American War of Independence
2 Inventor of cotton gin
3 Second son of Earl of Cavan. lived in Wiltshire
4 Elected to Congress in 1940
5 Created Baron Queensborough in 1918
6 Owner of Leeds Castle. Kent
7 Racehorse owner
8 Poet
9 US Ambassador to UK. 1957–61

LEONARD'S FAMILY TREE

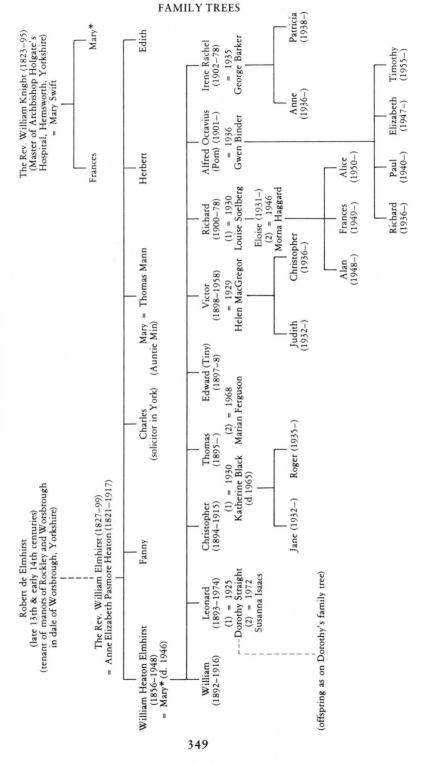

SOURCES AND NOTES

The quoted material not otherwise attributed is in the Dartington Hall Records Office.

CHAPTER 1 INTRODUCTION

1 'Only one thing about Nature was clear in the eighteenth century – that she abhorred a straight line. This was a favourite saying of William Kent.' Derek Clifford, *A History of Garden Design*, Faber & Faber, London, 1966, p.135.
2 Frances Cornford, 'Summer Beach'.
3 Anthony Emery, the historian of Dartington Hall and generally the authority I have borrowed from, wrote his book after the shields were painted and prefers the name Beornwynn. Anthony Emery, *Dartington Hall*, Clarendon Press, Oxford, 1973.
4 Undated note by Dorothy Elmhirst, 'Dorothy Whitney Elmhirst'.
5 Willie Elmhirst, *A Freshman's Diary 1911–1912*, Basil Blackwell, Oxford, 1969.
6 L. K. Elmhirst, *The Straight and Its Origin*, Willard Straight Hall, Ithaca, New York, 1975.
7 L. K. Elmhirst, *Poet and Plowman*, Visva-Bharati, Calcutta, 1975.
8 Victor Bonham-Carter and W. B. Curry, *Dartington Hall*, Exmoor Press, Dulverton, Somerset, 1970.
9 W. A. Swanberg, *Whitney Father, Whitney Heiress*, Scribners, New York, 1980.

CHAPTER 2 THE ENGLISHMAN

1 Much of this section draws on Leonard Elmhirst's unpublished account, written in 1966, 'Life at Laxton 1895–1903'.
2 Alfred Elmhirst interviewed by Michael Young, 1977.
3 Alfred Elmhirst interviewed by Michael Young, 1976.
4 Ibid.; and Richard Elmhirst interviewed by Michael Young, 1977.
5 'Life at Laxton.'
6 Leonard Elmhirst interviewed by Victor Bonham-Carter, 1958.
7 Edward Elmhirst, *The Peculiar Inheritance, A History of the Elmhirsts*, privately printed, 1951, p.117.

8   'Life at Laxton.'

9   Alfred Elmhirst to Michael Young, 5 June 1979.

10 'Life at Laxton.'

11 J. R. Currie, 'Leonard Knight Elmhirst', in Roger N. Dixey (ed.), *International Explorations of Agricultural Economics, A Tribute to the Inspiration of Leonard Knight Elmhirst*, Iowa State University Press, Ames, 1964, p.3.

12 Leonard Elmhirst to Mary Elmhirst, 15 July 1906.

13 'Life at Laxton.'

14 W. Storrs Fox to William Elmhirst, 22 February 1904.

15 'Life at Laxton.'

16 Ibid.

17 Ibid.

18 W. Storrs Fox to Leonard Elmhirst, 20 November 1907.

19 J. H. Appleton to Leonard Elmhirst, 27 October 1907.

20 Leonard wrote on 1 December 1967 to J. Thorn, Head of Repton, refusing to give money for a war memorial on the grounds that any money that was raised should be spent on single study-bedrooms. In an earlier draft letter to the headmaster in the same vein, dated 2 November 1938 but perhaps not sent, Leonard wrote that the 'argument was that group study and group dormitory and lack of any privacy were insurance methods against sex perversions and masturbation'.

21 Leonard Elmhirst to A. G. Grundy, 31 May 1934.

22 Leonard Elmhirst to William Elmhirst, 31 January 1915.

23 Leonard Elmhirst to Mary Elmhirst, 3 November 1912.

24 Leonard Elmhirst to Mary Elmhirst, 24 January 1915.

25 Note written by Leonard Elmhirst in 1974.

26 Leonard Elmhirst to William Elmhirst, 16 November 1913.

27 Eric James, 'A last eccentric', *The Listener*, 30 October 1980, p.574.

28 E. M. Forster, *Goldsworthy Lowes Dickinson*, Arnold, London, 1934, p.241.

29 Leonard Elmhirst in an undated memorandum, probably written while he was in India in 1915 and 1916, and referring to his work in Eastbourne in 1915.

30 Leonard Elmhirst to Dorothy Straight, 13 March 1923.

31 Graham Wallas, *The Great Society*, Macmillan, London, 1914.

32 Note written by Leonard Elmhirst in 1974.

33 G. Lowes Dickinson to Leonard Elmhirst, 6 May 1916.

34 Rachel Barker interviewed by John Lane, 1975.

35 Leonard Elmhirst interviewed by Victor Bonham-Carter, 1958.

36 Leonard Elmhirst to William Elmhirst, 20 June 1915.

37 Leonard Elmhirst to Mary Elmhirst, 16 June 1918.

38 Leonard Elmhirst to Alfred Elmhirst, 3 November 1915.

39 Leonard Elmhirst to Mary Elmhirst, 8 October 1915.

40 Leonard Elmhirst to Mary Elmhirst, 20 January 1916.

41 Leonard Elmhirst to Richard Elmhirst, 17 January 1917.

42 Leonard Elmhirst to William Elmhirst, 20 February 1917.

43 Leonard Elmhirst to Mary Elmhirst, 27 March 1917.

44 Leonard Elmhirst to William Elmhirst, 6 January 1917.

45 Leonard Elmhirst to Mary Elmhirst, 15 April 1917.

46 Leonard Elmhirst to Harold Angus, 15 November 1917.

47 Leonard Elmhirst's note, 'In Defence of Retreat', 1917.

48 'The first architect of union was Lionel Curtis of Milner's Kindergarten, who

resigned from his post as Assistant Colonial Secretary to the Transvaal in order to prepare a weighty memorandum outlining the advantages to the states of coming together.' John Selby, *A Short History of South Africa*, NEL Mentor, New York, 1975, p.182.

49 Quentin Bell, *Virginia Woolf*, Paladin, London, 1976, p.178.
50 Leonard Elmhirst to William Elmhirst, 26 October 1917.
51 Sam Higginbottom's words reported by Leonard Elmhirst interviewed by Michael Young, 1973.
52 Leonard Elmhirst to William Elmhirst, 13 June 1918.
53 Leonard Elmhirst's diary entry for 6 August 1919.
54 Leonard Elmhirst's unpublished account, written in 1966, 'Elmhirst'.

CHAPTER 3 THE AMERICAN

1 'Bring Her Home', *Shipyard Bulletin*, Newport News Shipbuilding, 1976.
2 Mark D. Hirsch, *William C. Whitney, Modern Warwick*, Dodd, Mead, Chicago, 1948, p.235.
3 Ibid., p.35.
4 Francis Bacon, quoted by M. Josephson, *The Robber Barons – the Great American Capitalists 1861–1901*, Harcourt Brace, New York, 1934.
5 Augusta Francelia Payne White, *The Paynes of Hamilton*, Tobias A. Wright, New York, 1912.
6 Frederick Clifton Pierce, *The Descendants of John Whitney*, Press of W. B. Conkey Company, Chicago, 1895.
7 W. A. Swanberg, *Whitney Father, Whitney Heiress*, Scribners, New York, 1980, p.167.
8 Henry Adams, *The Education of Henry Adams, An Autobiography*, Houghton Mifflin, Boston, 1918.
9 Barbara Goldsmith, *Little Gloria . . . Happy at Last*, Macmillan, London, 1980, p.91.
10 Dorothy Elmhirst, 'My talk in the Barn Theatre on the eve of my departure for Chekhov in America', 26 March 1939.
11 Leonard Elmhirst to Tony Soper, 6 January 1965.
12 Adams, op. cit.
13 Dorothy Elmhirst, note entitled 'Inagua South', 2 February 1959.
14 Quoted in Swanberg, op. cit., p.89.
15 'Inagua South', op. cit.
16 Ibid.
17 Susan Hammond interviewed by Michael Young, 1977.
18 Hirsch, op. cit., p.570.
19 Ibid., p.571.
20 'Inagua South', op. cit.
21 Ibid.
22 Ibid.
23 Ibid.
24 Ibid.
25 *Spence School Bulletin*, New York, 1955.
26 Hirsch, op. cit., p.599. It was put about and reported in the *New York Times* at the time of his death that his fortune was worth $21m. But there were no death duties then and executors were liable to exaggerate a bit (since there was no sanction) to make a better show on behalf of the dead.

27   B. H. Friedman, *Gertrude Vanderbilt Whitney*, Doubleday, New York, 1978.
28   Ibid., pp.230–1.
29   Karolyn Gould to Leonard Elmhirst, 6 February 1973 and 2 April 1973.
30   Andrew Gray, 'Mrs Gardner as Matchmaker', to be published in *Fenway Court*, the Annual Report of the Isabella Stewart Gardner Museum, Boston, Mass., in 1982.
31   Sir Thomas Wyatt, *Collected Poems*, edited Kenneth Muir, Routledge & Kegan Paul, London, 1949, p.7.
32   Department of Manuscripts and University Archives, Cornell University Libraries, Willard D. Straight Papers.
33   Quoted in Swanberg, op. cit., p.235.
34   Josephson, op. cit.
35   Hirsch, op. cit., p.565.
36   Ibid.
37   Swanberg, op.cit., p.237.
38   Herbert Croly, *Willard Straight*, Macmillan, New York, 1924, p.27.
39   Susan Hammond interviewed by Michael Young, 1977.
40   Karolyn Gould, unpublished note.
41   17 November 1909. Quoted in Swanberg, op. cit., p. 281, from the Department of Manuscripts and University Archives, Cornell University Libraries, Willard D. Straight Papers. The quotations from Swanberg, op. cit., below come from the same source.
42   21 November 1909, ibid., p.283.
43   Croly, op.cit., p.364.
44   Swanberg, op.cit., pp.292, 317.
45   Ibid., p.293.
46   Letters from Dorothy Whitney to Willard Straight between 25 December 1910 and 21 February 1911. Swanberg, op.cit., p.316.
47   5 February 1911, ibid.
48   15 April 1911, ibid., p.317.
49   30 July 1911, ibid., p.322.
50   Dorothy Elmhirst to Irene Elmhirst, March 1927.
51   Quoted in Karolyn Gould's unpublished note.
52   Ibid.
53   Ibid.
54   1130 Fifth Avenue is now classified as an 'official city landmark' by the New York City Landmarks Commission. It was at one time the headquarters of the National Audubon Society.
55   Croly, op. cit., p.459.
56   Herbert Croly, *The Promise of American Life*, Capricorn Books, New York, 1964, p.116. (First published 1909.)
57   Ibid., p.204.
58   Unpublished note by Leonard Elmhirst, 'The founding of *The New Republic* in 1912', 1971.
59   Alva Belmont was the domineering and socially ambitious mother who had forced the daughter of her first marriage, Consuelo Vanderbilt, into a miserable match with the Duke of Marlborough in 1895.
60   30 June 1918. Swanberg, op. cit., p.401.
61   6 August 1918. Ibid., p.402.
62   1 December 1918. Ibid., p.444.
63   Ibid., p.390. Willard Straight to Dorothy Straight, 31 March 1918.
64   Ibid., p.402.

65   Department of Manuscripts and University Archives, Cornell University Libraries, Willard D. Straight Papers.

66   Swanberg, op. cit., p.335.

67   Croly, *Willard Straight*, op. cit., p.567.

68   Ibid., p.568.

CHAPTER 4 TOGETHER

1   L. K. Elmhirst, *The Straight and Its Origin*, Willard Straight Hall, Ithaca, New York, 1975, p.21.

2   Ibid., p.16.

3   Dorothy wrote to Leonard's mother on 4 February 1925, 'Before I even knew Leonard I had heard of the magnificent thing he was doing. Mr Villard, the editor of our *Nation*, called me on the telephone one day in New York and said, "I have just been up to Cornell to speak at the Cosmopolitan Club. It is the only spot in the university where freedom of speech still exists, and the fact it exists there is due entirely to one young man called Elmhirst. I wish you could see him." That was my introduction to Leonard.'

4   Leonard Elmhirst to Mary Elmhirst, 28 September 1920.

5   Elmhirst, op. cit., p.22.

6   Ibid., p.23.

7   Krishna Kripalani, *Rabindranath Tagore*, Oxford University Press, London, 1962.

8   Rabindranath Tagore and L. K. Elmhirst, *Rabindranath Tagore, Pioneer in Education*, John Murray, London, 1961, p.50.

9   Kripalani, op. cit., p.20.

10   Ibid., pp.229–30.

11   Elmhirst, *The Straight*, op. cit., p.29.

12   Ibid., pp.29–30.

13   Ibid., pp.49–50.

14   Ibid., p.89.

15   Ibid., p.90.

16   Ibid., pp.87–8.

17   Leonard Elmhirst to Dorothy Straight, 16 October 1920.

18   Elmhirst, *The Straight*, op. cit., pp.108–9.

19   Dorothy Straight to Leonard Elmhirst, 9 August 1921.

20   Leonard Elmhirst to Dorothy Straight, 18 August 1921.

21   Dorothy Straight to Leonard Elmhirst, 19 August 1921.

22   Leonard Elmhirst to Dorothy Straight, 10 October 1921.

23   Leonard Elmhirst interviewed by Victor Bonham-Carter, 1958.

24   Leonard Elmhirst's diary, June 1920.

25   Note by Leonard Elmhirst, 'Farmhand at the Meridale Butter Farms', 1970.

26   Leonard Elmhirst's diary, 30 November 1919.

27   Elmhirst, *The Straight*, op. cit., p.8.

28   R. B. Nye and J. E. Morpurgo, *A History of the United States*, volume 2, Penguin Books, Harmondsworth, 1955, p.652.

29   A reference by Theodore Roosevelt to the supporters of *The New Republic*. See Herbert Croly to Dorothy Straight, 3 May 1918.

30   Nye and Morpurgo, op. cit., p.652.

31   Ibid., p.653.

32   Joseph P. Lash, *Eleanor and Franklin*, André Deutsch, London, 1972, p.280.

33 Rose Schneiderman and Lucy Goldthwaite, *All for One*, Eriksson, Middlebury, Vermont, 1967, p.147.
34 Lash, op. cit., p.280.
35 Dorothy Straight to Leonard Elmhirst, 19 September 1921.
36 Dorothy Elmhirst, undated note, 'Dorothy Whitney Elmhirst'.
37 Dorothy Straight to Leonard Elmhirst, 14 August 1923.
38 Herbert Croly to Dorothy Straight, 11 September 1920. Professor E. A. Stettner of the Department of Political Sciences, Wellesley College, Boston, Massachusetts, who is writing a life of Croly, has kindly made transcripts of these letters available. I could not read the handwriting of the originals.
39 Herbert Croly to Dorothy Straight, undated, late 1924 or early 1925.
40 Leonard Elmhirst to Dorothy Elmhirst, 22 August 1955.
41 Dorothy Straight to Leonard Elmhirst, 28 June 1921.
42 Dorothy Straight to Leonard Elmhirst, 16 July 1921.
43 Dorothy Straight to Leonard Elmhirst, 15 April 1922.
44 P. Spear, *The Oxford History of Modern India, 1740–1947*, Oxford University Press, London, 1965, p.336.
45 Ibid., p.245.
46 Ibid., p.341.
47 Kripalani, op. cit., p.266.
48 Leonard Elmhirst interviewed by Victor Bonham-Carter, 1958.
49 'Knowing, at that time, that the Liberal and the Labour Party in Britain were both pledged to implement the first half of this plan at an early date, I hoped and thought that the second half, whereby India was to achieve full independence as soon as either liberal-minded party came into power, would be enacted by Parliament less than ten years later and anyhow in the early thirties.' L. K. Elmhirst, *Poet and Plowman*, Visva-Bharati, Calcutta, 1975, p.29.
50 Kripalani, op. cit., p.246.
51 Elmhirst, *Poet and Plowman*, op. cit., p.20.
52 Ibid., pp.25–6.
53 Kripalani, op. cit., p.84.
54 Leonard Elmhirst to Sir Stafford Cripps, 3 August 1945.
55 Leonard Elmhirst to Irene Elmhirst, 6 December 1921.
56 Leonard Elmhirst to Dorothy Straight, 30 January 1922.
57 Elmhirst, *Poet and Plowman*, op. cit., p.144.
58 Ibid., p.54.
59 Dorothy Straight to Leonard Elmhirst, 29 May 1922.
60 Leonard Elmhirst to Dorothy Straight, 8 November 1922.
61 Gretchen Green wrote an autobiography, *The Whole World and Company*, John Day/Raynel Hitchcock, New York, 1936.
62 Tagore and Elmhirst, op. cit., pp.74–5.
63 Ibid., p.49.
64 Ibid., pp.63–4.
65 Ibid., pp.68, 79, 84.
66 Leonard Elmhirst to Dorothy Straight, 28 August 1923.
67 Leonard Elmhirst to Dorothy Straight, 21 August 1923.
68 Leonard Elmhirst to Dorothy Straight, 4 November 1923.
69 Leonard Elmhirst to Wyatt Rawson, 8 February 1925.
70 Leonard Elmhirst to Rabindranath Tagore, 28 June 1923.
71 Lady Ranu Mookerjee to Leonard Elmhirst, 28 September 1942.

72 Rabindranath Tagore to Leonard Elmhirst, 13 November 1922.
73 Sybille Bedford, *Aldous Huxley*, vol. 1, Collins and Chatto & Windus, London, 1973, p.316.
74 Note by Leonard Elmhirst, 'Tagore's visit to Argentina', 1961.
75 *Rabindranath Tagore: A Centenary Volume 1861–1961*, Sahitya Akademi, New Delhi, 1961, p.34.
76 *Testimonios sobre Victoria Ocampo*, López, Buenos Aires, 1962, p.321.
77 Rabindranath Tagore to Leonard Elmhirst, 10 July 1930.
78 Dorothy Straight to Leonard Elmhirst, 31 July 1924.
79 Leonard Elmhirst to Dorothy Straight, 16 August 1924.
80 Ibid.
81 Dorothy Straight to Leonard Elmhirst, 24 October 1924.
82 Leonard Elmhirst to Dorothy Straight, 13 October 1924.
83 Leonard Elmhirst to Dorothy Straight, 13 October 1924.
84 Leonard Elmhirst to Dorothy Straight, 25 November 1924.
85 Dorothy Straight to Leonard Elmhirst, 8 January 1925.
86 Margaret Isherwood, interviewed by Michael Young in 1977, said that when she went to the USA in the late 1920s 'it was a great astonishment to me to find the difference of treatment that I got in America. The approach of men to women was so much more considerate and they would be interested in what one had to say even.'
87 Leonard Elmhirst to Richard Elmhirst, 25 June 1923.
88 B. H. Friedman, *Gertrude Vanderbilt Whitney*, Doubleday, New York, 1978, p.469. The comment came from Harry Whitney, Dorothy's brother.
89 Dorothy Straight to Leonard Elmhirst, 14 August 1923.
90 Note by Dorothy Elmhirst, 'Dorothy Whitney Elmhirst', undated.
91 Susan Hammond to Michael Young, May 1977.
92 In this they were like one of their friends and heroes, Franklin Roosevelt, who was about the opposite of the Russians of the Gosplan who had so much influence on world thought in the 1920s and 1930s. 'Roosevelt was an intuitive politician, willing to experiment, working from day to day with a "let's see if it will work" technique. He was never a master planner, nor can one find in his New Deal any unity of programme. His greatest asset was his ability to discover, express and translate into action the trends of popular opinion.' Nye and Morpurgo, op. cit., p.664.
93 Harriet Martineau, *Society in America*, I, 1. Quoted in A. E. Bestor, *Backwards Utopias*, University of Pennsylvania Press, Philadelphia, 1950, p.1.
94 C. Nordhoff, *The Communist Societies of the United States*, Hillary House, New York, 1961.
95 R. M. Kanter, *Commitment and Community*, Harvard University Press, Cambridge, Mass., 1972.
96 D. Hayden, *Seven American Utopias*, Massachusetts Institute of Technology Press, Cambridge, Mass., 1976, p.3.
97 'We sung several songs on our knees, for we have become so used to standing on our knees, that it is almost as natural for us as it is to stand on our own feet. . . . Then Elder Brother said, let us arise from our knees and greet each other with a kiss of charity, then we may be dismissed. So we all went to hugging and kissing, and loved a heap. . . . It appeared to me that the heavens were opened and I was worshipping with the Angelic host. Some times the Brethren and Sisters were passing and repassing each other – sometimes hugging and

kissing the sweetest kisses that I ever tasted, for we felt love enough to eat one another up.' Quoted in Kanter, op. cit., p.48.

98 W. H. G. Armytage, *Heavens Below*, Routledge & Kegan Paul, London, 1961, p.438.

99 M. Young and P. Willmott, *The Symmetrical Family*, Routledge & Kegan Paul, London, 1973.

100 Note by Leonard Elmhirst, 'Time Budget 1934–35', 1934.

CHAPTER 5 THE ENGLISH EXPERIMENT

1 L. K. Elmhirst, 'Looking Back: Private Forestry', paper read to the Society of Foresters of Great Britain, January 1969, published in *Fifty Years On*, Oxford University Press, London, 1969, p.23.

2 Leonard Elmhirst to Dorothy Straight, 6 March 1925.

3 'Particulars and Conditions of Sale . . . of the Dartington Estate', Knight, Frank & Rutley, 1921, p.4.

4 'Particulars of . . . Dartington Hall', Michelmore & Son, Land Agents, Totnes, undated.

5 A. Emery, 'Dartington Hall, Devonshire', *Archaeological Journal*, Royal Archaeological Institute of Great Britain and Ireland, June 1960.

6 John Harvey to Leonard Elmhirst, 11 July 1958.

7 Leonard Elmhirst to Dr Margaret Galway, 2 January 1956.

8 Leonard Elmhirst to John Harvey, 6 January 1971.

9 Leonard Elmhirst to Dr Margaret Galway, 2 January 1956.

10 Leonard Elmhirst to John Harvey, 30 April 1963.

11 Leonard Elmhirst interviewed by Victor Bonham-Carter, 1960.

12 Arthur Champernowne and his wife were attached to the ruins. Chris Martin, the Dartington Hall Arts Administrator who was related to the Rev. J. S. Martin, Rector of Dartington, and thus to the Champernownes, wrote to Leonard on 13 May 1936, 'I recollect not long ago a curious conversation with Iris (Mrs Arthur). She was able to discuss Dartington, to be interested in much that was going on but some deep emotional chord was touched when she expostulated with me that the initials of the Trustees appeared on the drain pipes against the Great Hall and the White Hart.'

13 May Crook interviewed by Michael Young, 1977.

14 Ibid.

15 Dorothy Elmhirst's diary, 30 May 1925.

16 Ibid., 31 May 1925.

17 Rachel Barker interviewed by John Lane, 1975.

18 Dorothy Elmhirst to Leonard Elmhirst, 25 July 1925.

19 Sean O'Casey described Totnes when he later came to live in the town to allow his children to become day-pupils at Dartington Hall School. 'Apart from the quiet hurry of market day, gentleness is the first quality to give it; gentleness in its buildings, and in the coming and going of its people; and in the slow winding, winding of the River Dart from the moor to the sea. Oh, Lord, the natural lie of it is lovely. Except when visitors pour in during the brief summer, the town is so quiet that it looks like a grey-haired lady, with a young face, sitting calm, hands in lap, unmindful of time, in an orchard of ageing trees, drowsy with the scent of ripened apples about to fall, but which never do.' Eileen O'Casey, *Sean*, Macmillan, London, 1971, p.168.

20 Beatrice Straight interviewed by Michael Young, 1978.

21 Dorothy Elmhirst to Leonard Elmhirst, 25 July 1925.
22 Leonard Elmhirst to Dorothy Elmhirst, 22 July 1925.
23 Dorothy Elmhirst to Leonard Elmhirst, 23 July 1925.
24 Dorothy Elmhirst to Leonard Elmhirst, 15 March 1926.
25 Leonard Elmhirst to Mary Elmhirst, 28 March 1926.
26 Alfred Elmhirst interviewed in *Dartington Voice*, June 1976.
27 Dorothy Elmhirst to Leonard Elmhirst, 8 October 1925.
28 Clerk of Works was a title Leonard loved to use. He could not contain his excitement when it came out that Richard II appointed as Deputy Clerk of Works to Geoffrey Chaucer a John Elmhurst who might have been Leonard's ancestor. (Leonard Elmhirst to John Harvey, 28 August 1957.) Leonard's own unceasing interest in the details of building work going on at Dartington led the builders to describe him as 'the best Clerk of Works' they had ever encountered. (Bob Hening to Michael Young, August 1978.)
29 Anthony Emery, *Dartington Hall*, Clarendon Press, Oxford, 1973, p.112.
30 Bob Hening to Michael Young, August 1978.
31 *Yesterday's Village*, Dartington Village Archive, 1978.
32 Dorothy Elmhirst to Anna Bogue, 1 November 1926.
33 Anna Bogue to Leonard Elmhirst, 1 August 1927.
34 Walter Thomas to Dorothy Elmhirst, 10 August 1926.
35 Walter Thomas to Dorothy Elmhirst's secretary, 21 August 1926.
36 Emily Thomas interviewed by Michael Young, 1976.
37 Ibid.
38 Paula Morel interviewed by Michael Young, 1976.
39 Emily Thomas interviewed by Michael Young, 1976.
40 Dorothy Straight to Leonard Elmhirst, 31 August 1923.
41 Sybil Newman interviewed by Michael Young, 1977.
42 Richard Elmhirst interviewed by Michael Young, 1977.
43 Ann Collingbourne interviewed by Michael Young, 1978.
44 This account draws on the recollections of Jack Collingbourne in *Dartington Voice*, December 1978, and George Honeywill, interviewed by Anthea Williams, 1979.
45 W. G. Hoskins, *Devon*, Collins, London, 1954, p.298.
46 Michael Straight to Michael Young, September 1980.
47 Christine Raikes to Anthea Williams, February 1979.
48 Christine Raikes interviewed by Michael Young, 1978.
49 Joyce Carew, *Dusty Pages*, p. 77. (No publisher or date given.)
50 The Rev. J. S. Martin to Leonard Elmhirst, 16 July 1934.
51 Report from the Rev. R. A. Edwards to the Bishop of Exeter, January 1948.
52 Quoted in John Saville, *Rural Depopulation in England and Wales*, Routledge & Kegan Paul, London, 1957, p.201.
53 *Yesterday's Village*, Dartington Village Archive, 1978.
54 Michael Straight to Michael Young, 11 September 1980.
55 Ernest Clake interviewed by Anthea Williams, 1980.
56 Dorothy Elmhirst to Frances Livingstone, 11 February 1927.

CHAPTER 6 TO THE TOTNES STATION

1 Richard Elmhirst interviewed by Michael Young, 1977.
2 Leonard Elmhirst interviewed by Maurice Punch. Quoted in Maurice Punch, 'The Elmhirsts and the Early Dartington: A Neglected Experiment', *New Era*, January/February 1976, p.13.
3 Leonard Elmhirst to M. A. Strickland, 21 April 1943.
4 L. C. B. Seaman, *Life in Britain Between the Wars*, Batsford, London, 1970, p.109.
5 Alec Waugh, *The Loom of Youth*, Bles, London, 1955. (First published 1917.)
6 Robert Graves, *Goodbye to All That*, Jonathan Cape, London, 1929.
7 Ernest Raymond, *Tell England*, Cassell, London, 1922.
8 I am grateful to Raphael Samuel, of Ruskin College, Oxford, for emphasising the ramifications of this English movement which is so different from, although often allied with, Marxism or working-class socialism.
9 George Orwell, *The Road to Wigan Pier*, Secker & Warburg, London, 1965, p.182. (First published 1937.)
10 Ibid., p.221.
11 W. A. C. Stewart, *The Educational Innovators*, vol. 2, Macmillan, London, 1968, p.9.
12 W. H. G. Armytage, *Heavens Below*, Routledge & Kegan Paul, London, 1966, pp.374–5.
13 Ibid., p.334, quoting *Seed Time*, the quarterly of the Fellowship of the New Life.
14 Trevor Blewitt, *The Modern Schools Handbook*, Gollancz, London, 1934.
15 Leonard and Dorothy did visit A. S. Neill's Summerhill after their own school had opened. In 1927 they kept a joint diary for part of the year. For 24 January Leonard recorded, 'D and I visit Neill's school and are horrified at the mess and disorder and seeming chaos.'
16 'There is a certain Farm School in the Philippine Islands where some three hundred young boys work their own little holdings, build their own cottages, keep their own accounts, run their own municipality, tend their own livestock, and pocket their own profits. "All of our classroom work is in the nature of round-table discussions of stored-up experience", said the Principal.' Rabindranath Tagore and L. K. Elmhirst, *Rabindranath Tagore, Pioneer in Education*, John Murray, London, 1961, p.69.
17 See J. M. Hall, *Juvenile Reform in the Progressive Era – William R. George and the Junior Republic Movement*, Cornell University Press, Ithaca, New York, 1971. Also L. K. Elmhirst, *The Straight and Its Origin*, Willard Straight Hall, Ithaca, New York, 1975, p.56.
18 The Lincoln School's principles were set out by its founder, Abraham Flexner, in *A Modern College and a Modern School*, quoted in Stewart, op. cit., p.134.
19 Dorothy's notes on the first of Professor Dewey's lectures on 13 October 1921 reported that 'Human beings are what they are because of, and under the influence of, education in its broader sense – which is the sum total of contacts and relationships, direct and indirect, with other people who have in some way exerted influence'. One of the books in his recommended list for the course was Graham Wallas's *The Great Society*.
20 John Dewey, *The School and Society*, 1900; *The Child and the Curriculum*, 1902; *Moral Principles in Education*, 1909.
21 Rousseau would probably have attacked public schools for the same basic

reason as Leonard and the other writers just mentioned; or one could put it the other way and say that they reacted as they did partly because of what Rousseau had said. Here is Alec Waugh on a public-school education. 'It is inclined to destroy individuality, to turn out a fixed pattern; it wishes to take everyone, no matter what his tastes or ideas may be, and make him conform to its own ideals. In the process, much good is destroyed, for the Public School man is slack, easy-going, tolerant, is not easily upset by scruples, laughs at good things, smiles at bad, yet he is a fine follower. He has learnt to do what he is told; he takes life as he sees it and is content.' Waugh, op. cit., p.126.

22 *Emile for Today*, edited W. Boyd, Heinemann, London, 1956, p.11.
23 Ibid., p.33.
24 John Dewey, *The School and Society*, University of Chicago Press, 1956, p. 34.
25 John Locke, though his main conclusions were never so extreme, took a similar view about the paramount need to interest children. 'None of the things they are to learn should ever be made a burden to them or imposed on them as a task. . . . Children have as much a mind to show that they are free, that their own good actions come from themselves, that they are absolute and independent, as any of the proudest of you grown men, think of them as you please.' *Locke's Thoughts Concerning Education*, edited F. W. Garforth, Heinemann, London, 1964, p.166.
26 *Emile for Today*, op. cit., p.89.
27 Dewey, op. cit., p.14.
28 *Prospectus*, 1926.
29 Leonard Elmhirst to Edward Lindeman, 6 May 1927.
30 Leonard Elmhirst to Edward Lindeman, 7 January 1925.
31 *Outline of an Educational Experiment*, 1926.
32 *Prospectus*, 1926.
33 Ibid.
34 Thomas Pakenham, *The Boer War*, Weidenfeld & Nicolson, London, 1979.
35 *Prospectus*, 1926.
36 Leonard Elmhirst to O. N. Gorton, 14 June 1927.
37 Leonard Elmhirst to O. N. Gorton, 18 October 1928.
38 *Prospectus*, 1926.
39 Elmhirst, *The Straight*, op. cit., pp.78-9.
40 Michael Straight to Michael Young, 11 September 1980.
41 John Wales interviewed by Michael Young, 1973.
42 Mark Girouard, *Life in the English Country House*, Yale University Press, New Haven, Conn., 1978, p.23.
43 *The Chronicles of Froissart*, translated by Lord Berners, edited W. P. Ker, IV, p.331. Quoted in Girouard, op. cit., p.28.
44 Alfred Elmhirst to Michael Young, 17 August 1976.
45 'Report of meeting held to discuss plans and purposes of Dartington School', 11 September 1926.
46 Dorothy Elmhirst's diary, 24 September 1926.
47 Ibid., 25 September 1926.
48 Ibid., 26 September 1926.
49 Michael Straight to Michael Young, 11 September 1980.
50 Dorothy Elmhirst's diary, 27 September 1926.
51 Dorothy Elmhirst to Susan Swann, later Hammond, 15 March 1927.
52 Dorothy Elmhirst's diary, 8 October 1926.
53 Ibid., 15 October 1926.

54 Ibid., 28 September 1926.
55 Leonard Elmhirst interviewed by Michael Young, 1973.
56 Note written by one of the girl pupils about the first three terms of the school.
57 Dorothy Elmhirst to Vic Elmhirst, 2 March 1929.
58 Michael Straight to Michael Young, 11 September 1980.
59 Dorothy Elmhirst's diary, 24 June–5 July 1927.
60 Leonard Elmhirst, 'Report on Education Experiment, Dartington Hall, September to December 1926'.
61 Ibid.; and 'Safety Precautions', enclosure with a letter to parents, 28 September 1927.
62 Copy of a letter from Dorothy Elmhirst to unknown recipient, undated, probably February/March 1927.
63 Dorothy Elmhirst's diary, 5 March–20 March 1927.
64 S. R. Williams, 'Observations, Criticisms and Suggestions', undated.
65 Frederick G. Bonser and Virginia Bonser, 'Observations and suggestions relative to the educational experiment at Dartington Hall, June 1–June 20, 1928'.
66 Marjorie Wise, *English Village Schools*, Hogarth Press, London, 1931.
67 Ruth Ash interviewed by Michael Young, 1976.
68 Leonard Elmhirst to Winifred Harley, 30 January 1931.
69 It was later that, as W. B. Curry wrote about the only compulsory activity in the school, 'One new boy caused great merriment by announcing that he did not propose to "take" Useful Work.' Victor Bonham-Carter and W. B. Curry, *Dartington Hall*, Exmoor Press, Dulverton, Somerset, 1970, p.194.

CHAPTER 7 MICROCOSM

1   Ena Curry interviewed by Michael Young, 1979.
2   Leonard Elmhirst to W. B. Curry, 29 April 1930.
3   Dorothy Elmhirst to Anna Bogue, 10 April 1932.
4   Leonard Elmhirst interviewed by Maurice Punch. Quoted in Maurice Punch, 'Ecole paradis, A Short History of Dartington Hall School 1926–1969', unpublished typescript, 1970, p.13.
5   Curry wrote on 27 September 1944 to Peter Russell, Bertrand's third wife, about his son. 'A nice story for Bertie. Julian asked me one day whether I believed in God and I replied that I did not. He then asked whether I believed in Christ and I said that I believed there had been such a person and that he had been important. "Was he", asked Julian, "as important as you and Bertie Russell?" '
6   Bertrand Russell, *Principles of Social Reconstruction*, Allen & Unwin, London, 1917.
7   W. B. Curry, *The School and a Changing Civilisation*, John Lane The Bodley Head, London, 1934, p.23.
8   Victor Bonham-Carter and W. B. Curry, *Dartington Hall*, Exmoor Press, Dulverton, Somerset, 1970, pp.200–1.
9   See W. B. Curry, *The Case for Federal Union*, Penguin, Harmondsworth, 1939.
10 Curry, *The School*, op. cit., p.5.
11 Ibid., p.17.
12 Ibid., p.19.
13 Bonham-Carter and Curry, op. cit., p.197.

14 Curry, *The School*, op.cit., p.21.
15 Bertrand Russell, *Education and the Social Order*, Allen & Unwin, London, 1977, p.10.
16 *The School, Dartington Hall*, 1932, p. 11.
17 W. B. Curry, Report to the Trustees, July 1941.
18 Raymond O'Malley and Denys Thompson produced in the 1950s in five volumes 'a complete course in the use and understanding of English, designed for pupils of eleven to sixteen': *English One*, etc., were published by Heinemann. The same partnership was responsible for *English for Living*, published by Methuen, and *Rhyme and Reason*, an anthology published by Chatto & Windus in 1957. Raymond O'Malley wrote about his experience of crofting in the Western Highlands in the Second World War in *One Horse Farm*, Frederick Muller, London, 1948.
19 E. B. Uvarov and D. R. Chapman, *A Dictionary of Science*, Penguin, Harmondsworth, 1951. (First published 1943.)
20 Bonham-Carter and Curry, op. cit., p.164.
21 David Lack, *The Life of the Robin*, Penguin, Harmondsworth, 1953, p.21. (First published 1943.)
22 Leonard Elmhirst to Elizabeth Lack, 7 March 1973.
23 David Cabot to Leonard Elmhirst, 27 October 1967.
24 Mary Ogilvy to Leonard Elmhirst, 31 May 1967.
25 W. B. Curry, Report to the Trustees, Summer term 1937.
26 W. B. Curry to Bertrand Russell, 13 January 1934.
27 W. B. Curry to Bertrand Russell, 22 May 1934.
28 Katharine Tait, *My Father Bertrand Russell*, Gollancz, London, 1976, pp.122-3.
29 Sybille Bedford, *Aldous Huxley*, vol. 1, Collins and Chatto & Windus, London, 1973, p.264.
30 Ibid., p.293.
31 Lucie Freud to W. B. Curry, 17 September 1935.
32 W. B. Curry, *Education for Sanity*, Heinemann, London, 1947, p.103.
33 A. S. Neill to W. B. Curry, 26 July 1933.
34 Bonham-Carter and Curry, op. cit., p.172.
35 A. S. Neill to Bertrand Russell, 28 January 1931. Quoted in *The Autobiography of Bertrand Russell 1914-1944*, Allen & Unwin, London, 1968, p.187.
36 W. B. Curry to A. S. Neill, 4 July 1947.
37 A. S. Neill to W. B. Curry, 29 December 1932.
38 A. S. Neill to W. B. Curry, 24 January 1936.
39 W. B. Curry to A. S. Neill, 29 January 1936.
40 J. Harrison to W. K. Slater, 29 February 1936.
41 W. K. Slater to W. B. Curry, 25 February 1936.
42 John Dewey, *Moral Principles in Education*, 1909.
43 Curry, *The School*, op. cit., p.63.
44 Ibid., p.65. Curry recalled in another passage the pleasure that mixed baths could bring. 'I have a vivid recollection of an almost coal-black Negro from Africa coming to the Junior School, and the others clamouring for the privilege of sharing his bath because they were so fascinated by the beautiful glistening satin quality of his skin.' Bonham-Carter and Curry, op. cit., p.183.
45 Curry, *The School*, op. cit., p.66.
46 Susanna Isaacs, 'Bill Curry's Contribution', unpublished typescript, 1973.

47 Curry, *The School*, op. cit., p.71.
48 W. B. Curry, Report to the Trustees, July 1941.
49 W. B. Curry to W. K. Slater, 22 February 1936.
50 J. Harrison, Memorandum, 5 March 1936.
51 L. K. Elmhirst, 'Why Adult Education?', *Journal of the Working Man's College*, May 1963.
52 Leonard Elmhirst to B. G. Lampard-Vachell, 13 October 1948.
53 Leonard Elmhirst to J. E. Palmer, 23 April 1971.
54 Leonard Elmhirst to J. E. Palmer, 10 May 1971.
55 Peter Snape interviewed by Michael Young, 1977.
56 Bonham-Carter and Curry, op. cit., p.184.
57 Curry, *The Case for Federal Union*, op. cit., p.20.
58 Ibid., p.29.
59 Bonham-Carter and Curry, op. cit., p.197.
60 Dorothy Elmhirst to Leonard Elmhirst, 20 February 1941.
61 W. B. Curry, Report to the Trustees, February 1943.
62 Report by H.M. Inspectors on the Dartington Hall School, Inspected on 22, 23 and 24 November 1949.
63 Ibid.
64 Minutes of the Trustees' meeting, School Section, 20 July 1951.
65 W. B. Curry, Report to the Trustees, August 1953.
66 Bonham-Carter and Curry, op. cit., p.189.
67 Ibid., pp.188–9.
68 H. A. T. Child and L. A. Child, 'Dartington Hall', in H. A. T. Child (ed.), *The Independent Progressive School*, Hutchinson, London, 1962, p.43.
69 Ibid., p.45.
70 Leonard Elmhirst to Christian Schiller, 24 January 1968.
71 Royston Lambert, *The Chance of a Lifetime?*, Weidenfeld & Nicolson, London, 1975, p.314.
72 Leonard Elmhirst to David Cabot, 23 October 1969.
73 Lambert, op.cit., p.322.
74 Ibid., p.323.
75 Lambert said his only unequivocal success was the new nursery school opened without fees in the middle of the village. Ibid., p.329.
76 Ibid., p.327.
77 Royston Lambert, *Alternatives to School*, W. B. Curry Memorial Lecture, University of Exeter, 1972, p.9.
78 Lambert, *The Chance of a Lifetime?*, op. cit., p.330.
79 Lambert, *Alternatives to School*, op. cit., p.10.
80 Lambert, *The Chance of a Lifetime?*, op. cit., p.345.
81 It is very difficult to judge how Dartington children are different from others when they become adults; particularly when the sample of ex-pupils followed up in later life is as biased as it was in one ambitious study that has been done. See Maurice Punch, *Progressive Retreat*, Cambridge University Press, 1977.
82 Russell, *Education and the Social Order*, op. cit., p.91.

CHAPTER 8 THE LARGER SPIRIT THAT INFUSES ALL LIFE

1   This paragraph follows almost word for word what Leonard had earlier written in 'Siksha-Satra', Rabindranath Tagore and L. K. Elmhirst, *Rabindranath Tagore, Pioneer in Education*, John Murray, London, 1961, pp.79 *et seq.*

2   William Wordsworth, 'Intimations of Immortality from Recollections of Early Childhood', *Poetical Works*, Thomas Hutchinson (ed.), revised Edward de Selincourt, Oxford University Press, London, 1969, p.460.

3   In her farewell talk in the Barn Theatre in 1939 to 'members' of the estate, Dorothy said that in the seven years from 1918 to 1925 she found where she stood and what she believed in: 'The importance of the individual, the right of free speech, free press, the redistribution of wealth, democratic institutions, tolerance, an interacting spirit, a world brotherhood.' She was referring to the period in her life when she had been most radical in political terms.

4   Herbert Read, *The Philosophy of Modern Art*, Faber, London, 1952, p.18.

5   *Paintings, Sculpture, Furniture belonging to Mr and Mrs Leonard Elmhirst*, Newman Neame, London, 1951; foreword by Peter Cox.

6   Dorothy Elmhirst to Leonard Elmhirst, 16 October 1931.

7   Leonard Elmhirst's notebook on pots, 1967.

8   Ibid.

9   David Leach to Leonard and Dorothy Elmhirst, 14 November 1967.

10 Dorothy Elmhirst to the Hon. Secretary of the Dartington Parochial Church Council, 16 July 1948.

11 'It was the done thing to be a member of the Episcopal Church, or the Protestant Episcopal Church, allied as it was to the Church of England, with its appeal to conservative churchgoers "whose circle is so large that God is included in their visiting list". A Bishop of Massachusetts described it as "Episcopalian with leanings towards Christianity".' D. Wecter, *The Saga of American Society*, Scribners, New York, 1937, p.475.

12 Dorothy Elmhirst to Leonard Elmhirst, 7 October 1923.

13 Dorothy was still very close to Ethel after another war. She wrote to Leonard on 7 December 1946 about visiting Ethel at her house at Oyster Bay on Long Island. 'Then we talked about poetry and love and life and all the deep things of the heart that I tend to keep tightly locked away. It was strange how she opened all the doors, and how naturally we both got down to the level where two souls really meet. Nothing like that has happened to me in years – I mean that kind of communication with a friend. I'm afraid, like Bill, I reserve it all for my family.'

14 Now published as Dorothy Elmhirst, *My Special Anthology*, Dartington Press, 1979.

15 Dorothy Elmhirst to the Rev. R. A. Edwards, 6 August 1942.

16 Goldsworthy Lowes Dickinson said, 'I think that all forms of love, including the physical, point to something beyond.' E. M. Forster, *Goldsworthy Lowes Dickinson*, Arnold, London, 1934, p.219.

17 See Philip Toynbee, *Towards the Holy Spirit*, SCM Press, London, 1973.

18 Dorothy Elmhirst's notebook, September 1967.

19 Dorothy Elmhirst, note entitled 'Inagua South', 2 February 1959.

20 Dorothy Elmhirst's notebook, 1967.

21 Psalm 91.

22 I John 4.16.

23 Louise Croly to Dorothy Elmhirst, September 1939.

24 No source given by Dorothy.

25 Nancy Wilson Ross, who knew Dorothy well, said that Dorothy's favourite in the book that she kept by her bed was Sonnet X, not in the Anthology. Nancy Wilson Ross interviewed by Anthea Williams, 1977.

26 Arthur Waley, *The Way and Its Power – A Study of the Taote Ching and its Place in Chinese Thought*, Allen & Unwin, London, 1934.

27 Dorothy Elmhirst to Margaret Isherwood, 27 April 1947.

28 Dorothy Elmhirst, 'The Arts at Dartington', The Latin Press, St Ives, 1950.

29 Leonard Elmhirst to Gwen Elmhirst, 17 March 1958.

30 Forster, op. cit., p.141.

31 Rachel Barker interviewed by John Lane, 1975.

32 Sybille Bedford, *Aldous Huxley*, vol. 1, Collins and Chatto & Windus, London, 1973, p.247. Gerald had even more of an effect on Aldous than on Dorothy. 'It was now, in this summer that Aldous began to practise – with some difficulty – a kind of non-metaphysical meditation; what had started, at Gerald's instigation, as exercises in breathing and in mind control had led to this. . . . Aldous had already gone a good way – on his own and with Gerald Heard, absorbing, using, at that point what Gerald had to offer – towards a "religious solution".' Ibid., p.308. The year was 1935.

33 Dorothy Elmhirst's notebook, 1934 and 1935.

34 Gerald Heard's paper 'The World and Ourselves', quoted in Dorothy Elmhirst's notebook, 1967.

35 Dorothy Elmhirst's notebook, 1934 and 1935.

36 Ibid.

37 Gerald Heard to Dorothy Elmhirst, 10 May 1939.

38 Margaret Isherwood interviewed by Anthea Williams, 1977.

39 Dorothy Elmhirst to Margaret Isherwood, 18 December 1946.

40 Margaret Isherwood, *The Root of the Matter*, foreword by Gerald Heard, Harper, New York; Gollancz, London, 1954.

41 Margaret Isherwood interviewed by Michael Young.

42 Beryl de Zoete, *The Thunder and the Freshness*, Spearman, London, 1963.

43 Waley, op. cit., p.144.

44 Ivan Morris (ed.), *Madly Singing in the Mountains. An Appreciation and Anthology of Arthur Waley*, Allen & Unwin, London, 1970, p.119.

45 Anthony Stevens, unpublished typescript on the Withymead Clinic, Exeter, p.47.

46 Ibid., p.48.

47 Ibid., p.97.

48 Anthony Stevens interviewed by Michael Young, 1977.

49 Irene Champernowne to Leonard Elmhirst, 1 August 1969.

50 Stevens, op. cit., p.86.

51 Ibid., pp.86–7.

52 Dorothy Elmhirst to Juliette Huxley, 27 February, probably 1966.

53 Dorothy Elmhirst to Margaret Isherwood, 9 April 1952.

54 Stevens, op. cit., p.240.

55 Leonard Elmhirst to Irene Champernowne, 26 May 1970.

56 Leonard Elmhirst to Lord Butler, Master of Trinity College, Cambridge, 3 August 1972.

57 Leonard Elmhirst to Jack Kahn, 1 May 1973.

58 Leonard Elmhirst to Alan Bullock, 11 November 1971.

59   T. S. Eliot, 'Conformity to Nature'. Quoted in P. Abbs and G. Carey, *Proposal for a New College*, Heinemann Educational Books, London, 1977, p.47.

60   T. S. Eliot, *Notes Towards a Definition of Culture*, Faber, London, 1948.

CHAPTER 9 A NEW DAY FOR THE ARTS

1   *Miss Aunt Nellie, The Autobiography of Nellie Cornish*, edited E. Van Volkenburg and Edward Nordhoff Beck, University of Washington Press, Seattle, 1964, p.128.

2   Maurice Browne, *Too Late to Lament*, Gollancz, London, 1955, pp. 303–4.

3   Ibid., p.307.

4   Ibid., p.319.

5   Ibid., p.317.

6   Ibid., p.323.

7   Peggy Wales interviewed by Anthea Williams, 1979.

8   *News of the Day*, 24 June 1929. This was the estate news-sheet which went to everyone.

9   Miss Cornish visited Dartington several times. On her first arrival, as she tells in her autobiography, 'we were invited into the dining room for breakfast. A battery of huge platters under silver covers were aligned on the massive sideboard. With Richard Odlin as my guide, I discovered under these lids delectable kippers, lamb chops, and American ham and eggs. A butler who looked and played the part served us very formally and very politely. Much of my first visit to Dartington was spent visiting the activities, including the newly-equipped dance school where Louise Soelberg taught her classes. There I became acquainted with her fourteen-month-old daughter, Eloise, with whom I could play only when her very strict nanny graciously permitted it. Again I felt the whiff of English comedy.' *Miss Aunt Nellie*, op. cit., pp.225–6.

10   Catalogue of the Cornish School, undated, probably 1930s.

11   Dorothy Elmhirst to Mr Downing, 31 January 1933.

12   Bernard Leach, *Beyond East and West*, Faber, London, 1978, pp.167–8.

13   Ibid., p.161.

14   The support and the friendship continued. On 27 August 1969 Bernard wrote to Leonard, 'Your letter touched me to the quick. So generous. Covering years of unchanging support – you and dear Dorothy. I would never have been able to do those things without that help, and if it has had an effect which I don't even seek to assess – thank God!'

15   *Leach Pottery 1920–1952*, p.4.

16   Margaret Barr, Spring Term Report, 1931.

17   A previous show in the still ruined Great Hall apparently went much better though I cannot remember it myself. 'Not merely was the aim high: it was achieved; the second half of the programme equalled in actual result the greatest creative dancing I have seen. At one moment there were six or eight slender and impersonal female figures "clad in white samite, mystic, wonderful".' Maurice Browne, writing in *Theatre Arts*, October 1931.

18   Margaret Barr to W. K. Slater, 30 March 1931, enclosing General Outline for 'The Spring Festival'.

19   Beatrice Straight to W. B. Curry, 15 November 1933.

20   Kurt Jooss interviewed by Ruth Foster, 1973.

21   *Jooss Souvenir Book*, 1942.

22   Nancy Wilson Ross to Leonard Elmhirst, 30 December 1932.

23   W. K. Slater to Walter Gropius, 3 May 1933.

24   Leonard Elmhirst to Henry Morris, 26 January 1937.

25   Dorothy Elmhirst, 'My talk in the Barn Theatre on the eve of my departure for Chekhov in America', 26 March 1939.

26   Dorothy Elmhirst's tribute on the death of Michael Chekhov, *News of the Day*, 19 October 1955.

27   Beatrice Straight interviewed by Paula Morel, 1975.

28   Beatrice Straight interviewed by Michael Young, 1978.

29   Michael Chekhov, *To the Actor*, typescript, 1942, lodged at Dartington Hall, pp.iv–v. Later reworked by Charles Leonard in conjunction with Chekhov and published by Harper, New York, 1953.

30   Ibid., pp.3–4.

31   Sean O'Casey to Dorothy Elmhirst, 28 December 1936.

32   Eileen O'Casey, *Sean*, Macmillan, London, 1971, p.206.

33   Chekhov said that one kind of love is 'erotic love. . . . Even its two poles or extremes are more or less familiar to us: its highest aspects we refer to as platonic love and romanticism; the baser, lowest end is just animal gratification.' Michael Leonard, *Michael Chekhov's To the Director and Playwright*, Harper, 1963, p.19.

34   Dorothy Elmhirst to Margaret Isherwood, 2 September 1947.

35   Dorothy Elmhirst to Margaret Isherwood, 11 June 1948.

36   Leonard Elmhirst to Dorothy Elmhirst, 31 March 1937.

37   Dorothy Elmhirst to Kathleen Hull-Brown, 13 March 1942.

38   Dorothy Elmhirst to Mary Elmhirst, 7 August 1941.

39   Peter Cox interviewed by Michael Young, 1978.

40   Michael Chekhov to Dorothy Elmhirst, 25 October 1940.

41   Dorothy Elmhirst to Leonard Elmhirst, 25 August 1943.

42   Dorothy Elmhirst to Leonard Elmhirst, 5 February 1941.

43   Ibid.

44   Dorothy Elmhirst's garden diary, 10 December 1957.

45   Dorothy Elmhirst's talk to weekend gardening course at Dartington Hall, 18 September 1953.

46   Edward Hyams, *The English Garden*, Thames & Hudson, London, 1964, p.242.

47   Ibid., p.248.

48   Report by Dorothy Elmhirst, quoted in Victor Bonham-Carter, 'Dartington Hall 1925–56: A Report', vol. 3, 'Gardens', p.7.

49   Dorothy Elmhirst, *The Gardens at Dartington Hall*, C. Eric McNally, Dartington, 1961, p.23.

50   Leonard Elmhirst to Dorothy Elmhirst, 8 October 1952.

51   Dorothy Elmhirst, op. cit., p.6.

52   Dorothy Elmhirst's garden diary, 6 February 1944.

53   Ibid., 20 May 1943.

54   Dorothy Elmhirst, op. cit., p.12.

55   E. M. Forster, *Goldsworthy Lowes Dickinson*, Arnold, London, 1934, p.136.

56   Kathleen Hull-Brown interviewed by Anthea Williams, 1977.

57   Terry Underhill interviewed by Michael Young.

58   Dorothy Elmhirst to Margaret Isherwood, 27 April 1947.

59   Christopher Martin, Report to the Trustees: 'Plan for the Arts Department, 1941'.

60   Peter Cox interviewed by Michael Young, 1978.

61 Imogen Holst interviewed by Michael Young, 1977.
62 Christopher Martin, Report to the Trustees, November 1943.
63 The recollections in this and the following paragraph are from Imogen Holst, interviewed by Michael Young, 1977.
64 Leonard Elmhirst to Dorothy Elmhirst, 13 June 1948.
65 Dorothy Elmhirst to Leonard Elmhirst, 24 January 1952.
66 Dorothy Elmhirst to Leonard Elmhirst, 10 September 1957.

CHAPTER 10 TOWN – COUNTRY

1 Leonard Elmhirst to Dorothy Elmhirst, 13 March 1923.
2 Raymond Williams, *The Country and the City*, Chatto & Windus, London, 1973, p.248.
3 W. J. Durant, *Rousseau and Revolution*, Simon & Schuster, New York, 1967.
4 Leonard Elmhirst to the Rev. R. A. Edwards, 1 January 1947.
5 Leonard Elmhirst to William Weir, 12 August 1927.
6 Leonard Elmhirst to Captain L. F. Ellis, 10 February 1931.
7 Captain L. F. Ellis to Leonard Elmhirst, 20 February 1931.
8 Professor F. C. Bartlett to Leonard Elmhirst, 7 February 1934.
9 Leonard Elmhirst to Professor F. C. Bartlett, 10 February 1934.
10 L. K. Elmhirst, 'Some social implications in the economic planning of agriculture', June 1934.
11 Colin Ward, 'Say it again, Ben! an evocation of the first seventy-five years of the Town and Country Planning Association', *BEE*, November 1974.
12 Ibid.
13 Leonard Elmhirst's diary, 12 January 1918.
14 Leonard Elmhirst to A. R. Pelly, 2 December 1929.
15 Peter Self (ed.), *New Towns – the British Experience*, Charles Knight for the Town and Country Planning Association, London, 1972, p.23.
16 C. S. Orwin and W. R. Peel, *The Tenure of Agricultural Land*, Cambridge University Press, 1926.
17 Viscount Astor and Seebohm Rowntree, *British Agriculture*, Penguin, Harmondsworth, 1939.
18 Joe Duncan, *Agriculture and the Community*, International Bookshops Limited, 1921. Quoted in J. H. Smith, *Joe Duncan*, RCSS, University of Edinburgh in conjunction with the Scottish Labour History Society, 1973, p.202.
19 Leonard Elmhirst, draft Land Charter, undated, probably c. 1932.
20 The Land Trusts Association is affiliated to the Foundation for Alternatives, Adderbury, Oxon.
21 *Report of the National Parks Committee*, Cmd. 7121, HMSO, London, 1947, p.7.
22 *Report on National Parks in England and Wales*, Cmd. 6628, HMSO, 1945.
23 Leonard Elmhirst's notebook on his visit to the Berkshire Downs, July 1946.
24 Michael Straight, *Twigs for an Eagle's Nest*, Devon Press, New York/Berkeley, 1979, p. 125.
25 Sir Frederick Gibberd, 'The master design; landscape; housing; town centres', in Self, op. cit., p.90.
26 Bob Hening to Leonard Elmhirst, 11 October 1963.
27 Bob Hening to Michael Young, 4 January 1979.

28 Bob Hening to Michael Young, 11 August 1978.
29 Leonard Elmhirst to Sir Eric Savill, 16 August 1971.
30 Leonard Elmhirst to Dr J. W. Cook, 4 October 1962.
31 Bob Hening to Michael Young, June 1978.
32 Sir Desmond Heap, *An Outline of Planning Law*, Sweet & Maxwell, London, 1973, p.12.
33 Leonard Elmhirst to Elizabeth Chesterton, 27 October 1969.
34 Elizabeth Chesterton in association with William Holford and Partners, 'A report on Land Use in Totnes Borough and the surrounding area of Totnes Rural District', 1957.
35 Elizabeth Chesterton, 'Dartington Hall: A Study and Plan', 1965; Elizabeth Chesterton, 'Study and proposals for the future of the Dartington Hall Trust's land at Dartington, Shinner's Bridge and Cott', 1971.
36 *Totnes and Dartington Outline Plan*, Devon County Council, 1972.

CHAPTER 11 CULTIVATION OF THE LAND

1 L. K. Elmhirst, 'Some social implications in the economic planning of agriculture', address to the Agricultural Economics Society at Oxford, June 1934.
2 Graham Wallas, *The Great Society*, Macmillan, London, 1914, pp.347–8.
3 Leonard Elmhirst to Sir John Russell, 22 March 1960.
4 Some years before an expert observer had criticised Devon banks because horse-drawn implements had to turn so often. 'It is not merely that time is wasted over the constant turning, but a man gets thereby into a retail way of looking at things, and puts out of his consideration all schemes for handling crops on a large scale with the help of machinery.' A. D. Hall, *A Pilgrimage of British Farming*, John Murray, London, 1913, p.357.
5 Leonard Elmhirst to J. R. Currie, 13 July 1928.
6 J. R. Currie and W. H. Long, *An Agricultural Survey in South Devon*, Seale-Hayne Agricultural College and Dartington Hall, 1929.
7 J. B. E. Patterson, 'Cobalt as a Preventive of Pining in Cornwall and Devon', *Nature*, vol. 157, April 1946.
8 Roger Morel to Leonard Elmhirst, 17 June 1937.
9 W. K. Slater to Leonard Elmhirst, 22 June 1937.
10 Leonard Elmhirst to Frank Crook, 6 March 1970.
11 Stanley Morris (Head of the Agricultural Economics Department, University of Exeter), Report, August 1963.
12 Ronald Hawtin interviewed by Robin Johnson, 1980.
13 'The conference thus covered most of the fields of study commonly included under the title agricultural economics. The farm management men were given a brief look at the macro-economics of agriculture which dominated the fortunes of their farmers; the administrators and academic economists were given insights into the economics of the farm, and the adjustments which farmers were making in their practices to meet the changing trends in prices, costs and techniques. But Elmhirst felt strongly that friendly relations, though possibly begun in the conference hall, were best developed in less formal gatherings outside the official timetable. His generation had grown up making their own amusements at home; games had not become spoiled for the casual players by people getting too good at them, and amateurs at golf, cricket, or music could enjoy themselves, and entertain others, without comparison with

professionals on television or the radio. At Dartington and at later meetings of agricultural economists, impromptu concerts, picnics, golf matches, games of cricket or baseball according to the venue, boating parties and farm visits, prevented mental indigestion and encouraged friendships.' Edith H. Whetham, *Agricultural Economists in Britain 1900–1940*, Institute of Agricultural Economics, University of Oxford, 1981, pp.72–3.

14   Nils Westermarck (President of the International Association of Agricultural Economists), 'Foreword and Dedication', in R. N. Dixey (ed.), *International Explorations of Agricultural Economics*, Iowa State University Press, Ames, 1964, p.v.

15   *Weekend Review*, 14 February 1931.

16   John Pinder (ed.), *Fifty Years of Political and Economic Planning – Looking Forward 1931–1981*, Heinemann, London, 1981.

17   Leonard Elmhirst to Dorothy Elmhirst, 23 February 1941.

18   W. E. Hiley, *Woodland Management*, Faber & Faber, London, 1967, p.330.

19   W. E. Hiley, *A Forestry Venture*, Faber & Faber, London, 1964, p.117.

20   Ibid., p.19.

21   Bede lived *c*. A.D. 672–735.

22   L. K. Elmhirst, 'Outlook for Britain', *Journal of the Royal Forestry Society*, July 1973.

23   L. K. Elmhirst, 'The History and Development of the Dartington Woodlands, Devon', *Forestry*, vol. XLIV, No.2, 1971, p.312.

24   Hiley for one, with woodlands in mind and the need for the long view, regretted the 'overthrow of the British landed aristocracy by the far distant democracy of American farmers'. Hiley, *Woodland Management*, op. cit., p.21., quoting G. M. Trevelyan, *English Social History*, Longman, London, 1942, p.553.

25   Hiley, *A Forestry Venture*, op. cit., p.25.

26   Gladys Burr interviewed by Michael Young, 1976.

27   Dorothy Elmhirst to Pom and Gwen Elmhirst, 25 August 1943.

28   Stuart Bunce, Forester, Dartington Woodlands, interviewed by Anthea Williams, 1976.

29   Israel Sieff (Lord Sieff of Brimpton), *Memoirs*, Weidenfeld & Nicolson, London, 1970, p. 192.

CHAPTER 12 REVIVAL OF RURAL INDUSTRY

1   L. K. Elmhirst, 'Some social implications in the economic planning of agriculture', address to the Agricultural Economics Society at Oxford, 1934.

2   George Sturt, in one of the great classics of the countryside, showed the importance of local knowledge. 'And so we got curiously intimate with the peculiar needs of the neighbourhood. In farm-waggon or dung-cart, barley-roller, plough, water-barrel, or what not, the dimensions we chose, the curves we followed (and almost every piece of timber was curved) were imposed upon us by the nature of the soil in this or that farm, the gradient of this or that hill, the temper of this or that customer or his choice perhaps in horse flesh.' *The Wheelwright's Shop*, Cambridge University Press, 1934, p.17.

3   Dorothy Elmhirst to Leonard Elmhirst, 22 July 1925.

4   'Report on Weaving Department', *News of the Day*, 13 December 1927.

5   L. K. Elmhirst, *Faith and Works at Dartington*, 1937, p.7.

6 Dorothy Elmhirst's speech on Foundation Day, 4 June 1960. From 1942 onwards Foundation Day was held at Dartington on a Saturday in June. It was a gathering, with entertainments, for the whole estate and for the presentation of long-service awards.

7 Note by Leonard Elmhirst, 'Time Budget 1934–35', 1934.

8 Dorothy Elmhirst to Ruth Morgan, 28 May 1928.

9 Leonard Elmhirst to the Secretary of the Incorporated Secretaries Association, 3 May 1928.

10 Leonard Elmhirst to members of the estate, 18 September 1927.

11 *News of the Day*, 9 May 1930.

12 *News of the Day*, 25 May 1931.

13 The King v. Income Tax Commissioners, ex-parte Elmhirst, 1 King's Bench Division, Court of Appeal, 1935. Elmhirst v. Commissioners of Inland Revenue, 2 King's Bench Division, 1937.

14 Leonard Elmhirst to Peter Sutcliffe, 12 February 1948.

15 Leonard Elmhirst interviewed by Michael Young, 1973.

16 The giant firm of auditors was brought in by Leonard and they lived up to their reputation by introducing giant books for the accounts, eight feet by three. Leonard visited Christopher Addison, who had been Minister of Reconstruction in the wartime government and was to be Minister of Agriculture in the 1929–31 Labour Government and Commonwealth Secretary in the 1945 Labour Government. He recommended Price Waterhouse as the best firm of auditors there was. The British public and government would pay attention to anything they did.

17 Sybil Newman interviewed by Michael Young, 1977.

18 Ann Collingbourne interviewed by Michael Young, 1978.

19 Jack Collingbourne interviewed by Michael Young, 1978.

20 Jack Collingbourne's memoirs, 1978.

21 Jack Collingbourne interviewed by Michael Young, 1978.

22 Ibid.

23 F. A. S. Gwatkin to Leonard Elmhirst, 26 September 1934.

24 George Turner was manager of the saw mill, 1932–8.

25 W. K. Slater to F. A. S. Gwatkin, 7 January 1939.

26 Richard Elmhirst to Leonard Elmhirst, 31 December 1952. The reference is to Harper Adams Agricultural College, Newport, Shropshire.

27 A. R. Pelly to W. K. Slater, 21 June 1938.

28 Report to the Dartington Hall Trustees from J. V. Elmhirst, 15 May 1939.

29 Frank Walters interviewed by Michael Young, 5 March 1979.

30 Ibid.

31 Dorothy Elmhirst to Leonard Elmhirst, 15 December 1940.

32 Dorothy Elmhirst to Leonard Elmhirst, 19 January 1941.

33 Dorothy Elmhirst to Marjorie Wise, 3 September 1940.

34 Dorothy Elmhirst to Leonard Elmhirst, 6 April 1941.

35 Dorothy's chauffeur in New York, Matthew Hammill, regularly sent her expensive soap which she told him she delighted in. 'I don't think you could have chosen anything more welcome than this wonderful collection of soap and all the delicious cosmetics that are very necessary to a woman's person and very close to her heart.' (Dorothy Elmhirst to Matthew Hammill, 8 March 1944.)

36 Dorothy Elmhirst to Leonard Elmhirst, 22 September 1942.

37 Dorothy Elmhirst to Leonard Elmhirst, 1 October 1942.

38 *News of the Day*, 24 June 1941.
39 Letter from Dorothy Elmhirst in *News of the Day*, 8 July 1941.
40 Jack Collingbourne interviewed by Michael Young, 1978.
41 Dorothy Elmhirst to Leonard Elmhirst, 20 February 1941.
42 Dorothy Elmhirst to Leonard Elmhirst, 16 August 1942.
43 Dorothy Elmhirst to Leonard Elmhirst, 11 February 1945.
44 Dorothy Elmhirst to Leonard Elmhirst, 15 December 1940.
45 Peter Sutcliffe interviewed by Michael Young, 1980.
46 Dorothy Elmhirst to Margaret Isherwood, 17 February 1947.
47 Dorothy caught this habit of interrupting herself, for emphasis, from Leonard. 'Fatal' is one of Leonard's words, with just his intonation in that sentence.
48 Dorothy Elmhirst to Margaret Isherwood, 7 December 1948.
49 Dorothy Elmhirst to Margaret Isherwood, 7 March 1948.
50 Dorothy Elmhirst to Margaret Isherwood, 9 February 1951.
51 Dorothy Elmhirst to Margaret Isherwood, 8 September 1951.
52 Dorothy Elmhirst to Margaret Isherwood, 21 April 1948.
53 Dorothy Elmhirst to Margaret Isherwood, 11 October 1952.

CHAPTER 13 RETROSPECT

1 Ian Mercer, 'Appreciation of Leonard Elmhirst', *Journal of the Devon Trust for Nature Conservation*, Summer 1974.
2 Leonard Elmhirst to Dorothy Elmhirst, 27 May 1932.
3 Leonard Elmhirst to Dorothy Elmhirst, 22 October 1954.
4 Leonard Elmhirst to Milton Rose, 22 April 1969.
5 Dorothy Elmhirst to Margaret Isherwood, 11 June 1948.
6 Dorothy Elmhirst to Margaret Isherwood, 27 April 1947.
7 Dorothy Elmhirst to Leonard Elmhirst, 8 September 1953.
8 Peter Cox interviewed by Michael Young, 1978.
9 Imogen Holst interviewed by Michael Young, 1977.
10 Leonard Elmhirst to Dr D. Cook, 12 November 1968.
11 Dorothy Elmhirst, 'The Arts at Dartington'.
12 Lewis Mumford, *My Works and Days*, Harcourt Brace, New York, 1932.
13 Joseph P. Lash, *Eleanor and Franklin*, André Deutsch, London, 1972, p.396.
14 T. W. Elmhirst, 'Telephone Occasions in War', unpublished note, 1978.
15 C. R. Attlee to Leonard Elmhirst, 18 May 1946.
16 R. A. Armstrong to Leonard Elmhirst, 23 November 1972.
17 Leonard Elmhirst to Edward Heath, 25 November 1972.
18 Edward Heath to Leonard Elmhirst, 1 December 1972.
19 Leonard Elmhirst to Dr R. D. Whitehorn, 18 July 1962.
20 Miriam Adams interviewed by Anthea Williams, 1977.
21 Marion Iacopucci to Michael Young, 27 June 1980.
22 Leonard Elmhirst to Juliette Huxley, 25 May 1972.

INDEX